The Regulation of Behaviour

DEVELOPMENT IN LEARNING

BEHAVIOUR: LEARNING: EDUCATION

1

The Regulation of Behaviour

E. A. LUNZER

WITH CHAPTERS BY

N. MORAY

E. A. LUNZER AND J. F. MORRIS

STAPLES PRESS

First published 1968 by Staples Press
3 Upper James Street Golden Square London W1

Printed in Great Britain by
Cox & Wyman Limited
London, Reading and Fakenham

SBN. 286.62063.4

TO

JEAN PIAGET

RESPECTFULLY

AFFECTIONATELY

PREDICTABLY

CONTENTS

PREFACE

Development in Learning is a comprehensive introduction to the psychology of education, designed to serve as a basic text for students preparing for advanced diplomas and degrees in education or in psychology. While the level of treatment is often more detailed than might be thought necessary for students whose interest in psychology is less direct, e.g. for 3-year students in education, it is none the less hoped that each of these volumes will be useful to them also, especially as a work of reference.

The Regulation of Behaviour was not originally planned as a separate volume. Rather it was thought to devote one chapter, or at most two, to deal with the relation of learning theory to educational psychology. But to do so would have meant side-stepping the very real problems posed by the treatment of learning in classical psychology. It might have entailed paying lip-service to views with which the author profoundly disagrees, simply because they have been the orthodox views in psychology for a very long time, and to omit them would have been unthinkable.

These views are indeed set forth, I hope sympathetically, in the course of the rather lengthy first chapter, separate sections being devoted to each of the major thinkers of the early twentieth century. The remainder of the book is concerned, first, with the critique of this classical body of theory, and second, with the exposition and discussion of an alternative overall approach to the problems of psychology. I certainly do not think of this as entirely new. Indeed it will be obvious from the following pages that I owe so much to my teachers and contemporaries that perhaps only the putting together of it is new.

Be that as it may, I hope this synopsis may prove of some interest to 'academic' and/or 'pure' psychologists as well as to educationists. For one of the aims of the series is to lessen the gap between them, and at the same time to bring their shared interests to the attention of the wider public.

Doubtless the list of credits to conclude this preface could be spun as long as the chapter references. There are two that must not be denied, and whom it gives me the utmost pleasure to recall: Dr J. F. Morris, co-editor of the series, who bore with me through the several years of its gestation, and has so often listened patiently to quite wild ideas, offering sometimes damaging, but always sage and always sympathetic criticism; and to Mr P. Herriot, who carefully read the final MS, added many useful suggestions, and prepared a quite superb index.

CONTRIBUTORS

E. A. LUNZER, M.A., Ph.D., Senior Lecturer in Child Psychology, Department of Education, University of Manchester.

N. MORAY, M.A., D.Phil., Senior Lecturer in Psychology, University of Sheffield.

J. F. MORRIS, B.Sc.(Econ.), Ph.D., Senior Lecturer in Psychology, Manchester Business School (within the University of Manchester).

ACKNOWLEDGEMENTS

I WOULD like to express my thanks to J. Piaget and to Routledge and Kegan Paul Ltd for permission to reproduce extracts from *The Origin of Intelligence*, and to W. Heinemann for two extracts from *Play, Dreams and Imitation.* Thanks are due also to Prentice-Hall Inc. for permission to reproduce an extract from *Comparative Psychology*, ed. C. P. Stone. All these extracts appear in Chapter 5.

In respects of illustrations, acknowledgements are due as follows:

In Chapter 1: To Liveright and Co. for fig. 1 (from *Gestalt Psychology* by W. Kohler); to Routledge and Kegan Paul for fig. 2 (from *The Mentality of Apes* by W. Kohler); to Harper Bros. Inc. for fig. 3 (from *Productive Thinking* by W. Wertheimer); to Appleton-Century-Crofts for fig. 5 (from *Purposive Behaviour in Animals and Men* by E. C. Tolman); to American Psychological Association for figs. 7 and 8 (from articles by C. L. Hull in *Psychol. Rev*, Vols. 41 and 42); to *J. exp. Psychol.* for fig. 6 (from an article by E. C. Tolman, B. F. Ritchie and D. Kalish in Vol. 37); to B. F. Skinner and to Appleton-Century-Crofts for figs. 9 and 10 (from *The Behaviour of Organisms*).

In Chapter 3: to J. A. Deutsch and the Syndics of the Cambridge University Press, for fig. 7 (from *The Structural Basis of Behaviour*).

In Chapter 5: to Messrs M. E. Bitterman, J. Wodinsky and D. K. Candland and to the American Psychological Association, for figs. 1–4 (from Vol. 71 of *Amer. J. Psychol.*); and to H. F. Harlow, together with the APA (fig. 5, from *Psychol. Rev.*, Vol. 56), and with McGraw-Hill Ltd (fig. 6, from *Psychology; A Study of A Science*, Vol. II, ed. S. Koch.); and to Prentice-Hall Inc. (fig. 7, from *Comparative Psychology*, ed. C. P. Stone).

E.A.L.

The Regulation of Behaviour

1

Classical Theories of Learning

I. INTRODUCTION

THE FACT that learning occurs is obvious; so obvious that it is difficult not to take it for granted. What is more, many of the circumstances which favour learning are perfectly familiar: the intrinsic interest of the material, its novelty, the manner of its presentation, the motivation of the learner, his opportunities for practice and rehearsal, his intelligence. One does not need a psychologist to be reminded of these.

Yet there are many questions about which one would clearly like to know a great deal more. How much practice is needed for learning to be effective? Under what circumstances can one expect learning to occur 'in one'? What makes things easy or difficult to learn? Is it always true that the stronger the motivation the more effective is the learning? Is intelligence no more (and no less) than a measure of the rapidity with which the learner can learn? Is all learning of a kind: for instance, what is the difference between learning a fact (e.g. the logarithm of 1 is 0), acquiring a skill (e.g. the use of tables of logarithms), and mastering a conceptual discipline (e.g. an understanding of the principles of logarithms)? Of course skills are more complex than facts and disciplines involve more than one skill, but are there also differences in kind as well as differences in the amount to be learned?

Perhaps none of these questions admit as yet of an unequivocal answer. But this does not mean that we cannot go some way towards their resolution. To do this, more often than not the question itself must first be rephrased. There is nothing unusual about this, for the language of science is seldom co-terminous with that of common sense. But first of all one needs to question the obvious.

Science always begins by questioning the obvious. It is obvious that if one drops an object from a height it will fall to the ground, and that if one rolls a ball along a horizontal surface the ball will continue awhile in motion and then gradually come to rest. Just as physics began by questioning some of the more obvious facts about motion, so an important part of psychology begins by questioning the obvious facts about learning.

In what way does an organism that learns differ from one which does not? Is there some principle which is common to all instances of learning, and if so, what is this principle? To put the matter another way, suppose one had constructed a model, a machine which was capable of simulating some types of behaviour but one which could not learn, what would one need to add to this machine to make it capable of learning?

This second formulation is anachronistic. Psychologists began asking fundamental questions about learning about the turn of the century, while it is only since the last war that models of psychological processes have become increasingly possible. But it should be stressed that the relevant advances have been in the realm of electronics and engineering, for it is these which have made it possible to construct *working* models to simulate some points of theory. In so far as the theories elaborated in the preceding half century can be taken as specifications for the construction of working models, there is nothing very wrong in regarding these as theoretical models, and this is what we will do.

The reason that one is apt to take learning for granted is bound up with our conscious experience. Remembering what we have seen or what we have been told permeates every aspect of our social living just as much as motion permeates all physical processes. Forgetting seems to be no more than the complement of such learning, and it is just as universal. But the introspection of conscious experience offers no sound basis for the construction of an objective science. Moreover the advances that had been made in all branches of science, but especially in physiology, led men like Thorndike and Pavlov to recognize that psychology could not aspire to the rank of a science so long as it took ideas or mental events as its starting point.

The early behaviourists went so far as to exclude ideas from psychology altogether. Contemporary psychology is less chauvinistic and at the same time more objective in its aim: to establish precise relations between ideas and material events inside and outside the thinking subject. The point is that an explanation of learning or of emotion which is couched purely in terms of ideas (he will learn if he wants to learn: learning is effective if the learning is meaningful, etc.) is not an explanation at all. It may well be true at a descriptive level, but it is not science, for it makes no attempt to establish a bridge between mental and physical processes. It encapsulates the former and insulates them from the latter by providing them with a causality and an energy of their own, different from material causality and physical energy and incapable of precise conversion. The argument has been well put by Eysenck (1953) in his criticism of Freud.

Eysenck distinguishes between 'understanding' and 'explanation'. It is not that such 'understanding' is without value. It is of immense value to the novelist, the teacher, and the social worker, and to each of us in the handling of his everyday affairs. But it is not science.

The task of psychology is to pursue an objective approach to problems of behaviour to a point where it can lead to a model which will be adequate to elucidate some of the problems with which we began. But how is this objectivity to be achieved? Here at least, there is a considerable measure of agreement among all schools of psychology: by grounding the study of the interpretation of behaviour on what human beings and animals do, rather than what they think and feel. These are the primary data of psychology. As we have already said: ideas and feelings are not excluded: on the contrary, they are of the utmost importance. But psychology seeks to define their role and action more precisely by establishing their connexion with the behavioural data.

II. PIONEERS OF LEARNING THEORY: THORNDIKE AND PAVLOV

1. *Basic Similarity of Approach: Behaviour and Learning*

The scientific study of learning has its origins in the work of Thorndike and Pavlov, both of whom elaborated their ideas about the turn of the century. It is usual to stress the differences in their approaches. Both from the standpoint of historical accuracy and in order to bring out the essential characteristics of psychological inquiry, it is more important to see their similarity. In contrast to a great deal of the psychology that went before, both Pavlov and Thorndike sought to establish a model which would account for all of behaviour, and especially learning, based on the correlation between the behaviour of the subject and the contingencies in his environment. Before this time it was mainly in the field of perception that psychologists sought such objectivity. The study of thinking and emotion tended to be based largely on introspection. As to learning, although many of the techniques of objective inquiry had been elaborated in the pioneer studies of Ebbinghaus and Müller, these were confined to one aspect of learning only: rote memorization. The fundamental significance of learning in the achievement of nearly all complex mammalian behaviour was not fully appreciated, and memorization itself was thought of by Ebbinghaus more as a faculty of the mind, akin to intelligence, than as a process in the brain.[1]

[1] See Flugel (1933) and Spearman (1923).

Thorndike and Pavlov agreed in viewing the behaviour of organisms as a matter of response to stimuli. The subject is to be looked on as a machine which is responsive to environmental manipulation. It was known that the central nervous system mediates reflex connexions between certain kinds of environmental events and specific actions. These are the innate reflexes such as, in the human being, the knee-jerk reflex, the eye-blink reflex, pupillary contraction, salivation, and so on. Typical environmental stimuli which trigger these reflexes are, respectively, a tap on the patella, a puff of air against the eye, raising the intensity of illumination, the presence of a foreign substance in the mouth. There are many more innate reflexes. But if the brain is essentially no more than a complex circuitry connecting stimuli and responses, then clearly the one thing which differentiates it from machines known at the time is the fact that in the brain these connexions must be constantly changing as a function of the subject's experience. Animals, like human beings, are adaptive. Their characteristic mode of behaviour is subject to change, and in general the direction of change is one which favours their survival in a changing environment. Therefore the central problem of learning becomes that of discovering a principle (or a theoretical mechanism) which will account for such change.

This approach has two important characteristics. The first is the continuity between animal learning and human learning. In spite of the fact that there must clearly be differences between the two, the recognition of that continuity understandably constituted a great step forward. It was a reasonable hope that the objective study of simple learning in animals should throw light even on the most complex learning in human beings, and the hope has in fact advanced the inquiry. The second is that underlying the new conception of learning is the model of behaviour as consisting of responses to stimuli. Behaviour as such, we will suppose, poses no fundamental problem of analysis; it is made up of discrete units or responses, whose many interconnexions with one another and with the environmental stimuli account for all the complexity of adaptive behaviour. The critical problem is that of establishing the basic laws which govern the changes in these connexions: learning.

It appears to follow from this that if one can devise a theoretical model which is validated by careful experimental study of any one class of learning in any organism, the model should be valid for all learning in all organisms. In other words, it is supposed that there is only one kind of learning.[1]

[1] This is an initial supposition. We will qualify it somewhat in this chapter, and more considerably in those that follow.

However, as is well known, the model proposed by Pavlov and that put forward by Thorndike are very different, and both appear to be valid.

2. *Contrasts*

Pavlov's contribution to the psychology of learning was based largely on the studies of conditional salivation (Pavlov, 1941). Salivation is an innate reflex to the stimulus provided by a foreign substance in the mouth. If the introduction of such a substance is regularly preceded by some other stimulus, such as the sounding of a metronome, the salivation begins to occur earlier in the sequence of events: it becomes a reflex response to the metronome. But whereas the former is a fixed, innate 'unconditional', connexion, the latter is formed, or 'conditioned' by the contingency of the two stimuli, sound and food: it is also 'conditional' on the maintenance of that contingency, i.e. on the continued 'reinforcement' of the '*conditional stimulus*' (**CS**) by the presentation of the '*unconditional stimulus*' (**US**); it is therefore temporary, and not permanent, for if the experimenter chooses repeatedly to withhold the **US** after administering the **CS**, the conditional reflex (**CR**) is weakened and gradually disappears (*experimental extinction*).

Thorndike's inquiries began with the observation of the behaviour of cats, dogs and chicks in their attempts to escape from a confined space and reach a lure consisting of appropriate food (Thorndike, 1898). The puzzle boxes were devised in such a way that a relatively simple operation, or sequence of operations would suffice to cause the front of the box (slatted so that the food was visible) to drop. Thorndike noted that the animal invariably responded to the situation by trying out whatever movements had proved successful with similar situations in the past: thrusting a paw through the bars, scratching and clawing at various parts of the apparatus, hurling itself at the door, and so forth. If it succeeded in escaping, (and this did not happen always), then on subsequent occasions the time taken to escape gradually decreased, the fall off being rapid at first and then slowing down, but eventually reaching an asymptote when the animal pulled at the appropriate loop or depressed the right lever immediately on being placed in the box.

Thorndike also noted that animals which had persistently failed to master a problem did not profit by repeatedly watching another which was successful. There was no learning by imitation. He proposed to account for this sort of learning in terms of a number of principles of which by far the most important is the '*law of effect*'. All of the actions which the animal performed could be thought of as responses linked to the stimuli of the situation by bonds of varying strength; the effect of success was to increase the strength of the bond between the stimulus and the response which led to the success. Bonds linking the other responses with the stimulus were weakened, at least relatively to those of the successful responses.

Clearly, Pavlov's learning model is different from Thorndike's. They agree in asserting a change in connexion between stimulus and response. But in classical (Pavlovian) conditioning, the response is first triggered by the **US** in the form of an unconditional reflex and the effect of the learning is to create a new linkage with the **CS**, causing it to antedate the **US**, so that it is now a **CR** to the **CS** as well as **UR** to the **US**. Thorndike's model supposes some kind of pre-existing link between the stimulus and the to-be-learnt response. Reinforcement is contingent on the occurrence of the right response, and learning is a strengthening of the initial bond. Reinforcement learning is sometimes called '*instrumental learning*' or even 'instrumental conditioning', because the response is instrumental in bringing about the reinforcement.

Thus right from the start of the inquiry we are faced with two distinct models each designed to account for the essential facts of learning. There is no need to choose between the two. Most contemporary psychologists would agree with Skinner (1938) that both formulations correctly describe certain (different) aspects of the processes involved in learning. At the same time it will be argued that neither principle is sufficient to account for the complexity of behaviour, nor are the two taken together, at least in the form in which they were proposed by their authors.

We cannot in the present chapter undertake to describe the wealth of experimentation yielded by the various theoretical approaches to the problem of learning, nor is it proposed to offer a rounded picture of such theories, covering those areas which were subjected to direct experimental investigation and the extrapolations offered by their proponents to account for learning outside the laboratory.[1] Judged in the light of subsequent developments, the work of Thorndike and Pavlov has two important limitations. Neither devoted any great attention to problems of motivation in relation to learning, and neither put forward any clear model of the way in which the learning of discrete responses could lead to the emergence of complex and insightful behaviour. However, because

[1] Among the more useful introductory accounts, I would suggest Hill (1963). More technical presentations are numerous, some of the most important being Hilgard (1958), Osgood (1953), Koch (1959), Mowrer (1960, a and b).

of the very considerable influence of these two pioneers on subsequent developments, a word of amplification is necessary.

3. *The Heritage of Thorndike's Work and its Limitations*

Thorndike's chief contribution consists in his formulation of the law of effect, together with his insistence on the presentation of behaviour as made up of linkages between stimuli and responses. Thorndike went on to apply his methods of study to learning in human beings, claiming that similar principles were applicable: learning consists in the strengthening of connexions under the influence of the law of effect, the law of exercise, and the law of readiness. We have already noted the principal component of the law of effect: the satisfying consequences of a response operate in such a way as to strengthen the bond between that response and the stimulus which elicited it. Thorndike first proposed and later rejected the converse proposition: that responses which are followed by unsatisfying or punishing consequences will be weakened. Experiment had shown that, at least in verbal associate learning (learning to repeat a particular word after another, or a word after a number, or a number after a word, following on repeated presentations and reinforcements of correct responses), punishment (by a mild electric shock) did little to weaken wrong associations, and punishment of correct associations was actually more effective than the mere information conveyed by the statement: 'right'.

The law of exercise holds that practised connexions tend to be strengthened: once again, Thorndike later modified this law by the proviso that practice without 'knowledge of results' has little effect. Thorndike made little distinction between reinforcement and knowledge of results, assuming (a little naïvely) that knowledge that the result is correct is automatically reinforcing or satisfying, (and incidentally side-stepping the complex issues involved in *knowledge* of *results*). The law of exercise was thus subordinated to the law of effect. Finally, the law of readiness asserted that for a connexion which is ready to conduct, conduction is satisfying, while for a connexion unready to conduct, such conduction is annoying. This principle may be thought of as something of a catch-all. It seeks to account for all the phenomena generally described under the heading of psychological 'set' (the existence of which was established in the nineteenth century, notably by the Wurzburg school, see Humphrey (1951): e.g. if a subject is first told to reply to each word by supplying its opposite and then given a list of words, his reaction times are shorter than when the task is given separately for each word in the list).

At the same time, the law of readiness might be interpreted in such a way as to account for all the phenomena of interest: the intrinsically satisfying character of preferred modes of activity, and so on. In general, however, the principle is too vague to be more than a corrective to the law of effect, and is formulated at a descriptive rather than an explanatory level.

Thorndike's failure to find learning by imitation in animals led him to deny the existence of animal thinking and of animal intelligence in the then accepted sense (for at the time, the two were taken to be roughly synonymous). This should not be taken to imply that he also denied intelligence in human beings. Thorndike was in fact one of the pioneers of intelligence testing (Thorndike, 1925). Differences in intelligence were allied to the theory of connexions by allowing (a) that more complex sequences of connexions were possible given greater intelligence; e.g. puzzle boxes involving the sequential operation of two release mechanisms are vastly more difficult to learn; and (b) that human beings are capable of 'abstraction' i.e. of responding to some aspect of the stimulus rather than to the situation as a whole, e.g. to the meaning of a sentence rather than the individual words, to the number of a collection rather than to its individual elements, and so on. Given these connexions of varying complexity and the possibility of abstraction, learning for Thorndike remained a matter of trial-and-error. It is quite incorrect to assume that he thought of trial-and-error as blind, for the initial responses were seen as determined by previous experience.[1] Nevertheless, his connexionism did lead him to favour an inductive rather than a deductive approach to learning, e.g. mathematics, as well as perhaps an underestimate of the generality of conceptual structures (Thorndike, 1949). For Thorndike, just as later for Skinner, understanding a complex topic is merely a matter of being able to perform a large number of more or less simple, related actions (e.g. giving appropriate answers, carrying out appropriate calculations, etc.). It remains that although it is clear that Thorndike did think of complex behaviours and skills as made up of S-R bonds, he did not enter in any detail as to the proposed manner of their connexion in complex structures and still less as to the mode of operation of such structures.

[1] 'Nowhere are the bonds acquired with old situations more surely revealed in action than when a new situation appears. The child in the presence of a new object, the savage with a new implement, manufacturers making steam-engines or motor-cars, the schoolboy beginning algebra, the foreigner pronouncing English – in all such cases, old acquisitions are, together with original tendencies, the obvious determiners of response, exemplifying the law stated above' – Thorndike (1949) p. 110.

The law referred to is the law of association by analogy or, roughly, generalization, which is held to extend the acquisitions due to the operation of the law of effect.

4. *Pavlov's Contribution*

A similar limitation applies to the work of Pavlov. Indeed Pavlov made no attempt to extend his conception of learning to allow of its implementation in teaching. Nevertheless, Pavlov's conception of the activities in the brain which underlie its function in the control of behaviour is richer than Thorndike's. It was noted that Thorndike put forward and later dropped a negative corollary to the law of effect: i.e. a principle of weakening of bonds. Pavlov's use of the technique of conditional reflexes enabled him to demonstrate the operation of negative bonds: *inhibition*. Three examples may be cited. Withholding the **US** after the formation of a **CR** leads to experimental extinction; but if the **CS** is re-applied the following day without the **US**, the **CR** reappears: a phenomenon known as '*spontaneous recovery*'. Clearly, the positive connexion between **CS** and **CR** was not destroyed by experimental extinction; it was opposed by an inhibiting process. Similarly, if the **CS** is accompanied by, say, a loud noise, the **CR** fails to appear: a phenomenon sometimes referred to as '*external inhibition*', as opposed to the '*internal inhibition*' of experimental extinction and of delay. If the **US** is regularly withheld until, say, a minute, after the onset of the **CS**, the **CR** is also delayed, appearing just before the usual ('expected') time of the **US**. However, if an external stimulus is applied during the delay period, there is a paradoxical effect causing the **CR** to appear in spite of the inhibition of the delay: there has been inhibition of the inhibition, uncovering the excitatory process.

Both excitation and inhibition are subject to '*generalization*': if a **CR** is established to a pitch of a given tone, the **CR** also appears on presentation of other tones. If the **CR** is established to the appearance of a circular disc, it generalizes to an elliptical disc. If the latter is not reinforced by the **US**, there is '*differentiation*' or differential inhibition. Rounder forms elicit the **CR** and less round forms do not. (Presentation of intermediate forms were also found to bring about breakdown of behaviour and acute symptoms of nervousness; or '*experimental neurosis*'.)

Pavlov deliberately avoided the use of mental terms. The word 'expected' used earlier in brackets is a figure of speech. There is every reason to believe, with Pavlov, that processes of excitation and inhibition underlie the phenomena of consciousness. But they are in no sense the result of conscious processes, and it has been demonstrated that **CRs** can be established reflecting correct 'expectations' although the subject has no understanding of the situation (Merlin, 1961).[1]

[1] Adult subjects were required to press a button when told to press. Two bulbs were on display, one red, the other green. These lights were flashed at intervals.

It is important to note that inhibition is not a mere weakening of excitation or weakening of bonds, but a process in its own right. The importance of excitation and inhibition is generally accepted in psychology, as also are the 'laws' of generalization and differentiation. They have been extended and incorporated in the Hullian interpretation, which will concern us in Section V. But, once again, although Pavlov claimed that both these very elementary processes must underlie all nervous activity, he did not set out to show how complex skills and concepts were built up out of their interaction. His essays in this field were limited to two. First, the demonstration that if a sequence of positive (excitatory) and negative (inhibitory) stimuli is presented repeatedly, the subject builds up a '*dynamic stereotype*': the entire sequence of **CRs** can then be triggered off by a single **CS**, and it becomes increasingly difficult to modify the pattern by new differential reinforcement. Second, Pavlov believed that the system of permanent and temporary reflexes underlying the regulation of behaviour in animals was insufficient to account for the regulation of human behaviour; he suggested that in addition to this '*first signalling system*', human beings possessed a '*second signalling system*', based on language and the power of the word to signal or symbolize the percepts figuring as signals in the first signalling system. The regulation of human behaviour and thinking was thus a function of the interaction of the two systems. However, although the dynamic stereotype clearly answers to some of the characteristics of habitual behaviour, the concept is insufficiently elaborated to act as a model for the selectivity of attention and controlled anticipation which govern the performance of complex skills. Similarly, although the concept of the second signalling system anticipates the fundamental distinction which Piaget draws as between sensorimotor behaviour and representation, Pavlov himself never pursued the notion in any detail.

III. GESTALT PSYCHOLOGY

Perhaps the most significant problem raised by the work of Pavlov and Thorndike was whether the purposive and intelligent characteristics of behaviour could result from the interaction of simpler bonds between stimuli and responses. Pavlov and Thorndike held that they could, but

---

Flashing of the red light was always followed by a shock and the instruction 'press'. Heightened skin conductivity induced by perspiration (psycho-galvanic skin reflex) rapidly developed as a CR to the red light and not the green *before the subject could tell when he had to press.*

neither gave an adequate explanation of how they could. The group of psychologists who formed the 'school' known as 'Gestalt', whose leading figures were Wertheimer, Kohler, Koffka and Lewin, denied the possibility of providing such an amplification.

1. *Introduction*

According to the Gestalt school behaviour is a response made by the organism to its perception of the situation. An adequate analysis of the characteristics of perception provides the basis for an adequate account of intelligent behaviour and learning. Now perception, it was held, could not be described in terms of an aggregate of sensations yielded by the stimuli of the various parts of the thing perceived. Instead, perception can only be described, and explained, in terms of the 'total' stimulus. The total or whole has a form (German: *Gestalt*), which is more than the sum of its parts. What the subject perceives depends on the structure of the whole. Among the numerous experimental demonstrations carried out in support of this proposition we may consider first the phenomenon of closure: a drawing of a circle featuring a small gap in the circumference tends to be seen as a circle, the gap being overlooked; other conventional drawings of objects with missing parts are likewise identified, and remembered, as wholes. In general, whether some aspect of the stimulus is seen or overlooked is a function of the structure of the stimulus as a whole. For instance, in the figure shown below subjects fail to see the 'hidden' figure 4: the various parts of this figure belong to different structures. Yet, it is clear that the figure 4 is a much more familiar figure than other component figures which are seen.

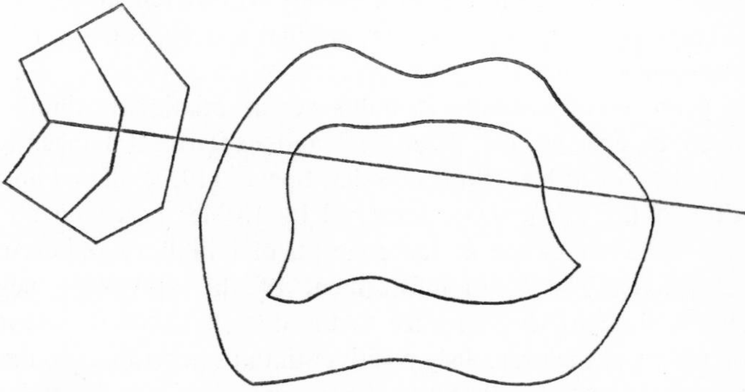

Figure 1. Hidden figure (from Kohler, 1929)

To this extent, Gestalt psychologists tended to minimize the importance of learning, as well as to deny the role of simple habits in the determination of behaviour: repeated presentation of a component should strengthen the bond between that figure and the response of perceiving it, yet such repeated presentation does not modify the perception of the complex figure. As to the characteristics of the visual field which determine the structure of what will be perceived, Gestalt psychologists draw particular attention to the properties of symmetry, continuity, proximity, closure, and 'good form' (e.g. a squarish figure is seen as a square rather than an oblong because a square is a better, more regular, simpler form). The discussion of perception as such forms the topic of Volume II, Chapter 1. Our interest here is merely to bring out the significance of the central concept of Gestalt or 'structure of the whole'.

2. *Relational Perception*

From the standpoint of Gestalt, behaviour, like perception, is a response to the properties of the whole. This is illustrated by a famous early experiment of Köhler (1929). The subjects were chicks: these were trained by selective reinforcement to peck at grains on the brighter of two cards. When presented with two backgrounds of which one was a card brighter than the originally positive one, and the other was the previously positive card, the chicks pecked at the now brighter card. Köhler's interpretation was that a response had been formed to a relation 'brighter', and not to an absolute stimulus. In general, Köhler argued that response is made to the relational properties of the situation as a whole. By the same token, the evidence of previous learning is reflected in the subject's ability to transpose a pattern of relations. An oft-quoted instance is the ability to transpose a melody in a different key, when none of the responses correspond to the original stimuli, but the relations between them do.

The problem of absolute stimulus versus relational stimulus has continued to exercise the theoretical and experimental ingenuity of psychologists for at least three decades. Spence (1937) offered an interpretation of the phenomena described by Köhler based on absolute learning. This makes use of the concepts of inhibitory and excitatory generalizations. The non-reinforcement of the previously negative stimulus is thought to generalize to the distant stimulus, just as the reinforcement of the previously positive stimulus generalizes to the near but previously negative stimulus. The subject's choice is determined by the difference between the residual excitatory tendencies after subtraction of inhibitory tendencies. Spence predicted, and found, that when the test situation involves two stimuli both greatly different from the orginal pair, response will be to the stimulus which is absolutely nearer to the previously positive stimulus. Although Spence's theory accounts for new phenomena, the balance of evidence favours a modification of Köhler's account. Thus absolute choices are favoured by successive presentation of positive and negative stimuli and relative choices by simultaneous presentation, where Spence would predict no difference (Baker and Lawrence, 1951). Riley (1958) presents evidence to show that the relational view can predict a decline in 'far transposition' if account is taken of the relation between both stimuli and the background illumination as well as between the intensities of the two stimuli considered by themselves. The most telling evidence is the physiological finding that action potentials in the retina are related to brightness contrast rather than absolute intensity (Motokawa, 1949). (At the same time it should perhaps be remarked that there is nothing necessarily mentalistic about relational response. Nothing could be simpler than to devise a two-way relay operated by the brighter illumination striking two photoelectric cells. But this was less obvious in 1929.)

However, from the point of view of a consideration of human learning it is instructive to note that seven-year old children effect 'far transposition' as easily as 'near transposition' where younger children are more influenced by the particular values of the stimuli. (Kuenne, Kendler, 1950). The intervention of a symbolic referrent serves to fix the relation and abstract it from its immediate context.

3. *Insight Learning*

We may now turn to the main contribution of Gestalt to problems of learning: the identification and characterization of insightful behaviour and insightful transposition. The Gestaltist account of learning rests largely on the observations carried out by Köhler on the behaviour of chimpanzees during the period of his imprisonment on the island of Teneriffe during the first world war (Köhler, 1925). Köhler observed that a chimpanzee, unlike a rat, is capable of using tools, e.g. using a box to climb on in order to reach a bun suspended from the ceiling of its cage, or of using a stick to rake in a banana. However, the animal is not born with these abilities. It appears to discover them as a result of successive restructurizations of its perceptions. A typical case of insightful learning is illustrated in Figure 2. The chimpanzee is inside a cage and the circles represent the bars. The lure is a banana. This is attached to a length of string which is anchored at one end to a heavy stone while the other is within the animal's reach. The problem cannot be solved by pulling at the string directly, but only by passing the string through the successive bars until the banana is near enough for the animal to reach it. Typically, the animal may go through three stages in trying to secure the fruit: (1) pulling in the direction of the string; (2) pulling the string in the desired direction of the fruit; (3) passing the string round the bars (successful solution). While some animals by-passed either (1) or (2), others went through all three stages. (2) represents a partial restructurization or a

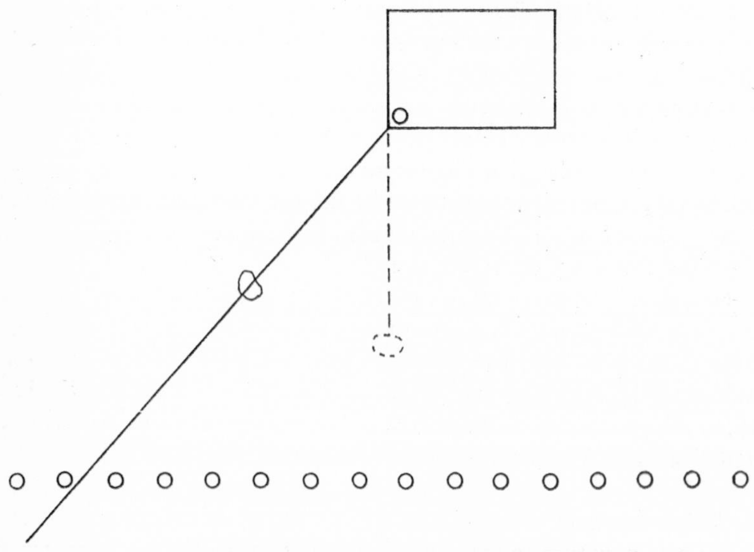

Figure 2. A Case of Insightful Restructurization (based on Köhler, 1925, p. 199)

'good error'; there is a partial 'insight' into the solution: the string and fruit must be dragged sideways. The 'good error' contributes to the final solution when the further problem of overcoming the obstacle of the bar is resolved. It is to be contrasted with (*a*) errors arising from the animal's limitations, e.g. the chimpanzee's inability to pile boxes on one another so that the structure will balance (the chimpanzee solves such problems readily enough, but the solution owes a great deal to the animal's agility, for his structures are always precarious, and sometimes unsuccessful); and (*b*) 'blind stupidities', as when the animal tries to apply in one situation a solution which was applicable to a totally different one, e.g. attempting to use a box (suitable for suspended objects), instead of a stick or a string to reach a lure outside the bars.

Köhler emphasizes two points. First, the animal's behaviour is not blind. It is a sensitive response to the structural relations existing in the situation as a whole. Even the 'blind stupid errors' are a response to some of its features: they are stupid only because they neglect others which 'should be' obvious. Second, the animal's behaviour itself has a purposive, directional character, and behaviour after solution reveals understanding: in future presentations, the problem is solved immediately or almost immediately; moreover, similar problems are solved with almost equal facility (*transposition*), e.g. an animal which has learned to use a stick as a rake to reach a banana, will break off a branch and strip it of its twigs to reach a bunch of grapes. Where Thorndike emphasized the gradual course of learning by trial-and-error, Gestalt psychology paid attention to the immediacy of insightful solution.

The main characteristics of insightful behaviour are therefore:

(1) Suddenness of solution.

(2) Immediacy and smoothness of behaviour after solution (e.g. unhestitatingly passing the string through each bar in succession in the problem illustrated).

(3) Ability to repeat solution without error on successive presentation of original problems.

(4) Ability to transpose the solution to situations exhibiting the same relational or structural features, but in a different context.

Where Köhler demonstrated the occurrence of insight and its correlates in the chimpanzee, Wertheimer (1945) illustrated the operation of similar principles in children's learning. Much of this work consists in the detailed discussion of a single group of problems: the solution of problems based on figures of equivalent area. Pupils taught by conventional demonstration were able to solve the problem of the area of the parallelogram (*a*) as shown in Figure 3. Many were at a loss when Wertheimer showed them (*b*). Some, after some hesitation, realized that (*b*) was merely a rotation of (*a*) but others remained at a loss. Yet a number of much younger children who knew nothing of Euclid were able, after appropriate experience, to solve all analogous problems by converting the figures to rectangles as in (*c*) and (*d*). Insightful solutions according to Wertheimer depend on the presentation of the problem in a way which will bring out the structural features of the situation.

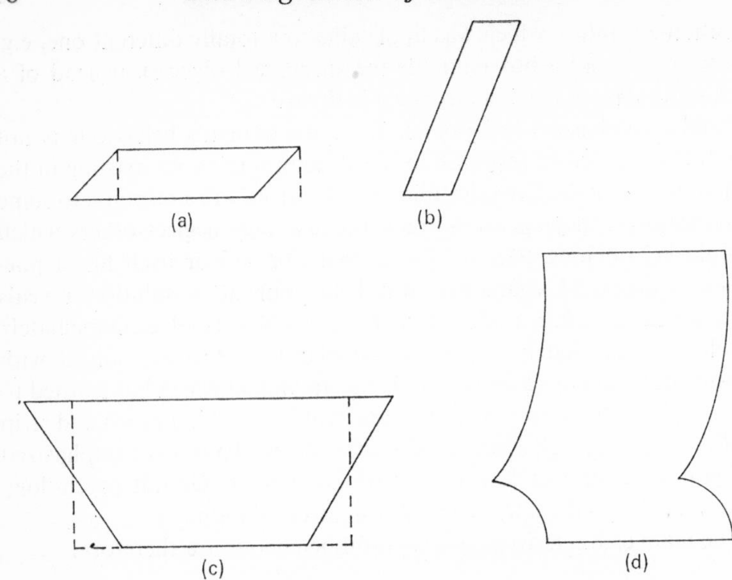

Figure 3. Problems used by Wertheimer (1945)

4 *Trace Theory of Memory*

On the face of it, the observations and demonstrations of Köhler and Wertheimer concern problem solution rather than learning. Indeed, Piaget (1959) argues that insight is not learning but merely the result of learning – on the basis of a semantic definition (learning must involve change of behavioural regulation over relatively long intervals of time), to which the present writer does not wholly subscribe. The question remains how Gestalt psychology accounts for the modification of behaviour over time and over successive presentations. This problem has been tackled by Koffka in terms of a theory of memory (Koffka, 1935). The essence of this theory is that each perception of a situation leaves a trace in the brain reflecting the structure of the percept. During the interval between memorization and recall, the trace undergoes changes in the direction of a more coherent structure. Thus, if the original situation consists of a two-dimensional figure involving some asymmetry, the trace will tend in one of two directions: either the asymmetry will be reduced, or it will be accentuated, for the structural properties of the trace force it to move either towards a maximum or to a minimum. The trace theory of memory is best illustrated in an example by Wulf (1922) purporting to show just such changes as those indicated when subjects are asked to reproduce figures after varying time intervals. Thus Figure 4 tended to be reproduced more as a dumb-bell (symmetry) or more as a bottle (accentuated asymmetry). More generally, we have already noted that Gestalt psychology seeks to interpret behaviour as a directional response to the structural properties of the stimulus situation. The trace theory of memory may be seen as modifying and amplifying this standpoint: the structure inherent in the stimulus communicates with relevant memory traces to yield the perceived structure. It is not difficult to see a direct filiation to Herbart's theory of apperception.

However, the theory of spontaneous structurization in the memory trace is not borne out by subsequent investigations. For instance, Gibson (1929) showed that errors in reproduction could be readily accounted

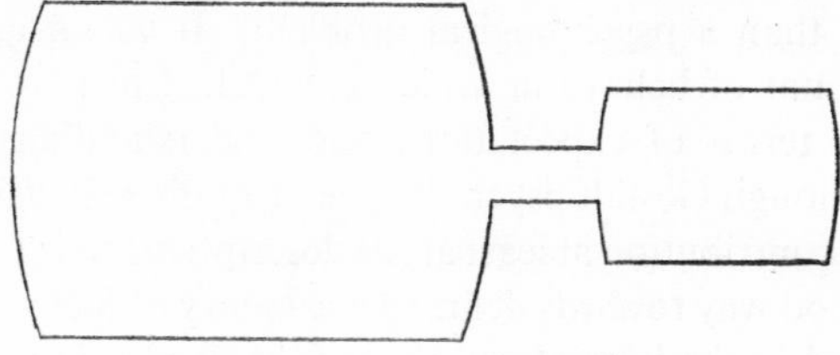

Figure 4 (from Wulf, 1922)

for in terms of the tendency to categorize the percept as a familiar figure; Zangwill (1937) showed that the errors of simplification and rationalization which occurred when the subject is required to recall or reconstruct the figure were recognized as such when he was asked to choose between the original figure and one which was close to his reproduction (i.e. the stored trace was not so degenerate as Wulf supposed: the subject constructs a figure which makes sense to him because of what we would call difficulty in access to store); finally, Hebb and Foord (1945) and others have shown that while errors increase with increase in the interval between perception and reproduction, there is no evidence that such errors are progressive (i.e. all pointing in the same direction: that of 'good form'). An excellent discussion of these and related problems is given by Riley (1963).

5. *Evaluation*

The reader may well share the present writer's doubts as to the adequacy of such terms as 'good structure', 'maximum' and 'minimum'. Presumably a dumb-bell is the minimum for Figure 4; but what is the maximum? and how are these concepts to be generalized for non-graphic material? The theory of spontaneous change in the memory trace is certainly inadequate and probably incorrect. The concept of structure itself in the hands of Gestalt psychology was no more than a beginning, and even the work of Piaget which extends it greatly leaves many unresolved problems.

Nevertheless, from the point of view of theoretical development, the historic significance of Gestalt psychology is unquestionably two-fold: (*a*) to highlight the gap between the simple connexionism of Thorndike and Pavlov and the complexity of behavioural regulation even in animals; and (*b*) to make it abundantly clear that the gap can only be bridged by advances in our understanding of the structure of connexions as opposed to a recognition of their mere existence (which is not enough), or even a fuller knowledge of the form which they take (this being more of a physiological than a psychological problem). It was suggested earlier that any account of behaviour which is couched in purely mentalistic terms, i.e. in terms of expectations and understandings is less than scientific. Although Gestalt psychology is mentalistic it was nevertheless an important contribution at least at the descriptive level: for it described and went a good way towards defining a category of fact which had been largely ignored in the laboratory, i.e. insight. It also initiated a fruitful body of research into what is still one of the most inadequately explored domains of psychology: memory. Yet, as a theory of learning, it is sketchy and also one-sided. In particular, even if one allows that learning can occur as a result of insight, it is very clear that the gradual learning that yields a negatively accelerated curve, which was first discovered by Ebbinghaus and subsequently reflected in the experiments of Thorndike, is so fundamental and pervasive that no theory can afford to ignore it – and no more can the practical worker, e.g. the teacher. The problem, after Gestalt psychology, was, and remains, to arrive at a model which will begin not only to describe but also to account for both kinds of learning.

IV. TOLMAN'S PURPOSIVE BEHAVIOURISM

1. *Introduction*

The work of Tolman constitutes a lifelong essay in this context. Tolman called himself a purposive behaviourist, and his reflections and formulations were an attempt to integrate the observations of Gestalt psychology within the framework of a stimulus-response approach. There are three features of his work which are determinant.

(1) '*Molar behaviourism*'. While adhering to the S-R orientation, Tolman emphatically rejected the conception that behaviour could be interpreted in terms of mere physiological responses: 'muscle twitches'. Psychology, for Tolman, was concerned with the making of inferences and predictions about the relations between stimuli and responses in various situations, but the stimuli were conceived more as total situations and the responses as 'total performances', i.e. as goal-directed manipulations of the environment (cf. Tolman, 1959, p. 95).

(2) *Use of intervening variables.* Tolman sought to explain behaviour and learning in terms of the expectancies of the subject. Behaviour was determined by the expectancies which the subject formed as a result of his existing perceptions and his previous experiences. Learning was essentially a matter of modifying expectancies and forming new ones. Such expectancies have the status of intervening variables; i.e. they are inferred by the psychologist from the relations between the various features of the situation (which he controls) and the characteristics of performance that he observes.

(3) *Eclecticism and experimentalism.* Where Hull tried to construct a unified system which would be sufficiently complete to function as a model for the interpretation of all aspects of behaviour and learning, Tolman remained sceptical as to the feasibility of such an enterprise. In particular, he hypothesized that there were at least three levels at which learning could occur: conditioned reflex, trial and error, and inventive learning, suggesting that the 'laws' governing each successive level incorporated those of the preceding level together with some new ones (Tolman, 1932, Chapter 23). In point of fact, the 'laws' are not so much laws as relations deemed to be relevant and worthy of investigation, e.g. the effect of drive or demand (as defined, for example, by deprivation of food and/or water), the structure of the problem (e.g. the complexity of a maze and the relations between the constituent paths and cues), the capacity of the subject (rat *v.* chimpanzee, etc.), relation to previous learning. The position is eclectic in that Tolman interjects no new relations but seeks to establish where such variables as demand, previous learning experiences, contiguity of instrumental action and reinforcement, or structure of the problem are relevant and where they are less relevant. The first group is taken over from Thorndike and Pavlov via Guthrie,[1] while the last is the specific contribution of Gestalt psychology. But at

[1] Guthrie was an early theorist who adopted from Pavlov the principle of conditioning as such, i.e. that a response which follows a stimulus on one occasion tends to be triggered off when the same stimulus is repeated, and little else (e.g. he rejected

the same time Tolman's position is an out-and-out experimentalist position precisely because his 'laws' are relations to be investigated rather than accepted generalizations of fact. In a later presentation, Tolman (1949) distinguished no less than six varieties of learning (see under 5).

From the theoretical point of view, it is instructive to compare Tolman's position with that of Köhler and Koffka on the one hand and on the other that of Thorndike and Hull.

2. *Comparison with Gestalt psychology*

Any attempt at a generalized theory in psychology is greatly influenced by the particular classes of events or typical situations from which the generalization is made (cf. Morris, 1951). Where the theory is at an early stage of evolution, the typical situation is apt to be singular. The starting point for Gestalt psychology was the organization of perception in the visual field. Hence, in spite of the potential explanatory power of the trace theory of memory, the purposive character of behaviour is interpreted largely in terms of the perceptual coherence of the situation as such, and the subject is seen as the more or less insightful *observer*. For Tolman, the typical situation is the rat in the maze (see especially Tolman, 1938). As a result Tolman sees the structure less as a set of relations among the parts of the object and more as a description of the action possibilities which it holds for the subject. Thus, in Figure 5, the various points along

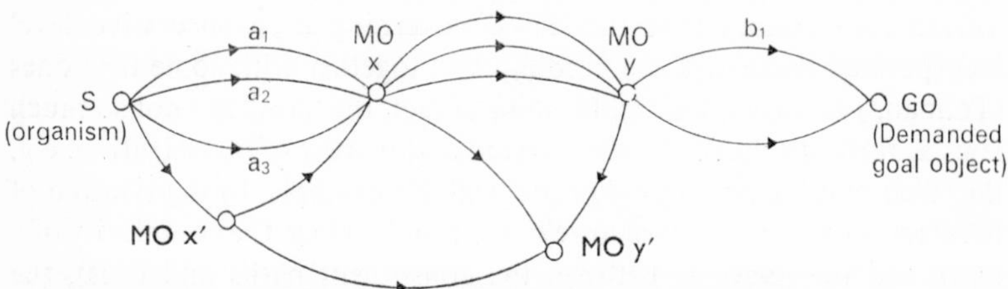

Figure 5. Schematic representation of means–end dependencies (based on Tolman, 1932)

---

the explanatory role of inhibition). The variety of behaviour and learning was accounted for by assuming that every stimulus differs in greater or lesser measure from every other stimulus, so that the response which occurs to a new stimulus will reflect its similarity to previous stimuli. The 'theory' was too simple and too abstract to be very fruitful experimentally. Perhaps one of Guthrie's major claims to fame is that he saw the possibility of 'one-trial learning'. Indeed Guthrie went so far as to maintain that all learning is one-trial learning (cf. Hilgard, 1958, Chapter 3, Mueller and Schoenfeld, 1954, Guthrie 1959).

the paths S—M O_x—M O_y and S—M O_x'—M O_y'—M O_y are thought of as intermediate means objects sub-serving a common goal, G; and the path M O_y—G O is seen as a final common path. In effect Tolman recognizes explicitly that the subject must learn these means-end dependencies through his actions and their results. Although I am not aware that Tolman has said so in so many words, it seems to follow that even where the entire path is within full view of the subject, the means-end dependencies which it involves cannot be assumed to be present for the subject in the same fulness as they are for the psychologist who designed the set-up: the subject's perception is a function of his previous experience with analogous dependencies. In this sense, Tolman's position anticipates that of Piaget, and has clear implications for the importance of sound 'programming' in education. For Tolman, as for Piaget, the means-end characteristics of the object are apprehended by the subject only as a result of his 'commerce' with it.

3. *Comparison with other behaviourisms*

Tolman's position represents an advance on that of Thorndike in its attempt to specify the structure of complex behaviour. This it does through the intervening variables which take the form of means-end dependencies. At the same time what proved to be one of its most fruitful assumptions in terms of experiment was the denial of the law of effect. Where Thorndike had based his view of learning on the assumption that S-R bonds are strengthened by their rewarding consequences, Tolman made a distinction between performance and learning. What is learnt, for Tolman, is the behavioural connectedness of the various parts of the field, i.e. that the performance of **x** in relation to **y** leads to **z**. The essential prerequisite for such learning, apart from the capacities of the learner, is the contiguity of these parts, the experience that behaviour **x** in relation to stimulus **y** leads to stimulus **z**, not the experience of reward **z** following behaviour **x**. In spite of this Tolman's indebtedness to Thorndike is greater than his indebtedness to Pavlov, both because of his emphasis on instrumental learning and because he did not, like Hull, use the concepts of generalization and of inhibition in any systematic way. The role of reward, for Tolman, is to determine the direction of behaviour, given the motivation. Learning, it is held, can take place in the absence of reward. The presence of reward may have the additional effect of producing enhanced attention to a means stimulus, but apart from this it does not critically alter S-R tendencies. The *effect* of learning is not usually apparent except in a situation where differential behaviour has differential consequences.

This is because behaviour is purposive. The critical experiments are those on *latent learning*, beginning with the study of Blodgett (1929).

Blodgett ran three groups of rats in the same maze over a period of seven to nine days. The first group was consistently fed in the goal-box at the end of each run; the second was not fed for the first six days but was fed on days seven, eight and nine, while the third group was fed on the third day. The learning of the first group showed the familiar exponential (negatively accelerated) curve, both in terms of errors and in terms of time. The second group showed little improvement over the first eight days (although there was some, particularly in terms of errors), and a sharp decline in time and errors on the eighth (after the first experience of feeding). The performance of the third group, after the third day, was similar, save that the decline was less sharp (since even the learning of the first group was far from complete after only three days at one trial per day).

Taken in relation to Thorndike's law of effect, Blodgett's experiment marks out an entirely new dimension of behaviour. But taken in relation to Hull's elaborated system of behaviour in which reinforcement is still a cornerstone the experiment is far from definitive. In particular, it is virtually impossible to show in experiments of this type that there has not been some reinforcement, e.g. that provided by escape from confinement, or by the experience of novelty itself. Granted such minimal reinforcement, Hull like Tolman would predict a sharp decline in errors following the enhanced incentive, while preserving the critical role of reinforcement in the original learning (see next section).

Blodgett's experiment was the forerunner of many. In addition to those which closely resemble Blodgett's prototype (1), three further types of latent learning experiment have been distinguished. (2) Free exploration in the maze without feeding may be followed by feeding directly in the goal-box, to determine the effect of such feeding on the subsequent performance in the maze itself; (3) the reward may be present for both experimental and control groups from the start of the experiment, but the former is satiated for the reward until the critical test run; (4) the conditions are similar to those in (3), but the experimental group are initially run under some strong irrelevant drive, e.g. both limbs of a T maze contain water and only one contains food: the experimental group is thirsty but not hungry during the training runs, while during the test runs they are hungry but not thirsty. All these experiments have been reviewed by Thistlethwaite (1951) and, again, by MacCorquodale and Meehl, (1954). Results are far from conclusive. Although latent learning is apparent in most of the studies based on designs (1), (2) and (3) it is not shown in some of them, nor in the majority of those with design (4). Since some latent learning would be predicted by a sophisticated (Hullian) reinforcement theory as well as by a cognitive behaviourism, and since the latter can predict failure of latent learning under some conditions (e.g. when the distraction of irrelevant incentive is so strong that the means-end dependencies which need to be learnt are ignored), the present writer cannot resist the conclusion that the detail of these rat experiments is of more specific interest to the student of rat behaviour than it is to the student of behaviour in general. But – be it noted – one is wise after the event.

Contrasting Tolman's view with that of Hull, a first and abiding difference lies in the importance which the latter attaches to reinforcement. Perhaps the majority of the remaining differences may be summed up by the statement that Tolman's position is centralist while the Hullian position is peripheralist. What this means is that Tolman attempts to map out the determinants of behaviour in terms of means-end expectancies which he sees as relations between processes in the brain subserving a wide variety of equivalences, while Hull attempts to reduce such equivalences to differential strengths among competing S-R tendencies. Hull's conception of the S-R bond is much more like the 'muscle-twitch' which Tolman rejects.

Hence the numerous experiments designed to show the importance of place-learning as opposed to response-learning, e.g. in the situation illustrated in Figure 6. Tolman, Ritchie and Kalish (1946) predicted that animals trained to run from S_1 to F_1 would continue to run to F_1 from S_2 even though the response involved is now a right turn and not a left, while those trained to turn left to F_2 would now turn right to F_2 from the new starting point. This group of experiments is reviewed by Restle (1957) who notes that neither place-learning nor response-learning is universal: what is learnt is a response to cues. Whether place cues or movement cues are predominant depends largely on the specific character of the situation. Thus in an overhead maze, place cues predominate; in an enclosed maze response cues predominate. Again, one is thrown back on the realization that the experiment designed to be critical and general is specific to the species studied.

More generally, however, because Hullian theory envisages the possibility of integrating stimulus response bonds into 'habit-family hierarchies', deductions from experiments conceived in a centralist vein are rarely conclusive, for the 'orthodox' (Hullian) position itself provides for the elaboration of such general action tendencies.

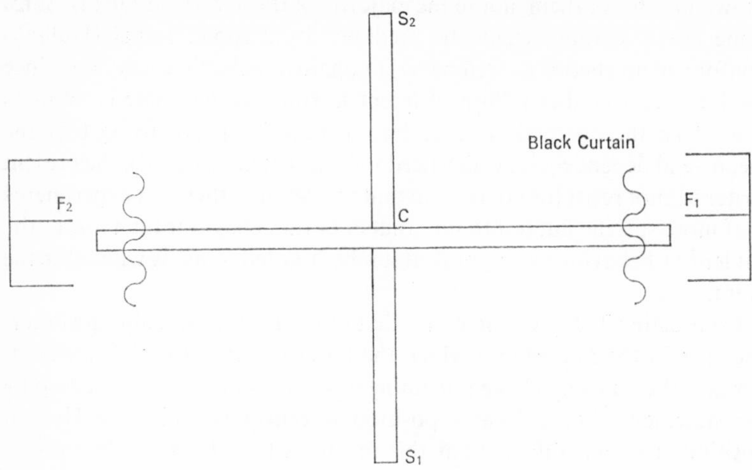

Figure 6. Place Learning (based on Tolman, Ritchie and Kalish, 1946)

4. *Vicarious trial-and-error*

Tolman's contention that the behaviour of rats in mazes is conditioned by 'expectancies' rather than by 'habit' is supported by the observation of what he calls 'vicarious trial-and-error' (**VTE**). In the maze this is the tendency for the rats to peep into alleys without entering them. A similar tendency to explore the possibilities before action (more properly, to engage in partial preliminary actions which do not commit the subject to the complete action and permit of a return to the starting point) was observed by Muenzinger (1938) in the discrimination apparatus known as the Lashley jumping-stand. (The animal is placed on a platform from which it is required to jump towards one of two doors differentiated both by their position and by their stimulus value, e.g. one is black while the other is white: jumping to the correct door is rewarded because this is loosely hinged and the animal lands on a food platform, while jumping to the incorrect door is punished by a fall into a net.) Tolman takes the occurrence of **VTE** as evidence for a cognitive approach to learning, and it is quite possible that if the experimentation on learning had been conducted entirely from the hypothesis of habit formation, its existence would have been overlooked. But, once again, it is not critical evidence against the latter, for it is arguable that exploratory behaviour as an intermediate response between an initial S and a final R is a highly reinforced mode of response, one which allows for the operation of further mediating stimuli and the elaboration of effective habit-family-hierarchies[1] (see Spence, 1945).

5. *Historical significance of Tolman's work*

Tolman himself has repeatedly described his own work as 'programmatic' (e.g. Tolman, 1949, 1959). Similar criticisms have been made by Hilgard (1958) and Meehl and MacCorquodale (1954). This stricture needs to be taken in conjunction with the observation that Tolman's scope was a large one: to provide a comprehensive approach which would cover all fields of behaviour and learning. Part of the difficulty (but only a part) lies in the diversity of the processes to be explained.

Reference was made earlier to Tolman's suggestion that there were at least three levels of learning: conditioning, trial-and-error, and inventive ideation, and that the 'laws' applicable to these successive levels must be of increasing complexity. He returned to this topic later, this time suggesting six varieties of learning, and offering suggestions as to the laws which would be applicable to them (Tolman, 1949). These areas are: (1) learning of 'cathexes', i.e. rewarding or punishing nature of goal object (e.g. that a particular food is hunger reducing, or that an electric shock is pain producing); (2) learning of 'equivalence beliefs', e.g. that swimming a flooded maze is equivalent to wading a less flooded maze (Macfarlane, 1930, showed that rats who had learnt the latter transferred readily to the former); (3) formation of 'field expectancies', i.e. the means-end expectancies upon which most of Tolman's work was concentrated, as in place learning and latent learning; (4) formation of 'field cognition modes', including 'set of rules about time, space, force and quantity . . . and these we carry around with us from one specific situation to another, so that they govern our specific apprehensions, i.e. our field expectancies'; (5) the acquisition of drive discrimination, e.g. to distinguish appropriately between the hunger and thirst conditions in a T maze when food is found in one limb and water in the other; and (6) the patterning of motor behaviour. Tolman suggests, tentatively, that the kind of conditioning by contiguity emphasized by Guthrie may be most relevant to (6); he has no suggestions to offer for the laws governing (5); he supposes that (1) may be a class of learning to which Hull's hypothesis of need-reduction may be most appropriate. This leaves (2), (3) and (4), representing the more complex behavioural organizations. It is suggested that the first of these, (2), may be acquired by a process to which both need-reduction and expectancies are relevant, while (3) is a class covered more exclusively by

[1] See p. 41.

the latter. Finally, as to (4), an area covered extensively by Piaget, Tolman has no suggestions to offer, merely emphasizing its importance.

In 1932, Tolman had offered what amounts to three sets of laws of which each successive set would incorporate the previous sets, each set providing for the learning of behaviour at a different level. The 1949 formulation tackles the same problem from the opposite end; for the division is in terms of behavioural categories. It brings out both the positive and the negative aspects of Tolman's work. Its essentially programmatic character is evident in the tentative way in which varying approaches to learning are assigned to each of the categories. It is even more manifest in Tolman's unwillingness to commit himself with respect to category (4). There is even lack of system in the arrangement of these categories, for a logical arrangement would be: (1), (6), (2), (3), (4). (I can think of no evidence that animals, or even human beings, learn to discriminate among their drives (5), although there is plenty of evidence that they learn to behave differently according to which drive is in operation. But, all that is needed for this is that the drive shall operate as a stimulus, and this is rather an aspect of all learning than a separate kind of learning.)

It was argued earlier that Tolman's 1932 laws were not so much laws as statements of what variables might prove relevant. This is no less true of the 1949 version. In this sense Tolman's work is more of a mapping of the area which needs to be covered by theory than itself a theory. This is its historical significance. Tolman's work acted as a challenge to psychologists in that he stressed the sort of learnings which in fact occur and which merit investigation, laying particular stress on those aspects which seemed by their complexity to defy an approach in terms of simple connexions betweeen S and R. This, in itself, would hardly represent much of a contribution, were it not for the fact that, together with his collaborators, Tolman repeatedly pointed out ways of investigating these areas in the laboratory – as in the latent learning and place learning investigations or in the study of **VTE**.

But there is one more serious limitation which merits a word of comment before we pass to 'learning theory' proper. It is that Tolman deliberately confined himself to the study of the rat. It will be shown in Chapter 5 that such a limitation can imply a serious restriction both in the accuracy of interpretation and in the range of the inquiry. Not only does this account for his failure to find anything very significant to say about (4), but it also seriously detracts from the conceptual usefulness of his concept of 'cognitive map'. As will be apparent from a consideration of the work of Piaget (see Chapter 5, Section IV), there is a real distinction between the ability to select an appropriate detour at a choice-point and the ability to reconstruct, or represent, a 'map' of the maze.

V. HULLIAN THEORY

The work of Hull and his associates represents a comprehensive attempt to provide a complete account of organized behaviour and complex learning based on the stimulus-response hypothesis: i.e. that behaviour is a matter of responses to stimuli. It incorporates the most significant principles of Thorndike and Pavlov, albeit in somewhat modified form. At the same time a number of additional features provide for the construction of a theoretical model which will account for the more complex forms of behaviour and learning revealed by Gestalt psychology or by Tolman. No one reading this chapter, or any other psychological work on learning can be unaware that there are many theories of learning. Yet the terms 'the theory of learning' and 'learning theory' are commonplace in psychology. Thus a particular phenomenon in education, say the effectiveness of short, spaced learning periods (see Volume II, Chapter 4), or the ineffectiveness of teaching the contrasted spellings of homonyms at the same time, may be said to be deducible from 'learning theory'. When the term is used in the singular form, the reference is to Hullian theory. This is not to say that such processes as generalization and differentiation, inhibition, or the effectiveness of rewards were first introduced by Hull. The point is that they were incorporated by Hull into a comprehensive theory.

Had the Hullian synthesis been successful in the light of subsequent developments in psychology, this section might well have figured right at the start of our discussion of learning, in the interests of clear exposition of an authenticated interpretation, or at the end, as a historical synthesis of all that went before. It is here in the middle, because, at least in the opinion of the present writer, and probably of most of his contemporaries, the attempt was unsuccessful, and most of the specifically Hullian concepts are mythical entities. The chapters which follow will be concerned to show why. Anticipating: because behaviour is not a matter of response to stimuli. But we may note right from the start that no one since Hull has tried to repeat his attempt at a Newtonian synthesis. Contemporary psychologists, apart from a few eminent adherents of Hull, are usually content to limit the range of their interpretation to more limited aspects of behaviour.

However, Hullian theory has more than a mere historical importance. For viewed from this less ambitious standpoint of its ability to map out some relevant aspects of behavioural organization and to describe its laws at least partially, the contribution of Hull and his followers is probably equal to any. The limitations of Thorndike and Pavlov lay (*a*) in their failure to show how connexions between stimuli and responses could yield complex behavioural organizations, and (*b*) in their failure to bring out the role of motivation in behaviour and learning in a systematic and experimentally testable form. Hullian theory may be looked on as an extension of their principles aimed at overcoming both these limitations.

Hull has given a detailed and axiomatic presentation of his theory together with a fair body of relevant evidence, in the course of two major works (Hull, 1943 and 1952). There is neither scope nor justification for following this presentation in the present chapter, which has the very limited aim of bringing out the most salient features of the system as a system and of illustrating some of the areas in which it has proved most successful. Unless otherwise indicated laws attributed to Hull may be found set out in detail in at least one of the above volumes.

From this point of view, the principle features of the system may be assumed under a number of sub-section headings.

1. *Reinforcement, learning and performance*

The distinction between performance and learning is familiar from the work of Tolman. Hull incorporated this same distinction by postulating that the occurrence of behaviour in the presence of the stimulus is a function of many factors including the presence of sufficient motivation or drive. Learning, however, is taken to be essentially a matter of increase in the strength of the positive bond between **S** and **R**. The bond itself is, of course, not observed, and has the status of an 'intervening variable'. It is termed '*habit strength*' (sHr). The growth of habit strength is held to be a function of reinforcement, and reinforcement is defined as the reduction of a drive or need. Any R which occurs in the presence of an S and is followed by reduction of a need acquires a stronger bond with antecedent stimuli. Experiments carried out with the rat indicate that the increase is exponential and asymptotic. This, of course, is the familiar negatively accelerated learning curve found as early as Ebbinghaus.

The principle of learning by need-reduction is of course an attempt to give greater precision to Thorndike's law of effect. More important, however, is the separation of performance and learning which enables Hullian theory to account for most of the phenomena of latent learning.

Learning results in observable performance only when there is sufficient drive. A second feature of the system, which it shares with most other theoretical formulations, and one which corresponds with most of the observed phenomena of learning, but not all, is the assumption that change in the strength of association is gradual (although negatively accelerated) and incremental. Guthrie alone, among learning theorists, proffered an all-or-none formulation, but Gestalt theory came close to it. However, Hullian theory can accommodate the phenomena of insight, as will be seen under sub-section 5.

2. *Incentive and drive*

Learning itself cannot be observed directly. It is inferred from the characteristics of performance. In an experimental investigation, the most readily accessible of such characteristics are the latency of response, its strength and its resistance to experimental extinction (see above, p. 5). These characteristics of performance are held by Hull to be a function of '*reaction potential*' (**sEr**), itself an intervening variable. While habit strength is a function of previous reinforcing experiences, reaction potential is a complex function. Its chief determinants, together with habit strength, are drive and incentive. *Drive* is held to be a physiological response to the presence of a need and the intensity of drive is determined experimentally by manipulating such needs as hunger and thirst. Drive is then a function of the length of deprivation (of food or water). Experiments by Miller and others show a precise relation between each of the parameters of response (or performance) and length of deprivation, with previous experience (habit strength) held constant.

It is of some importance to note that the intensity of behaviour (or of the inferred reaction potential) appears to be a function of motivation in general, '*generalized drive*', and not only of the relevant deprivation, '*relevant drive*'. Thus, although hungry rats run more quickly to a food reward, after a longer food deprivation, they also run more quickly to a food reward after water deprivation. The concept of generalized drive assumes particular importance in Miller and Spence's extensions of Hullian theory, involving the assumption that *anxiety* is a learnt, generalized drive (Dollard and Miller, 1950, Spence, 1956). This idea has been followed by Eysenck (1957) and his collaborators in this country. Furneaux predicted, and found, that students at the university level who rated high on a measure of anxiety tended to perform better at their examinations (Furneaux, 1957). On the other hand, there is little evidence that anxiety is an asset in the earlier stages of education. Although Lynn

(1959), found some association between the measure of anxiety and reading in a select group of children, the present writer found that all types of maladjustment and unsettledness are associated with retardation (Lunzer, 1960), and Rushton (1966) found a significant negative correlation between anxiety and success at the '11 plus' selection examination. Similar findings have been reported by Hallworth (1961) in relation to children of secondary school age.

Even in the rat, the interaction of various types of motivation is a complex process (Spence, 1956, pp. 189 ff.) and not a mere summation. There is also good ground for the 'Yerkes-Dodson hypothesis' (Yerkes and Dobson, 1908) that intense motivation acts as a positive spur for simple tasks, but tends to disrupt integration (and therefore learning) when the task is more complex. The suggestion has been substantiated both for rat learning (Broadhurst, 1957) and for chimpanzee learning (Birch, 1945a), and there is good reason to believe that a similar principle holds true of human learning also. The investigation of drive continues to be a useful field of inquiry which promises to enhance our understanding of the mechanisms underlying human behaviour in an educational context. But Furneaux's findings are consistent with the common sense hypothesis that students who are anxious about their success ('relevant anxiety') will spend more time on their books than those who regard their period at the university as the holiday of a lifetime. It is altogether likely, following the Yerkes-Dodson hypothesis, that unless this anxiety is immediately inhibited when the book is opened, anxious students will tend to get less out of their study than their unworried colleagues. But the restriction is important. For if the anxiety is 'relevant', there is every reason to predict that it will be allayed when the learning task begins, so that disruption is minimal, while if it is irrelevant, generalized anxiety, the inception of the task will not dispel it and disruption will continue. The difficulty of investigations in this field are largely centered around the difficulty of devising methods which will discriminate effectively between generalized and relevant anxiety.

In a rat experiment, drive (**D**) is a function of length of deprivation. *Incentive* (**K**) is a function of the size of the reward which the animal finds on completion of the response. Since the Hullian system is a strict S-R system which will not allow mentalistic expectancies, **K** is deemed to be mediated by the anticipatory goal reactions, r_G, which are supposed to intervene between **S** and **R** (see sub-section 4). Be that as it may, there is overwhelming evidence that rats run faster to a sizeable reward than they do to a niggardly reward. The reader who is fond of a bit of logical analysis can easily satisfy himself that the hypothesis that drive interacts with habit strength will readily explain the second and third types of latent learning described in the last section while the role of incentive is particularly relevant to the original Blodgett experiment.

3. *Generalization and inhibition*

(*a*) The principal facts about stimulus generalization were established in Pavlov's laboratory. Hull's conception of learning is instrumental (Thorndike type) rather than classical conditioning. However, the concept of generalization is taken over from Pavlov, together with its corollary that response to a stimulus which is similar to the original stimulus under which conditioning occurred will be weaker than the original response, in proportion to the degree of dissimilarity.

It should be stressed, however, that the issues are by no means so simple as this would imply. In particular, it is difficult to establish precise boundaries between the weakening effect of generalization *per se* and those of differential inhibition. For if a response has been established to, say, a light stimulus of a given intensity, it is no use repeatedly administering a stimulus of some different intensity to find an average value for the effect of generalization. If the second stimulus is reinforced, there is new learning as well as generalization, and if it is not reinforced there is differential inhibition. There is some evidence that if one examines only the first application of the generalized stimulus (which means using different subjects for each point along the generalization continuum) the generalization is complete and immediate (see the review by Mednick and Freedman, 1960).

The issue is further complicated by the concept of '*afferent stimulus interaction*', which is a necessary corollary to the S-R approach. There is no guarantee that the subject will obediently be conditioned to what the experimenter chooses to regard as 'the stimulus'. It is therefore proposed that the bond is established with all incoming signals, and that these interact to yield a stimulus complex. Most psychologists are bound to agree with Hebb (1949) that the concept of stimulus interaction is impossibly vague (see Chapter 3).

There is an important variant to the orthodox Hullian approach which appears to have originated with Spence (1937). Let us suppose a simple discrimination experiment in which the subject is required to choose between a black disc and a white disc, the position of these discs (left or right) being varied according to some random method of arrangement. Any response made by the subject can then be taken as (i) a response to the position (since his choice must be for the left or the right hand disc), and (ii) a response to its colour (since he is bound to choose either white or black). If the response is reinforced, two bonds are strengthened, the position bond and the colour bond, and if it is not, both are weakened, (by inhibition, see below). To this couple one may add the consideration that the subject's previous choice may have been to the same position or to the same colour, or both, or any of the opposite trio. Extending the concept of 'stimulus' to these relations with the subject's previous behaviour (and there is very good experimental ground for doing so, beginning with the study of Krechevsky (1932)) then the number of 'stimuli' (in what sense is the rightness of a right object following choice of a left object an 'afferent' process?) becomes potentially infinite and must clearly vary with the capacity of the subject (e.g. a double alternation problem in a maze, L L R R L L R R . . . , is relatively easy for the human adult and impossibly difficult for the rat). But, even more telling, the problem of which of these 'stimuli' is the 'leading' stimulus, with which others 'interact', and whether any of these 'stimuli' exists for the subject ('is noticed') becomes crucial and cannot be resolved in terms of the **S-R** approach, which assumes the stimulus as the starting point for behaviour. The entire process of behaviour and learning becomes much more tractable if one begins at the other end, by assuming that in any given situation, the functional properties of the stimulus are *selected* by the subject in accordance with his endowment (fish, rat, monkey or human being, see Chapter 5 and Bitterman, 1965) and his previous experience – which is the point of view shared by the present writer with Piaget, Sutherland, Mackintosh, 1964, and Broadbent, 1958 – although the last named of these may not have suspected the company that they kept until these lines were written).

The definition of the 'stimulus' is rather a tangled skein, and the definition of generalization is very much dependent on that of the stimulus. Nevertheless, the fact of stimulus generalization can be taken as proven: it cannot be defined for all situations, but it can be defined in privileged situations such as laboratory conditioning. Nor is there much doubt that the process is at work in all behaviour. No one is therefore inclined to quarrel with Hull in adopting it from Pavlov, and in showing its operation in instrumental conditioning. Generalization as at present understood leaves many problems unresolved; but it seems more likely that the concept itself will come to be refined, than that it will ever need to be dropped.

(*b*) Inhibition is another concept which Hull took over from Pavlov, but in this case with a considerable shift of emphasis. Inhibition for

Pavlov is bound up with the *organization* of reflexes. Although 'internal inhibition' was shown in experimental extinction and in such phenomena as the delayed conditional reflex, Pavlov tried to relate these phenomena to 'external inhibition', shown in the inhibitory effect of irrelevant stimuli. Differential inhibition is seen as a particular case of external inhibition, and the interaction and conflict of the two processes, excitatory and inhibitory, is dramatically revealed in experimental neurosis. More generally, the organized interaction of the two processes is held to account for the smooth (and rigid) performance of habitual sequences: dynamic stereotypes. Also, the control of attention is taken to be directly dependent on the function of reciprocal induction: the tendency for any strong excitatory process to inhibit other processes, and for strong inhibitory processes to disinhibit others. Very strong stimuli were shown to produce 'supra-marginal inhibition'; all reflexes are inhibited, and the subject 'freezes into immobility'. Monotonous repetition of inhibitory stimuli was found to induce a condition allied to hypnosis, and one which passes over into sleep. This was attributed by Pavlov to a 'spread of inhibition over the cortex' – a concrete neurological hypothesis which has since proven to be far too simple (see Chapter 2, and Magoun, 1963).

It should be said in passing that the concept of negative induction or 'reciprocal inhibition' has ever since been widely accepted, not only for its explanatory power, but also, and especially, for its usefulness in psychotherapy. Many readers will be familiar with Watson's impressive conditioning of Little Albert, who was first trained to fear a rabbit by coupling the sight of the rabbit with a loud noise, and then gradually led to accept the animal by having it brought nearer and nearer during mealtimes, (Watson, 1957). Essentially the same method is now quite widely used in the cure of neurotic symptoms (see, e.g. Wolpe, 1958), even though it is not a panacea (Eysenck, 1957).

By contrast with Pavlov's emphasis on the role of inhibition in the regulation of behaviour, Hull's account is based on an inhibition which is held to be an inevitable accompaniment of the performance of any individual response, whether or not it is reinforced. This '*inhibition of reinforcement*' (which had itself been observed by Pavlov) is held to be closely allied with fatigue, and to be directly proportional to the amount of 'work' done (as shown, e.g. by measuring the speed of experimental extinction when an animal is required to press a lever for a food reward, the resistance of the lever being varied by a spring). During the course of exercise, the response is held to acquire '*reactive inhibition*', whether or not it is reinforced. As the response is repeated, the inhibition accumulates. When the animal ceases to respond, it dissipates rapidly: hence the spontaneous recovery shown by Pavlov.

However, in addition to such reactive inhibition which dissipates with rest, Hull postulated another kind of inhibition, '*conditional inhibition*'. Following Miller and Mowrer (Hull, 1943), he argued that the fatigue of reactive inhibition should act as an irritant or drive, and that the non-execution of response should be reinforced by the reduction of that drive, since, when the animal rests, he is not responding. Hull suggests that, as response is maintained, so the tendency not to respond continues to be reinforced; and he argues further that this conditioned inhibition summates with reactive inhibition, and the two together act in the opposite direction to reaction potential, so that the '*effective reaction potential*' can be calculated by subtracting the total inhibition (generalized, since inhibition like excitation is subject to generalization) from total (generalized) positive reaction potential.

Hull's account of inhibition has been severely criticized on several grounds (Koch, 1954). In particular one does not see why reactive inhibition should not multiply with conditioned inhibition instead of being added, since one is a drive and the other a negative habit. Eysenck (1957) even goes so far as to make it multiply with positive habit strength to yield a negative result, and with negative conditioned inhibition to yield a positive result. One may perhaps be pardoned for regarding this as a kind of mathematical gymnastics when carried out upon such tenuous constructs. In particular, the derivation of conditioned inhibition seems to me to be somewhat illogical, for the cessation of a response upon its completion is not at all the same thing as not responding before its inception.[1] Very generally, however, one might reasonably conclude that Hullian theory and experiment have yielded a positive advance in relation to Pavlov's treatment by highlighting the effect of 'fatigue' and demonstrating its close relation to inhibition. At the same time the attempt to focus the interpretation of inhibition on what happens within the given S-R bond, to the neglect of its role in the organization of behaviour looks like a retreat in relation to Pavlov's grandiose vision.

4. *Secondary reinforcement and the goal gradient*

The concept of secondary reinforcement, like many others, is one which Hull adopted, and partly adapted, from Pavlov. Frolov, one of

[1] It is the dependence on drive reduction which makes the relation implausible. There is nothing implausible in supposing that the effort involved in exertion is directly conditioned to the situation which released that exertion, tending to inhibit its tendency to act as a releaser in the future. This is practically a primary datum of common observation.

Pavlov's collaborators, had succeeded in establishing a conditional reflex to a neutral stimulus, a black square, using a previously conditioned stimulus, a metronome, to take the place of the *unconditional stimulus* for salivation. The original **US**, food, was never presented in the course of these second-order conditioning trials, although it was essential to continually reinforce the metronome independently. Under conditions of classical conditioning, second-order conditioning is difficult to form and higher order conditioning impossible: the experiment requires the non-reinforcement of the intermediate stimulus when it is preceded by the second-order stimulus, and therefore there is a strong tendency for differentiation, i.e. the metronome will be positive when alone and inhibitory when preceded by the square.

However, the strength of secondary conditioning is easier to demonstrate in instrumental learning. Bugelski, following a lead by Skinner, found that after rats had been trained to depress a lever in an experimental 'Skinner-box' to actuate the food mechanism and release a food pellet, the course of experimental extinction was less rapid if the depression of the lever continued to actuate the mechanism with its characteristic click (although no food was given) than when it was disengaged. Clearly, the click had acquired secondary reinforcing properties. In an even more striking experiment, Cowles (1937) was able to train chimpanzees to use chips in a slot machine to secure food, and then go on to solve a succession of discrimination learning problems (choosing the correct box out of five boxes), when the sole reward was the presence of a chip in the positive box.

Secondary reinforcement is closely linked with the phenomenon of the *goal gradient*. Under classical reinforcing conditions, delay in the administration of the unconditioned stimulus (**US**) tends to seriously impair the formation of the **CR**, the optimal interval being of the order of half a second. In instrumental learning an animal can be trained to execute a long series of actions, e.g. run a complete maze to gain a food reinforcement. Hull's interpretation is that the intermediate stimuli acquire secondary reinforcing potential, thus greatly extending the range of time over which the primary reinforcement can operate.

In spite of the fact that the primary gradient of reinforcement is overlaid even in animal learning by the intervention of secondary reinforcers, its influence is still marked, as is evident in a simple maze running experiment where rats will run faster as they near the final stretch. Much the same may well be true of human learning, which is doubtless one of the reasons why the practice of regular examinations has been so widespread a feature in most educational systems (there are others, e.g. to test the effectiveness of the teaching).

The capacity to work for long range reinforcers is one which may be expected to discriminate among species and also among individuals within a species. Young children, and defective children, require constant and immediate reinforcement (praise or knowledge of success) while older children can reasonably be expected, and presumably should be expected, to work without such automatic reinforcement. Nevertheless, there is some reason to doubt whether such long-range reinforcers as prizes or marks in examinations can be regarded as strict instances of 'reinforcement'. They appear to function as motivators of behaviour rather than as reinforcers of learning (see Chapter 7). Turning back to secondary reinforcement in Hullian theory, its importance will emerge more clearly in the course of our consideration of the antedating response which forms the topic of the next sub-section.

5. *The antedating response*

The concept of the antedating response is undoubtedly the linchpin of the entire Hullian system. It is supposed that, in addition to the effect of reinforcement in strengthening the bond between the initial stimulus and the initial response, reinforcement acts so as to cause some portion of the final response to antedate its original stimulus and attach itself to the initial stimulus. For instance, in a straight alley leading to a goal-box, the presence of food in the goal-box strengthens the tendency to run down the alley from the point of release; but it also causes some of the behaviour of the goal-box to occur at the point of release: salivation. Salivation is only a part of the total response in the goal-box, which includes chewing and swallowing. It is the detachable part of the goal response, and it is this detachable part which is antedated and becomes attached to the initial stimulus. While the entire goal response, R_G, can only be performed when food is present, this fractional goal response, r_G, (students like to call it 'little Argy') tends to accompany the entire sequence of behaviour, being conditioned to all the stimuli that the subject encounters.

The concept of the antedating response is clearly much the same as that of the conditional reflex itself. The principal differences are two. First, Hull recognized that the **CR** is not in all respects identical with the **UR**; and, second, Hull chose to make the conditioning dependent on reinforcement in the sense of need-reduction. By no means all of his followers have accepted this formulation. For instance, Mowrer (1950, 1960a) prefers to think of conditioning in Pavlov's sense. Thus, in conditioning fear to an anticipated shock, a rat can be trained to move from one compartment to another to avoid the shock. The avoidance reaction is an unconditioned response to shock, and has little to do with shock termination (the reader will recall the earlier argument on conditioned inhibition).

Many writers who otherwise follow Hull also choose to regard conditioning as independent of need reduction, so favouring a dual learning theory: conditioning, and instrumental need reduction (see the discussion in Osgood, 1953, pp. 462 ff., and, especially, Skinner's sharp distinction between elicited responses and operant responses, noted in the next section).

Be that as it may, the fact of conditioning is indisputable. The concept of the antedating of responses underlies at least three of the most powerful aspects of the Hullian system: incentive learning, insight and the habit-family-hierarchy.

(*a*) *Incentive motivation.* Experiments carried out by Crespi (1942) and by Spence and his followers demonstrated clearly that the speed of running in rats varies with the magnitude of the reinforcement they have been accustomed to receive. Moreover, if the reinforcement is increased there is a sharp rise in performance; if it is decreased performance shows a sharp drop. The relevant literature is fully discussed by Spence (1956). The variation of performance with incentive was attributed by Hull to an expectancy factor, **K**. But neither Hull nor his followers were content to think of this in purely mentalistic terms. The origin of **K** is attributed to the r_G mechanism. The occurrence of the fractional responses itself gives rise to stimuli associated with the goal-box and behaviour in the goal-box: r_G gives rise to s_G. These s_G have secondary reinforcing properties, giving rise in turn to an energizing force, **K**, which varies with the magnitude of the incentive. We have had to refer to the role of **K** already in bringing out the systematic way in which 'learning theory' differentiates between learning and performance (habit strength and effective reaction potential). The latter is taken to vary with incentive just as it varies with drive. If we add the inhibitory effects on response tendencies, but conveniently forget about generalization (to avoid complicating the formula unduly), we have

$$_S\mathbf{E}_R = \mathbf{D} \times \mathbf{K} \times {_S\mathbf{H}_R} - (\mathbf{I}_R + {_S\mathbf{I}_R})$$

Incentive motivation clearly plays an important role in behaviour. It has already been suggested that the Hullian interpretation of latent learning is largely based on this concept. Thus, in the Blodgett type experiment, it can be argued that the minimal reinforcement yielded by escape from confinement, or by the satisfaction of curiosity, was sufficient to establish a potentially stronger **sHR** in favour of the correct maze responses: the introduction of the reinforcement immediately yielded a strong incentive factor **K**, and hence a powerful **s$\bar{\text{E}}$R** for the correct responses.

The concept of incentive motivation may, indeed, be pushed further, as it has been in the work of Spence (*op. cit.*), who regards all learning as essentially a matter of strengthened reward expectations, depending on the number of times reinforcement has been experienced, the amount of reinforcement, and the length of the chain of responses from the initial stimulus to the reinforcement (see last section on goal gradient). Hull (1943) leant rather more heavily on the concept of primary reinforcement, and on the influence of habit strength (**sHR**) together with primary drive in determining behaviour, **s$\bar{\text{E}}$R**, while allowing some explanatory role to the antedating response, to secondary reinforcement, and to incentive motivation, **K**. In the hands of Spence, the order of importance is reversed: learning is more a matter of association between stimuli and reinforcers, *via the* $\mathbf{r_G}$ *mechanism,* than of association between stimuli and responses. Apart from the italicized 'explanation', the position is remarkably close to Tolman's sign-significate expectation; as Spence himself points out (*op. cit.*, p. 152). However, in fairness to Tolman, it should be added that he never accepted the interpretation of behaviour as essentially a chain of responses, in which each successive stimulus elicits a chosen response (by virtue of the balance of **sHR**, $\mathbf{r_G}$, **K**, **IR**, **sIR**, and so on, attaching to the various alternatives), and each response brings its consequent stimuli, and this paradigm is *the* hallmark of Hull's theory and its variants. Tolman preferred to think of sign expectation as a field-structure; and, although this is more of a speculative description than a theoretical model, it is less open to the objections raised in the next chapter.

(*b*) *Insight and the habit-family hierarchy.* Let us consider first a conditioning experiment carried out by Shipley (1933) with human subjects. The experiment involves two parts: first, a conditioned blinking response was established to a faint light using a sharp tap on the cheek as the unconditional stimulus; the second step was to establish a conditioned finger withdrawal to the tap on the cheek, using a mild electric shock to the finger as an unconditional stimulus. When the light (which had never been paired with shock) was now shown (without tap or shock) it elicited not only blinking but also finger withdrawal. This is not a case of second-order conditioning; it would have been if the order of these steps had been reversed: but in fact when the original **CR** to the light was formed, the **US** itself (tap on cheek) was not yet associated with shock as **CS**. Hull

(1935) takes this experiment as one of the neatest demonstrations of *mediation* by $\mathbf{r}_G$: the occurrence of the blink is held to elicit fractional shock stimuli and these mediate the finger withdrawal. The function of mediation by $\mathbf{r}_G$ is therefore to bring about a linkage or closure between two independently learned connexions. It is the contention of 'learning theory' that the perceptual restructurization demonstrated by Köhler's insightful apes amounts essentially to this.

Consider, next, a famous experiment by Maier (1929) demonstrating reasoning in the white rat. The rats were trained to reach a raised table-top for a reward, using any one of three ring ladders from the floor; they were next trained in the geography of the table-top itself, which was such that water could be reached by starting down an alley from one position only, corresponding to the head of one of the previously learned ladders, a position which was inaccessible from the other ladder head. The test was to start the animal hungry from the floor. The majority in fact chose to run up the ladder which led to food, i.e. the rats had put together two bits of evidence. In a discussion which has achieved even greater fame than Maier's article, Hull schematized the situation as shown in Figure 7.

Hull argued that the animal at S is not neutral as between W_1 and W_2, since W_1 has responses attached to it which have become conditioned

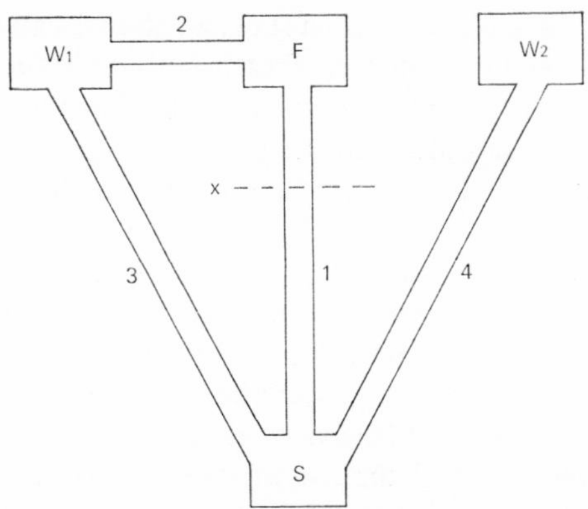

Figure 7. Schematic illustration of the mechanism of insight (based on Hull, 1935)

S is the starting platform; W_1 and W_2 are platforms where the animal finds water; F is the food platform. Before the introduction of the barrier X, the animal has received equal training on paths 1 and 2 under food deprivation, followed by paths 3 and 4 under water deprivation. The test consists in starting the animal at S, hungry but not thirsty.

to F_1 where W_2 has not. Therefore, response associated with taking that alley will have greater reaction potential attaching to it: r_F is antedated to Sw_1 and rw_1 which is present at S; but since r_{W_1} is present, so is s_{W_1} (for each fractional response is sensed by the subject), and s_{W_1} will elicit r_F, and hence s_F, with the attendant secondary reinforcement and incentive value.

However, the classical insight experiments are those of Köhler (1925) described in Section III. Birch (1945b) carried out an investigation designed to establish whether the insight shown by Köhler's apes was largely independent of experience, being a function of perceptual re-structurization. His results are conclusive. When presented with a problem requiring the use of a T-shaped stick as a rake or hoe to pull in a banana only two of his six chimpanzee subjects were successful. None had had any previous experience with stick problems, but one had frequently been observed playing with sticks in its living quarters: this animal, Jojo, was the only one to exhibit insightful behaviour – a smooth and purposeful solution. The success of the other animal gave all the appearance of chance. The animals were then given sticks to play with over a period of three days and gradually came to use them increasingly: first in manipulatory play, but later instrumentally, as an extension of the arm – chiefly in prodding one another! The second development seemed to arise quite naturally out of the first. When playing with a stick, an animal's attention may be drawn to some other object and it reaches towards it without relinquishing the stick; the stick is bound to follow the arm. After the experience of free-play with sticks, all of the animals were successful not only in the original problem, but in several others more complex (e.g. problems requiring the re-orientation of the stick, the use of a small stick to rake in a longer one, etc.). Birch's findings are entirely consonant with Piaget's observations of his own children (see Chapter 5, Section II).

Birch's evidence is taken by Hull (1952) to support an interpretation similar to that of the Maier-type experiments. Insight depends on the assembly of separately learnt behaviour segments: reaching out with the hand (well-established) and the use of the stick as an arm-extension (established in the course of play). The mediating response is the incipient hand-reaching (incipient because, in the problem situation, the animal is not actually holding the stick and must therefore inhibit (or desist from) overt hand-reaching to first grasp the stick). Hull deduces that, in the course of repetitions of the insightful solution, the instrumental grasping of the stick becomes conditioned not only to the mediating stimulus (self-stimulation of incipient hand reaching) but also to the terminal stimulus of eating the fruit. In other words, the appropriate response is reinforced not only by mediated, secondary reinforcement, but also by primary reinforcement. Two conclusions follow. First, that inasmuch as insight depends on the putting together of two established sequences, the learning difficulty will centre on the point of juncture: past this point, as before it, behaviour will be smooth. Second, insightful learning is not necessarily immediate but more often progressive; in other words the probability that insight will occur at the point of juncture will rise with successive trials until the point is reached when the behaviour is no longer insight but a habit. Both conclusions may be attested by experiment as well as by everyday observation.

Nevertheless, as Hull himself is aware, the central difficulty of his formal explanation is that the stick cannot be used like a hand to grasp the fruit but only to rake it. Such variation in behaviour is accounted for by a principle of response-oscillation.[1] Granted the variation, reinforcement alone will ensure the strengthening of the adaptive raking behaviour. However, the account is not entirely convincing in view of the immediacy of solution:

> '... the animals who had failed to obtain the food in their initial attempts at the problem ... after the stick-play ... upon being admitted to the problem cage, ran at once to the grill, picked up the stick and swept the food into reach, took it in hand and ate ... Only one animal, Alf, prefaced his use of the stick with an attempt directly to reach the food by means of a non-instrumentally-augmented direct extension of his arm.'
>
> (Birch, 1945b, p. 376.)

> 'It is important to remember that at no time during the stick-play period were any of our animals ... observed to use the stick as an instrument by means of which a distant object was swept into reach. What was developed ... was an arm-stick-extension pattern and not a stereotyped reaching sweeping movement.'
>
> (*Ibid.*, footnote.)

(*c*) *The Concept of the Habit-Family-Hierarchy*. Since Birch speaks of 'an arm-stick-extension pattern', one is led naturally to examine the way in which Hullian theory provides for the acquisition of such

[1] This states that the final choice of **R** is not absolutely determined by the equation roughly given on page 37. The $_S E_R$ attaching to each of the possible responses is held to fluctuate from movement to movement albeit within fairly narrow limits, so that it can happen that a theoretically weaker **R** will displace a stronger.

behavioural equivalences. This is the mechanism of the habit-family-hierarchy described by Hull (1934). The habit-family-hierarchy is a composite structure arising out of two sets of **S-R** relations. One is the separate conditioning of several responses to the same stimulus, giving rise to a divergent pattern: a single **S** linked with several **R**s. The second is the convergent pattern, where several **S**s each have links with the same **R**. Suppose now that the divergent pattern forms an initial node for several lines of behaviour (**S-R** chains), while the convergent pattern forms a terminal node. Such a structure will arise quite naturally not only in the spatial sense where several alternative routes co-exist but also in the behavioural sense where several lines of behaviour, each giving rise to their respective proprioceptive and exteroceptive stimuli, all lead to the same end. The clearest examples are the equivalence of motor responses: running, crawling, hitching from one point to another, or perceptuo-motor responses: head-turning and eye-movement.

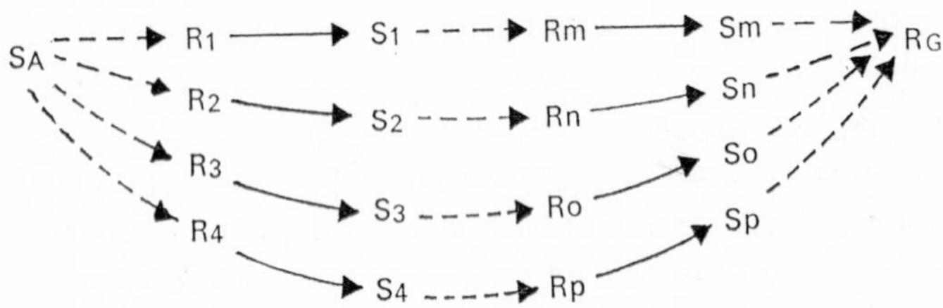

Figure 8. Diagram of a Habit-Family-Hierarchy (from Hull, 1934)

Once again, the r_G mechanism may be invoked to deduce that, in an extended behaviour sequence in which one only of the alternative paths has been learned (e.g. a maze with a roundabout route and a shorter route diverging and converging on the same points, but where the shorter route has been learnt separately, and not beginning from the start of the maze) all of the possible routes will be available to the subject, and he will prefer the shortest. For since r_G is evoked at the choice-point all the alternative responses will be weighted with an incentive value based on r_G-s_G, *in inverse proportion to their distance from the final node*. Even though the shortest may not have been executed previously in the particular context, it achieves a higher probability of occurrence because the initial response within that line of behaviour is strongly favoured by r_G.

It should be abundantly clear that the habit-family-hierarchy is the equivalent in Hullian theory to the means-end-field or cognitive map in

Tolman's theory. It is also quite close to Piaget's concept of the schema as a set of behavioural equivalences (Chapter 4, Section II).

But there is a certain lack of elasticity about the concept in the form in which it was originally elaborated. This arises out of the fact that the mediating r_G-s_G are thought of more as intervening variables determining the selection of the eventual **R** than as internalized thinking behaviour. Intervening variables are taken to be activated simultaneously, presumably in the period between the presentation of **S** and the determination of the first **R**, which will commit the subject to one of the alternative lines of behaviour. It will be argued that such an interpretation leads to consequences that are untenable (Chapter 3, Section II). To go back to the Birch experiments, even if one grants that the existence of a habit-family-hierarchy relating to hand and arm movements enables the stick-learning in general to be much more effective than it otherwise would, it is difficult to see how the hand-arm-hierarchy could favour the choice of the raking movement which is peculiarly adaptive for sticks but not for hands. Since the problem is clearly soluble by overt trial-and-error, an interpretation which provides for the possibility of internalized trial-and-error would be more plausible.

6. *Evaluation*

Hullian theory is first and foremost an extension to Thorndike's approach incorporating many of the physiological principles established in Pavlov's laboratory. Behaviour is taken to be more or less adequately represented as a chain of links each consisting of a set of stimuli and an eventual response, the two being connected by a number of intervening variables. Stimuli and responses are taken to be observable and definable: the first in terms of intensity and of difference from other stimuli (as in generalization), the second in terms of occurrence or non-occurrence, and also in terms of amplitude (e.g. speed of running), of latency (the delay between stimulus presentation and recorded response), and of resistance to extinction (following experimental withdrawal of the reinforcer). Both stimuli and responses are thought of as having exact analogues *within* the organism: the stimulus trace and the effective reaction potential. Intervening variables are not observable, nor do they have any direct analogue *outside* the organism, but they are said to be inferrable from the systematic ways in which variations of response are linked with variations of antecedent conditions (e.g. of deprivation, of practice, of reward experience).

So far the Hullian model is quite close to that of Tolman. The principal differences are threefold. First, the systematic formulations are much tighter and much freer from cognitively loaded terms. In particular, the concept of the antedating response and its attendant response-produced stimulus, r_G-s_G, constitutes an attempt to provide a strictly behavioural substitute for the frankly mentalistic 'means-end readiness'. Similarly, the habit-family-hierarchy, closely linked with conditioning experimentation by its use of the same antedating, mediating response, is or should be a more precise and testable concept than the cognitive map. In the second place, there is a constant attempt to lend substance to the intervening variables postulated by the system by showing precise quantitative dependencies between variations in antecedent variables and variations in response. Finally, Hullian theory is much more of a unified statement of principles than can be found in the work of Tolman. Where Tolman offers a variety of kinds of learning and a variety of principles which might be relevant to each, Hull argues for a closely knit set of interdependencies taken to characterize all of behaviour and all of learning. The result is the fairly complex system we have tried to outline in the previous pages. Inevitably, we have had to look at the Hullian constructs one at a time, and it is not altogether easy to envisage the way in which they interact within the system. The reader may well find that he is helped to do so at this stage by studying the flow-diagram in Chapter 3 (Figure 2), together with the explanatory notes.

For all that, it is our contention that the Hullian synthesis is misconceived, being based on inadequate analysis of the sort of processes which can properly be ascribed to the organism. The chief criticisms are set out in detail in Chapter 3, Section II. They may be summarized as follows:

(1) The assumption of a 1:1 correspondence between the physical stimulus **S** and the cues that regulate the behaviour of the subject is formally simple but theoretically unsatisfactory. In the first place, it is not a behaviouristic construct but a mental one, closely modelled on the philosophers' sense-datum. In the second place, it turns out to be quite unworkable, for it relies on the very vague notion of 'stimulus-interaction' which, if followed through to its logical conclusions, would lead to untenable consequences. In the third place, the analysis of behavioural regulation attributed to the subject follows too closely the restrictions that are more properly applicable to a description of what must be established by the observer in testing his explanations: the observer needs to anchor his formulations by reference to 'stimuli' and 'responses', but it does not follow that the behaviour of the subject is accountable in similar terms.

(2) The regulation of behaviour cannot be explained in terms of a

succession of discrete responses if the observed response depends on the simultaneous operation of a large number of processes, partly overlapping and independent, partly hierarchical. Yet this is unquestionably the case in all skilled behaviour, and this includes ordinary locomotion in a multi-sensible environment as well as more obvious skills like the use of language and playing a musical instrument.

(3) The hypothesis of a 'drive' which is quite separate from behaviour, being an immediate response to an organismic need, and which simply interacts with the behavioural tendency (habit-strength) is theoretically redundant and experimentally improbable. It is designed to account for such experimental facts as the data of latent learning experiments and the variation of response measures attendant on variations in deprivation. But the same facts could be equally accounted for in terms of a truly 'hierarchical' model of behaviour, in which the concept of drive would enter as the activation of a general schema including several alternative lines of behaviour, rather than as a separate construct (see Chapter 6, Section IV).

For all these criticisms, it is difficult to overestimate Hull's contribution to psychological thinking, for his influence on research and theory has been greater than that of any other figure in the present century. And even the most telling and fruitful researches which point to alternative interpretations have frequently been inspired directly by his formulations, either as attempts to verify them or as deliberate demonstrations of their inadequacy. Nearly all would agree that any theory is no more than an imperfect approximation, and one that advances understanding by inspiring productive research is good, even if this leads to its own infirmation.

More than that, it is possible to list at least eight ways in which Hullian theory has led to a more coherent ordering of the facts of behavioural regulation:

The first two are general.

(1) The attempt to arrive at an integrative yet systematic view of behaviour remains a challenge which must eventually be faced. There is a fundamental continuity between the behaviour of a rat in a maze and that of a scientist in his laboratory or the pupil in his classroom – or the schizophrenic patient in the consulting room, just as there are obvious differences, and one cannot hope to understand the latter unless one can also analyse the former. If the following chapters represent an attempt to offer a more up-to-day synthesis, based on recent advances in several fields, it is also one which is incomparably less rigorous, which means that

its scientific usefulness (as opposed to its pedagogic value) may be more questionable.

(2) Hull's uncompromising behaviourism (i.e. his refusal to admit explanatory constructs which themselves imply the knower and the wisher, or the little man in the machine) is still an essential ingredient of all fundamental research. In the final analysis, all psychological explanation must be in terms of relations of implication and interdetermination of physical events (events in the brain). The same holds true of his uncompromising quest for explanations which lead to testable conclusions: a theoretical interpretation which cannot be infirmed is one which needs to be sharpened – or else discarded.

(3) In spite of the fact that many have been led to question the concept of drive in the particular form of a response to physiological need, the experimental fact of systematic variation in the intensity of behavioural arousal remains unquestioned. Equally unquestioned is the fact that one of the ways in which such dependence can be assessed most unambiguously is that where the variation in drive intensity results more or less directly from deprivation of food or water. It is probably no exaggeration to say that Hull and his associates were the first to bring the variables of motivation under experimental control. Perhaps the most significant finding here is that the strength of drive is correlated with the intensity of behaviour, but uncorrelated with the amount of learning which results from such behaviour.

This does not mean that the learning behaviour of a pupil in a classroom is correspondingly dependent mainly on food deprivation, or even on the administration of artificial or extrinsic secondary reinforcers, e.g. praise, high marks, etc., but it does mean that any analysis of all the motivational factors which do operate (including, e.g. confirmation of a strategy or mode of attack by the consistency with which it leads to predicted and coherent results) should ultimately be formulated in ways that are equally testable.

(4) The facts of secondary reinforcement in instrumental learning (as opposed to second-order conditioning) were extensively tested in Hull's laboratory. Their importance is enhanced rather than diminished in the measure that one is led to question the validity of the distinction between primary and secondary reinforcement (as I do in Chapter 4, where I put forward the hypothesis that reinforcement occurs wherever the inception of a line of behaviour results in the input which facilitates the running off of a pre-existing schema).

(5) No less significant than the role of drive in learning is the role of

learning in drive. Drive presents itself as a simultaneous variation in the strength of activation of related behaviours. That is how Skinner views it, as we will see, and that, too, is how the present writer prefers to regard it. Such variation can be most readily demonstrated by manipulating conditions of deprivation: unlearned drive. But variations in the strength of behaviour can also be induced by the presentation of environmental conditions which have been associated with noxious or reinforcing consequences. Secondary reinforcers have 'drive inducing properties', i.e. they lead to the activation of behaviour in varying strengths. The maintenance of direction in human behaviour depends in large measure on such learned drives. Because the arousal is contingent on environmental stimulation, it shows greater fluctuation in the measure that the behaviour of the subject brings about changes in input. These effects have been subjected to more detailed study by Hull's successors, especially Miller (see Miller, 1959) and Mowrer (1960a). Theoretical considerations and the findings of recent research lead one to question (*a*) the concept of drive as a 'stimulus' (Chapter 3); (*b*) the notion that social behaviour is mediated entirely by secondary drives (Chapter 4, Section III, Chapter 6, and Volume II, Chapter 2); and (*c*) the notion that all drive is ultimately attributable to a primary physiological deficit (Chapters 3 and 4, Section III). But the role of learned connexions in the activation of behaviour, i.e. secondary drive, remains a central theme in psychology, whether theoretical or applied.

(6) Hull's goal-gradient hypothesis is a hypothesis only in respect of its systematic formulation in terms of the r_G mechanism. As a description of the fact that in any serial task the last elements of the series (along with the initial) are acquired first, or that in maze-running, goal-pointing blinds tend to be entered more frequently, or that in the execution of any goal-oriented behaviour, the intensity of arousal rises as the subject reaches cues associated with the completion of the task, it has the status of well-attested experimental fact.

(7) The concept of insight is not fully accounted for in terms of the antedating reaction and the habit-family-hierarchy. An adequate analysis of insightful learning needs to take at least the following three aspects into consideration: the equivalence of alternative lines of behaviour or strategies within a schema; the role of 'discovery' or schematically oriented trial-and-error behaviour in the acquisition of such a structure; and the part played by the synthesis of constituent sub-schemata in the process of its construction. But it is to Maier, Hull and Birch that we are principally indebted for an appreciation of the role of learning in the

formation of insight (which enters into both the second and the third aspect), and more especially the significance of the acquisition of behaviour appropriate to the junctures between separately acquired lines of behaviour (being part of the third aspect).

(8) The concept of the habit-family-hierarchy has been criticized earlier on two grounds. The $\mathbf{r_G}$-$\mathbf{s_G}$ attaching to the several alternative lines of behaviour are held to be activated simultaneously, thereby tending to exclude the operation of genuine internalized trial-and-error (Tolman's **VTE**). Conversely, the resultant behaviour is thought of as a succession of discrete responses, thereby excluding the consideration of simultaneous strategies in the determination of observable behaviour (see Chapter 4, Section II). Both limitations arise more or less directly out of the confusion between the observer's definition of the stimulus and the perceptual processes attributable to the subject and similarly between the observer's definition of response and the subject's executive behaviours (see Chapter 3, Section II). Nevertheless, the habit-family-hierarchy marks a limited advance on Tolman's cognitive map insofar as the r_G is accorded a quasi-behavioural status instead of being regarded simply as a kind of foreknowledge.

Leaving aside questions of simultaneity, the notion that intelligent adaptive response arises out of the prior intervention of learned internalized behaviour, mediating the determination of the observed behaviour, is one which is almost certainly very close to the truth, and one which has inspired a great deal of fruitful research, particularly in the treatment of language. To this we must briefly turn, although its fuller consideration must be reserved for Volume II.

7. *Language as a Mediating Response*

Language as a mediating response enters in an explanatory role both in the earlier work of Kuenne (1946) and in the more recent studies by Kendler, e.g. Kendler (1963). Kuenne found that four-year-old children, having learned to choose the larger of two shapes, were able to transpose the relation *larger* when required to choose between two shapes differing not too greatly from the training stimuli (near transposition), but they were unable to do so when the size difference between the training pair and the test pair was greatly increased (far transposition), and instead chose the object the actual size of which was nearest to the original positive stimulus; seven-year-old children made relational responses whatever the absolute dimensions of the stimuli. She noted that they were also more often able to give a general description of the basis of their choices, and argued that the use of the word 'larger' mediated the correct (relational) response. Kendler (1963) tested the hypothesis that spontaneous verbalization mediated the response pattern of older children by testing the effect of provoked verbalization, predicting that this technique would affect older children less than younger. Thus, in one experiment, the subject might be presented with a large black square contrasted with a small white one. Choice of the first object is consistently rewarded. However, one group of children were instructed to say '*black*' when making their choice, a second group to say '*large*' while a control group made no provoked and overt verbalization. The criterion test was the number of trials to learn to choose a large white square against a small black one and a small white square against a large black one: choice being in terms of the originally verbalized cue (colour) but with reversal of values. It was found that both four-year-olds and seven-year-olds who had been saying *large* were greatly hindered in their learning of the new task by the intruding mediating response (which was irrelevant), as compared with the non-verbalizing controls; four-year-olds who had been saying *black* (relevant, reversal, mediation) were rather better, but seven-year-olds as predicted were not helped by the provoked mediation – presumably because they used sub-vocal language spontaneously. Although the results of any one such inquiry are seldom conclusive, several other investigations, reviewed by Blank in Volume II, Chapter 3, all point in the same direction.

The intrusion of vocal or sub-vocal speech in the determination of overt behaviour is at least one step away from the Hullian conception of the mediating r_G. In other words, it does not imply the simultaneous spread of fractional responses to all possible response-tendencies which we have just criticized. Also recognition of the mediating function of language is still a very long way from an explanation of the origin of language acquisition, the complexity of language behaviour, and the nature of representation. Nevertheless these researches and their interpretation were more or less directly inspired by Hullian thinking. We must note at least two more general attempts to account for linguistic behaviour in terms of the r_G mechanism. The first, by Mowrer (1960b), is an analysis of language communication. By way of example, it is argued that the sentence '*Tom is a thief*' leads to an anticipation of dishonesty in Tom by a simple conditioning process. The word '*Tom*' evokes a fractional, imaginal, component of the reaction to Tom, the word '*thief*' to that which would be evoked by such an individual; attaching the mediating '*thief*' response to the mediating '*Tom*' response will therefore be conducive to its evocation by the full stimulus, Tom, who of course evokes '*Tom*'. This sort of analysis is little more than an exposure of the inadequacy of the strict Hullian r_G construct. For instance, how would it be extended to: '*If Tom is a thief then I am a Chinaman*' so as to cover the equivalence of that sentence, for speaker and listener, with '*Tom is as honest as the day is long*'? Neither the syntactic nor the semantic aspects of language can yield anything to this mode of approach.

Osgood (1957) offers a much more sophisticated analysis, but one which still owes something to Hull's concept of the habit-family-hierarchy (see also Osgood and Sebeok, 1965, pp. 95 ff. and 126 ff.). Osgood distinguishes between linguistic *decoding* being the process executed by the listener, who obtains information from the sound patterns emitted by the speaker, and linguistic *encoding*, being the process executed by the speaker who converts the information which he intends to convey into language expression. Each of these activities comprises three levels of organization: a representational level, corresponding to the semantic function of language, an integrational level, corresponding to its grammatical or structural features, and a skill level, governing the actual production of sounds by the speaker and, to a lesser extent, their monitoring by the listener. Confining our attention to the behaviour of the former, the determination of response involves the simultaneous participation of all three levels. It is postulated that there is a hierarchical relation between the three levels in so far as determination at the higher level restricts the field of possibilities at the lower (e.g. granted the intention to transmit a particular sort of message, say a question, one is restricted as to the grammatical patterns which would be appropriate). Moreover, within each level, the determination of response reflects the transitional probabilities of the language, so that the field of possible responses constitutes a habit-family-hierarchy.

This way of attacking the problem of language implies a conception of behavioural organization which is very close indeed to that which is presented in Chapter 4 of the present volume. Indeed, Osgood's analysis owes rather more to the constructs of information theory than it does to Hull, for the simultaneous operation of processes at three levels (actually, many more than three may be operative in practice, since there will usually be more than one determinative process within each of Osgood's major levels) seems to me to be quite contrary to Hull's conception of the habit-family-hierarchy. Osgood's account of the way in which the child may be supposed to acquire the meaning of words as mediating responses is rather closer to Hull, and similar to that of Mowrer. But inevitably the fractioning of behaviour which results from treating each successive overt behavioural unit (e.g. the word) as the 'real' response makes it very difficult to render a coherent analysis of the acquisition of syntax.

VI. SKINNER'S DESCRIPTIVE BEHAVIOURISM

1. *Introduction*

It is not easy to switch from an examination of Hullian theory to an outline of Skinner's approach. The difficulty springs from the fact that although many of the terms are the same (stimulus, response, reinforcement, secondary reinforcement, drive), and method of experimentation is not entirely dissimilar (Skinner prefers to substantiate his generalizations by reference to the performance of a single individual, but the changes imposed on antecedent conditions, e.g. deprivation, are often identical), yet the frame of reference is quite different. There is one sense in which one may observe a continuity between Thorndike, Hull and Skinner: their approach to psychology is behaviourist. This means that each of them sees the task of psychology as primarily one of accounting for differences in observed behaviour, and especially gross or molar behaviour, by reference to differences in the conditions under which it is seen to occur. To this extent, Skinner, like his predecessors, may be counterposed to the psychologies of the nineteenth century which were primarily concerned to account for differences in the mind of the subject. Moreover, Skinner is as uncompromising as any of these others, less ready to compromise than Tolman, and much less compromising than Gestalt psychology.

But there is also a discontinuity which it is important to realize in order to understand what Skinner is about. And it is more far-reaching, for it counterposes Skinner not only to Thorndike and his successors, but also to his mentalistic predecessors, right back to Descartes. We have to recapitulate four centuries of history in not many more sentences. Before Descartes it was generally understood that there was mind and there was matter, and the former, being endowed with sensation, could know the latter. (There was also a great deal of disputation as to whether this was a very significant aspect of mind, or whether, as the idealists maintained, the only true knowledge was that which could be attained by pure reasoning.) Descartes showed that the subject's (mind's) awareness of the object (matter) was necessarily indirect – mediated by activity in the sensory nervous system. The latter is quite unlike the object of sensation, and the awareness could exist not only in the absence of the object (hallucination), but also in the absence of activity in the more distal parts of the sensory system (sensation experienced in a phantom limb after amputation – the techniques of direct stimulation of the brain were still a long way off). Not surprisingly, Descartes' analysis triggered off a great flowering of idealistic philosophies, both in the form of the subjective idealism of Berkeley and Hume (who now took the mental 'sense datum' as the ultimate object of knowledge), and in the new rationalist constructions of Spinoza, Leibnitz, and Hegel (Kant defies this kind of summary categorization). More important, from our point of view, is the fact that it was also the point of origin for the birth of experimental psychology in the nineteenth century. Since this required the precise measurement of variation in physical stimuli, as well as the precise recoding of certain properties of response (notably reaction time), it could not easily have emerged before the necessary technological advances had been accomplished.

Granted that mind cannot directly know matter, this does not mean that mental events are independent of material events. The new dualistic science of psychology of the nineteenth century (for Descartes himself had been a dualist and not a pure idealist) set itself the task of formulating precise correlations between the variations of physical events in the environment (the stimulus) and consequent states of the subject (mind). We may denote this as a psychology of

S—M—(R).

The real concern of psychology is the middle term, mind, but the way to establish scientifically valid propositions about it is by noting the way in which its states co-vary with states of the physical antecedents (S). Since the states cannot be observed directly by the experimenter, we have to rely on the subject's description or report of these states (R). However, it was assumed all too easily that such reports would be completely accurate; the interest was not in the reports as such; and because they were direct descriptions of M and not different events from which one would have to *infer* the state of M, the role they played in explanation was minimal, which is the reason for the bracket.

We have already seen that the assumption that reports about mental states could be relied on implicitly proved to be unfounded. More important, the psychology of mind implied too great a discontinuity between animal and man. No less important, the study of reflex mechanisms in physiology indicated the probability that mental events were themselves attributable to similar, but more central mechanisms. Hence the break-away from mentalistic psychology inaugurated by Pavlov,

Thorndike and Watson. But the break was not complete. Psychology was still concerned primarily with the central term. However, to say useful things about it, we no longer rely on correlations between the stimulus and the verbal report of the subject: instead we establish correlations between stimulus and the behaviour of the subject (response). Thorndike's psychology is often described as an **S-R** psychology. So it is, but the characterization is insufficient for the present analysis. For Thorndike was principally concerned to establish the conditions which strengthened or weakened the *bonds* between stimuli and responses, and the dash is too inconspicuous and ambiguous a symbol to denote these. Moreover, Thorndike, like all the psychologists we have examined in this chapter, took it for granted that there is some correspondence between the physical stimulus and some process in the organism, and likewise between the observed response and some mechanism within the organism (the potential response or the response tendency), even if he was less systematic in his formulations than Hull. Therefore a more adequate characterization would be:

S—|S-R|—R

where the prime interest is in the middle term, about which inferences are made from the correlations between the two extreme terms.

We have already seen that Gestalt psychology challenged the atomistic bonds between S and R, preferring a construct which would characterize the structure of the field as a whole. These Gestalten were denoted primarily in cognitive terms, but were also supposed (especially by Köhler) to correspond with field-states of the brain. Hence one might write:

S—G(B)—R

since the Gestalten are inferences from the observed correlations between stimulus conditions and the responses of the organism.

Similarly, both Tolman and Hull offer sophistications of Thorndike in which the interactions of a relatively large number of intervening variables take the place of the S-R bonds, and both might be written:

S—Σ(I.V.)—R

even though the intervening variables (I.V.) are different in the two cases.

More generally, the formula

S—X—R

may be seen to cover every theoretical approach to experimental psychology from Wundt to the post-Hullians, and in every case the prime object of psychology is the elucidation of the states or processes in the organism (X) by inference from correlations between S and R. It is this meta-psychological premise which is challenged by Skinner, most eloquently in his article *Are theories of learning necessary?* (reproduced in Skinner, 1959), but, more or less explicitly, throughout his writings.

Contrary to all other behaviourists (and, for the record, I include myself, being a behaviouristically-flavoured disciple of Piaget), Skinner denies that psychology should be primarily concerned with the description of this middle term X, representing states or processes in the organism inferred from behaviour. Psychology is defined as the science of behaviour, and it begins and ends with the description of behaviour, or, rather, with the description of correlations between behaviour and any determinants which may prove to be relevant, whether in the environment (S) or in the previous behaviour of the subject. It is not a set of inferences from behaviour about something else (either in the mind or in the brain), but a set of statements about behaviour itself. Of course Skinner does not mean any statements which describe any behaviour, but statements which have some generality, and preferably, perfect generality. For he, like anyone else, has sought to establish precise laws governing the correlation between significant aspects of behaviour and objective determinants (outside the organism). What is more, he has been at least as successful as any. The point is that, having established such laws, he regards them as quite sufficient in themselves. They are not intended as descriptions of anything except behaviour, and any 'intervening variables' he may appear to use in their expression are to be taken as no more than convenient shorthand expressions for the facts of behaviour and their relations with relevant conditions. Therefore, to characterize his approach, I would write:

$$Y—R$$

where Y includes the S of the previous formulae, but also anything else that may prove relevant (such as the history of previous behaviours of the subject and such conditions of the experimentation as deprivation history, etc.), and where the prime interest centres on R, the middle term X having dropped out.[1]

[1] The above discussion relies on a different categorization from the twofold categorization of theories represented in Chapter 3, Section I. All three are valid. The criterion used here is essential to an understanding of Skinner. It is irrelevant in Chapter 3 because there is no other comprehensive theory which it would help to define other than in purely negative terms: 'different from Skinner'.

2. *The Concept of Operant Behaviour*

We noted in Section II that the kind of behavioural change studied by Pavlov was fundamentally different from that studied by Thorndike, and their use of the term 'reinforcement' differed correspondingly.[1] In the last section we showed how Hullian theory was (in part) an attempt to weld the two conceptions into a systematic whole. Skinner's approach to the study of behaviour begins with a recognition of their essential difference which may seem deceptively simple, but which carries with it a radically different conception both of the stimulus and of the response.

Salivation is an instance of a reflex form of behaviour which may be seen to be *elicited*, prior to any learning. by an unconditional stimulus: the presentation of food in the mouth. It is also subject to learning by the process of conditioning: repeated presentation of the **US** immediately following on that of a conditional stimulus (**CS**). Reinforcement consists of such presentation, and its effect is that the reflex comes to be elicited by the **CS** as well as by the **US**. The laws governing the regulation of such reflex behaviour were studied by Sherrington (integration of unconditional reflexes), and by Pavlov (extension to conditional reflexes). They are re-stated by Skinner (1938, Chapter 1) with some changes in emphasis. These are not important to our present purpose. More important is the recognition that the amplitude of reflex is a significant measure of conditioning and also reflects the intensity of the stimulus. By the same token, in the study of the Pavlovian process of conditioning, considerable interest may attach to the formulation of laws governing the length of delay between presentation of a **CS** and the observation of the **CR**. The system of elicited reflexes is termed by Skinner the system of reflexes of Type **S**, and the laws of learning appropriate to it are said to be the laws of conditioning and extinction of Type **S**.

If we now consider the course of events when an animal learns to escape from a Thorndike puzzle-box, we find it to be quite different. Say the correct behaviour is to tread on a lever, we cannot say that it is elicited by a stimulus. What stimulus? The lever is not an unconditional stimulus for treading, and if it were what would be the conditional stimulus? The terminology is inappropriate. What happens is that the animal operates on the environment, and the effect of the operation is to produce the reinforcement (say escape and food). Skinner's own subsequent work with pigeons (summarized in Skinner, 1953) rules out any possibility of basing an interpretation on the elicitation of the response by the stimulus of the

[1] '*Reinforcement*' is used by Pavlov to designate the presentation of the US, e.g. meat powder; Thorndike uses it to refer to an extrinsic reward.

lever. If the experimenter arranges matters so that when the bird finds itself in the experimental cage it will receive food from a hopper every time it raises its head, the bird will repeatedly do just this. And if the reinforcement is now withheld until the bird stands on its toes, this behaviour too can be strengthened. Here there is no obvious external stimulus whatever to elicit the behaviour. The experimenter simply waits for the *operant* behaviour to occur and reinforces it when it does, thereby raising the probability of its occurrence on future occasions. Because the behaviour is emitted by the organism, and not elicited by any recognizable stimulus (Skinner allows that there may be stimuli of some sort operating, but they are not under the experimenter's control), and because the general characteristic of such behaviour is that the subject operates on the environment to produce the reinforcement, it is termed an *operant reflex*, or a reflex of Type **R**, and the laws appropriate to its study are the laws of conditioning and extinction of Type **R**. The first states that when an operant is followed by presentation of a reinforcing stimulus it is strengthened, the second, that when it is not followed by such reinforcement its strength is decreased.

The importance of the distinction between the two kinds of reflex is that it enables Skinner to pursue the elucidation of operant learning without contaminating the analysis by the introjection of notions applicable only to conditioning of Type **S**. In particular, since there is no eliciting stimulus, delay of the reflex cannot serve as a measure of its strength. Similarly, we do not find a correlation between the strength of an operant and its amplitude (the rat does not press harder on the lever the more often it is reinforced, and our own well-ingrained habits are not performed with exceptional vigour). But there remains the question of how one can study the strength of an operant. Allied to this are the questions: how can one define a reinforcement without invoking the concept of need? in what way does operant learning lead to adaptive behaviour if it is not elicited by environmental stimuli? how can Skinner's simplified and descriptive approach deal with motivational variables like drive?

3. *The Regulation of Operant Behaviour*

(1) *Conditioning of Operant Behaviour.* Let us begin with the question of the effect of reinforcement. A reinforcing stimulus is defined as any stimulus the presentation of which has the effect of raising the strength of an operant behaviour. Such was the formulation in 1938. By 1953, Skinner had come to recognize a second kind of reinforcement. The strength of an operant may also be increased by the withdrawal of an

aversive stimulus. For instance, a rat will learn to operate a lever to avoid an electric shock and a child learns to say 'Please' to avoid an angry look. The strength of an operant is defined as the probability of its occurrence. Of course one cannot observe a probability, but one can observe a frequency. In practice therefore, what Skinner does is to measure the frequency with which a response is 'emitted' during a specified period of time, i.e. *the rate of response*.

But here we encounter a snag. For right from the start Skinner established that a few reinforcements were sufficient to produce a constant rate of response – say every ten to fifteen seconds for lever-pressing by a rat. Further reinforcements served only to maintain this rate, not to raise it.

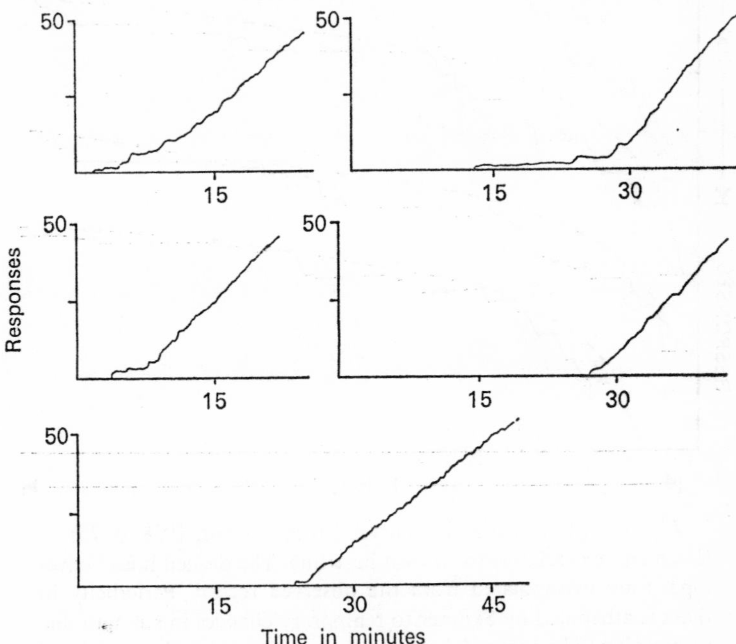

Figure 9. Five Records of Changes in Rate of Response with constant reinforcement (from Skinner, 1938, p. 68)

(The curves are cumulative; the record moves upwards a constant interval each time the subject responds and does not move back down. Therefore the slope of the curve at any point reflects the rate of response. A horizontal line indicates failure to respond.)

The differential effect of the number of reinforcements becomes much more apparent when the reinforcement is discontinued. In other words, the strength of the operant may be assessed by the shape of its curve of extinction: the absolute number of unreinforced responses and the rate of their emission. The asymptote of these curves (see Figure 10), representing the total number of responses to be expected sooner or later, was termed the *reflex reserve* (Skinner uses the term reflex to include operant

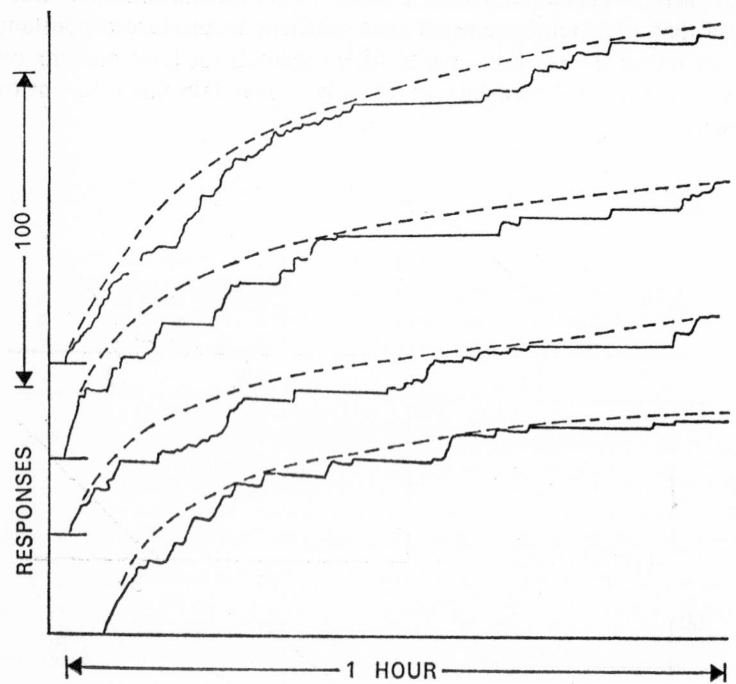

Figure 10. Four extinction curves (from Skinner, 1938, p. 75) (Each curve is relative to its own base line. The dashed lines ('envelopes') are extrapolated from the observed record. Periodicity in these is attributed by Skinner to temporary changes in strength due to emotion. The interval between the asymptote of the 'envelope' and its base is the estimate of 'reflex reserve'.)

behaviour). The reflex reserve was used to estimate changes in the strength of an operant due to conditioning. As is obvious from an inspection of Figure 10, the reflex reserve as an absolute measure of the conditional strength of an operant is only very tenuously supported by the actual behaviour observed. As Skinner's thinking developed, so he came to relinquish this quest for absolute laws, and with it, the concept of the 'reflex reserve'. What remains is the observation that the probability of a response can be manipulated by the contingencies of reinforcement in broad accordance with the laws of conditioning and extinction of Type **R**. And the descriptive formulation is one that cannot be gainsaid.

(2) *Reinforcement.* Let us return to the question of the definition of the operant and the reinforcer. Skinner (1953) defines any single occurrence of a specified behaviour as a *response*, while the class of such behaviours, if it does not fall under the heading of Type **S**, is termed an operant. Thus, in the case of a pigeon, a single instance of head-raising would be a response, while the behaviour of head-raising would be an operant. The terminology is unfortunate, since 'response' suggests an eliciting stimulus, but one must put this out of mind. Inevitably, the identification of a response and that of an operant are interdependent. But Skinner is more daring than this. For he makes the definition of both depend on that of the reinforcer – and vice versa. An operant is any specifiable class of behaviour the frequency of which can be manipulated by the administration of a reinforcer (or by the withdrawal of an aversive reinforcer), and a reinforcer is any stimulus the presentation (or withdrawal) of which increases the strength of an operant.

The definitions look circular and they are. But Skinner is quite correct in contending that there is nothing vicious in the circularity. On the side of the reinforcer, it is not the case that the class is left wide open. On the contrary, in the vast majority of cases, repeated presentation of a stimulus leads to habituation or adaptation. Repeated presentation of food to a hungry animal, or, generally, of praise to a child, does not.

We have already seen in our examination of Hullian theory that the role of *secondary reinforcers* in instrumental (operant) learning was first noted by Skinner. Working with rats which were reinforced with food delivered by a mechanical hopper, he found that when he had run out of food, the sound of the mechanism alone was sufficient to reinforce an operant. In itself, this looks like an application of Pavlovian (Type **S**) conditioning to the conditions of operant learning. For one would presume that the acquisition of reinforcing properties by a stimulus is an instance of type **S** conditioning. Mowrer (1960a) is particularly insistent on this mode of analysis. But Skinner is usually less interested in fine theoretical distinctions of this sort. More important to him is the fact that once it is granted that any stimulus may acquire secondary reinforcing powers, the distinction between primary and secondary reinforcement ceases to be of any great significance. Both may be recognized as reinforcers by their effects: increasing the strength of operant behaviour.

Skinner (1953) notes the value of secondary reinforcers in bridging the gap between pre-current operants and long-range reinforcing consequences. 'When a man puts storm windows in his house in October because similar behaviour last October was followed by a warm house in January, we need to bridge the gap between the behaviour in October and the effect in January. Among the conditioned reinforcers are verbal consequences supplied by the man himself or his neighbours' (p. 77). At least by implication, Skinner is here recognizing the physiological fact that reinforcement cannot operate to strengthen a behaviour unless the trace of that behaviour is still active at the time of reinforcement. In other words, a long-delayed reinforcer is not a true reinforcer but a mediated reinforcer.

The concept of reinforcement is further extended with the introduction of the concept of the *generalized reinforcer*. A (secondary) reinforcer is said to become generalized when its presentation is associated with that of a primary reinforcer under more than one condition of deprivation. Attention, approval and affection are cited as instances of generalized reinforcers. The reference to conditions of deprivation seems to the present writer to be an unnecessary concession to Hullian theory.

The notion that approval or, especially, affection are secondary reinforcers is infirmed by recent observations and experimentation (see Chapter 4, Section III and Chapter 6 of this volume, and Volume III Chapters 2 and 4). Which is not to deny that some tokens, e.g. money (also noted by Skinner), do appear to serve as generalized reinforcers as a result of a learning process. The question is whether reinforcement is limited to the reducers of primary need states and secondary reinforcers. In one significant passage, Skinner seems to allow for the contrary:

> 'It is possible that some of the reinforcing effect of "sensory feed-back" is unconditioned. . . . The baby's rattle is an example [Skinner is clearly referring to the circular reactions described in Chapter 5, Section II.] . . . Any organism which is reinforced by its success in manipulating nature, regardless of the momentary consequences, will be in a favoured position when important consequences follow.' (Skinner, 1953, p. 78).

I find it difficult to see how there can be sensory feed-back unless there has been pre-determination of a favoured sensory input by a 'strategy', a 'schema', or a 'plan'. Otherwise 'feed-back' becomes synonymous with 'input', and the mechanism would serve to strengthen any and every random behaviour. Here, as elsewhere, it requires only a little push to bring Skinnerian theory quite close to our own position: that reinforcement follows automatically on the unimpeded execution of an initiated strategy (Chapter 4, Section IV). The obstacle is Skinner's preference for a purely descriptive formulation.

However, as Skinner himself is not slow to point out, the descriptive standpoint has not stood in the way of far-reaching and valid experimental discoveries. Among the more significant of these, one would certainly include Skinner's investigations into the effects of *partial reinforcement*.

Skinner (1959, p. 87) describes how he hit upon the idea of partial reinforcement by accident: he was trying to study operant conditioning with less expenditure in rat food, and decided to offer reinforcement at one minute intervals ('Thrift, my dear Horatio'). There were two results: the supply of food lasted longer and the rats stabilized at a constant rate of responding. However, having discovered the effectiveness of partial reinforcement, Skinner proceeded to explore the relation between rate of reinforcement and the course of conditioning and extinction. Genuine scientific advances often (Skinner would say invariably) have nothing to do with testing elaborate theories. The facts of partial reinforcement may be summarized as follows:

(i) The most effective schedule for initial conditioning is a constant reinforcement, especially if one is also concerned with the shaping of a complex operant.[1]

(ii) Once an operant has been established, the use of partial reinforcement can lead to considerable increases in the rate of response and in the number of trials to extinction.

(iii) Reinforcement at regular time intervals has the effect of producing periodicity in the rate of response which reflects the reinforcement interval: the delay since the last reinforcement functions as a discriminative stimulus. Regular ratio reinforcement (every fifth, tenth, hundredth response) has an analogous effect: the recent reinforcement is a discriminative cue which lowers the probability of reinforcement, so that the rate of response is not even but builds up from each reinforcement.

(iv) A high and steady rate of response may be secured by using an irregular schedule. Instead of reinforcing every *n*th response, the experimenter reinforces one in *n* responses on average.

(v) It is usually necessary to proceed by stages, beginning with a higher ratio and reducing it gradually, in order to build up a high and steady rate of response with a very low reinforcement ratio.

[1] See below, p 66.

(vi) The rate of response is a function of several variables, including the degree of deprivation ('drive'), the size of reinforcement (corresponding to 'incentive'), and the emotional state of the subject.

True to his descriptive standpoint, Skinner is much more concerned with establishing the facts relating to partial reinforcement than with providing a theoretical model to explain them. In 1938 he went so far as to offer what amounted to a 'compound unit' interpretation: the reinforced operant consists in the emission of several lever presses rather than one. This explanation hardly accounts for the fact that under conditions of partial reinforcement the number of responses to extinction exceeds that found under constant reinforcement even when the opportunities for response are widely spaced, e.g. in a T maze, one arm of which is reinforced (Weinstock, 1954). Also to be explained is the finding that if one response has been given constant reinforcement and the other partial, the subject will prefer the former in a choice situation even though the latter yields more trials to extinction (Mason, 1957).

Partial reinforcement effects have been the subject of experimental and theoretical debate for thirty years. Among the suggested interpretations one may cite the secondary-reinforcement hypothesis, viz. that non-reinforcement itself becomes a secondary stimulus for positive response, since the trace of empty goal-box behaviour is reinforced on the next occasion. This interpretation, due to Denny (1946) is infirmed by the Weinstock experiment. Weinstock's own 'discrimination hypothesis' is more difficult to refute: the animal fails to discriminate between acquisition and extinction trials. However, this interpretation, too, can hardly stand alone, since it does not explain the very great rise in rate of response found in Skinner's experiments when the animal is free to respond all the time. Also, it is suspiciously anthropomorphic: 'acquisition and extinction trials' are definitions properly applicable to the behaviour of the experimenter, not to that of the pigeon or the rat. Amsel (1958) offers a 'mediation' hypothesis: non-reinforcement sets up a conditioned frustration response to the initial situation, and this in turn comes to function as a stimulus for positive behaviour by subsequent reinforcement. In effect, what the mediation hypothesis achieves is to credit the trace with greater permanence. It is a variant of secondary reinforcement. Mowrer's two-factor hypothesis (1960) is very similar. Mention should also be made of Deutsch's monitoring hypothesis: he supposes the existence of an analyser which is sensitive to the number of responses the subject has made; the rise in threshold (and consequent extinction) of the response comes to be governed by the presence or absence of stimulation from this analyser (Deutsch, 1960, p. 82, and see Chapter 3, Section IV for a general survey of Deutsch's theory).

The phenomena of partial reinforcement are complex and not easy to explain. I suspect that they are partly the resultant of emotional effects (Amsel and Mowrer) and partly attributable to monitoring processes. Mowrer (1960a) provides a lucid account of the most salient work, and a more comprehensive set of references may be found in the review of Lewis (1960). The reader may well come to two profound conclusions. First, that Skinner's discovery of partial reinforcement is of the greatest theoretical interest, and raises problems which are very central to an understanding of behavioural regulation. And, second, that the present writer is unwilling, and probably incompetent, to take any very firm stand.

The implications of partial reinforcement may be dealt with more summarily, because they are more obvious. Skinner (1953) amuses himself and his reader by proposing applications to gambling which should be profitable to bookies. In a more serious vein, programmed instruction cannot easily be based on partial reinforcement. The teacher is constantly concerned with the build-up of new behaviour regulations, much less with ensuring a high rate of perseveration in discrete responses.

But quite the most general lesson to be gleaned from the scientific approach to learning (from Pavlov and Thorndike on) is that what the pupil learns is not confined to the supposed content of the lesson. The laws governing changes in the regulation of behaviour apply equally to the learning of attitudes, the reinforcement of anxiety-induced behaviour, and the reinforcement of error-behaviour. It is in these areas that partial reinforcement may be expected to exert very far-reaching effects. Partial reinforcement is almost certainly at work in perpetuating unadaptive social behaviour, tale-telling, whining and importunity, showing-off, and so on. For it is characteristic of our response to such behaviour that the latter still achieves its desired effect at irregular intervals. Periodic punishment is quite ineffective against such an aperiodic schedule of reinforcement, which means that the teacher must provide conditions whereby an alternative and more acceptable 'operants' will be more regularly reinforced. For punishment does not weaken the strength of the behaviour; it merely inhibits it in the presence of the discriminative stimulus of the threat.

An equally significant consequence of partial reinforcement is that whereas correct learning will be reinforced part of the time whatever the conditions of instruction, unless careful attention is paid to the programming of the curriculum, there will be abundant opportunities for wrong behaviours (errors) to occur, errors which from time to time lead to a correct 'answer', and hence to reinforcement. The pupil is systematically acquiring the wrong methods of attacking the tasks he is set. This is an inevitable consequence of 'incidental learning'. One of the most obvious and insidious examples is apparent guessing behaviour (in fact use of insufficient cues or inadequately articulated solution strategies), for instance, in the acquisition of mathematical and reading skills.

(3) *Definition of an Operant.* On the side of the operant, Skinner's approach (practically) enables him to cut right through the atomism which is inherent in the **S-R** formulations of Thorndike and Hull, and even of Tolman. An operant is a functional unit which can be identified by the result that it achieves. Skinner's earlier experiments required the depression of a lever by a rat in a 'Skinner-box'. He did not record the precise movements used in doing this. What he did record was the fact that the lever had been depressed, and this achievement defined the operant. The presentation of a pellet of food each time the mechanism had been actuated was sufficient to secure a high rate of response after a very few (sometimes just one) combinations. Pigeons have been trained to execute complex routines like turning in a figure of eight, using the technique of 'shaping' to be described below. Here it is the complex routine which constitutes the operant, for it is this which occurs with increased frequency. Krasner (1961) reviews no less than thirty-one studies in which reinforcement was used to increase the frequency of some aspect of verbal behaviour – by definition, an operant (the study was first published in 1958). The subjects, usually students, were reinforced with an '*uh-huh*' or a '*that's interesting*' each time they introduced a sentence with '*I think*' or '*It seems to me*', or each time they made up a story about an animal rather than one about a man or a woman, or each time they used one of several optional words in a sentence-building task rather than another, and so on. Each of these aspects of verbal behaviour is therefore an operant.

This formulation undoubtedly implies that an operant representing a larger segment of behaviour (an instance given in *Verbal Behaviour*, 1957, is the phrase '*The truth, the whole truth and nothing but the truth*') may itself be made up of, and contain, operants representing smaller segments. It is also entirely consistent with the notion of a larger operant constituted by a number of alternative smaller operants – in other words, of a family of behaviour sequences, linked by a common end. This would be the counterpart in Skinnerian theory to the habit-family-hierarchy. But it would also be closer to the concept of the *schema* (to be developed in

Chapter 4) as a set of related strategies or lines of behaviour. One reason is that Skinner insists, correctly, that the large segment is reinforceable as a whole, and in its own right; another is that his concept of drive as change in the strength of a group of operants (see below) is consonant with our own (neo-Piagetian) conception of drive as the intensity of evocation of a strategy; another is that Skinner's insistence on 'multiple causation' implies the simultaneous functioning of several operants, a notion the importance of which I will be at some pains to stress at several points in this volume.

However, an extension of the concept of the larger operant to cover the functions of the schema remains more of a possibility than an actuality in the work of Skinner. Multiple causation is introduced to account for the determination of verbal behaviour, for instance to show that a speaker's actual choice of words may be determined by several causes – as when a speaker reporting on his attempts to hunt panda in China declared that his plans 'had not panned out' (example given in Skinner, 1953). More often, Skinner's distinction between larger and smaller units relates to his discussion of the acquisition of 'fine-grained responses' on the one hand, and to the shaping of behaviour on the other. Neither can be properly reported without first showing how, in Skinner's view, operant behaviour, although not elicited by a stimulus, can yet be brought under stimulus control. To this we now turn.

(4) *Bringing the operant under stimulus control.* Depressing a lever is not elicited by the lever. Yet it cannot be done in the absence of the lever. Nor without guidance from perceptual input deriving from the lever. To this extent the sight of the lever constitutes a *discriminative stimulus* for the operant. The operant is reinforced when performed in conjunction with the stimulus. This is a case where performance would not be possible in the absence of the stimulus. (In Piaget's language, the stimulus is an 'aliment'.) But this is not a necessary condition for the intervention of discriminative stimuli. If a rat is reinforced for depressing the lever whenever a light is showing and unreinforced in its absence, the light comes to function as a discriminative stimulus. This of course parallels the phenomenon known to Pavlov as the inhibition of differentiation in the context of elicited reflexes. Skinner, while retaining the term differentiation, prefers to reserve the term 'inhibition' for the action of external inhibitors (see Section II). But he recognizes an interaction between the differentiated branches of the original operant – a process which he designates by the term 'induction'. Induction is a generalizatory process which depends on the communality of the two situations, (here, light and

no light, the communality being the presence of the lever, etc.). It has some affinity with Hull's 'afferent stimulus interaction', and is somewhat suspect on similar grounds (see Chapter 3). I find it a pity Skinner did not explore further the possibilities inherent in Pavlov's brilliant analyses of the interaction between inhibitory and excitatory processes. The reason, of course, is to be found in his positivistic attitude. Inhibition is a physiological process, and Skinner is concerned with behaviour. The trouble is that the recognition of generalization tells us nothing about the lines of generalization (what situations will be reacted to by the learner as effectively similar to the original learning situation), and on this kind of issue Skinner's treatment is far from convincing.

Be that as it may, Skinner's recognition of the difference between the eliciting stimulus and the discriminative stimulus constitutes a tremendous step forward *vis-à-vis* the **S-R** conception of the stimulus, one which is frequently missed. For as Verplanck (1954) points out, the **DS** is not a physical variable as such, but the cue to which the subject reacts. So long as no differentiation is made there is no **DS**. This is a recognition which comes very close to the conception of the filtering action of the comparator system to be developed in Chapter 4, which is itself largely inspired by the ideas of Broadbent and Sutherland.

Generally speaking, the process of operant conditioning is viewed by Skinner as the outcome of a three-term contingency. An operant is strengthened when it is reinforced in the presence of (or following on) a **DS**. The operant is then differentiated with respect to the **DS**. The strength of the differentiated operant becomes the probability of its occurrence in conjunction with the **DS**. The differentiating role of the **DS** is used by Skinner to great effect in what he calls the shaping of the operant. An operant cannot be reinforced until a response has occurred. The technique of shaping behaviour consists in reinforcing any behaviour which is remotely like the desired operant. Once this has become stabilized, the experimenter withholds the reinforcement until the subject has gone a step nearer the performance he wishes to obtain, and so on. In one experiment, a rat was conditioned in this way to get a marble from a rack, pick it up with its forepaws, carry it across a cage to a vertical tube two inches high, lift it up, and drop it into the tube. The eventual operant involves not only the 'chaining' of the several steps involved, but also the use of the discriminative cues of the rack, the marble, and the tube. Using the same principles, pigeons have been trained to play skittles, to turn figures of eight, to adjust the intensity of illumination, and so on. As Verplanck (1954) has commented, the skill of Skinner and his pupils as animal trainers cannot by itself be taken as evidence for the adequacy of his analysis. But it is difficult to deny that it testifies to its relevance: it must be partially adequate or it could not work.

One element in the formation of operants is therefore the chaining of responses, including of course the reinforcement of the use by the subject of response-produced discriminative stimuli. A second element which receives considerable stress in the work of Skinner is the argument that the fineness of differentiation in operant behaviour reflects the subtleties of the reinforcement procedures. Examples given by Skinner include the acquisition of language, drawing from copy and playing music by ear (Skinner, 1953, 1957). To take the first: a child or a foreigner learning language may often be content when he is able to produce recognizable approximations to the speech in his surroundings. If the response required is '*water*' and he says '*orter*' or '*vorter*' the operant is reinforced. But at least in the case of the child finer differentiations will be required later: approval will be given or withheld in the measure that his speech approximates to the accepted phonetic characteristics of his community. The mimic trains himself to go even further, reproducing inflexions and the subtleties of phonation which he finds in the model. He is using finer **D** Ss because his success as artiste or as life and soul of the party is contingent on their use. Similarly the poor copyist is sensitive only to gross differences between the disposition of lines in the original and his copy, while the skilled draughtsman is able to reflect subtler nuances in the former. The latter has a greater 'behavioural repertoire', i.e. he has more operants at his disposal from which to choose.

Skinner (1953, pp. 117 ff.) writes as if the behaviour of both may be seen as an approximation to a point-to-point correspondence. I do not believe this analysis is adequate, because I do not believe that the components in the regulation of behaviour are identical with the components of the observed behavioural product – i.e. the performance. (See Chapter 4, Section II. 8.) Thus, in considering the behaviour of the copyist, what we have to take into account is not the set of all possible lines which he might draw and from which he must choose, but rather the relations between the members of this set, for it is these that govern the decision processes he must make (usually unconsciously). Given the three drawings of Figure 11, the similarity of the first pair does not derive from a greater point-to-point correspondence than that which exists between the second and the third. Nor can it be adequately explained by anything so vague as field-properties. It derives from the fact that the decision processes required, and also their input and output, are identical save for one element, the termination of the first continuous stroke. Because of his tendency to identify fine-grain control with point-to-point correspondence, and the sequencing of observed behaviour with the sequencing of decision procedures, Skinner's analysis falls short of the schematic account given in Chapter 4. Nevertheless, the recognition of multiple causation could almost bridge the gap. Once again, Skinner's lack of interest in such things as 'decision processes' proves an obstacle to the development of a more comprehensive and unified point of view.

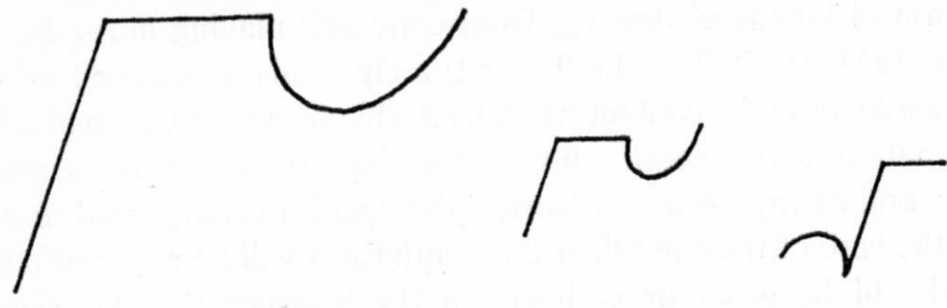

Figure 11: To illustrate problem of copying

Be that as it may, the application of Skinnerian principles to the technique of programmed instruction envisages not only the progressive build-up of more complex operants by a process of chaining, but also the differentiation of operants by the judicious use of fine-grain stimulus control. To take an example from the teaching of reading. It makes sense to begin by drawing the attention of the learner to the contrastive significances of graphemes, using sharply differentiated letters and word forms, e.g.

pit *bag* *run*;

before introducing finer-grain contrasts such as *bad* – *bat*. At the same time one needs to avoid the incidental acquisition of misleading and inadequate behavioural strategies which would result from an exaggerated delay in introduction of the finer **D**Ss.

4. *Verbal Behaviour*

Several references have been made already to Skinner's reflexions on language. I have no doubt whatever that the greatest fault of Skinner's extended essay on *Verbal Behaviour* (1957) is its length. It runs to 470 large pages. Vygotsky's *Thought and Language* (1962) is about half as long, and Chomsky's *Syntactic Structures* (1957) about an eighth. All three are seminal works. But one suspects that their richness of content is an inverse function of their length. (Readability is a reverse J-function!) However, few who have had anything very fundamental to say about the regulation of behaviour at the level of strict experimental control have cared to examine the implications of their work for the most specifically human of skills except in the most general terms. Osgood and Skinner are exceptions, and it is no mean achievement.

Even allowing for its verbosity, it is not easy to do justice to so large a treatise in a few sentences, but a summary is what is needed here, and the following will have to do. Skinner's main points are:

(i) The psychological study of language has been hindered by an obsession with meaning. To speak of the meaning of a speaker's utterance is to suggest an analysis of the ideas which antedate it. This is apt to lead to an infinite regress: in order to have the idea he must previously have the idea of the idea, and so on. Skinner's analysis starts with language as behaviour. 'Meaning is not a property of behaviour as such but of the conditions under which it occurs' (p. 13). Language behaviour is to be thought of as a 'repertoire' of operants and the psychological study of language is a study of the conditions for the acquisition of these operants and of the contingencies (of discriminative and reinforcing stimuli) which determine the probability of their occurrence.

(ii) A unit of language behaviour is simply a segment which may be rendered more or less probable by appropriate manipulation of **DS** and **RS**[1] contingencies. A word is very often a unit, but a longer phrase may likewise function as a unit. A phoneme may function as a unit in the acquisition of a new word (p. 62). A speech pattern or 'frame' is also a unit (p. 336). The unit is of course the operant, and the acceptance of units of varying lengths is consistent with that of operants of varying length.

(iii) Language begins as communication. To give a full account of an episode in which communication occurs one needs a sort of zig-zag model which contains the responses both of speaker and of listener. The roles are alternate, and the responses of one participant function as stimuli for the other. Reinforcement occurs when a partner offers a reinforcing stimulus (does what is required, or signifies understanding or approval), or withdraws an aversive stimulus (implied threat: e.g. '*What do you say?*' to a child who has received a gift).

(iv) Thinking and planning are forms of verbal behaviour in which the speaker acts as his own interlocutor. The fact that the language is subvocal is irrelevant to this.

[1] Reinforcing stimulus, see p 59.

(v) In shaping an operation in a pigeon like turning in a figure of 8, the trainer waits for the first approximation to be emitted and builds progressively from this. The acquisition of verbal behaviour in a child is made easier by the fact of *echoic behaviour*. Reinforcement is offered whenever the child emits a response which is similar to the stimulus he is given. In time, the range of responses that he emits in the presence of a verbal stimulus preceded by '*Say*' (explicit or implicit) is narrowed. Once the child has acquired the requisite minimal operants for the reproduction of new words, phonemes, a new operant can be shaped in one: '*Say "alligator"*' – '*Alligator*'. The process does not depend on a faculty of imitation, merely on the reinforcement of responses which are imitative (pp. 59–62).

(vi) Once an operant has been learned under optimal **DS-RS** contingencies (e.g. in the presence of a glass of water: '*Say "water"*' – '*Water*' – '*Good boy. Have a good long drink!*'), control of the operant is extended to more remote stimuli (e.g. thirst) and even to other words, the verbal context providing the **DS** for the emission of the operant in question (e.g. '*If one is really thirsty, the best thirst quencher is . . .*'). Such transfer of stimulus control is an instance of 'induction'.

(vii) Skinner distinguishes four categories of verbal operants by the criterion of the class of **DS** and **RS** contingencies with which they are associated. These are: (*a*) The *mand*, wherein the speaker manipulates the interlocutor by getting him to do something. (*b*) The *tact*, corresponding to a less direct manipulation of the audience, e.g. by providing information about some state of affairs. (*c*) The *intraverbal operant*, (e.g. *if . . . then*) where the D Ss are speech patterns and transition probabilities, and the R Ss are the reinforcements obtained following the use of the operant in a speech frame, or following a previous verbal sequence, usually in the form of an indication that communication has occurred without 'loss of information'. (*d*) The *autoclitic*, representing the use of speech to refer to speech (e.g. '*What I said was*', '*Listen*', etc.).

(viii) Verbal behaviour is the most conspicuous illustration of the phenomenon of 'multiple causation'. Quite generally, the occurrence of a given word in a verbal context is a function both of antecedent environmental conditions and of the intraverbal context, i.e. of the previous sequence of words.

(ix) Verbal behaviour provides the clue for all the 'higher functions' in human behaviour. It is reinforcing (to Skinner especially) to control one's environment. It is effective to set up secondary verbal reinforcers in the form of such verbal responses as 'It looks as if I'm on the right lines', and these are reinforced. It is also effective to write down one's utterances in the form of text, for they can then be revised and improved. Such behaviour is reinforced. The emission and subsequent editing of trial verbal behaviour is all that one means by thinking. Writing one's words instead of emitting them vocally or subvocally sometimes helps in the subsequent 'editing'.

Several references have been made already to the experimental substantiation of Skinner's descriptive approach in the context of verbal behaviour. The fact that it gives rise to correct predictions is proof of its relevance. It remains that as an interpretation of the very complex processes involved in language behaviour, Skinner's formulations are far from adequate. We may gain a better idea of their strengths and shortcomings by reviewing each principle in turn.

(i) It seems to me that Skinner's recognition that, in an important sense (my qualification), the meaning of an utterance (of whatever length) is a reference to the contexts which determine its probability of occurrence is an enormous step forward. It makes possible a *rapprochement* between the psychologist's treatment of language and the linguistic analysis of an 'idiolanguage' (the complete description of the language of one individual 'informant').

Attempts to define meaning without reference to the complete set of contexts are bound to lead to grossly impoverished definitions. Perhaps the most significant of these is Osgood's 'semantic differential' (Osgood, Suci and Tannenbaum, 1957). Meaning, for Osgood, is a mediating response, and the characteristics of this response can be measured by asking a subject to locate the word along a variety of bipolar continua, e.g. good – bad, sweet – sour, strong – weak, etc. Subsequent analysis of the subject's responses enables the assessor to summarize the 'meanings' of the concepts (words) by locating them in a three-dimensional 'space', as the resultant 'meanings' seem to differ principally with respect to the subject's evaluation of the concept as good or ill, his estimate of its potency or strength, and of its activity. Now I believe that Osgood's method constitutes an invaluable technique for the study of varieties of personality integration as well as for the measurement of attitudes. But I fail to see how it can possibly yield a useful measure of meaning in a linguistic sense. This type of analysis cannot but lead to absurd approximations: a 'spider' is rather like an 'alligator', a 'mother' is rather like a 'church', 'edible' means something like 'loveable', 'motor-car' is similar to 'eagle', and so on. Instructive for a Freudian 'depth-analysis', but useless for that of language. In effect, Osgood is unwittingly restricting meaning to connotative meaning as opposed to denotative meaning.

The point is that Osgood's test situation is itself a particular context or set of contexts, and the 'meaning' which it yields is circumscribed by these contexts. By contrast, Skinner's definition refers to the set of all possible contexts. But Skinner's definition removes 'meaning' from our analysis of the subject and transfers it to the environment. Now it is true that all the contexts relevant to the occurrence of an utterance could not possibly be active at the same time within the subject's mind or brain, and all are relevant to its meaning *in general*. But unless the connexions established within the subject's brain were modified by these contexts, they could not be operative in the determination of his behaviour. It seems to me that these considerations compel us to make the sort of distinction which is envisaged in Chapter 4, Section II between *schema* and *strategy*. The schema represents the set of all possible behaviours, while the strategy represents those connexions which are active at the given time.

The reinstatement of the subject as something more than a 'source of a succession of operants' enables one to broach problems which are all too liable to escape the investigator who is over-impressed by the parsimony of Skinner's constructs. For instance, the psychological analysis of language must be capable of dealing with the problem of forward reference which is a very common feature of language ('Although it is sunny I had rather not be without my umbrella'), and especially so in inflected languages like Latin. As a matter of fact, forward reference is not only the very basis of Yngve's analysis of sentences in terms of 'mean depth', but is also essential to Chomsky's analysis of transformational grammar (see Volume II, Chapter 6). Similarly, the refusal to examine the way in which the multiple determinants interact within the subject obscures the very real differences that exist between the processes of the speaker or writer and those of the listener or reader.

(ii) Skinner's recognition of the essential unity of longer as well as shorter operants (I would call them 'strategies') is one of the most powerful of his insights. What is lacking is an adequate analysis of the relations between the two. There is all the world of difference between a formula ('*All's well that ends well*') and a speech pattern ('*If . . . were . . . then . . . would be . . .*'). One cannot explain the latter simply by pointing to the unity of the former. It demands a properly hierarchical account of the determination of language behaviour, and this Skinner does not give.

(iii) Skinner's requirement that the analysis of language behaviour and language learning must take into account both speaker and listener is an admirable caution. The recognition finds a powerful application in programmed learning where the immediate reinforcement which might be given by an ideal listener is automatically provided by the form of the programme. But, characteristically, Skinner neglects the role of spontaneous practice and self-reinforcement in language learning (see under vi).

(iv) May be considered along with (ix).

(v), (vi) Echoic behaviour is accepted by Skinner as a fact. It is a fact, and one that can be used to advantage, as it is used in programmed learning. Here, very generally, concepts are defined verbally, and the learner is required to repeat the definitions as given. But such memorization is made very much easier by the use of the 'prompt' (a part, or nearly all, of the sequence is given and the subject is required only to provide the missing portion), combined with techniques of 'fading', i.e. reducing progressively the completeness of the prompt and thereby increasing the size of the operant. Using Skinner's terminology (with which there is no ground to quarrel), the subject who is copying the printed text or reading it is using textual cues; when he supplies a missing word, he is using intraverbal cues; later still, when he supplies the required formula and applies it correctly, he is using contextual or situational cues. Thus the entire course of learning depends on the conditioning of new and more powerful discriminative cues to the operant, in accordance with the principle of induction.

However, to return to the role of echoic behaviour in language learning, while Skinner is justified in recording its facilitatory role in the interpersonal situation where the child reproduces the word or phrase in its entirety in the form in which he has heard it, he leaves out of account the part of spontaneous rehearsal and approximation in imitation. Imitation, we are told, is not a faculty. Faculty is almost a rude word in psychology. But while it is true that the behaviour of listening is quite different from that of speaking, and, in general, the behaviour of observing a model is different from that of copying, children and primates generally imitate (Chapter 5, Section IV). Not only are the cues from their own behaviour, and their own persons, assimilated to analogous cues from the behaviour and appearance of the model, but the enhancement of these similarities is self-reinforcing. The study of speech development in the first year of life consists in large part of recording how the infant learns to perfect the strategies required to produce at will the sounds of his native tongue in the course of circular reactions which are essentially trial-and-error (reinforcement being a function of proximity of the sound to an internalized model – see Volume II, Chapter 5, the author of which is one of the pioneers in this field). By the same token, there is reason to believe that correct reproduction of the speech patterns of the native tongue is contingent on the prior elaboration, again through trial-and-error, of syntactic strategies which offer successive approximations to the syntax of the mother-tongue (Braine, 1963; Bellugi and Brown, 1964; and see Volume II, Chapter 6).

(vii), (viii) Categorization is often a useful step in the direction of explanation, and Skinner's categorization of the functions of language has a reasonable claim to our attention. In particular, the distinction between the mand, which serves the function of manipulating the behaviour of the audience, and the tact, which communicates information to the audience (or to the speaker acting as his own audience) is a helpful beginning. Similarly, one needs to recognize that language includes many elements whose explanation must depend more on the grammar of the language than on its semantic function – the intraverbal operant. But this sort of categorization is only a beginning, and rapidly breaks down, because of the fact of multiple causation, which Skinner recognizes, and because of the hierarchy implied by the interaction of strategies (or 'operants') of varying lengths. For instance, if a mother tells her child (as parents will) '*Be a dear and get me my scissors which you'll find in the drawer of my work-basket*', the utterance as a whole is a mand, the second portion is a tact, and several of the words are primarily intraverbal operants. But over and above this the utterance may communicate impatience, or a mutual affection and understanding, depending on the tone and the situational context: it is therefore a tact. Similarly the word '*my*' is partly a tact although mainly intraverbal, because, taken by itself, its informational contribution is negligible. And so on. By the same token, when one says: '*I see that Mr Wilson has had another rebuff*', the '*I see that*' may be an autoclitic in the formal sense, averting the audience to the fact that what one is about to say was conditioned by reading a newspaper, but it has this function only if the remark is an opening gambit. If it is uttered in the course of a political discussion, its function is little more than '*er*': the speaker utters a formula to gain time.

Quite generally, Skinner's categorization, though not without value, sits in uneasy alliance with his recognition of multiple causation. This is because he has not followed through the full implications of the latter. From the point of view of the analysis of the regulations implied in linguistic behaviour, Osgood's recognition that there is always an interaction of processes at (at least) three levels – semantic, grammatical, perceputo-motor – seems to the present writer to be far more fruitful.

Speech is certainly a sequence of sounds. But it is a modulated sequence. Semantic and syntactic determinants are superposed on motor determinants in respect of inflexion and pitch as well as of lexis and phonation (e.g. stress and pause). The psychological as well as the physical explanation demands a sort of Fourier analysis.

(iv), (ix) That thinking usually involves language is true. It is also clear that thinking is inextricably bound up with language. The idea does not precede its formulation in language, for it only achieves precision in the course of such formulation. But this does not imply at all that thinking is reducible to language. For, as Vigotsky (1962) points out, there is language before thought and there is also thought before language. All thinking involves representation, i.e. the reconstruction of reality (the possible input) by the manipulation of symbolic strategies which yield a symbolic input. Language itself is a form, the most flexible form, of representation. But Piaget (1951) has shown that at least four forms of representation seem to develop simultaneously: language, deferred imitation, play and imagery. Because language is a complex system of symbols or conventional signs which do not involve similarity of perceptual input in relation to the signified, and even more because the moment to moment organization of language behaviour obeys rules which are internal to the language, grammar, and shows only the most limited correspondence with the sequences of the signified, the use of language as a vehicle of thought is a comparatively late development, much later than the acquisition of language itself.

The temporal relations between representational behaviour and the signified may be of three sorts; the former may follow the latter, or it may accompany it, or it may antecede it. Observation of children's language and play shows this to be a natural order (Buhler, 1933). Even when the representation antecedes the direct behaviour, the process may have little of the constructiveness of thinking. It seems probable that the power of thinking depends on two closely related developments. One is the tendency for representation to proceed from both ends: the reconstruction moves to and fro from the initial state to the final envisaged end and back, progressively closing the gap between them by reconstructing the actions which lead from the first to the last (Bartlett, 1958). The other is the progressive elaboration of the systems of structural equivalences that makes such to- and fro-ing possible, as studied especially by Piaget (see Volume II, Chapters 8–10, 13). Linguistic formulation is an effective vehicle for thought because it fixes the successive moments in immediate memory so that they are available for the construction and validation of further relations. Although it is difficult to avoid the hypothesis of a prior 'intention' which activates the language itself, and gives it direction, this is no more than the vaguest anticipation of the form of the end-product, sufficient to provide an initial overall strategy, but one which is subject to constant amplification, refinement and revision in the course of the representation itself.

All this is no more than the briefest survey of the problems of language and reasoning, problems which are by no means fully resolved, and whose more detailed treatment is reserved for Volume II. But it is sufficient to show why Skinner's merely descriptive approach to human as well as animal behaviour leads to a neat side-stepping of the most crucial issues.

5. *Skinner's treatment of emotion and drive*

By contrast with his extensive theoretical and experimental treatment of reinforcement and of language, Skinner's discussions of drive and emotion are quite short, and our own review of his position can be correspondingly short. Skinner recognizes that motivational variables play a considerable part in influencing the probability of occurrence of an operant. Moreover, they can be brought under experimental control by appropriate techniques. In a telling analysis of his approach to psychological problems in general, Skinner (1938) has this to say about drive. Say an animal has learned a particular operant, e.g. running a straightway to obtain a food reward, and we find that the behaviour does not occur. Failure of the response may be due to a variety of causes: the animal may fail to respond because training has been insufficient and has been extinguished by non-reinforcement; alternatively, the learning may be adequate, but failure of response may be due to lack of hunger (drive); alternatively, learning and drive may be adequate, but failure of response is due to a conflicting aversive response: the animal is afraid; finally, the failure of response may be due to any combination of the three variables. But this does not mean that the psychologist has no means of distinguishing between them. If he limits himself to the single observation, there is no way of deciding. But by appropriate control experiments, decision becomes an easy matter (at least in principle). If the animal responds at a high rate in other experimental situations for a food reward, one can rule out lack of drive; if intensity of drive is increased by increasing deprivation and response remains low, then the failure again must be due to insufficient learning or fear. Since fear is correlated with the presence of physiological symptoms such as urination and defecation as well as increased heart-rate, etc., if these symptoms are absent, then lack of learning is rendered more probable. And so on.

Drive then, appears as a temporary change in the strength of a group of operants, defined by the particular antecedents which induce it. Skinner's treatment of emotion is essentially similar. Fluctuations in the extinction curve shown in Figure 10 are attributed largely to temporary states of emotion, generated by the animal's own behaviour and the input which results. The same technique has also been extended to the study of the effects of anxiety and of drugs on the intensity of the operant.

On the theoretical side, Skinner's formulations are characteristically negative. Drive is not a stimulus, and it is not a response to a need. It is not a stimulus because the only sense in which it could be so described would be that of a construct: an intervening variable – and Skinner has no use for these. To argue that it is a response to a need would lead to confusion. It is common both in human beings and in animals for a subject to refuse certain types of food and accept others. How is one to account for the behaviour of a child who refuses his main course (or eats it slowly without relish) but laps up the dessert? Skinner's effective way of cutting the Gordian knot is to say quite simply that he has a strong drive of one sort and a weak drive of another – as evidenced by his behaviour.

The weaknesses of Skinner's position are perhaps more obvious than its strengths. His investigations of drive have been limited. Negative general formulae are a poor substitute for the detailed studies of the acquisition of secondary drives by Miller and others such as Mowrer, Sheffield and Amsel. Viewed from the very general standpoint of the applicability of psychological theory and findings to practice, the most significant facts relating to drives are bound up with the realization that the motivational aspects of behaviour are themselves subject to learning and forgetting. Particularly noteworthy are the observations that environmental cues are capable, as a result of conditioning, of arousing aversive behaviour, anxiety (Miller) and enhanced positive appetitive behaviour (Mowrer, Sheffield, Amsel). All of these researches were inspired more by the Hullian tradition. The fact that they were originally conceived in the orthodox belief in need-reduction, and that their authors have never fully abandoned the concept of the drive as stimulus is a comparatively small price to pay.

Nevertheless, it seems to the present writer that the notion of the drive as stimulus rests on a false conception of the nature of behaviour regulation (see Chapter 3). Skinner's conception of drive as no more than variation in the strength of specific behavioural arousal is entirely consistent with contemporary physiological approaches as well as with conceptions deriving from cybernetic analogues (Chapters 3, 4). It is certainly true that it becomes difficult to make a sharp distinction between drive and emotion while confining oneself to the study of their effects on gross behaviour. But this itself is probably a strength rather than a weakness. Our understanding of the causes of moment to moment variation of general and especially of specific arousal is still in its early beginnings, and clarification is almost certain to come more from physiological and interdisciplinary research than from the testing of *a priori* constructions based on supposed correlations between 'stimuli' and 'responses' (see the criticism of these concepts in Chapter 3).

6. *Evaluation*

In spite of Skinner's fairly consistent resistance to theoretical unifications, his achievement has been spectacular not only in its practical implications but also in the clarification of theoretical issues. Of course the reason is that Skinner is deeply concerned with theory in one sense: to establish perfectly valid and general laws concerning the precise relations between observed phenomena. And he is deeply committed to the experimental method which consists in isolating the reactions in which one is interested, and observing their effects as it were *in vitro*. His descriptive laws are not descriptive at the level of crude observation and statistical summary (rats learn more effectively when maintained on a relatively low diet; boys tend on the whole to be superior to girls in arithmetic and inferior in language, etc.). The concepts with which he is concerned, reinforcement, operant strength, the discriminative stimulus, etc., are concepts of high generality – and the circularity of their definitions testifies to the degree of their abstraction. As we have seen, the circularity is no obstacle to precise identification in concrete situations.

Skinner's objection to theory centres on the Hullian attempt to use behavioural observation as a jumping-off point for the elaboration of a system of relations between constructs whose status is midway between that of mathematical abstractions and states or processes in the organism. Now as we will see in Chapter 3, the Hullian position represents a sort of *reductio ad absurdum* of Thorndike's naïve assumption that behaviour is somehow made up of bonds between stimuli and responses. Skinner's counter to this position was undoubtedly a liberating influence. The chief features of this, as noted already, were (i) recognition of the difference between elicited responses and spontaneous operants; (ii) recognition of the role of discriminative stimuli (cues); (iii) recognition of operants of different lengths; (iv) recognition of multiple causation; (v) a theoretically neutral conception of drive, being a convenient term for the description of systematic influences on the strength of an operant. It seems to me that in every one of these respects, Skinner's formulation represents a fruitful advance on that of Hull. Together, they lead to a conception of behaviour which is free from the atomism which characterizes all previous formulations since Thorndike, even including Tolman, who never succeeded in resolving the contradictions posed by the **S-R** approach. I see no reason to doubt that the effectiveness of Skinner's formulations in practical applications is due quite largely to the emancipation from a too limiting theory.

On the other hand, Skinner's work has several limitations. And they too derive from his restriction to a purely descriptive set of laws. The most general limitation is his unwillingness to examine more closely the structure of behavioural regulation. Thus, although he recognizes operants of varying lengths, he does not consider the relations between them, beyond a very general assumption of multiple causation. The result is (i) a tendency to regard the larger operant as no more than the summed result of putting smaller operants end-to-end (in shaping behaviour), and (ii) an even stronger tendency to limit the analysis of overt behaviour by excluding any consideration of decision processes which are not themselves observable, but the intervention of which can be reliably inferred from the course of behaviour, e.g. in drawing a line, when to stop. These restrictions have the further consequence that a vague relation termed 'induction' is invoked much too easily to account for facilitations and interferences of all sorts, from perceptual generalization to insightful transposition, and including even the substitution of appropriate lexical units in syntactical frames.

The truth is that Skinner's contribution does not amount to a comprehensive analysis of behaviour, nor indeed is it intended as such. Skinner himself would prefer to take the stand that the descriptive and experimental approach has led to correct generalizations in some areas – which have very wide implications, from pigeon training to programmed learning and from lever pressing to verbal behaviour: other laws remain to be established using similar methods. But he is not entirely consistent here, and many of his reflexions in *Science and Human Behaviour* and in *Verbal Learning* do suggest an unwillingness to even consider the role of anticipatory and regulating strategies, the way in which equivalences develop, the range of such equivalences (including differences in the degree and type of generalization shown by different species), and above all the unique features of behaviour which is representational or symbolic.

VII. CONCLUDING REMARKS

All of the theories and researches which have been reviewed in this chapter are linked by a common thread. It is their adherence to the experimental method. All have this in common too: a belief in the continuity of the mechanism governing the regulation of behaviour in animals and in human beings, and hence in the relevance of animal experimentation for the study of human learning. One might indeed go further, for with the single exception of Pavlov, all of the major theorists whose work has been reviewed in this chapter tend more or less explicitly to the belief that the major laws which determine the regulation of animal behaviour are also those which are relevant to human behaviour, with the implication that differences between species are relatively unimportant for theory. A respect for the experimental method and a recognition that problems of human psychology are biological problems and reflect processes which are at least in part common to all organisms whose behaviour is modified by experience; these we can accept as a *sine qua non* for scientific study. Conversely, the assumption that the principles governing the regulation of behaviour are common to all species, implying that phylogenetic advance brings only quantitative changes, is one which has come to be very seriously questioned in recent years. Already we have seen reason to question treatments of language and thinking which fail to take account of the distinctive functional relations implied by behaviour which is representational. Throughout these volumes, the reader may find further evidence of phylogenetic and ontogenetic changes with respect to the kinds of learning that occur, and especially with respect to the extent of the generalization to which they give rise.

There is little advantage in attempting to summarize the content of previous sections, for section summaries should serve as they stand. I have tried to suggest that there is a continuity in the theoretical and experimental advances made during the first half of this century, which is approximately the period covered in this chapter. The basic orientations characterized in the preceding paragraph were already explicit in the work of Thorndike and Pavlov. The very general principles established by the latter, and the focus on instrumental behaviour and learning established by the former, remain prominent features of most of the succeeding work. Behaviourism itself, at least in the sense of a dissatisfaction with accounts which are based exclusively on the psychologist's intuition of cognitive organizations existing within the subject (animal or human), is common to nearly all. Gestalt psychology is something of an exception, and it has been suggested that Tolman's work was essentially an attempt to comprise the findings of Gestalt psychology within a behaviourist framework. The attempt remains loosely organized and programmatic, and Hullian theory seeks to provide a tighter and more materialist (less cognitive) set of constructs to account for the phenomena revealed both by Gestalt and by Tolman himself and his co-workers.

Among the principal contributions of the Hullian approach, we noted the establishment of certain clear relations between motivational conditions of drive and incentive and the observed behaviour. Motivation itself was shown to be largely a product of learning, through the intervention of secondary reinforcers. The analysis of insight mechanisms representing the combination of previously learned segments of behaviour, offered at least a partial explanation of the process. The notions of the antedating goal reaction and the habit-family-hierarchy have been criticized on the ground that they do not allow for the simultaneous action of multiple processes in the determination of continuous behaviour, being limited by the atomism which is inherent in all **S-R** formulations. Nevertheless, the first and the second have served their turn in bringing to light some of the ways in which the intervention of language and representation may 'mediate' between the input and the final form of response in a variety of experimental settings.

The work of Skinner was shown to be a liberating influence mainly because of his clear recognition of the fact that behaviour is not merely a sequence of elicited responses but consists largely in the spontaneous 'emission' of 'operants' controlled by environmental cues. At the same time the restriction to merely descriptive laws stands in the way of a structural analysis of the hierarchical relations between the several determinants of observed behaviour. Therefore Skinner's treatment of language is only partially adequate and his analysis of representational mechanisms, especially thinking and planning, is little more than an intellectual *tour de force*.

Psychology does not stand still, and the pace of theoretical and experimental advance has increased rapidly of recent years. Undoubtedly, one of the principal factors has been the growing scope of our understanding of the physiological bases of behaviour. Therefore Chapter 2 is devoted to a brief survey of these developments, more authoritative than could have been provided by the present writer. Chapter 3 surveys a number of trends, some recent, others which, although not recent, have only become influential in psychology since 1950. I have tried to offer a more thorough critique of the **S-R** approach, and at the same time to prepare the ground for a formulation of certain ways of thinking about behavioural regulations which I take to be increasingly common among contemporary workers in the field. This is the task undertaken in Chapters 4 and 5. It will be shown that the work of Piaget, covering a period of more than forty years, is entirely consistent with this more contemporary approach, and largely anticipates it, even though the problems studied are often very different.

Since the implications and applications of this new approach receive only partial treatment in the present volume, for the specific development in human learning and its conditions are dealt with more fully in Volumes II and III, the very general questions posed by way of introduction to this chapter must be dealt with elsewhere. What we have established already is this. That there is every reason to believe that questions concerned with the causes of human behaviour and the nature of human learning can be studied fruitfully if we accept that they are essentially physical processes, governed by laws, and open to investigation by appropriate observational and experimental techniques, informed by theories which are constantly revised and overhauled – or replaced and absorbed by better ones.

REFERENCES

AMSEL, A. (1958). The role of frustrative non-reward in non-continuous reward situations. *Psychol. Bull.*, **55**, 102–119.

BAKER, R. A., and LAWRENCE, D. H. (1951). The differential effects of simultaneous and successive stimuli presentation on transposition. *J. Comp. Physiol. Psychol.*, **44**, 378–382.

BARKER, R., DEMBO, T., and LEWIN, K. (1941). Frustration and Regression. *U. of Iowa Studies in Child Welfare*, **18**, No. 1.

BARTLETT, F. C. (1958). *Thinking: An Experimental and Social Study.* London: George Allen and Unwin.

BELLUGI, U., and BROWN, R. (1964). The acquisition of language. *Mon. Soc. Res. Child Dev.* **29**, No. 1 (Serial No. 92).

BERLYNE, D. E. (1960). Les équivalences psychologiques et les notions quantitatives. In Berlyne, D. E. et Piaget, J., Théorie du comportement et opérations. *Etudes d'épistémologie génétique*, **12**, 1–76.

BIRCH, H. G. (1945a). The role of motivational factors in insightful problem solving. *J. Comp. Psychol.* **38**, 295–317.

BIRCH, H. G. (1945b). The relation of previous experience to insightful problem-solving. *J. Comp. Psychol.* **38**, 367–383.

BITTERMAN, M. E. (1965). Phyletic differences in learning. *Amer. Psychologist*, **20**, 396–410.

BLODGETT, H. C. (1929). The effect of the introduction of reward upon the maze performance of rats. *Univ. of California Publications in Psychology*, **4**, 113–134.

BRAINE, M. D. S. (1963). The ontogeny of English phrase structure: the first phase. *Language*, **39**, 1–13.

BROADBENT, D. E. (1958). *Perception and Communication.* Oxford: Pergamon.

BROADHURST, P. L. (1957). Emotionality and the Yerkes–Dodson law. *J. Exp. Psychol.* **54**, 345–352.

BUHLER, C. (1933). The child and its activity with practical material. *Brit. J. Educ. Psychol.* **3**, 27–41.

CHOMSKY, N. (1957). *Syntactic Structures.* The Hague: Mouton.

COWLES, J. T. (1937). Food tokens as incentives for learning by chimpanzees. *Comp. Psychol. Monogr.* **14**, 1–96.

CRESPI, L. P. (1942). Quantitative variation in incentive and performance in the white rat. *Amer. J. Psychol.* **55**, 467–517.

DENNY, M. R. (1946). The role of secondary reinforcement in a partial reinforcement learning situation. *J. Exp. Psychol.* **36**, 373–389.

DEUTSCH, J. A. (1960). *The Structural Basis of Behaviour.* London: Cambridge U.P.

DOLLARD, J., and MILLER, N. E. (1950). *Personality and Psychotherapy.* New York and London: McGraw-Hill.

EYSENCK, H. J. (1953). *Uses and Abuses of Psychology.* Harmondsworth, Middlesex: Pelican.

EYSENCK, H. J. (1957). *The Dynamics of Anxiety and Hysteria.* London: Routledge.

FLUGEL, J. C. (1933). *A Hundred Years of Psychology, 1833–1933.* London: Duckworth.

FURNEAUX, W. P. (1957). *Student Selection.* Report to the Imperial College of Science and Technology.

GIBSON, J. J. (1929). The reproduction of visually perceived forms. *J. Exp. Psychol.* **12**, 1–39.

GUTHRIE, E. R. (1959). Association by contiguity. In Koch, S. (ed.) *Psychology: A Study of a Science. Vol. II. General Systematic Formulations, Learning and Special Processes.* New York and London: McGraw-Hill, 158–195.

HALLWORTH, H. J. (1961). Anxiety in secondary modern and grammar school children. *Brit. J. Educ. Psychol.* **31**, 281–291.

HEBB, D. O. (1949). *The Organisation of Behaviour: A Neuro-psychological Theory.* New York: Wiley.

HEBB, D. O. and FOORD, E. N. (1945). Errors of visual recognition and the nature of the trace. *J. Exp. Psychol.* **35**, 335–348.

HILGARD, E. R. (1958). *Theories of Learning.* (Second ed.). London: Methuen.

HILL, W. F. (1963). *Learning: A Survey of Psychological Interpretations.* London: University Paperbacks.

HULL, C. L. (1934). The concept of the habit-family-hierarchy and maze learning. *Psychol. Rev.* **41**, 33–54 and 134–152.

HULL, C. L. (1935). The mechanism of the assembly of behaviour segments in novel combinations. *Psychol. Rev.* **42**, 219–245.

HULL, C. L. (1943). *Principles of Behaviour: An Introduction to Behaviour Theory.* New York: Appleton-Century-Crofts.

HULL, C. L. (1952). *A Behaviour System.* New Haven: Yale University Press.

HUMPHREY, G. (1951). *Thinking: An Introduction to its Experimental Psychology.* London: Methuen.

KENDLER, T. S. (1950). An experimental investigation of transposition as a function of the difference between training and test stimuli. *J. Exp. Psychol.* **40**, 552–562.

KENDLER, T. S. (1963). Development of mediating responses in children. *Mon. Soc. Res. Child Dev.* **28**, No. 2, 33–48.

KOCH, S. (1954). Clark L. Hull. Section 1 in Koch, S. *et al. Modern Learning Theory*, New York: Appleton-Century-Crofts.

KOCH, S. (ed.) (1959). *Psychology: A Study of a Science, General Systematic Formulations, Learning and Special Processes.* London: McGraw-Hill.

KOFFKA, K. (1935). *Principles of Gestalt Psychology.* New York: Harcourt Brace.

KOHLER, W. (1925). *The Mentality of Apes.* London: Routledge.

KOHLER, W. (1929). *Gestalt Psychology.* New York: Liveright.

KRASNER, L. (1961). Studies of the conditioning of verbal behaviour. In Sol Saporta (ed.), *Psycholinguistics: A Book of Readings*, pp. 75–96.

London and New York: Holt Rinehart and Winston. (First published in *Psychol. Bull.* **55**, 148–70 (1958).)

KRECHEVSKY, I. (1932). 'Hypothesis' versus 'chance' in the pre-solution period in sensory-discrimination learning. *U. of California Publications in Psychology*, **6**, No. 3, 27–44.

KUENNE, M. R. (1946). Experimental investigation of the relation of language to transportation behaviour in young children. *J. Exp. Psychol.* **36**, 471–490.

LEWIS, D. J. (1960). Partial reinforcement: a selective review of the literature since 1950. *Psychol. Bull.* **57**, 1–28.

LUNZER, E. A. (1960). Aggressive and withdrawing children in the normal school. *Brit. J. Educ. Psychol.* **30**, 119–123.

LYNN, R. (1959). Two personality characteristics related to academic achievement. *Brit. J. Educ. Psychol.* **29**, 213–217.

MacCORQUODALE, K., and MEEHL, P. E. (1954). Edward C. Tolman. Section 2 in Estes, W. K. *et al. Modern Learning Theory*. New York: Appleton-Century-Crofts.

MacFARLANE, D. A. (1930). The role of kinaesthesis in maze learning. *U. of California Publications in Psychology*, **4**, 277–305.

MAGOUN, H. W. (1963). *The Waking Brain*. (Second edition) Springfield, Ill.: Charles Thomas.

MAIER, N. R. F. (1929). Reasoning in white rats. *Psychol. Monogr.* **6**, No. 29.

MASON, D. J. (1957). The relation of secondary reinforcement to partial reinforcement. *J. Comp. Physiol. Psychol.* **50**, 264–268.

MEDNICK, S. A. and FREEDMAN, J. L. (1960). Stimulus generalization. *Psychol. Bull.* **57**, 169–200.

MERLIN, V. S. (1961). The dynamics of 'transfer' of conditioned reflex connexions from one signal system to the other. In O'Connor, N. (ed.) *Recent Soviet Psychology*. Oxford: Pergamon.

MILLER, N. E. (1959). Extensions of a liberalised S-R theory. In Koch, S. (ed.) *Psychology: A Study of a Science. Vol. II. General Systematic Formulations, Learning and Special Processes*. New York and London: McGraw-Hill, 195–292.

MORRIS, R. (1951). *The Quality of Learning*. London: Methuen.

MOTOKAWA, K. (1949). Physiological induction in human retina as a basis of color and brightness contrast. *J. Neurophysiol.* **12**, 475–488.

MOWRER, O. H. (1950). *Learning Theory and Personality Dynamics*. New York: Ronald Press.

MOWRER, O. H. (1960a). *Learning Theory and Behaviour*. New York: John Wiley.

MOWRER, O. H. (1960b). *Learning Theory and the Symbolic Processes.* NewYork: John Wiley.

MUELLER, C. G., and SCHOENFELD, W. N. (1954). Edwin R. Guthrie. Section 5 in Estes, W. K. *et al. Modern Learning Theory.* New York: Appleton-Century-Crofts.

MUENZINGER, K. F. (1938). Vicarious trial and error at a point of choice. I. A general survey of its relation to learning efficiency. *J. Genet. Psychol.* **53**, 75–86.

OSGOOD, C. E. (1953). *Method and Theory in Experimental Psychology.* New York: Oxford University Press.

OSGOOD, C. E. (1957). Motivational dynamics of language behaviour, in Jones, M. R. (ed.) *Nebraska Symposium on Motivation.* Lincoln: University of Nebraska Press.

OSGOOD, C. E., and SEBEOK, T. A. (ed.) (1965). *Psycholinguistics: A Survey of Theory and Research Problems,* with *A Survey of Psycholinguistic Research, 1954–1964* by Diebold, A. R. Jr. Bloomington: Indiana U.P.

OSGOOD, C. E., SUCI, G. J., and TANNENBAUM, P. H. (1957). *The Measurement of Meaning.* Urbana: U. of Illinois Press.

PAVLOV, I. P. (1941). *Lectures on Conditioned Reflexes.* (2 volumes). London: Lawrence and Wishart.

PIAGET, J. (1951). *Play, Dreams and Imitation in Childhood.* London: Heinemann.

PIAGET, J. (1959). Apprentissage et connaissance. In Gréco, P. et Piaget, J., Apprentissage et connaissance, *Etudes d'épistémologie génétique,* **7**, 21–67.

RESTLE, F. (1957). Discrimination of cues in mazes: a resolution of the 'place-*v.*-response' question. *Psychol. Rev.* **64**, 217–228.

RILEY, D. A. (1958). The nature of the effective stimulus in animal discrimination learning: transposition reconsidered. *Psychol. Rev.* **65**, 1–7.

RILEY, D. A. (1963). Memory for form. Chapter 7 in Postman, L. (ed.), *Psychology in the Making.* New York: Alfred Knopf.

RUSHTON, J. (1966). The relationship between personality characteristics and scholastic success in eleven-year-old children. *Brit. J. Educ. Psychol.* **36**, 178–184.

SHIPLEY, W. C. (1933). An apparent transfer of conditioning. *Psychol. Bull.* **30**, 541.

SKINNER, B. F. (1938). *The Behaviour of Organisms: An Experimental Analysis.* New York: Appleton-Century-Crofts.

SKINNER, B. F. (1953). *Science and Human Behaviour*. New York: Macmillan.

SKINNER, B. F. (1957). *Verbal Behaviour*. London: Methuen.

SKINNER, B. F. (1959). *Cumulative Record*. London: Methuen.

SPEARMAN, C. (1923). *The Nature of Intelligence and the Principles of Cognition*. London: Macmillan.

SPENCE, K. W. (1937). The differential response in animals to stimuli varying in a single dimension. *Psychol. Rev.* **44**, 430–444.

SPENCE, K. W. (1945). An experimental test of the continuity and non-continuity theories of discrimination learning. *J. Exp. Psychol.* **35**, 253–266.

SPENCE, K. W. (1956). *Behaviour Theory and Conditioning*. New Haven and London: Yale University Press.

SUTHERLAND, N. S. (1959). Stimulus analysing mechanisms. In *Proceedings of a Symposium on the Mechanisation of the Thought Processes*. Vol. II, pp. 575–609. London: H.M.S.O.

SUTHERLAND, N. S., and MACKINTOSH, J. (1964). Discrimination learning: non-additivity of cues. *Nature, Lond.* **201**, 528–530.

THISTLETHWAITE, D. (1951). A critical review of latent learning and related experiments. *Psychol. Bull.* **48**, 97–129.

THORNDIKE, E. L. (1898). Animal intelligence: an experimental study of the associative processes in animals. *Psychol. Rev. Monogr. Suppl.* **2**, No. 4 (whole No. 8).

THORNDIKE, E. L. (1925). *The Measurement of Intelligence*. New York: Bur. Publ., Teachers' College, Columbia U.

THORNDIKE, E. L. (1949). *Selected Writings from a Connectionist's Psychology*. New York: Appleton-Century-Crofts.

TOLMAN, E. C. (1932). *Purposive Behaviour in Animals and Men*. New York: Century.

TOLMAN, E. C. (1938). The determiners of behaviour at a choice point. *Psychol. Rev.* **45**, 1–41.

TOLMAN, E. C. (1949). There is more than one kind of learning. *Psychol. Rev.* **56**, 144–155.

TOLMAN, E. C. (1959). Principles of purposive behaviour. In Koch, S. (ed.) *Psychology: A Study of a Science. Vol. II. General Systematic Formulations, Learning and Special Processes*. New York and London: McGraw-Hill, 92–157.

TOLMAN, E. C., RITCHIE, B. F. and KALISH, D. (1946). Studies in spatial learning. II. Place learning versus response learning. *J. exp. Psychol. 36*, 221–229.

VERPLANCK, W. S. (1954). Burrhus F. Skinner. Section 3 in Estes, W. K. *et al. Modern Learning Theory*. New York: Appleton-Century-Crofts.

VIGOTSKY, L. S. (1962). *Thought and Language*. New York and London: John Wiley.

WATSON, J. B. (1957). *Behaviourism*. (Revised edition) Chicago: Phoenix Books.

WEINSTOCK, S. (1954). Resistance to extinction of a running response following partial reinforcement under widely spaced trials. *J. Comp. Physiol. Psychol.* **47**, 318–322.

WERTHEIMER, M. (1945). *Productive Thinking*. New York: Harper.

WOLPE, J. (1958). *Psychotherapy by Reciprocal Inhibition*. Stanford, Cal.: Stanford U.P.

WULF, F. (1922). Über die Veränderung von Vorstellungen. *Psychol. Forsch.* **1**, 333–373.

YERKES, R. M. and DODSON, J. D. (1908). The relation of strength of stimulus to rapidity of habit-formation. *J. Comp. Neurol. Psychol. 18*, 459–482.

ZANGWILL, O. L. (1937). An investigation of the relationship between the process of reproducing and recognizing simple figures with special reference to Koffka's trace theory. *Brit. J. Psychol.* **27**, 250–276.

2

Brain Mechanisms and Learning

NEVILE MORAY

IT IS not necessary to understand how an internal combustion engine works in order to be able to drive a car, nor to understand the intricacies of electronics in order to do calculations on a digital computer. But in both cases at least the beginning of an acquaintance with the mechanisms involved will lead the user to appreciate their capabilities more fully; to appreciate when a situation arises in which the mechanisms may get into difficulties; to identify faults; to realize the need for repairs and servicing and above all, to use the machines in the best possible way so as to maximize their efficiency and usefulness. The same can be said of a knowledge of brain mechanisms for the educationalist. What we know of the mechanisms of learning will not allow the sudden magical improvement of teaching techniques, or the massive imparting of information or skill to the refractory student; but it may make the person who has such an acquaintance more aware of the nature of the organism with which he or she is dealing, and the kind of goal towards which the teacher should aim in order to make the best use of the machinery of the brain.

I. A BASIC DESCRIPTION OF LEARNING

If a living organism is to survive in the world in which we live, it must be aware of the state of its surroundings, and must make a response to those surroundings. At least it must seek out a source of energy when its bodily reserves are run down, it must seek water when it is depleted and thirsty, it must avoid predators and seek out its prey, and so on. Let us therefore begin by making a kind of formal diagram of the situation. We can represent the organism as receiving a large number of stimuli, and as making a large number of responses to them.

Sometimes more than one stimulus may call up the same response. In some cases there may be several responses which are made to the same stimulus. And of course by making the diagram so formal, we are concealing the enormous wealth of phenomena which are covered by the words 'stimulus' and 'response'. When speaking of humans, there are many things which are stimuli and many things which are responses apart from the obvious biological needs; such things as requests, promises, advertisements, daydreams, the wishes of others, our own aspirations. But more importantly, in the diagram below, we have omitted one very important feature – the provision for learning. We have drawn the diagram as if the organism of which we are thinking has only a certain fixed set of responses to a certain well-defined set of stimuli. And of man, above all other animals, this is totally untrue.

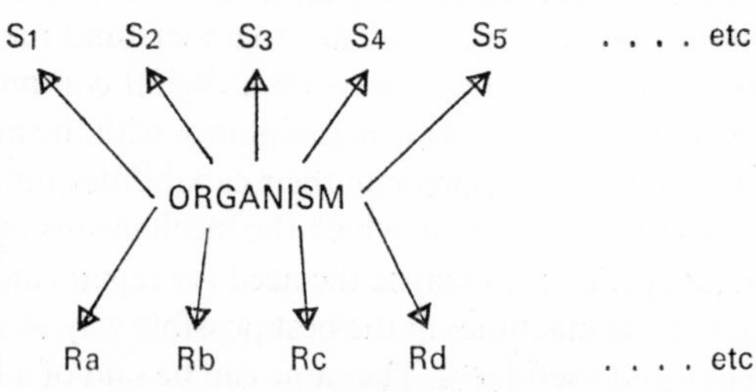

Figure 1

The question of 'innate' as against 'learnt' or 'acquired' elements of man's make-up is a vexed, and probably a misleading one. Nowadays biologists and ethologists such as Tinbergen and Lorenz have taught us to use the word 'instinct' to refer to a well-defined and clearly marked-out kind of behaviour. The mating patterns of birds, breeding habits, foraging and fighting habits – these are in lower animals 'instinctive' not merely if they are inborn, but when the pattern of behaviour is stereotyped, is shown by all members of the species on the first opportunity for its occurrence without practice, and consists of an elaborate sequence of specific responses to specific stimuli.

In this sense, it seems likely that there are *no* such instincts in man. Instincts as McDougall talked of them are so vague as to be unusable by psychology today in a serious scientific sense; and Freud's use is little more than saying that most men have certain biological and psychological potentialities which can often act as the driving forces which lead to action being initiated.

Instinct in the lower animals consists in the 'wiring diagram' of that computer we call the brain being given, to a very large extent, at birth, the connexions being made by the action of the genes in the chromosomes of the cells passed on from the parents. In man the brain is not completely 'wired up' at birth, and indeed rewiring, the recombination of the paths along which information flows through the brain, continues throughout life. This we call learning.

Learning is the way in which animals adapt to new situations, situations which have not necessarily been the common experience of all their ancestors for hundreds or thousands of generations, but rather new situations which vary from day to day, and even from hour to hour. As such, the chance of survival of such an animal, once it has emerged from the helpless state in which it is born, is immeasureably greater than that given by instinct. What we see as we look at animals higher and higher up the evolutionary scale is the gradual increase in the importance of learning as a way of adapting to the world, from very simple responses in the first place until finally even the immensely elaborate patterns of sexual behaviour upon which depend the survival of the species become far more determined by learning than by instinct. Man is the supreme learner (Roe and Simpson, 1958; Dethier and Stellar, 1964; Maier and Schneirla, 1935).

How then should we redraw our formal diagram of the nature of the organism responding to the world? At one time one set of stimuli give rise to one set of responses; later the relationships differ. Some stimuli produce responses which did not exist before, some responses which used to exist disappear. And certain combinations of stimulus and response become rearranged. Consider the next diagram:

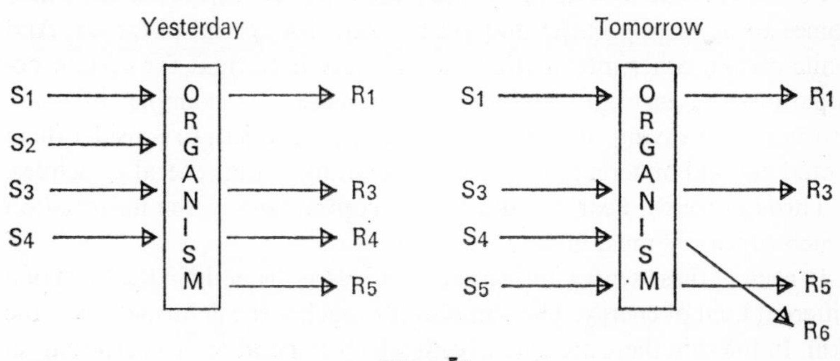

Figure 2

This diagram summarizes the basic requirements for any system, whether an organism or a machine, which learns. It must take in information from the world around it, it must make responses, and it must be able to alter the relationships between the stimuli and the responses. We will examine the function of the brain from these three points of view; how it organizes its responses, and how it alters the way in which the one initiates the other. In addition we shall have to look at several other properties of the human brain which while not directly concerned with learning are none the less essential to its efficient functioning.

II. AFFERENT PROCESSES OF THE BRAIN

1. *How the brain acquires information*

The world around a man consists of information. It flows into his brain through his sense organs and along his nerves. Traditionally there are said to be five senses, sight, hearing, touch, taste, and smell. But in fact there are many more. We are sensitive to temperature, to disturbances in our posture, to the state of distension of our stomach, to the state of our muscles (whether they are being strained), to the position of our limbs, to vibration, and so on. But whether the information is about the world outside, or about the state of some organ or organs of our body, it is possible to point out some general principles which apply to all the senses, and it is around such general principles rather than through a detailed discussion of each sense, that our discussion of the mechanisms of perception will be arranged.

From the point of view of teaching human beings, it is probably true to say that the most important of the senses are vision, hearing, and touch. We do not in practice often pay much attention to the information which comes to us through taste and smell except for special purposes. And while certain other information may be very important for certain occupations (balance and bodily position sense, for example, in many sports such as diving, and in professions such as ballet), to consider them would not add materially to our understanding of the general principles.

Through touch, hearing, and vision, comes most of the information which educators must impart.

In each of these senses, information arrives at the body in the form of a different kind of energy. The stimulus for touch is the deformation of the skin. In the skin there are special cells which respond to this deformation by sending a signal to the brain, along the nerves which connect the area of the body touched to the deeper parts of the central nervous system. In hearing, the information reaches the body in the form of pressure waves in the air, sound waves, which stimulate special cells in the ears, modified nerve cells, which again then send messages along nerves to the deeper parts of the brain (van Bergeijk *et al.*, 1961; Wever, 1949). The mechanisms of the ear are such that the waves of pressure in the air are amplified and changed into vibrations in the fluid of the inner ear, the cochlea. In the cochlea the movements of the fluid displace the basilar membrane whose properties allow it to act as a rough analyser of the frequency of the incoming sound waves, so that different cell groups are stimulated by sounds of different pitch. And finally, the eye receives information in the form of electromagnetic radiation, waves of energy closely related in their nature both to wireless waves and to X-rays and gamma rays, and which stimulate cells at the back of the eye (the cells which, together with a complicated network of nerve cells which allows one part of the visual stimulus to interact with other parts, make up the 'retina'), which are modified to absorb this kind of energy and respond to it by sending messages along nerve fibres to the brain (Gregory, 1966). Typical pathways of the three sense modalities are shown in Figure 3.

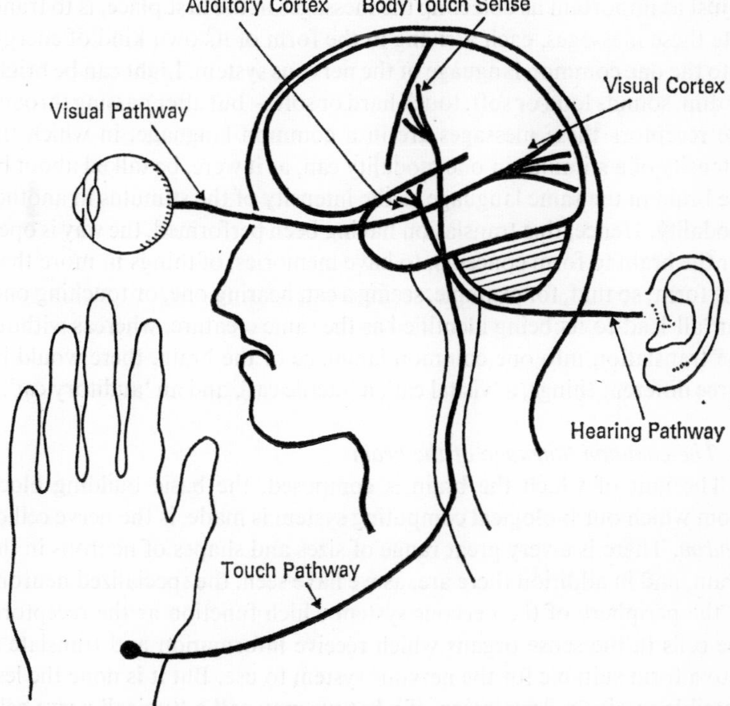

Figure 3. General picture of sensory pathways and areas of the brain involved in sensory perception.

Optic nerve fibres carry information about the pattern of retinal stimulation and hence about the nature and size and shape of the thing at which we are looking. In a similar way the other two senses give us information about other aspects of the thing observed, with the provision that touch is of use only when the thing is very near us. But as we saw above, these messages reach us in very different languages. The sheer amount of physical energy needed to deform the skin and so stimulate a touch receptor is immensely greater than the amount needed to stimulate the cells in the retina of the eye, which are sensitive to the smallest amount of physical energy which physicists believe can exist in the physical universe. The job of the various sense receptors, the nerve cells which lie at the body surface or in special sites within it to detect messages is therefore one of *translation*. They detect the stimuli, the information from the outside world, and send it on to the brain. But an equally important task, which is not often stressed in books about the nervous system, but which is just as important as detecting the messages in the first place, is to translate these messages, each arriving in the form of its own kind of energy, into the one common language of the nervous system. Light can be bright or dim, sounds loud or soft, touch hard or soft – but after passing through the receptors these messages are in a common language, in which the intensity of a stimulus in one modality can, as it were, be talked about by the brain in the same language as the intensity of the stimulus in another modality. Hence, this translation having been performed, the way is open for the brain to form concepts, to have memories, of things in more than one form; so that, for example, seeing a cat, hearing one, or touching one, can all lead to its being identified as the same creature, whereas without the translation into one common language of the brain, there would be three different things, a 'visual cat', a 'tactile cat', and an 'auditory cat'.

2. *The common language of the brain*

The unit of which the brain is composed, the basic building block from which our biological computing system is made, is the nerve cell or *neuron*. There is a very great range of sizes and shapes of neurons in the brain, and in addition there are, as we have seen, the specialized neurons in the periphery of the nervous system which function as the receptors, the cells in the sense organs which receive information and translate it into a form suitable for the nervous system to use. But it is none the less possible to give a description of what we may call a 'typical' nerve cell, whose properties are those which are found by and large in the whole nervous system (Stevens, 1966). Figure 4 shows such a neuron.

The nerve cell consists of the cell body, with its internal structures such as the nucleus which are concerned with its inherent organization and function, its metabolism, and so on; and a number of extensions which stick out from the cell body. Some of these are short, and are called the *dendrites*, while one of them is usually much longer and is called the *axon*. The cell body and the dendrites receive messages from other cells, and the neuron transmits messages along the axon to stimulate, in its turn, other neurons or other cells. The actual size of the cell body is very

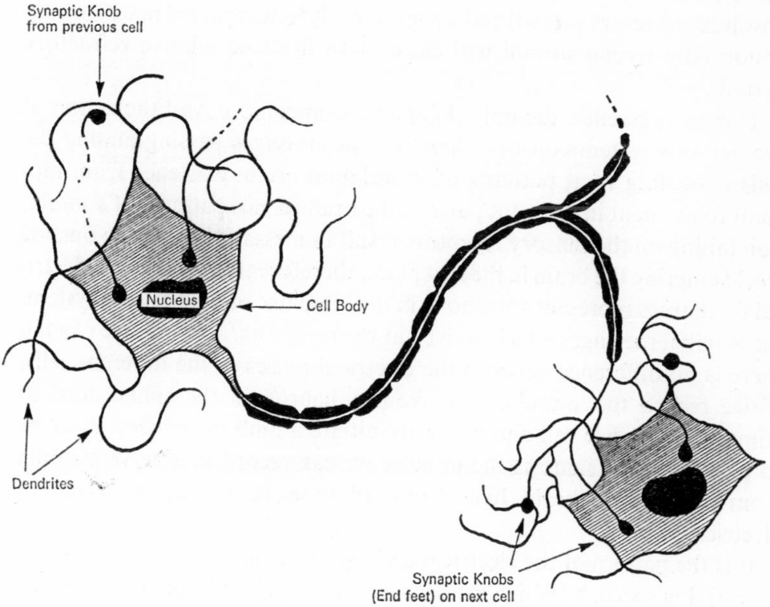

Figure 4. The nerve cell

small, very rarely as large as 1/10 of a millimetre across, and usually very much smaller, and the axon is generally proportionally narrow. But the length of the cell can be very great. For example, the axons which run from the spinal cord to the small muscles of our hands and feet must be several feet long, and in large animals very considerably longer. In all, it is usually said that there are some 10,000,000,000 neurons in a mature human brain.

The fundamental property, the fundamental statement which can be made in the language of the nervous system is in fact extremely simple. If a stimulus of sufficient strength falls on the dendrites or the cell body of a neuron, then a small pulse of electricity, rather less than 1/10 of a volt and with a duration of about 1/1000 of a second passes along the axon from the cell body. When it arrives at the end of the axon it causes very rapid changes in the chemistry of the region where the endfeet of the axon abut on to the dendrites and cell body of the next cell, as a result of which that cell in turn is stimulated. After a cell has fired there is a short period, about 1/500 sec., during which it will not fire again (the absolute refractory period) and a considerably longer period in which only abnormally strong stimuli will cause it to fire (the relative refractory period).

This is, in essence, the only thing a neuron can do. And the action of the nervous system consists, therefore, in messages passing among the cells indicating what patterns of stimulation are in existence from moment to moment in different parts of the brain. Since patterns of stimulation falling on the sensory receptors result in messages about the outside world entering the brain in the first place, therefore these flickering electrical discharges represent somehow, in the language of the nervous system, the original messages which arrived at the receptors. As far as we can tell there is no difference between the electrical pulses of the different cells. If we record the impulse sent from a neuron in the spinal cord to stimulate a muscle cell and hence to initiate a limb movement, it seems to be exactly the same as the impulse we can record in a nerve running from the eye to the brain. In each case all we see is a small, quick pulse of electricity.

It is the pattern of the electrical activity of the brain, a pattern both in time and in space, by which messages are distinguished from one another, and their several effects are brought about. For example, the intensity of the stimulus which stimulates a neuron makes no difference to the size of the nervous impulse. Each neuron has a threshold excitability such that if the stimulus which arrives at the cell body or the dendrites is very weak the cell will not fire at all, and no message will be transmitted along it. If the threshold is exceeded, then the message is always the same size, even when the stimulus is very much stronger. Most neurons receive the endfeet of at least several hundred axons from other cells, and most of them likewise stimulate many other neurons, so that the possibilities for very complicated patterns of information flowing through the brain are great. Information from different sources can be added by two messages converging onto a single cell, and certain cells have the property of inhibiting the activity of others, so that messages can be blocked, or their routes through the nervous system altered (Young, 1964; Eccles, 1953; Stevens 1966).

Since the size of the impulses does not alter when the stimulus changes in intensity, an obvious question is to wonder how weak or strong stimuli are represented in the nervous system. What is the difference between a message signalling a bright light and one signalling a dim light? between light and heavy pressure, between soft and loud sounds? The answer is a very clear example of the 'common language' of the nervous system into which the receptors translate the information arriving from the outside; for in every sense modality, and indeed throughout the entire nervous system, intensity of stimulation is signalled by the rate at which nerve cells fire. The size of the impulse does not change as the stimulus becomes stronger, and the speed at which the message passes along the nerves (some hundreds of feet a second) does not change. But the stronger the stimulus, the more frequently the impulses occur, so that for example a nerve carrying information about the brightness of light from the eye to the brain will fire perhaps thirty times a second in dim light but nearly 300 times a second in bright light. Whatever the sense modality, whatever the stimulus, what we experience as an increase in sensation involves an increase in the rate of firing of the relevant nerve cells.

3. *The organization of a sensory pathway*

Given that the receptors have, then, translated the message which they receive from the environment into nervous impulses, what happens to the message after it leaves the receptors?

Firstly, there may be limits on the kind of information which can be conveyed. In general, if the stimulus is constant, the response of the brain will become reduced as time passes. The nervous system is first and foremost sensitive to change, either in time or space. Moreover there are, for any species of organism, only certain kinds of images the receptors can send. Very few animals have colour vision. The frog's eye does not respond to stationary objects, and seems only to have few kinds of response, to movement, to the pressure of small dark objects, to decreased brightness, and to curved edges – all characteristics either of the insects on which it feeds or to the approach of possible danger (although the latter would not be recognized in detail). Some species can tell a vertical from a horizontal rectangle, but not when they are both tilted through 45°.

If we look more closely at one of the pathways in Figure 3, we see that impulses are shown running from the ear, for example, to the *auditory cortex*, that part of the surface of the brain which is concerned with the final analysis of sounds. But in such a simple diagram, there is much that is omitted. A more accurate picture is given in Figure 5. Here we see that in fact the pathway from the receptors to the cortex is interrupted several times. Now this cannot be because it is impossible to have nerve cells

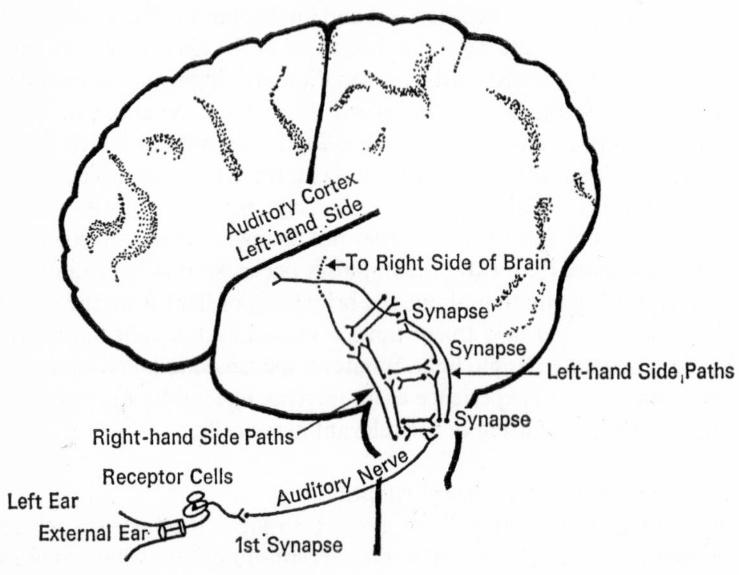

Figure 5. The nerve pathways of the sense of hearing, showing the way in which the path is interrupted to allow for interaction and the processing of messages on their way to the brain

longer than this, since as we saw in the section about the language of the nervous system there are in fact nerve cells which are very much longer than the distance from the ear to the auditory cortex. Instead, what these relay stations in the nervous pathway represent is the fact that the analysis of the incoming messages is not done as a whole by one part of the brain but is performed piecemeal at different moments as the messages pass inward from the periphery to the central nervous system.

The *cortex* of the brain is the great outer layer of nerve cells which we see when we look at the outside of a brain. And it is well established that there are separate regions concerned with different functions. These are outlined in Figure 6. Each of the main sensory modalities (the traditional 'five senses') is represented by groupings of cells, and these areas of the brain are connected with other areas by the axons of the cells which dive deep into the brain below the surface and convey impulses to other *nuclei* as the groups of cells within the brain are called.

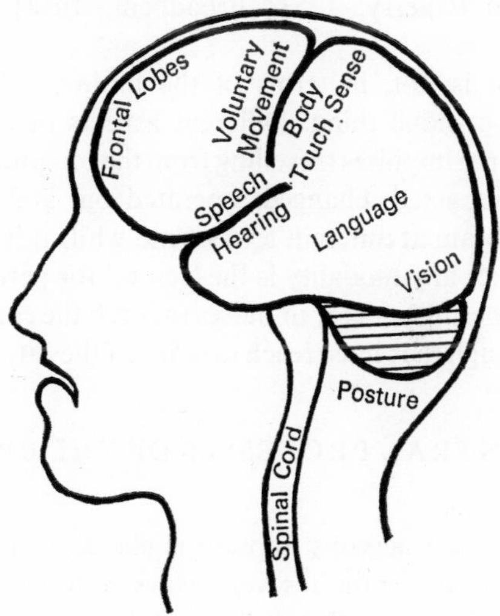

Figure 6. The areas of the brain involved in various functions

The cells in the part of the brain which forms the cortical area of any sense modality are concerned with the analysis of meaningful patterns. Thus an animal in which the cortex has been damaged may often still be able to discriminate between simple pure tones of different pitch, between sounds of different loudness, or between lights of different brightness. But it will no longer be able to recognize patterns of sounds: if the damage is to its auditory cortex (Neff and Diamond, 1958), or (if its visual cortex has been damaged) to recognize objects in the visual world (Cowey and Weiskrantz, 1963; Lashley, 1960). In man the cortex is similarly necessary for pattern recognition, patients whose cortex has been badly damaged often being able to respond to sounds which are little louder than a normal person can hear, but being unable to respond to meaningful words or patterns of noise.

The lower parts of the sensory pathways apparently are able, in the absence of the cortex, to analyse simple messages, although probably they do not do so if the cortex is intact. And yet other nuclei in the sensory pathway perform other tasks, such as comparing the stimuli received by the two eyes, or measuring the difference in time of arrival of sounds at the two ears (the latter being the basis of our ability to localize sounds in space, and hence of our ability to listen to one person when several are speaking at once) (Cherry, 1953; Broadbent, 1958; Moray, 1959; Treisman, 1966).

Thus perception is not, in terms of the brain mechanisms which mediate it, an all-or-none thing. Different aspects of the information contained in the nerve impulses travelling from the receptors to the central mechanisms are extracted, changed, operated on, and handed on to other parts of the brain at different levels. And while it is often said that the sensory cortex of any modality is the 'centre' for perception of such information, it is not sufficient for impulses to reach the cortex for them to be perceived, although they must reach that area if they are to be analysed.

III. CENTRAL PROCESSES OF THE BRAIN

1. *Habituation and sleep*

Since the nature of the nervous impulse is electrical, it is possible to record the activity of the brain in several ways, either by placing a very fine needle in the brain itself, or by placing metal electrodes on the outside of the skull and in both cases then passing the tiny electrical currents so detected through amplifying apparatus until they become big enough to record. When we do this we often find that while there is plenty of activity in a cortical area the animal or person appears not to be noticing anything. In one experiment a cat was forced to listen to a series of loud clicks for several hours while the response of the brain, and also the behavioural response of the whole animal, were observed and recorded. Initially the cat looked around and pricked up its ears whenever a click came, but later, when it had heard many such clicks, it drowsed without showing any behavioural response. Yet at that time the cells in the auditory cortex were actually more active than at the beginning of the experiment. In an experiment with human beings, the electrical responses were recorded by means of external electrodes attached to the skin while the subjects were asleep. Tape-recordings of names were played to them, and even when they did not wake up and did not report hearing anything, or dreaming, and while the brain rhythms were those of sleep, it was possible to see the brain responding more vigorously to their own names than to neutral names. Furthermore, it is quite possible for people to go to sleep for several seconds or more while having their eyes open, and even while continuing to behave adaptively with sensory input continuing, despite the fact that as far as they are concerned they perceive nothing (Oswald, 1962).

2. *Arousal and attention*

These findings lead us to consider the role of a part of the brain which is not specifically concerned with perception, or indeed with any particular job, but rather with the overall level of activity in the brain, the so-called *reticular arousal system*. This lies in the deepest parts of the brain, and is evolutionarily very old, suggesting that it is an important mechanism for the brain to possess. The function of the arousal system is to keep the brain at an optimal level of activity. Input through the sense organs stimulates the arousal system to activity, and the latter in its turn, when aroused, stimulates the sensory systems into a state of high sensivity. Conversely, if the arousal system is inactive (as in sleep), then the sensory systems tend to become insensitive, and so, even if information reaches the cortex, it may not be perceived if the overall level of arousal is low (Samuels, 1959; Oswald, 1962; Kleitman, 1963).

This relation between sensory input and arousal is very important practically, since a very uniform environment, in which there is not much variation in light and noise level, and where a person is comfortably warm may tend to reduce the level of arousal, and hence make a person less efficient at taking in information from his surroundings. This in its turn will lead to a further reduction in the level of arousal, and the person will become drowsy and inattentive. In its extreme form this problem becomes that of the vigilance or 'watch-keeping' task, where without some aid few people can maintain vigilance for more than about half an hour (Broadbent, 1958; Buckner and McGrath, 1963). It follows from this that while noise is usually undesirable in an environment because it interferes with communication, a certain amount may actually be desirable in that it keeps the arousal system at a reasonably high level of activity and hence actually improves the efficiency of the brain as a whole (Solomon *et al.*, 1961; Magoun, 1963).

3. *The coding and storage of information*

Before moving on to consider the way in which responses are prepared and organized, there is an important point to be made concerning the way in which the performance of the nerve cells of the brain are related to the performance of the man as a whole in perceptual tasks.

If we measure the accuracy of perception by doing careful scientific experiments on perception under the very best conditions, we come away with the impression that the sensory system of the brain is extraordinarily sensitive. Thus the ear can detect sounds between pitches of roughly 15 cycles per second and 15,000 cycles per second, and can discriminate many thousands of different pitches in between. In the same way the number of different loudness levels which can be detected for a note of a given pitch is enormous. If to this we add the number of different colour gradations and brightness gradations that can be distinguished, and sensitivity to touch, to temperature, and so on, it is extraordinary that we cannot handle information arriving from outside us at a greater rate than we do. But in fact, the simplest possible stimulus-response situation, say pressing a buzzer as quickly as possible when it buzzes beneath your finger, takes about $\frac{1}{8}$ of a second. And as soon as the task becomes at all complicated the rate at which we can respond begins to drop with great rapidity. Despite the very large number of categories and the great sensitivity of the nervous system when it is given plenty of time and absolutely optimal conditions, the way in which our overall behaviour is related to a real life situation is comparatively coarse and slow.

To take a very simple case, if a person is given a large number of pieces of coloured paper, all equally bright, and asked to sort them into piles of the same colour, no other instruction being given, he will usually only use about eight categories, however wide the range of colours may be. The performance which we expect from a person cannot be directly predicted from a knowledge of the absolute sensitivity of the basic units of the nervous system. The properties and modes of function of the total person give a picture very different from the properties of the individual parts, although there is no reason to doubt that the overall properties are explicable in terms of the properties of those parts when the analysis is taken down to the right level with appropriate precision (Summerfield, 1962; Miller, 1956; Garner, 1961).

IV. MECHANISMS OF RESPONSE

1. *The role of feedback in behaviour*

To all intents and purposes, all responses consist in the activation of muscles by means of impulses in nerves running from the central nervous system to the limbs, leading to movements of some part of the body. There are some other systems, for example the liberation of chemicals such as the adrenalin compounds into the blood under the stress of emotion, but they subserve the preparation of the body for muscular action. Whether we make a gesture, or speak, or wink, we activate some group of muscles and cause them to contract. The problem of learning what response to make consists, at one level, in learning which groups of muscles to activate so that the correct gesture (including here the movements of the throat muscles in speech) will be made.

But a moment's consideration will show that this is a far over-simplified picture. Hardly ever do we in fact make the same movement twice, even when the thing we are trying to do is the same. This is particularly true of the very important class of movements which constitute the skills which we exercise in everyday life. Thus in driving a car, in playing a game such as tennis, even in handwriting, we have a particular result to achieve (to keep the car within certain limits of position on the road, to return the service to a particular part of the court, to write a particular word). But however many times we do these things it would be, for the most part, quite incorrect to call them conditioned reflexes, even when they are highly practised. Most accurate movements result from an initial impulse to action which sets the limb in motion, followed by a series of 'feedback' actions in which the position of the limb is controlled and corrected as it approaches its target.

If we consider the case of steering a car round a corner, the importance of feedback is particularly apparent. We move the wheel initially to the position which past experience leads us to believe will steer the car round the curve of this particular sharpness. As the slight bumps in the road alter the position of the car, or as the slight movements of our feet on the accelerator lead to variations in the speed of the car, and hence to slight variations in the line it takes through the corner, so we make one or two corrective movements, based on the information which has been 'fed back' through the various sense receptors, eyes, muscle position, and so on. And this cycle of movement-feedback-movement-feedback is repeated until the desired final position or result of movement is achieved.

In the case of the car this can be seen very clearly, but there are more subtle feedback loops which control movement and muscle position which are constantly in operation and of which we are quite unaware. In fact in many cases quite peripheral parts of the nervous system look after the adjustment, and the brain itself may not be implicated. Thus the position and amount of tension in muscles and joints is constantly being controlled by nerve fibres which take account of the demands of posture from moment to moment, and in the learning of 'motor skills', as skilled movements are sometimes called, it seems likely that one of the things that happens is that the brain learns to send finer and finer control commands to the muscles, as well as learning what movements to try to make. As learning progresses, these adjustments become more and more automatic.

2. Feedback and learning

The importance of 'feedback' for understanding the mechanisms of learning cannot be overemphasised. In one form or another it can be regarded almost as the central concept, both theoretically and practically. It involves essentially the idea that learning and adjusting to the requirements of the world does not merely include a stimulus, a learner, and a response; but that there is a closed loop between the learner and the environment. The environment makes a demand on the learner, be it a question from a teacher, a signal to cross a road, or a twinge of a nerve which causes a pain to be felt. As a result the learner does something which makes a difference in his relation with his environment. And following on that, *if he is to learn, it is essential that a signal of some kind be received back from the environment to tell him whether his response was correct or incorrect.* In this sense, a learning situation is one where the environment interacts with the learner. The learner does not merely react to the environment.

A moment's reflection on the last paragraph will make it clear that no learning can ever take place without feedback. In that sense it is conceptually central to the mechanisms of learning. But at a purely practical level its importance can be readily demonstrated. For example, it is possible to manufacture goggles which reverse the visual image of the world, so that everything on the wearer's right is now on his left and vice versa. The initial effect is completely to disorientate a person. He puts out the opposite hand to grasp something which another person gives him; he turns to the left when he means to turn to the right, and so on. Within a few hours he has, however, begun to adapt to the situation, and eventually it is possible even to ride a bicycle, and it appears, from what people who have worn the glasses say, that 'the world looks normal' (Taylor, 1962). But a very interesting fact emerges when we look at the first few hours of adaptation. If the person wearing the goggles walks about, then he begins to adapt; but if he is pushed in a wheel-chair, he does not. It is essential both to the adaptation of movement, and to the reorganization of the perceptual processes themselves that he make movements and see the result. Again, if two kittens are reared from birth in the dark, then when they first encounter the world of visual objects they are unable to respond to it. If at this time they are given visual experience that is controlled in such a way that one moves about and the other is only passively moved, while both receive the same amount of stimulation, then the actively moving kitten learns to see very quickly, while the passively moved one does not (Gregory, 1966; Smith and Smith, 1962; Held and Hein, 1963). The relation between the input to our brains, our response to it, and further input which allows us to assess the effect of the responses, is vital to the development of the healthy efficient nervous system (Solomon, *et al.*, 1961; Riesen, 1961).

3. *Memory*

It is logical to move on from here to a discussion of memory, and the difference between short-term and long-term memory. We have seen that feedback is of vital importance for learning. A direct corollary of this is that a memory of the stimulus which was received and the response which was made must be retained until the feedback signal is received as to whether the response was correct or not, and therefore whether it should be used again if that stimulus recurs. Clearly many of the things which we perceive we do not remember for a long time, whereas on the other hand there are many things, both facts and skills, which we retain almost indefinitely in our memories. It is therefore necessary to distinguish between the two kinds of memory, even if there is some doubt as to how far they need to be represented in the brain by different mechanisms.

A practical demonstration of the difference is shown by the following experiment, devised by the Canadian neuropsychologist Hebb. A series of lists of ten numbers, in random order, is prepared. Each list is read to a listener at a rate of one number every second, and after each list the listener immediately tries to repeat it back. It will be found that most people only get about seven of the numbers correct if they have to give them in the correct order. If however, every fourth list is actually identical, then even if the listener does not realize that this is the case, his performance on that one list gradually begins to creep up until he is eventually getting it completely correct. If however only every seventh list is identical, then there is virtually no improvement (Hebb, 1961; Melton, 1963).

The implications of this experiment are twofold. In the first place, when a person is trying to learn something, it must be reinforced quite quickly in time, and secondly, even if something is remembered quite well for a few moments, unless it has been transferred to the long term memory there will not be a permanent record of it in the memory for future use.

There is also a body of direct physiological evidence for a difference between short- and long-term memory. In accidents involving concussion there is always a gap of at least a few seconds and generally of minutes for events just before the accident, as if those memories had not had time to become firmly established in the physical structure of the brain (Russell, 1959, Richter, 1966). And experiments have been carried out to prove this. If a rat is required to learn to go to one shape and avoid another, and just after it has been rewarded for the right or punished for the wrong response it is given a powerful electric shock to the brain, then it never learns to make the discriminative response. But if on the other hand a period of several minutes is allowed to elapse between the reward or punishment and the shock, then it will learn (Deutsch, 1962). Several other experiments have confirmed this result.

From the above experiments we may be tempted to conclude that certain common methods of teaching a learner are far from being optimum. And it is such considerations among others that has led to the development of teaching machines with their emphasis on immediate knowledge of whether the response was right or wrong. If a learner is asked to give an answer, to make a response, and only gets feedback hours or days later when his work is eventually returned, it is far from easy for the brain to associate the 'correct' or 'wrong' signal with the actual making of the response. In general, the closer together the stimulus, response, and feedback knowledge of results, the more efficient is likely o be the learning.

V. THE PHYSIOLOGICAL PROCESSES OF LEARNING

1. *Kinds of learning and forgetting*

We are moving on towards a consideration of the fundamental mechanisms of learning. The actual way in which memories are physically embodied in the brain, whether as patterns of pathways among the nerve cells, with different patterns representing different pathways, or as changes in the chemical components which make up the cell are at present unknown, although there are signs that within the next ten years this problem may be solved. There is however a good deal known about the mechanisms which allow such learning to take place.

There are several different kinds of learning. And we are not at present able to say with certainty that there is only one mechanism which represents them all. Indeed the evidence rather points to the contrary.

A rather obvious dichotomy is one which we have already mentioned – that between repetitive responses where the same stimulus is presented and the same response is required on each occasion, and the type of performance better called a skill, in which there is a goal to be achieved, but no fixed, set pattern of responses which inevitably lead to it. Moreover classical conditioning *à la* Pavlov, in which an inbuilt physiological response is conditioned, may be very different from 'operant conditioning' where any bit of spontaneous behaviour which occurs may be used to produce the response by shaping it as a function of reinforcement. And yet again, more complicated kinds of problem solving, and ultimately reasoning and the use of language to formulate possible responses without actually making them may very well require different mechanisms.

Evidence in this direction comes from the effect of electro-shock experiments such as that quoted above in which the brain of the rat received a strong shock during learning. Different kinds of learning show very different resistance to such treatment. Some kinds of learning disappear completely under the impact of the shock, others hardly at all. With some tasks the acquisition of learning is slowed or prevented by shock but the retention of the task once learnt is not affected.

This leads us to consider in what ways learning may be prevented or, once acquired, impaired. In the first place, failure to produce the correct response may be due to a failure to perceive the stimulus, question, etc., and this in its turn may be due to a failure of attention, a lack of clarity in the presentation, and so on. Thus the relevant information may never enter the nervous system at all. In the second place, there may be a failure due to the similarity either of the stimulus, or of the response, to another stimulus or response, so that the brain fails to choose the correct response to go with the particular stimulus. Thirdly, it is possible that even though the memory has been firmly laid down in the physical structure of the brain, it may be lost from the memory store, either through brain damage, through the loss of cells with age, or some other way. Surprisingly, the evidence seems to suggest that this may be rather rare. Memories, once laid down, seem to be astonishingly stable, and what is more, some feature of the organization of the brain seems able to cope with the loss of substantial amounts of nervous tissue without much obvious loss in the way of specific learning or memories. The final thing that might happen, however, and which is closely linked with the previous suggestion, is that although the information is stored in the brain it is impossible for the person to use it. This seems to be the case in certain kinds of language defects arising from brain damage. One day the patient may describe an ashtray as '*what you put out cigarettes in*'; and the next day be unable to recall the word for cigarette, but say that it is what is stubbed out in ashtrays (Osgood and Miron, 1963). It seems that the information is still there, but that the mechanisms for retrieving it from the memory store when it is required are defective.

2. *The mechanisms of learning*

The discovery of some of the details of the physical basis of learning has been one of the most exciting events in physiological psychology in the last few years. It has been known from time immemorial that reward and punishment determine whether or not an animal or a person will learn things; but while a large amount of empirical data, both informal and from the laboratory had been gathered, there was until recently no real knowledge of what happened in the brain when these things had their effect.

In the last few years, the work of Professor Olds has opened up a completely new line of approach to these topics. We saw earlier in this chapter that it is possible to record the electrical activity of the brain and also to stimulate the brain. It is in fact possible to record and stimulate single cells or small groups of cells, and by means of careful operations to do so while an animal is fully conscious and walking about its cage.

Olds has found that there are several quite precisely localized areas of the brain which, if stimulated, lead to learning. These areas are buried deep in the older parts of the brain, in the hypothalamic region which is overlaid by the cortex as is shown in Figure 7.

A typical experiment on these so-called 'self-stimulation' areas is shown in Figure 8.

When the animal presses the bar, the result is that a very weak shock is delivered to the hypothalamus of its own brain. After three or four presses the animal continues to press the bar faster and faster, and may continue for hours at a time. In a similar fashion it will learn to run a maze if the 'reward' is self-stimulation instead of the more ordinary food for a hungry animal (Olds and Milner, 1965). The learning is very fast, and very stable. The animals seem to choose it in preference to various other rewards such as mating, or even in preference to food for moderate levels of hunger. It is further known that these areas of the brain are involved in the control of other forms of motivation such as hunger, thirst, and sex, and therefore there can be little doubt that in looking at these mechanisms we are really looking at something very closely connected indeed with the actual physical embodiment of the learning process. The effectiveness of self-stimulation, indeed, can be increased

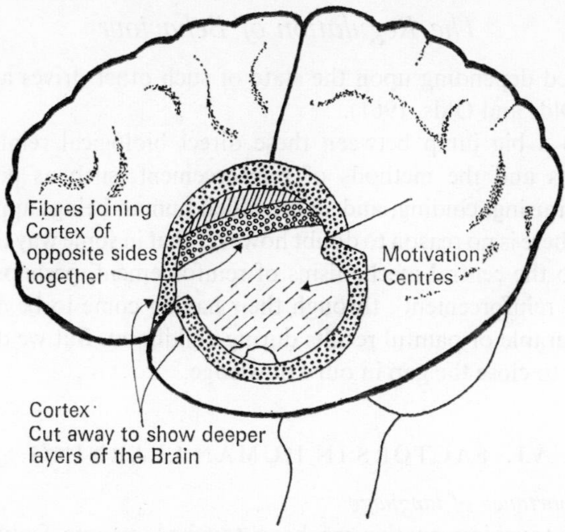

Figure 7. Cutaway view of the brain to show how the areas concerned with motivation are buried deep below the cortex. Stimulation to these areas can produce patterns of behaviour related to food seeking, thirst, mating, or can, when the stimulating electrodes are placed appropriately, cause learning to occur.

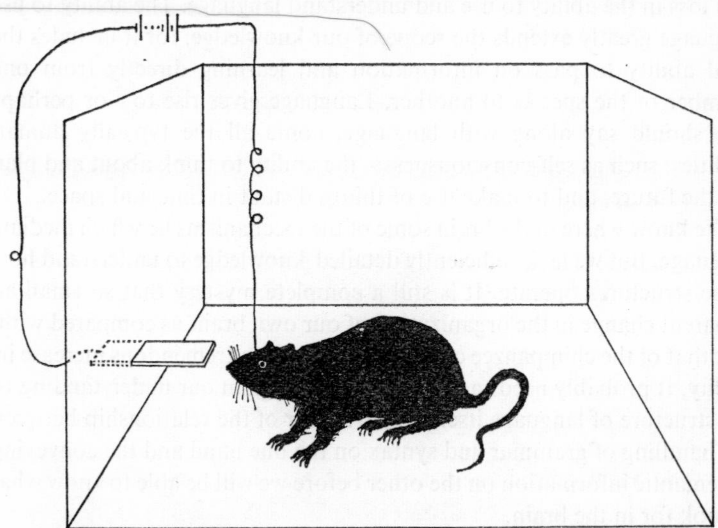

Figure 8. A self-stimulation experiment. When the rat presses the lever, it is given a slight electric shock to the reinforcing areas of the brain indicated in Figure 7. The result is that it presses the bar more and more frequently.

or decreased depending upon the state of such other drives as hunger, sex, etc. (Olds and Olds, 1961).

There is a big jump between these direct biological reinforcement mechanisms and the methods of reinforcement, such as persuasion, cajoling, praising, chiding, and so on which human beings apply one to another. There is no reason to doubt however that in some way their effect is linked to the central mechanisms of reinforcement, perhaps through 'secondary reinforcement', through their having come to be associated with pleasurable or painful results during childhood. But we do not yet know how to close the gap in our knowledge.

VI. FACTORS IN HUMAN LEARNING

1. *The importance of language*

Indeed, in touching on this we have touched on one feature which distinguishes man from all the other animals and which has tremendous implications – the possession of a language of the richness and grammatical complexity which human language embodies. Language itself is represented in the brain. We can identify areas damage to which results in a loss in the ability to use and understand language. The ability to use language greatly extends the scope of our knowledge, for it includes the vital ability to pass on information and learning directly from one member of the species to another. Language gives rise to – or perhaps one should say along with language, come all the typically human abilities, such as self-consciousness – the ability to think about and plan for the future, and to make use of things distant in time and space.

We know where in the brain some of the mechanisms lie which mediate language. But we lack sufficiently detailed knowledge to understand how these structures operate. It is still a complete mystery that so small an apparent change in the organization of our own brain as compared with, say, that of the chimpanzee can give rise to such a tremendous increase in ability. It probably needs a major breakthrough in our understanding of the structure of language itself, in particular of the relationship between the handling of grammar and syntax on the one hand and the conveying of semantic information on the other before we will be able to know what to look for in the brain.

2. *The frontal lobes*

It has been said that the typically human traits are localized in the frontal lobes of the brain (see Figure 6). But while it is true that damage to these areas produces some very strange defects of behaviour, it cannot be said that they are concerned with 'specifically human' abilities. It has been known for many years that if these parts of the brain are removed, either by surgery or in an accident, then very marked changes in personality may occur. The person may become careless, irresponsible, coarse in his language, and perhaps prone to stealing and to behaviour which in general seems completely irresponsible. This led to the suggestion that in some way the 'conscience' was localized here. But if the description of the change is examined carefully, and compared with the changes which are seen in monkeys and apes following similar operations, this rather exotic suggestion is found to be unnecessary. Rather, the frontal lobes seem concerned with inhibiting responses, and perhaps in some way with an ability to concentrate on a task, and more modern operations can selectively remove small areas of brain tissue from this area with often beneficial results to the patient, and without any of the severe personality changes which were associated in earlier years with what was then extremely severe damage to the brain (Warren and Akert, 1964).

3. *Age, development and the nervous system*

The topic of the development of the nervous system and its changing properties as a function of age have been left to last, until this rough sketch of the overall properties of the mature nervous system had been completed. But there is a reason for this. The nervous system of the newly born child is not a nervous system that has properties which resemble an adult nervous system at all closely.

At the beginning of this chapter we pointed out that whereas an animal which relies mainly on instincts can be thought of as having in its skull a computer whose wiring diagram is more or less complete at birth, one relying on learning as its means of adaptation to the demands of the world in which it finds itself is rather inefficient at first, although as it develops it becomes more and more efficient, and can ultimately surpass in performance and versality the 'pre-wired' brain. Humans, more than any other animal, rely on learning. Hence the nervous system of the new-born child is not an elaborate computer so much as a kit of bits and pieces for a 'do-it-yourself' design which is wired up as life progresses.

At birth, many of the nerve cells are not sufficiently well formed to conduct impulses properly, and it is for this reason that many things simply *cannot* be taught to a new-born or young baby. Thus toilet training, walking, and of course speech, all must wait for some time. During the first few weeks of life the nerve cells develop, and begin to function properly, and as they do so the information begins to pour into the brain, and the brain to organize itself under the impact of the need to process the information. It is not too much of an exaggeration to say that not merely does the child learn how to behave, but the brain itself changes and learns how to learn. One clear indication of the complexity and slow speed of development is seen in the changes in E E G rhythms. Earlier we saw how one can detect characteristic patterns of brain activity by recording the electrical rhythms picked up through the skull, showing different patterns, for sleep or arousal, brain disease, and so on. The brain of the new-born child shows very little in the way of brain rhythm changes; and during the first years of life it is possible to see the patterns of activity becoming more complex as the organization of the brain continues. The final adult patterns may not be found until well into the teens (Grey-Walter, 1959).

The systematic unfolding of brain potential depends on a number of external factors. Defects in diet, maltreatment to the brain leading to physical damage, and so on, may injure its development. Yet the brain does show remarkable powers of adaptation even to quite severe damage, if it occurs early, before the self-organization has proceeded too far. Thus, the mechanisms for language usually lie on the left side of the cortex, the corresponding region on the other side of the brain having different functions. Damage to this area in an adult may result in permanent language deficiency, while following a corresponding lesion in the brain of a child whose language learning has not proceeded very far, the opposite side of the brain may take over (Penfield and Roberts, 1959).

But in addition to such gross factors which may hinder or help in the development, there are more subtle effects dependent upon the functioning of the brain itself. There is abundant evidence that the brain requires stimulation if it is to develop. Animals reared in the dark have defective vision when they finally enter the light. Humans with congenital cataract whose sight is given to them when they are adults have tremendous difficulty in learning to see. They cannot initially recognize even simple geometrical shapes without handling them, and the learning is a very slow and painful process (von Senden, 1960; Gregory and Wallace, 1963; Riesen, 1958). Dogs reared in a very protected environment where there are no hard objects are defective in their response to painful and dangerous stimuli. It seems likely that these results can be generalized to human babies. Indeed they suggest that the more an animal relies on learning, the more important is a rich, varied environment full of stimuli in the very first weeks and months of life, if the brain is to organize itself effectively.

Among these early effects are those dependent upon the contact with a mother. Social deprivation in young animals is extremely deleterious for their future social development, and since the critical period for this is so close to that for the general development of the nervous system, it seems likely that social contact has in some way a particularly important role in the response of the brain as it develops to the calls made upon it (Harlow, 1964).

Even a cursory glance at a young child will make one realize the avidity with which it seeks new stimuli, and responds to new situations. This drive continues throughout life, and it can be helped or hindered by all those who have contact with the child.

CONCLUSION

The full complexity of the brain, even of the rather slight amount of knowledge which we have discovered about it, cannot be dealt with within the confines of several volumes, let alone a chapter. But it is important for anyone teaching to realize that the mechanism of the brain responds to the way in which the whole person is treated. Like any piece of mechanism there are right and wrong ways of using the brain. The first will get the best from it, the second may damage it or even break it. To say that man's brain is a 'mechanism' need not lead us to say man is 'nothing but' a machine, if by this we mean his value is lessened. Rather, the extraordinary capacities of human beings should make us place a higher value on the biological mechanisms of which they are made, and keener to make the most of the material with which we have been provided.

REFERENCES

BEACH, F. A., HEBB, D. O., MORGAN, C. T. and NISSEN, H. W. (ed.), (1960). *The Neuropsychology of Lashley*. New York and London: McGraw-Hill.

BERGEIJK, W. van, PIERCE, J. R., and DAVID, E. E. (1961). *Waves and the ear*. London: Heinemann.

BROADBENT, D. E. (1958). *Perception and Communication*. London: Pergamon.

BUCKNER, D. N., and MCGRATH, J. J. (1963). *Vigilance: a Symposium*. New York and London: McGraw-Hill.

CHERRY, C. (1953). Some experiments on the recognition of speech with one and with two ears. *J. Acoust-soc. Amer.* **25**, 975–979.

COWIE, A., and WEISKRANTZ, L. (1963). A perimetric study of visual field defects in monkeys. *Quart. J. exp. Psychol.* **15**, 91–116.

DETHIER, V. G. and STELLAR, E. (1964). *Animal Behaviour.* New York: Prentice-Hall, Foundations of Modern Biology.

DEUTSCH, J. A. (1962). Higher Nervous Function: the Physiological Bases of Memory. *Ann. Rev. Physiol.* **24**, 259–286.

ECCLES, J. C. (1953). *The Neurophysiological Basis of Mind.* London: O.U.P.

GARNER, W. R. (1962). *Uncertainty and Structure as Psychological Concepts.* New York: Wiley.

GREGORY, R. (1966). *Eye and Brain.* London: World University Library, Weidenfeld and Nicolson.

GREGORY, R. and WALLACE, J. (1963). Recovery from early blindness: a case study. *Experimental Psychology Society.*

GREY-WALTER, W. (1959). Intrinsic Rhythms of the brain. In *American Handbook of Physiology*, Volume I. 279–299.

HARLOW, H. F. and HARLOW, M. K. (1964). Love in infant monkeys. In Coopersmith, S. (ed.) *Frontiers of Psychological Research: Readings from Scientific American.* San Francisco: Freeman, 125–8.

HEBB, D. O. (1961). Distinctive features of learning in the higher animal. In J. F. Delafresnaye (ed.), *Brain Mechanisms and Learning.* Oxford: Blackwell. 37–53.

HELD, R., and HEIN, A. (1963). Movement-produced stimulation in the development of visually guided behaviour. *J. comp. Physiol. Psychol.* **56**, 872.

KLEITMAN, N. (1963). *Sleep and Wakefulness.* Chicago: Univ. of Chicago Press.

MAGOUN, H. W. (1963). *The Waking Brain.* Springfield, Ill: Charles C. Thomas.

MAIER, N., and SCHNEIRLA, T. (1935). *Principles of Animal Psychology.* New York and London: McGraw-Hill.

MELTON, N. (1963). Implications of short-term memory for a general theory of memory. *J. Verb. Learn. Verb. Behav.* **2**, 1–21.

MILLER, G. A. (1956). The magical number seven $\pm$ 2. *Psychol. Rev.* **63**, 81–97.

MORAY, N. P. (1959). Attention in dichotic listening: affective cues and the influence of instructions. *Quart J. exp. Psychol.* **11**, 56–60.

NEFF, W. D., and DIAMOND, I. T. (1958). The Neural Basis of Auditory

Discrimination. In Harlow, H. F. and Wolsey, C. N. (ed.), *Biological and Biochemical Bases of Behaviour.* Madison: Univ. of Wisconsin, 101–122.

OLDS, J. and MILNER, P. (1964). Positive Reinforcement produced by electrical stimulation of Septal area and other regions of rat brain. In Isaacson, R. L. (ed.), *Basic Readings in Neuropsychology.* New York: Harper.

OLDS, J. and OLDS, M. E. (1961). Interference and learning in paleocortical systems. In J. F. Delafresnaye (ed.), *Brain Mechanisms and Learning.* Oxford: Blackwell, 153–188.

OSGOOD, C. E., and MIRON, M. S. (1963). *Approaches to the Study of Aphasia.* Urbana: Illinois U. P.

OSWALD, I. (1962). *Sleeping and Waking.* Amsterdam: Elsevier.

PENFIELD, W., and ROBERTS, L. (1959). *Speech and Brain Mechanisms.* O.U.P.

RICHTER, D. (1966). *Aspects of Learning and Memory.* London: Heinemann.

RIESEN, A. H. (1961). Studying perceptual development using the technique of sensory deprivation. *J. Nerv. Ment. Dis.* **132**, 21–25.

ROE, A., and SIMPSON, G. (1958). *Behaviour and Evolution.* New Haven: Yale U.P.

RUSSELL, R. (1959). *Brain, Memory, Learning.* London: O.U.P.

SAMUELS, I. (1959). Reticular Mechanisms and Behaviour. *Psychol. Bull* **56**, 1–25.

SENDEN, M. von (1960). *Space and Sight.* London: Methuen.

SMITH, K., and SMITH, W. (1962). *Perception and Motion.* Saunders, Philadelphia.

SOLOMON, M. *et al.* (1961). *Sensory Deprivation.* Cambridge, Mass.: Harvard Univ. Press.

STEVENS, C. (1966). *Neurophysiology, a primer.* New York: Wiley.

SUMMERFIELD, A. and LEGGE, D. (1961). Information theory and perception. In J. Cohen (ed.), *Readings in Psychology.* London: Allen and Unwin, 236–248.

TAYLOR, C. (1962). *The Explanation of Behaviour.* London: Routledge & Kegan Paul.

TREISMAN, A. (1966). Our limited attention. *Adv. Sci.* pp. 600–611.

WARREN, J., and AKERT, K. (1964). *The Frontal Granular Cortex and Behaviour.* New York: McGraw-Hill.

WEVER, E. G. (1949). *Theory of Hearing.* New York: Wiley.

YOUNG, J. Z. (1964). *A Model of the Brain.* London: O.U.P.

3

Structural Interpretations of Behaviour and Learning

I. S-R AND STRUCTURAL APPROACHES: BASIS OF DISTINCTION

1. *Psychology as the Functional Analysis of Processes deemed to occur in the Brain*

THE LAST chapter was concerned to trace the main lines of the development of behavioural theory from its origins to the systematic version of Hull and his followers. The approaches of Gestalt psychology and of Tolman, although very different in flavour, were considered at the same time. The reason is that the considerations which they urged were precisely those that led to the eventual form of what has been termed 'learning theory', and their interpretation has contributed largely to its key concepts: the fractional or mediating response, incentive motivation, stimulus interaction, and habit-family-hierarchy.

It was conceded at the end of the last chapter that Hullian theory had stimulated a vast amount of precise experimentation and that it had contributed to several new discoveries. Nor are we disposed to stress the argument that few of the predictions which follow from the theory can be made to apply easily outside the laboratory situation, for this need be no more than a comment on the youthfulness of psychology as a science. Nevertheless, it will be argued in the present chapter that the basic framework of Hullian theory is misleading and the model which it implies is inadequate. On the positive side, an alternative type of approach will be advanced, one which for want of a better term, I shall call 'structural'. However, it should be stressed that no one is inclined to quarrel with any body of experiment in so far as it offers correct *descriptions* of a significant body of facts. And this is clearly the case in respect of the experimental work on, for example, incentives and drives, in so far as this stems out of Hullian theory and is consonant with it. But there is very good reason to take issue with the *explanatory* laws of 'learning theory': with the proposition that drives are direct or indirect responses to biological needs, that they exist as variable 'drive stimuli' exercising a precise influence on the reaction potentials of 'responses', likewise with the proposition that behaviour consists essentially in a sequence of responses to stimuli, and so on. The reader who is relatively new to the subject should perhaps be reminded that terms like drive stimulus, habit strength, reaction potential or mediating stimulus are not observable characteristics of the nervous system. They have the status of intervening variables the existence of which might relate some of the observations of behaviour with some of the observations of its antecedents. Even though Hull and his followers acknowledge that they should in time be discoverable in the nervous system, they rarely if ever consider just what form they might take, and indeed they regard such attempts on the part of psychologists as unprofitable and unscientific speculation.

The warning against neurological speculation is partly justified. One of the most seminal works to have appeared in the not so distant past is Hebb's neurophysiological essay *The Organisation of Behaviour* (Hebb, 1949). There are few contemporary psychologists who do not owe something to Hebb's challenging ideas regarding the ways in which successive hierarchies of behaviour are formed, to his trenchant criticisms of the then dominant Hullian system, and to his endeavour to provide a possible rapprochement between psychology as the science of the regulation of behaviour and neurophysiology as the study of the way in which the central nervous system achieves this regulation. Yet within a very few years of its publication, many of the specifically neurological speculations contained in this work were proved unsound. (Its chief weaknesses concern the attempts at localization of functions in the cortex with an attendant neglect of what have since proved to be quite crucial relations between cortical, palaeocortical and subcortical functions, together with his hypothesis of neurobiotaxis (growth of nerve tissues) as the neural mechanism underlying learning.) There is little to be gained in trying to improve on Hebb's work by building card castles on the shifting sands yielded by more recent discoveries – such as the role of R.N.A. in learning, the reinforcing function of palaeocortical areas, and the arousal functions of the reticular system. Those who work in these fields wisely confine their interpretations to the levels of behavioural organization in which their experiments offer a secure anchorage.

Be that as it may, the present writer is not in the least competent to indulge in neurological speculations – or even to follow intelligently those of others, and little attempt will be made in this direction. But the criticism of the Hullian system goes deeper, for its lack of concern with neurology has led not only to a (justifiable) failure to specify neurological correlates for its constructs, but to the elaboration of constructs of a purely mathematical kind, for which no neural basis is even possible. Psychology therefore tends to become the study of the mathematical relations between certain selected frozen aspects of behaviour and of the environment instead of the study of behaviour itself as the resultant of complex processes. We contend that these processes need to be studied; moreover, speculation in regard to their functional interrelations is essential even if speculation with regard to their anatomic localization is unwarranted and unnecessary. In the discussion which follows (which is far from orginal, even though it draws on several sources), there will be occasion to hypothesize quite a num ber of hypothetical functional entities. Although no attempt will be made to specify anatomic localizations for these, it will be assumed that they do correspond to systems within the brain, and that their interrelations with one another correspond to real processes. At the very least, they must be possible processes. This is in some contradiction to the relations between the Hullian intervening variables, which are generally no more than mathematical constructs. And since behaviour clearly does derive from neural mechanisms, I will apply the same treatment to the variables of 'learning theory', to see what we would need to assume if we wanted to construct a 'brain' and a 'body' on its basis. I believe that the reader is very likely to conclude, with perhaps the majority of contemporary psychologists, that this kind of 'brain' is in the highest degree unlikely.

2. *A Categorization of Psychological Theories based on the role of the Stimulus*

Undoubtedly the most important single difference between the various streams of learning theory considered so far and the structural approach consists in the use or non-use of the stimulus as an explanatory concept. From the S-R point of view, the organism is thought of as active in response to stimuli. Behaviour is made up of responses to stimuli. If there were no stimuli, there would be no behaviour. The end-state towards which behaviour tends is a state of rest. For the purpose of this argument, the approach may be named 'reactive'. From the point of view of the structural approach, the organism is seen as spontaneously active. Behaviour is responsive to stimuli, but it is not made up of responses to stimuli. If there were no stimuli (in the environment), the organism would seek stimuli. There is no end-state for behaviour in general, for the organism is constantly active. There are ends for particular segments of behaviour, but these lead only to switching in the control of behaviour, not to its termination.

The distinction is drawn rather eloquently by Miller, Galanter, and Pribram (1960). It is anticipated to some extent by Lewin (1936) and by Hebb (1949).

A science can only be experimental if it specifies the operations that it performs and the data which it observes. Moreover both the operations and the data must be objective: in other words they must be expressed in terms such that the same operations can be repeated by another and the same observations will be made. This is why the concepts of stimulus and response are central to experimental psychology. The stimulus is useful in defining the operations that one performs and the response in defining the observations which one makes.

The use of objectively defined environmental stimulus variation dates from the very beginnings of experimental psychology. The recognition of the importance of the behavioural response dates only from the turn of the century. That is why nineteenth-century psychology was most fruitful in the area where behaviour is minimal, the psychology of perception.

However, granted the experimental manipulation of stimuli and recording of responses, experiment may be used to substantiate any one of three types of theory. Stimuli and responses may be studied from the reactive standpoint and the object of psychology may be thought of as the making of inferences about the connexions between environmental stimuli and responses. Alternatively, the standpoint may be reactive but the inferences may be about connexions of a different sort, e.g. meanings or events in the brain. Finally the standpoint may be biological or cybernetic (see p. 167). In this case, the connexions which are inferred are in practice never connexions between environmental stimuli and responses.

Given this categorization, the term 'stimulus-response theory' is often used for the first category. Its proponents include both Pavlov and Thorndike on the one hand, and Hull and his followers on the other. The second category includes what Hilgard (1958) describes as cognitive psychologies: Tolman and Köhler and Koffka. Hebb (1949) is probably intermediate between the second and third category. This includes Lewin, perhaps all of modern ethologists, and Piaget. Among its earlier adherents one might include Dewey and MacDougal. I believe it also includes Skinner.

This is by no means the only way of categorizing these various theories.

A far more usual way is to bracket Piaget along with Tolman and Gestalt psychology among the cognitive approaches, with a larger, complementary, behaviourist category to include not only Thorndike, Pavlov and Hull, but also Skinner and the cybernetically influenced approaches of Deutsch, Sutherland, Broadbent, and others. I have no wish to quarrel with this categorization, which is based on whether or not the set of explanatory constructs is allowed to include such terms as 'knowing', 'anticipating', 'understanding' or 'structuring', etc. But I believe the categorization based on the use of the stimulus and response to be a valid alternative cross-categorization, and I have adopted it because it seems to serve the interests of the present exposition (see Figure 1).

	Behaviourist	*Intermediate*	*Cognitive*
S-R 'reactive'	Thorndike Hull	Lloyd Morgan	(Locke, Hume)
Intermediate	Osgood? Harlow Pavlov Hebb	Tolman	'classical' Gestalt psychology
Structural	Skinner Deutsch	Lorenz Broadbent G. Miller (and present writer)	Lewin Piaget

Figure 1. A Cross-categorization of some Learning Theorists (The categorization is necessarily arbitrary. Piaget is less of an extreme cognitivist than Lewin, and Hebb is probably nearly as structural as Skinner. Similarly a good case could be made for moving Harlow nearer the (vertical) centre, and so on.)

The vertical categorization in Figure 1 is useful in bringing out the limitations in the work of Gestalt psychology and of Tolman (see Ch. 1), and in explaining the appeal of the S-R approach to would-be hard-headed experimentalists. It also brings out the strength of Skinner's pragmatic approach which enables him to avoid nearly all the bogs of confusion upon which the castle of 'learning theory' is constructed: Skinner's refusal to regard the stimulus as the source of all behaviour, together with the elasticity of his concept of the operant as a 'functional unit' justify his inclusion in our third category (see p. 78). Piaget's almost exclusive interest in epistemology (the fundamental character of 'knowledge'), together with his propensity to rely heavily on the interpretation of the unstructured verbal behaviour of his subjects in making inferences about processes deemed to regulate their activity must undoubtedly render him suspect to experimentalists in our third category (e.g. Broadbent, Deutsch) as well as in our first. This is liable to obscure the similarity of Piaget's concept of 'assimilation' to the notions of 'analyser' (Deutsch, Sutherland), of 'comparator' (Mackay), and of 'filter' mechanisms (Broadbent); or that of the concept of learning or adaptation as resulting from the interaction of assimilation and accommodation to the cybernetic concept of feedback; as well as the affinity between Piaget's notion of the structure of inferences as constituting a 'schema', and the cybernetician's attempts to establish a correspondence between the processes of reasoning in the human subject and the structure of a computer programme (Newell, Shaw and Simon, 1958). Finally, the present categorization highlights the differences between the *Zeitgeist* of the thirties, influenced largely by the bankruptcy of introspection in psychology and the seductions of the (then) new movement of positivism in philosophy (sanctioning the use of purely mathematical constructs as intervening variables), and that of the post-war era, influenced by developments in physiology, in ethology and in computer technology. In this sense, and in defiance of the calendar, one is inclined to rank Skinner and Piaget among the 'moderns', and several of their younger, and often brilliant, contemporaries, among the 'ancients'.

II. CRITIQUE OF THE HULLIAN MODEL

1. *The Model implied by Hullian Theory*

The construction of functional models of processes or 'flow diagrams' is commonplace for psychologists with an interest in cybernetics. It is less usual among adherents of older types of theory. Nevertheless, since one must admit that behavioural regulation can only occur as a result of specific processes, it seems a legitimate test of any theory, and we will therefore examine the model which seems to be implied by Hullian theory.

It was said earlier that, from the point of view of the S-R type of theory, the object of psychology is the making of inferences about the connexions between environmental stimuli and responses. Let us follow the argument through. To study the behaviour of a subject in an experimental setting, we need to define that setting, to vary it in precise ways, and to note the variations in behaviour. The procedure is illustrated diagrammatically in Figure 2.

We maintain as many conditions invariant as possible, and control the variations of one, noting the changes in behaviour. It is convenient to regard the subject as a black box (thereby acknowledging our relative ignorance of neurophysiological mechanisms). To make deductions about the workings of the black box, we note the correlations between input and output, between stimulus and response. Let us add at once that there is nothing wrong with this. It is difficult to see how else one could go about the business of conducting experiments (although there are many variations, such as the use of statistical techniques to overcome the inevitable errors of measurement as well as our inability to reproduce situations exactly).

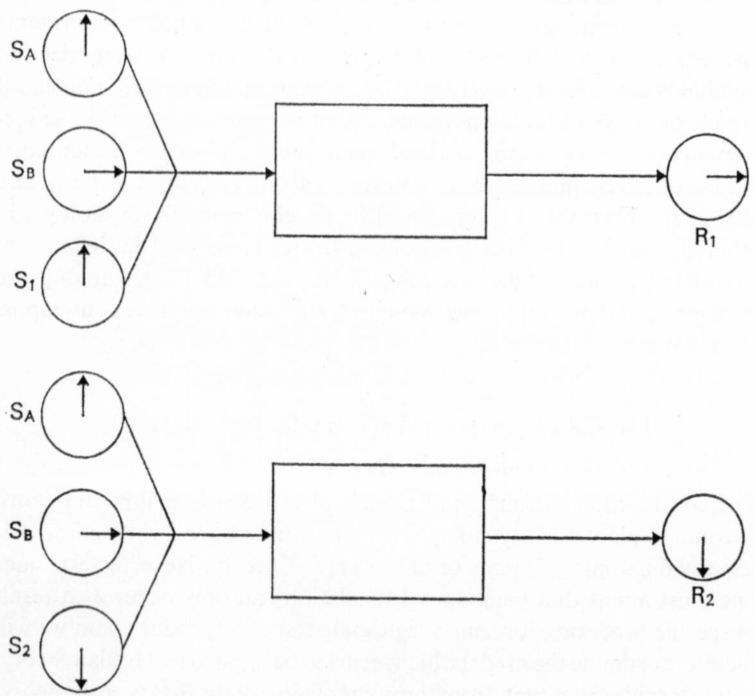

Figure 2. Simplest Diagrammatic Representation of Learning
S_A and S_B represent two of the many stimuli acting on the 'black box' which have remained constant: S_1 has been varied to yield S_2: R_2 is observed to differ from R_1.

However, in order to move from the mere description of what occurs in the experiment to its explanation, one needs to make some hypotheses concerning what takes place in the black box, hypotheses which may be verified or infirmed by our results. Indeed this is the object of undertaking the experiment in the first place.

Figure 3 is a diagrammatic representation of the principal assumptions about the black box made in Hullian theory. We may note that all the elements which now figure in the box are 'intervening variables'. All of these are assumed to vary simultaneously (or in succession) and to react upon one another along the lines indicated by the arrows. In order to simplify the picture, I have assumed that the stimulus conditions include only two aspects, 'stimuli', to which the subject is sensitive. Similarly, I have assumed that he is capable of only three responses, with bonds linking each of the two stimuli to two of the three responses. The picture would of course cease to be a possible diagram if one tried to represent all of the responses available to the organism and all the discriminations of which it is capable – even if one confines himself to the rat.

There are a number of features of this mode of interpretation the significance of which can easily be missed:

(1) It assumes a 1–1 correspondence between every discriminable feature of the environment, **S**, and some variable in the organism, usually termed **s**.

(2) The only actions actually carried out by the black box are taken to be the observable **R**s, or smaller fractional responses modelled on these. To put the matter another way, all of the terms which will ever enter into the behaviour of the box are assumed to be there from the start, being elements whose strength may vary, usually between zero and some asymptote, but even when their strength is zero, they are none the less present. There is no switching; the circuitry is ready-made and not self-adjusting.

(3) All of the variables shown at any level (i.e. belonging to the same category and figuring within the same column) are assumed to function (vary) simultaneously, thus modulating all of the organism's response tendencies (momentary effective reaction potential of each response).

(4) With a single exception, the variables merely modulate the other variables with which they are connected; they do not, either singly or taken in conjunction with one another, activate other variables or render them inactive. This is essentially the same point as was made under (2). The single exception is the decision procedure **D P**, which

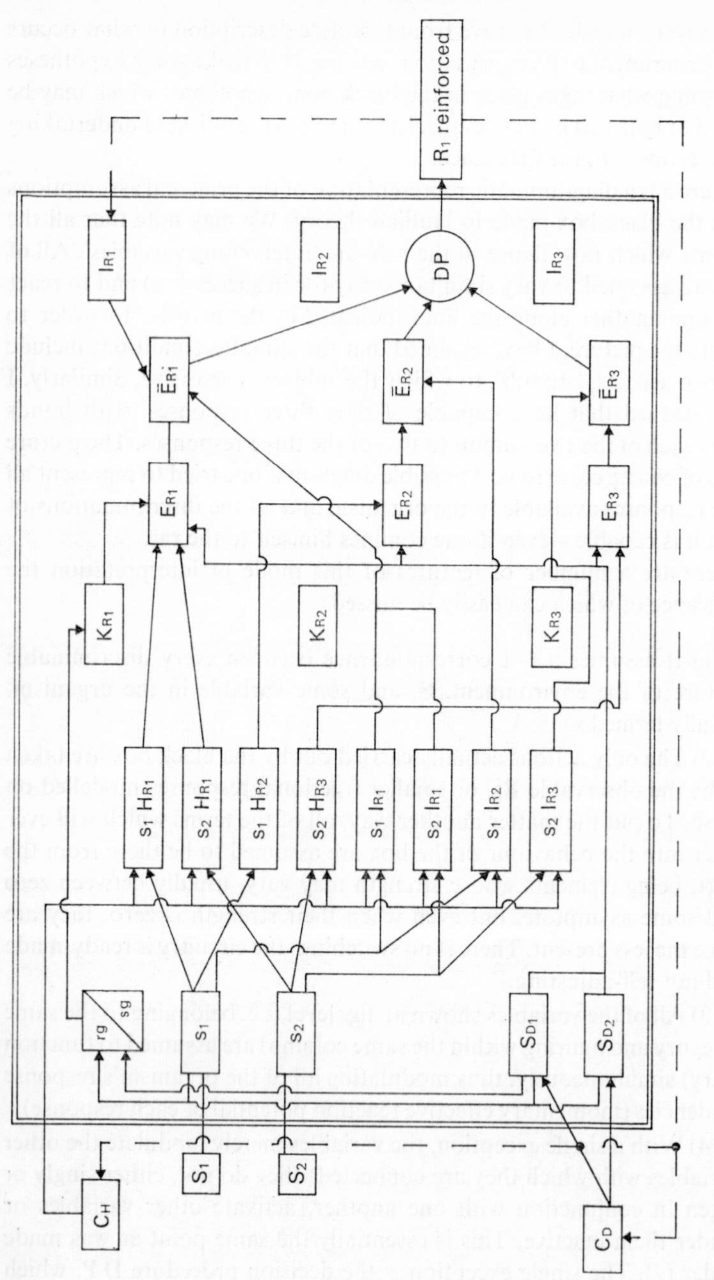
R1 reinforced
IR1
IR2
IR3
DP
ĒR1
ĒR2
ĒR3
ER1
ER2
ER3
KR1
KR2
KR3
S1 HR1
S2 HR1
S1 HR2
S2 HR3
S1 IR1
S2 IR1
S1 IR2
S2 IR3
rg
sg
S1
S2
SD1
SD2
S1
S2
CH
CD

Figure 3

Figure 3. A flow-diagram based on 'learning theory'

C_H = Historical antecedents of the experiment.

S_1, S_2 = Two features of the stimulus conditions.

C_D = Drive conditions: it is assumed that two drives are present, e.g. hunger and anxiety, and that their effects will summate (the Miller-Spence hypothesis).

Together, these three groups constitute the antecedent variables. It is further assumed that only one behaviour is observed, R_1, and that it is reinforced, resulting in a reduction of one of the needs, that corresponding to the first of our two drives.

All the remaining terms are 'intervening variables', and are therefore located inside the black box, represented by the heavy rectangle. Arrows represent the successive modulating effects exercised by the various terms on one another. Continuous lines are used to represent effects deemed to be operative at the start of the trial, while dotted lines indicate connexions which become effective as a result of behaviour in the first trial, R_1, reinforced with respect to D_1. Nodal bifurcations represent effects acting in parallel, in accordance with the usual convention. Dotted connexions may be thought of as feedback.

s_1, s_2 = Stimulus traces corresponding to the two aspects of stimulation, S_1, S_2.

S_{D1}, S_{D2} = Drive stimuli resulting from C_D.

$s_1H_{R_1}$, $s_2H_{R_1}$, etc., represent habit strengths of responding to s_1 with R_1, etc. It is assumed that, by virtue of previous conditions, the first response has become attached to both stimuli, the second response to the first stimulus only. Only these connexions are therefore represented. This eases the burden on the reader, but it is a kind of cheating, for if one follows the system through strictly, it seems necessary that every stimulus is always attached to every response, even if the connexion sH_R be of zero strength. The effect of conditioning may then be to raise it.

$s_1I_{R_1}$, etc. = conditioned inhibition attaching to the various stimulus-response connexions. The above comments again apply.

E_{R1}, E_{R2}, E_{R3} = reaction potential attaching to the three responses. In accordance with the requirements of the theory, all the drive states react on all responses. However, differential effects will be manifest as a result of reinforcement history, when incentive effects, K, should prove more discriminating.

$\bar{E}_{R1}$, etc. = effective reaction potential attaching to each of the three responses. This is affected by its corresponding E, by its several sI_R, and by the fatigue effects I_R, when these become operative.

K_{R1}, K_{R2}, I_{R1}, etc., represent the respective incentive strengths and

Figure 3—contd.

reactive inhibitions attaching to the three responses. It may be noted (i) that each of these terms is shown as specific to a response only, as are the E and $\dot{E}$ terms (see Ch. 1, p. 37); (ii) the singleton K which becomes operative does so as a result of the r_G-s_G mechanism; the remainder are shown, although not operative, being at zero strength; the same holds of the I_2 terms. In this respect the diagram is fuller than for the H terms where zero strengths were omitted.

D^3 P is a decision procedure, being a comparison of the relative strengths of the three $\bar{E}$s, and resulting in R_1.

Turning now to the feedback mechanisms:

Since there has been reinforcement, the original drive conditions C_D are altered, by the diminution of D_1.

s_1 and s_2, and also both s_D are now capable of evoking r_G, and hence s_G; the K term, although attaching to both the stimulus aspects, s_1 and s_2 (since both were present initially), is confined to the successful response R_1, and will therefore increase its effective reaction potential on the next occasion.

Both $s_1H_{R_1}$ and $s_2H_{R_1}$ are increased (by primary reinforcement) shown operating on C_H.

The two sI_R terms relating to R_1 are increased, as a result of the increase in I_{R_1}, and will counteract in some measure the increase in sH_{R_1}.

The two s become conditioned to one another, and severally, as well as jointly, they become capable of evoking s_G. An alternative way of representing these changes is to go through the general term C_H outside the box.

Finally, it should be added that, strictly speaking, we should represent not only the H terms linking s_1 with R_1, s_2 with R_1 separately, but also the sH_R (and sI_R) corresponding to their conjoint operation. This seems to be implied by the concept of stimulus interaction! As is pointed out in the text, this is not only difficult to represent diagrammatically, even for only two stimuli and three responses, but also impossible to conceive in the organism, for the number of cells needed to realize it would be virtually infinite.

dictates that of any two incompatible responses, the response having the greater momentary effective reaction potential will occur, and the other will be inhibited. This in accordance with Pavlov's principle of reciprocal inhibition.

(5) The **s** which are taken to be direct outcome of the **S** are, to all intents and purposes, sensations, while those which are mediated by

the **r** (fractional responses), are to all intents and purposes fractional traces of sensations, or images – this in spite of the militant behaviourism (anti-cognitivism) of the theory.

2. *Critique of the Hullian concept of Stimulus*

The diagram shown in Figure 3 is not one which is to be found in any 'orthodox' textbook. As was said earlier, proponents of Hullian theory have not concerned themselves with models or flow diagrams. It differs chiefly from diagrams which do appear elsewhere in that it attempts to portray as many as possible of the elements which are assumed to be present and to vary – at least in a limited model. This is deliberate. For it brings out the impossibility of the theory as a viable representation of what might happen in the brain. The difficulty centres on the number of elements which one would need to assume in the brain, and the number of simultaneous modulations which are supposed to occur.

Consider first the **H** and **I** connexions. If Pavlov's demonstration of the conditioned reflex is to be taken seriously (and there is no more well-established principle in psychology), then one must conclude that any response can be conditioned to any stimulus. But since, according to Hullian theory, the effect of conditioning (through reinforcement) is merely to modify the strengths of existing **H**s and **I**s, and not to set up new connexions, the number of these bonds (most of which will be at zero strength) becomes astronomical. For granted that there are something of the order of 10^9 cells in the brain, this is nothing like enough to mediate the number of bonds that would be needed to establish 1–1 connexions between every discriminable stimulus and every available response, even if the number of these is thought of as fairly modest. It might be, if one considers only the connexions between the universe of stimuli taken singly and the universe of responses – for the number of such connexions is merely the product of the two, say a million bonds for a thousand stimuli and a thousand responses. But the principle of stimulus interaction entails that we have to allow in addition that any combination of stimuli can be conditioned to any response. Given a thousand stimuli, this yields $1{,}000 \times 2^{1{,}000}$ H bonds, and as many I bonds (cf. Broadbent, 1958, p. 38, and Schutzenberger, 1962). Hebb, 1949 (p. 15) criticizes Hull for introducing the principle of afferent neural interaction on the grounds that, while it yields an *ad hoc* explanation of some facts, it detracts from the definiteness of inference. But the principle rests on the firm ground of the interaction of stimuli established in Pavlov's laboratory (summation of stimuli, differentiation of combined stimuli and stimuli in isolation when the former are positive, the latter negative, etc.). It is essential to the Hullian system and not at all optional. One might add that even if we allow some limit to the number of combinations of stimuli which the subject can differentiate, say 4 or 5, this certainly reduces the number of elements to more credible dimensions, but still not enough.

The most salient difficulties attendant to the Hullian system are bound up with the concept of the stimulus, i.e. of the 1–1 correspondence between discriminable properties of the environment and the bonds attributed to the subject. Which is why Skinner rejected the universal applicability of the concept, substituting the distinction between elicited responses, to which it is held to apply, and emitted operants to which it is inapplicable. As we will see, this does not by any means imply that the activity of the subject is independent of the environment with respect to this, the largest category of his behaviour. For one is bound to recognize that behaviour is regulated by discriminating cues. The questions centre entirely on how these are to be incorporated into an explanatory model.

Thorndike recognized that human subjects react to *aspects* of the physical stimulus, extending this notion not only to the redness of red objects but to the fiveness of five. Spence, not confining himself to human behaviour, suggested the universal applicability of this more generalized notion of stimulus, arguing that every discriminable property of a stimulus situation (position, size, colour, shape, etc.) contributes to its own specific habit strength. But Thorndike failed to analyse the implications of his recognition. Spence (1937) held that the increment in habit-strength must be automatically triggered off by reinforcement if a stimulus aspect is discriminable – a proposition which is not supported by the evidence showing that those aspects which have assumed significance in the past history of the (animal) subject not only gain in effectiveness but also tend to weaken the effectiveness of others equally discriminable (Lawrence, 1949, 1950; Sutherland, 1959; Mackintosh, 1965; Sutherland and Mackintosh, 1964). Such findings are what one would expect in accordance with Pavlov's concept of reciprocal inhibition, but this plays only a small part in the Hullian system (see above). In Chapter 1, we alluded to the intractability of alternation, and especially double alternation, strategies for the Hull-Spence model. They necessitate a stretching to the limits of the r_G-s_G mechanism, with, of course a corresponding increase in the number of **H** and **I** elements attributed to the brain. Spence's explanation leads to the further proposition that where two objects differ in several dimensions the subject will always select those combinations which have been most frequently reinforced, a proposition now known to be quite false. Chapter 5 includes a more detailed account of Harlow's work on the formation of learning sets. Once a discrimination reversal learning set had been formed, Harlow could repeatedly observe animals selecting the less-rewarded of two objects quite consistently (Harlow, 1944). The non-reinforcement of the previously reinforced object acts as a cue to the animal to switch to the strategy of selecting the other object by virtue of its previous training to do likewise with other *quite different* pairs. Here again, the Hull-Spence theory can try to invoke the r_G-s_G mechanism for a *post hoc* 'explanation'. I have already stressed the mathematical objection. But there is also a more general objection: the appeal of the theory derives from its reliance on the solid objective properties of stimulus and response as opposed to cognitive imponderables; the more one introduces the faint images of sensations and responses, the clearer it becomes that far from being a scientific and materialist system it relies constantly on unobserved and unobservable paramental entities. (This of course is what is implied by Hebb's critique of afferent interaction.)

Nor are the weaknesses of this theory confined to its use of the stimulus concept in interpreting complex behavioural strategies. The primary facts of perception discussed in Volume II, Chapter 1 make nonsense of the supposed 1–1 correspondence between **S** and **s**. The Gestalt concept of perception was criticized in Chapter 1 on the grounds of the vagueness of the notion of 'good form', and the attribution of form perception to the structure of the object, to the neglect not only of learning, but also of the unlearnt structurizing activity of the subject. But the facts to which these psychologists pointed are irrefutable and they render it impossible to use the stimulus as a point of departure for explanation. Consider only the phenomena of size and form constancy and the ability of the subject to perceive a stable world when his eyes and head are constantly moving. In point of fact, 'learning theory' has no means of handling effectively the problems of perception (even though a single author, like Osgood, 1953, is able to write with brilliance and immense learning on each in turn).

3. *Drive and Need-Reduction*

Doubtless the theory could more easily dispense with its specific theoretical postulates regarding drive than those that concern the stimulus. Although the more's the pity, since some of the most beautiful work inspired by it has been that of Miller on the conflict of fear and hunger and related problems (see Miller's own review, 1959). Nevertheless, the hypothesis of the identifiability of drives with physiological needs is infirmed both by the physiological evidence and by the behavioural. On the physiological side, Deutsch (1960) has assembled an impressive body of experimentation to substantiate his view that appetitive behaviour in hunger and thirst is activated by analysers which are responsive to quite specific conditions in the body, and triggered off by other analysers which are independent. The point is that the two mechanisms are separate, and the off-analyser is not related to need-reduction. The conclusions of a recent comprehensive review by Rosenzweig (1963) point in the same direction. On the behavioural side, Harlow's studies of attachment behaviour in young rhesus monkeys and of the interplay of curiosity and security-oriented activity demonstrate clearly that neither can be regarded as a learned response pattern deriving from the reinforcement of hunger by secondary reinforcement (see Chapter 4 and Harlow, 1961). The general implications of this work are consonant with the ethologists' account of the activation of hierarchically organized instincts, of which a very brief account will be given below. This is not to deny that the shifting of attention and the maintenance of direction in behaviour must be governed by precise physiological determinants. But it does invalidate the Hullian hypothesis that behaviour is the product of drive and habit strength triggered by the stimulus. For, on the contrary, the effect of such activation is, quite generally, to cause the organism to seek specific kinds of stimulation, which is the essence of Deutsch's theory. Similarly, this evidence does not support the proposition that the end of behaviour is the satisfaction of a need, but rather that the subject's activity shows a tendency to channelling in specific directions either until certain terminal actions have been performed (Lorenz), or until certain terminal signals have been received (Deutsch), when activity does not cease but alters in direction as other directive strategies take over.

However, the evidence here is less conclusive, since both the activation and the de-activation of specific drives like hunger and thirst usually operate in such a way as to reflect the need-states of the organism, even though the two mechanisms seem to be independent.

4. *The Nature of 'Response'*

Our first criticism focused on the use of the stimulus in Hullian theory. We have to make a parallel distinction between the legitimate use of the response as a somewhat arbitrary means of defining experimental findings and hypotheses, and its illegitimate use in the explanation of behaviour regulation. The distinction will enable us to overcome the artificial representation of behaviour as consisting in a sequence of discrete units.

It seems to me to be more correct to think of behaviour as consisting essentially of several layers of overlapping sequences. Every such sequence may be thought of as made up of units, but the units are of varying lengths. The passage from one such unit to another is governed by a decision procedure and this decision procedure is the nearest approach in the system to the old-fashioned concept of response. Generally speaking, the relation between the layers may be hierarchical, in the sense that the decision procedures governing the sequence of units in the lower-order layers are determined by strategies (or switching instructions) dictated by the higher-order layers. Such strategies take the form of sets of 'if ... then' instructions; i.e. they have a degree of indeterminacy, the eventual determination of the behaviour being a combined function of the strategy and the input (the blanks after the 'if' having been filled by the environment). However, the hierarchical arrangement is probably far from complete, and there seem to be cases, perhaps numerous, where the 'lower-order' sequences yield information which leads to revision or modification of 'higher-order' instructions.

The clearest illustrations of such overlapping are to be found in the most complex of skilled activities, notably in the field of language. Consider the behaviour involved in framing a sentence (see Volume II, Chapter 6). It is reasonable to suppose that this is initiated by an intention to convey a certain meaning. We do not need to assume that the meaning is precise before the utterance is made. It need only be sufficiently so to activate a strategy for framing a particular type of sentence, and (again probably simultaneously) to exercise a selective facilitation on the availability of relevant words. If the sentence is simple enough, there need be no intervening stage between the overall sentence strategy and the actual production. But even here there is a complex system of controls and of feedback to regulate pronunciation, voice production and so on. If this feedback is disturbed in any way, the speech becomes uncontrolled and there may be sharp swings and over-correction in voice production, repetitions of previously uttered material, intrusions of forward material, stammering, etc. The actual framing of the first word and the resultant feedback finally determines its successor, and so on. But this is only the final determination, since the realm of possibilities has already been sharply narrowed by the meaning to be conveyed and the sentence type. Moreover, such features of speech as pitch and stress are superimposed on the lexical material and are themselves governed by control strategies operating at the same time as the lexical control. The control hierarchy becomes even more complex if the sentence is at all complex. Thus, in the sentence 'I should be most upset if my dog were to be run over by a lorry', there are, in addition to the strategies governing the overall meaning and the conditional grammatical form, separate strategies governing the two parts. For instance, it is quite unnecessary to assume that a decision must be made at the outset as to whether the second part will be cast in the active or passive. Moreover, events that occur at a lower level may act back on a higher-order strategy. For instance, I might say: 'I should be most upset – did you know I have a dog?', where the determination of the word 'dog' as yet unspoken activates a new uncertainty and switches in a new controlling strategy. But in general, the hierarchical organization prevails, with the result that the sentence and inflexion strategies are operative over longer periods than lower-order mechanisms, and are 'switched off' only after all the successive delegated tasks have been accomplished.

All of the foregoing may be summed up by saying that behaviour does not consist of a sequence of responses; it is a network which approximates to a hierarchy of sequences, in which several sequences must be assumed to be simultaneously active at any level.

We have criticized the over-simplification of the 'stimulus' in the S-R-S-R-S-R paradigm, and the above discussion points to a corresponding over-simplification of 'response'. But a parallel criticism may be made of the relation between them. For to the concepts of the discrete stimulus and the discrete response there corresponds that of the trigger relation between the first and the second. Now there is no doubt that sequential switching mechanisms are involved in the regulation of behaviour, and such switchings do imply that the specification of input triggers specified output controls at various levels. But this is not the only way in which input and output are related. For in the final analysis much of the regulation of behaviour is achieved by the continuous control of the stimulus. Consider the behaviour of tracing a line. It is patent nonsense to argue that this is made up of a succession of partial tracing behaviours wherein each section of the line (how long?) is a stimulus which triggers a short stroke. The initial behaviour may be said to be triggered, but the maintenance of direction is not triggered by perception: it is under the continuous control of perception. What probably happens is that an initial direction is 'computed' on the basis of the 'fit' between the perception of the line, that of the tracing, and the kinaesthetic feedback; at the same time the comparator system (see next chapter) is set to detect any marked deviations between line and tracing: the behaviour then continues smoothly until the comparator registers a deviation, this is immediately passed back to a correction strategy, and appropriate correction is computed, or it is automatically triggered on the basis of previous computation (habit), and behaviour continues.

Driving a car and rowing a boat are more complex instances of this continuous regulation of behaviour by the stimulus. The considerations involved are referred to in more detail in Chapter 4 and in Volume II, Chapter 4. There is a partial recognition of the difference between the triggering and regulatory functions of stimuli implicit in Skinner's sharp distinction between the eliciting stimulus (the **US** and **CS** in Pavlovian conditioning) and the discriminating stimulus (cueing functions of the environment in the direction of spontaneous 'operant' behaviour) (Skinner, 1938). However, there is one feature of behavioural control which is absent from Skinner's treatment. This is the fact that all organisms are able to do several things at once. We have already noted that several events may occur simultaneously in the regulation of any particular aspect of behaviour. The point is that no organism is ever confined to one kind of regulation at a time.

It has been said that Napoleon could make love to a mistress, read a dispatch, dispatch a message and dispatch an enemy all at the same time. He was quite remarkable. But anyone is able to breathe and watch the scene at the same time. And both actions undoubtedly involve very complex regulations, as does the maintenance of heart-rate, of body temperature and so on. The point is that these are effected by different mechanisms which for the most part do not interfere with one another. And exactly the same is true of the regulatory mechanisms involved in driving a car and carrying on a conversation, when both are sufficiently developed as skills (see Volume II, Chapter 4). As Moray has noted already in Chapter 2, they can very easily interfere when the skills are insufficiently automatized, or when the execution of both simultaneously requires the subject to cope with the unexpected. In terms of the model to be presented in the next chapter, in the measure that different comparators and different strategies involve different units, simultaneity of action is possible and essential. In the measure that there is overlap, there will be mutual inhibition, with a consequent disruption of one or both behaviours. The overlap is especially likely in strategies requiring conscious attention and verbalization for their operation. This is one of the principal reasons why it is so difficult for one who has become perfectly fluent in a skill to appreciate the problems of another who has not. This, of course, is one of the central themes of this book, and we will return to it in Volume II, Chapter 14.

Enough has now been said to bring out the complex character of behavioural regulations. It is against this background of regulating mechanisms that one needs to consider the problem of learning. For if behaviour is more than a sequence of responses to stimuli, then learning cannot be simply described as some modification in the strengths of the bonds that unite these two terms.

I need not repeat that this kind of criticism does not invalidate the utility of the concept of secondary reinforcement, or of studies of incentive, the interaction of conflicting drives, etc. But enough has now been said to nullify the claim of Hullian theory to provide an explanatory framework around which all of our findings on behaviour can be organized. Not only is the study of learning completely cut off from perceptual and physiological inquiry, but even within this field, the main tenets of the theory have been shown to yield a model which would be impossible of realization and would lead to conclusions totally at variance with observation and experiment. It might still be argued that it provides the only attempt at a coherent presentation, that at least some of its deductions appear to be well-founded, and that, because they are quantitatively framed, they have been and may continue to be fruitful in stimulating research and thinking. The last point is acknowledged by Hilgard (1958) to be somewhat exaggerated as regards the claim for precise quantification. For the rest, it might command some approval if no alternative approach existed. I believe that, even fifteen years ago, no general alternative was available. But an alternative has crystallized and found expression in the work of many eminent workers in quite distinct fields. To this we now turn.

III. TWO SORTS OF BLACK BOX

We began by acknowledging the inevitability of specifying attributes of input and output in the conduct of psychological experimentation, and we recognized that these could conveniently be labelled stimuli and responses. The task of psychological explanation was to offer hypotheses as to what intervened between input and output – what goes on in the black box.

Black boxes are of (at least) two kinds. Consider first a teleprinting machine, the sort that will copy faithfully the sequence of holes in a punched paper tape, reproducing the tape exactly (the various combinations of holes represent, of course, figures or letters). With such a machine as this the sequence is: switch on the machine, feed your tape, the machine automatically and immediately 'reads' your tape, and 'punches' another just like it (as well as giving you a typed transliteration of the patterns of holes). But compare this with a digital computer. A computer requires a programme of instructions and (usually) a set of data. The effect of the programme is to set its connexions so that it is ready to operate in the precise manner that you require *when it receives the data*. The programme (which usually takes the form of a punched tape) is not fed directly into the computer but into a satellite machine, the 'reader'. The computer itself already has a programme, a master programme called a 'supervisor'. This ensures that it will (when it is ready) pick up your programme from the tape reader. We assume that it has done so and that your data tape has also been fed. There is still no guarantee that the machine will 'read' your data in the manner that you intend. Whether it does or not depends on the adequacy of the programme you wrote (as every programmer learns to his cost). Your data is not a *direct* input to the computer.

Or compare the behaviour of traffic-lights with that of a policeman. As you cross the mat short of the lights, so the mechanism ensures that the lights will turn in your favour within a prescribed delay interval; as you approach the manned crossing, there is no guarantee that the policeman will notice you (although in some circumstances you may be better off).

Reverting to the first example, the teletype machine is inert until you switch it on, and its response to the stimuli (punched holes) is direct and automatic: we may therefore say that the stimulus triggers the response. By contrast, the computer (we are not concerned with the tape reader) operates on its programmes, which may or may not direct it to search for the data, and thereupon to categorize them and operate on them in specified ways. The sequence is in no sense triggered off by the data, although the data undoubtedly function as stimuli in the broad sense of Figure 2.

Reverting to the main topic which is the analysis of behaviour, the role of the stimulus as trigger is the chief point of difference which separates the stimulus-response type of theory from what we have termed the structural approach. The student of psychology begins (or should begin) by observing behaviour. He notes the setting in which it occurs (we may call this the complex of physical stimuli) and also the sequence of the behaviour itself. If he arrives at an interpretation of the mechanism which governs the behaviour he tests this interpretation by varying the setting and establishing whether the changes in behaviour accord with his predictions. He is therefore tempted to cast his interpretation in the same terms as his observations and predictions: first, and most simply, as **S-R** bonds (as Thorndike did, always allowing that our student has already made Thorndike's tremendous leap in overcoming the temptation to accept mental categories like wishes and images as a sufficient explanation in themselves), and then (if he is as sophisticated as Tolman or Hull) in terms of **S-O-R** bonds, the **O** standing for organism. The stimulus is held to trigger reactions in intervening variables sited in the organism and these in turn determine the response. In other words, everything that happens in the organism is seen either as a direct consequence of a physical stimulus (e.g. the drive stimulus, S_D), or as the reaction of some simple variable to it – when the value of that variable is attributed not only to the stimulus but also to one or other aspect of the history of the subject (e.g. habit strength, attenuation caused by generalization, conditioned inhibition).

The structural approach rejects such an interpretation. It sets out from the proposition that the subject is always active; his activity is not triggered off by the stimuli but by the 'programme' which is built in (to his nervous and endocrine system) and which is also modified in the course of experience. The stimuli that he encounters merely channel his reactions in the first instance (although they are also instrumental in the modification of the programme which we call learning). Whether or not he encounters them depends on the programme. Also, one cannot simply assume that a physical stimulus, or even a set of physical stimuli, will be the same for all subjects. The physical stimulus is a necessary condition for certain events in the organism (perceptions, judgements, decisions) but it is by no means a sufficient condition.

Therefore, an important distinction must be drawn between the study of the sensitivity of end-organs (e.g. the powers of resolution of the retina or cochlea), a psychophysical study which determines what *might be* perceived by a given subject, and the study of perceptual categorization, or of what *is* perceived (see the distinction between discrimination and classification made by Vernon in Volume II, Chapter 1). The former corresponds to the reader in the analogy of the computer. To study it, one provides controlled conditions and maximal motivation; such study is easiest in adult human subjects where the task can be explained verbally (e.g. to listen for a sound on a pure tone amplifier) and the experimenter can request a verbal response; it is less easy, but still feasible, with animal subjects, where conditioning (classical or instrumental) is the obvious method; and most difficult with very young children, where the process merges all too readily into categorization and higher order regulations.

But it is the latter which intervenes in the regulation of behaviour.[1] In general, one can only infer what a subject has perceived at any moment by noting the way in which his behaviour is adapted to his environment, i.e. what differentiations he makes. There is no ground whatever for taking our introspectible 'feel' of perception as the starting point and concluding that to every categorizable aspect of the environment there corresponds a sort of sense-datum, and then extending the model to include hypothetical determinants of behaviour such as drive stimuli and minimal response-produced stimuli ($\mathbf{s_G}$). On the contrary, all the evidence indicates that the only safe ground is to accept that the most significant characteristic of perception is the decision-making to which it gives rise. For instance, in a discrimination learning situation, the task of the subject (whether imposed by the experimenter or self-imposed) may be to keep alternating his choices between two objects. Here the perceptual categorization is the selection of some aspect of the physical stimulus (e.g. position, colour or shape) *with reference to a previous selection and categorization.* Now in the light of the exigencies of the (perhaps artificial) environment, that principle of selection may be right or wrong. If it is right it will be reinforced (e.g. by a reward or by verbal approval) and if it is incorrect it will not be. If reinforced it will be strengthened and if not then some other principle of selection has a greater chance of becoming operative. But the important theoretical point to appreciate is that what is reinforced is the decision itself: the 'strategy' (Bruner, Goodnow and Austin, 1956); the 'learning set' (Harlow, 1949); the 'plan' (Miller, Galanter and Pribram, 1960) or the 'schema' (Piaget, 1950) – for all these bewildering terms cover much the same idea. It is not strictly speaking the response to the stimulus, or to an aspect of the stimulus, or even to an aspect of the sequence of stimuli. For the fact that I chose a circle last time and decide to choose a square this time is not an aspect of the stimuli at all: it is an aspect of my behaviour in relation to them, which is a very different kettle of fish. That is why the Hull-Spence sophistication of **S-R** is misleading.

IV. STRUCTURAL MODELS OF BEHAVIOUR – I: THE ETHOLOGICAL MODEL OF N. TINBERGEN

A consideration of Figure 1 suggests that although several contemporary approaches to behaviour imply a structural outlook, the polarization of

[1] See also next chapter, pp. 157ff.

theories in one direction or another along the axis structural-reactive does not obey any strict chronological sequence. Perhaps the very complexity of the instincts of insects combined with the limitations in their capacity for learning compel the naturalist to interest himself in the role of pre-programming in their behaviour. Hence, even the work of Fabre and others in the nineteenth century foreshadows a more contemporary approach than that of Thorndike and Hull.

It is therefore inevitable that the contemporary psychologist like Deutsch or Harlow will often turn for inspiration to the work of ethology, even though the more limited part of learning in the behaviour of lower orders prevents one from expecting even the most perfect ethological interpretation to provide adequate explanations of, say, human behaviour. While quite primitive organisms appear to be capable of some learning (for instance, conditional reflexes have been established in planaria), the part of learning in the regulation of behaviour appears to increase as one ascends the phylogenetic scale. What is more, as will appear in Chapter 5, new kinds of learning emerge at higher evolutionary levels. But all learning is grafted on to a pre-existing organizational framework; it is essentially a modification to a pre-existing programme. That is why it is useful to begin by considering the nature of such a programme.

Modern ethology provides a convenient starting point. For much of ethology deals with species whose behaviour appears to be largely governed by built-in mechanisms: birds, fishes, insects. Moreover, right from the start, ethologists have set out to base their theory construction on the careful observation of the behaviour of animals in their natural state. Instead of beginning with a ready-made formula – that behaviour consists in responses to stimuli – ethologists have preferred to begin with an atheoretical but detailed topography of the behaviour evinced by selected species and of the manner in which this is adapted to its biological conditions of existence. The observations themselves enable the scientist to recognize a patterning in the behaviour, and it is only at this point that theory begins to emerge. Ethology deals first of all with the description of the various patterns and the study of their interrelations, and secondly with the construction of a theoretical model of the regulatory mechanisms which seem to underlie these interrelations. Here experiment again comes into its own: behavioural or psychological experiment consisting in controlled modification of the input (stimulus conditions), and, latterly, physiological experimentation such as the elicitation of behaviour patterns by direct electrical stimulation of the brain.

The attempt to define experimentally the precise role of instinct in animal behaviour is largely associated with the work of Lorenz and his school. At least two popular accounts of some of this work and its underlying theory are available. They are Lorenz's *King Solomon's Ring* and Tinbergen's *Social Behaviour in Animals* (Lorenz, 1952; Tinbergen, 1953).

The behaviour of many animals, and in particular, birds, fishes and insects, appears to be dominated by a highly characteristic patterning which is intimately linked to the biological needs of the species, and varies in precise ways from one species to another. Lorenz finds it useful to draw a distinction between searching behaviour and *consummatory behaviour*. Consummatory behaviour differs from search behaviour in that the components and patterning of such behaviour tend to exhibit an astonishing rigidity and uniformity which is 'species-predictable' and therefore assumed to be genetically determined. The species-predictable components of consummatory behaviour are termed *instinctive movements*.

Perhaps the best known example of such patterning is the mating behaviour of the three-spined stickleback which was first analysed by Tinbergen. During the breeding season the male stickleback undergoes a number of bodily changes of which the most prominent is a change in colour: the underbelly becomes red. Following is a brief summary of Tinbergen's account, slightly paraphrased. The males isolate themselves from the school and select territories which they defend against rivals. Such fighting behaviour is highly characteristic. Even more common than actual fighting is threat, which often proves effective in persuading other males to withdraw. When the male is undisturbed it begins to build a nest. The nest is a hole in the sandy bottom of the pond lined with algae stuck together with a gluey secretion from the fish's kidneys. When the nest is finished, the male changes further in colour, so that his appearance is even more arresting. He will then parade up and down his territory. The females cruise in schools and are at this time distinguishable by a silvery gloss and especially by their swollen underbellies due to the bulky eggs in their ovaries. A male will react to seeing a female entering his territory by executing a characteristic zigzag 'dance', swimming away from the female, then turning abruptly towards it with open mouth, usually stopping just short of the female and turning away again. The female may swim away and escape, and will do so if she is not ready to mate. If she is ready, she stops and adopts a more or less upright attitude. The male then turns and swims towards the nest. The female follows.

At the nest, the male turns on its side, its snout facing the entrance. The female wriggles past and enters the nest. The male prods her tail-base with his snout. After a time, she spawns. The male then enters, pushing her through, and fertilizes the eggs. He then chases the female off the nest and repairs it. Now he will continue to look after the eggs by fanning with his tail to ventilate them. He will stop fanning when the young hatch some seven to eight days later and will guard the young fish. To protect them from possible danger, he will capture them in his mouth when they swim too far from the nest. Within about two weeks, the young will be swimming further, and the male's protective instinct will have begun to wane. He loses his colouring and rejoins the school, while the young form a school of their own.

If such behaviour is called instinctive, it is because of its rigidly determined, yet sequential character. The cycle as a whole falls into a number of distinct phases: establishment of a territory, nest-building, courting and mating, fanning, guarding. Within these phases, there is a close linkage between specific instinctive movements and the stimulus patterns capable of eliciting them. Both the movements themselves and the patterns are largely, and some would say entirely, innate. To take an example, the stimulus for the zigzag dance is the sight of the female in the territory. By introducing artificial models bearing a greater or lesser resemblance to the female stickleback, Tinbergen was able to discover what were the precise characteristics of the visual stimulus to which the male was responding. It appeared that the most important feature was the enlarged belly: where a most lifelike model of a female stickleback without the protruding belly might not elicit the dance, any tubular object of the right size would do so if it had a bulging lower half. Such a perceptual feature, or set of features, is termed an *innate release mechanism*, or **IRM**. In co-operative instinctive activity, the instinctive movements on the part of the one partner often or usually provide the **IRM** for related instinctive movements on the part of the other. Thus the stopping of the female provides the **IRM** for swimming to the nest, the swimming away of the male provides the **IRM** for the following of the female, and so on.

But the **IRM** only functions as such for the period when the instinct is operative. Until the nest is ready, the sight of the female will not elicit the dance; until the female is ready to spawn, the courtship dance will not elicit the readiness posture; and so on.

What has been said so far might appear to suggest that instinctive movements always appear with the same intensity if they appear at all, and that the **IRM** likewise operates in an all-or-none fashion. Both of these impressions would be false. Depending on the strength of the instinct, the animal may react with greater or lesser intensity (i.e. persistence) of instinctive movements in response to more or less adequate stimulation. Where the instinct is strongly operative, even a weak stimulus, i.e. one which lacks its most significant feature (e.g. a silver female without the swollen belly) may still elicit a weak instinctive movement. Conversely, when the instinct is weak, even a fully adequate **IRM** may elicit only a flagging response. According to Lorenz, certain instincts may be so strong in some animals that instinctive movements will be performed in the absence of any stimulation. This phenomenon, admittedly rare and difficult to prove, is termed '*Leehrlaufreaktion*'.

The intensity of an instinct may therefore be measured by the readiness of the animal to respond to a more or less adequate **IRM**. It also determines at least in part the general degree of 'arousal' exhibited in restlessness or 'searching behaviour'. Such intensity is determined partly by the animal's own previous activity (e.g. the courting phase of the mating instinct is initiated by the completion of nest-building), partly by environmental stimuli (e.g. the migratory instinct in birds, which is determined by the length of the day).

Not all the features of instinctive behaviour are entirely innate. Many 'instinctive movements' appear to be uninfluenced by the environment, at least after birth or hatching. But in many cases the **IRM** is only partly determined by heredity and admits of important environmental modification. Usually this sort of 'learning' is very rapid and irreversible. For instance, the following reaction in newly-hatched goslings studied by Lorenz depends on the experience of the chicks immediately after hatching. Such chicks follow the first large moving object that they see. Usually this will be the mother. But by hatching eggs in an incubator and arranging to be present himself when the chicks emerged, Lorenz was able to get them to follow him and ignore the goose. Evidently the learning involved takes place very rapidly. It is irreversible in the sense that a chick that has once started to follow the goose cannot be trained to follow a man or some other animal, and vice-versa. This phenomenon is termed 'imprinting'. It is not confined to release mechanisms but extends to some kinds of instinctive behaviour. For instance, the full song of certain song-birds is partly determined by the hearing of song from birds of their own species or of a related species. Once it has been established, it will not alter (see Thorpe, 1956). Imprinting is often regarded as a form of conditioning. Strictly speaking, it is a form of differentiation', this being a general function of the higher nervous system found also in the conditional reflex. But it differs sharply from the latter in that conditional reflexes are characteristically temporary and modifiable while imprinting is irreversible.

Now generalizations about an entire science are bound to be oversimplifications. Nevertheless, two conclusions seem to be warranted. First behaviour in lower orders is very largely effected by pre-programmed 'instinctive' regulating mechanisms. Second, a consideration of the nature of this pre-programming leads to a theory which is very much closer to the second kind of black box than it is to the first.

In what is perhaps the most useful up-to-date general account of ethology written for psychologists, Hess (1962) draws attention to the hierarchical structure of behavioural organization as envisaged by Tinbergen and others, and to the role of the **IRM** in mediating this hierarchy. Behaviour as a whole is thought of as a function of hierarchical instincts such as the reproductive instinct. The activation of the major instinct by its own appropriate **IRM** (increase in length of day) leads to the activation of search mechanisms at the next level governing the selection of territory, itself conditioned by a variety of **IRM**s (reactions to other males, etc., for outside the reproductive season, sticklebacks swim in shoals). The finding of an appropriate territory in turn facilitates the operation of **IRM**s concerned with fighting, nesting, courting, etc. (Some doubt exists as to whether some components of these behaviours have the character of 'pure' instinctive behaviour, unmodified by the environment.) Below the level of such 'molar behaviour, Tinbergen notes a similar hierarchical organization mediating the control of the swimming musculature and regulated by mechanisms of nervous feedback (corresponding to the **IRM** at the higher levels). Such a hierarchy had previously been observed by Weiss, and Tinbergen proposed that the whole of behaviour could be conceived as a hierarchical schema in which the ethological hierarchy is superimposed over the physiological. An interesting corollary to this is that it seems to imply that whereas the interrelations between behaviours at the physiological levels depend on neuro-muscular co-ordinations, those at the higher levels depend largely on mutual inhibitions (Pavlov's reciprocal inhibition). The whole structure is illustrated in Figure 4.

Inevitably, human psychology is very much more bound up with development and learning than the psychology of birds and fishes. But this does not mean that the regulating mechanisms which have been shown to function in these are irrelevant to human learning. Two of them

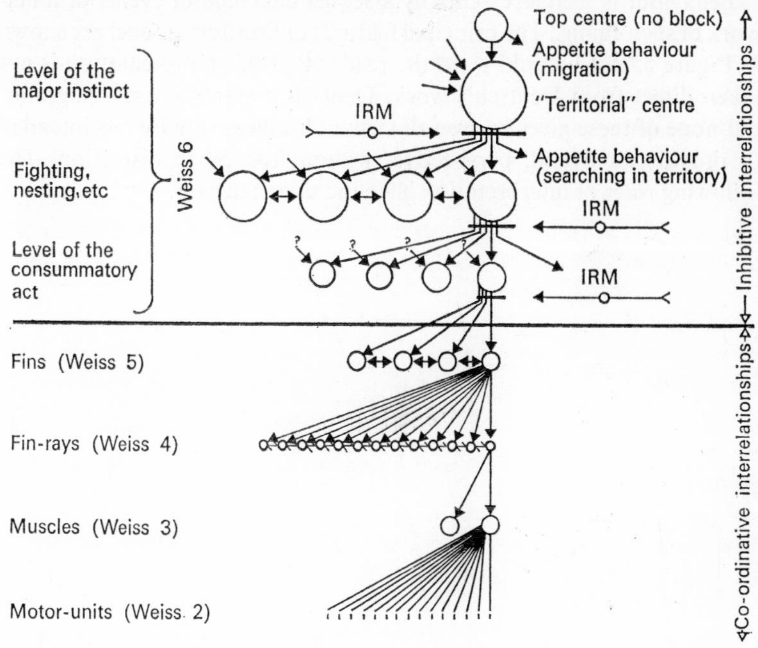

Figure 4. Organization of instinctive behaviour (from Tinbergen, 1950)

stand out: the hierarchical structure of behavioural organization, and the **IRM** mechanism. Both will be taken up again in the next chapter.

We will conclude the present chapter by considering the attempt of a psychologist to provide an account of learning within the context of a mechanism modelled on the **IRM**.

V. STRUCTURAL MODELS OF BEHAVIOUR– II. DEUTSCH'S THEORY OF LEARNING

1. *The Model*

The theory advanced by Deutsch (1960) is probably the most clearly defined attempt at providing a general behavioural model based on cybernetic or structural principles as opposed to **S-R** principles. It incorporates several features which seem to be well-founded in experiment and essential to the sort of model one must take to underlie the organization of behaviour and learning. The suggestions which will be made in the next chapter owe much to Deutsch.

Behaviour is seen as essentially a sequential chain of events or a network of such chains. The principal features of Deutsch's model are shown in Figure 5. But I would warn the reader that this representation is not taken direct from Deutsch's work. Deutsch presents several diagrams, but none of these gives an overall view of his ideas. Figure 5 is intended to provide an overall perspective, without too much distortion. The following rules of interpretation have the same purpose.

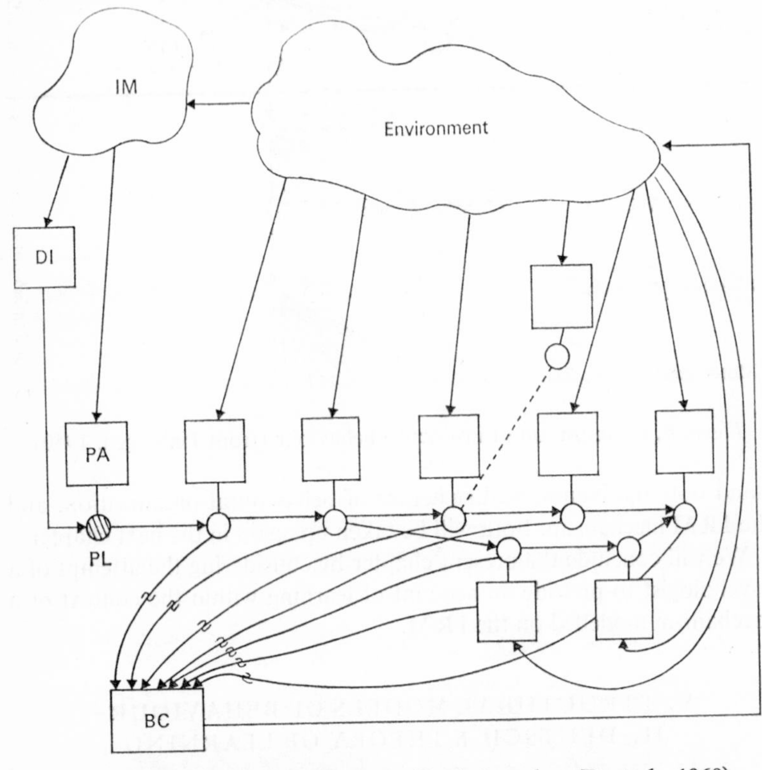

Figure 5. Regulation of behaviour (freely based on Deutsch, 1960)

IM = Internal medium
BC = Behavioural control
DI = Drive initiator
PA = Primary analyses
PL = Primary link

O Link
□ Analyser
------
learnt connexion

(1) A behavioural chain is activated by a specific centre termed a *primary link*. Primary links are responsive to specific physio-chemical

states within the organism, e.g. cellular dehydration in the case of thirst.

(2) Generally speaking, behavioural chains are made up of one primary and several secondary *links*. Every such link is connected to its own specific *analyser* from which it may receive signals. With the exception of the primary link, each link is also connected to the effector (muscular) system of the organism, so enabling it to exercise control over behaviour.

(3) Analysers are responsive to specific cues or combinations of cues in the environment (specific sorts of visual or audial stimulation, etc.) or in the internal medium (kinaesthetic cues, etc.). Such combinations are pre-programmed by heredity.

(4) When a primary link is excited, the excitation is transmitted along the chain of secondary links, exciting each in turn. This transmission of excitation continues until the activity of the primary link is switched off. This will occur when the analyser attached to the primary link begins to transmit sufficiently powerful signals to it. In general, the cues to which this analyser is sensitive correspond to a condition opposite to that which produces the primary irritation (e.g. hydration in the buccal region).

(5) Any secondary link which is thrown into an excitatory state as a result of the activation of the primary link will pass that excitation on to its successor unless it is also being stimulated by its own analyser.

(6) When a secondary link receives excitatory impulses from a primary link and at the same time receives stimulation from its analyser, it ceases to transmit the excitation along the chain to other links more remote from the primary link; at the same time it assumes control of motor output, causing behaviour to vary. The form of this control is quite specific. Motor output is varied in such a way as to maximize the stimulation from the analyser: so long as the stimulation is increasing the direction of behaviour is maintained; any tendency to decrease in impulses from the analyser causes variation. The effect of course is that an animal will 'approach' the source of stimulation (turn and move towards an audial cue, look at and approach a visual one, etc.).

(7) When the stimulation from the analyser is maximal, the link ceases to control the behaviour. In general, before this point is reached, control will have been assumed by its predecessor, i.e. the link nearest in line in the direction of the primary link (since excitation to links more remote has already ceased), due to the activity of *its* analyser (see (6)).

Before considering how Deutsch envisages learning within such a system we have to clarify how the system works so far. The simplest way to grasp it is to imagine a maze with just five distinctive cues from the starting-box to the goal-box: S_1, S_2, S_3, S_4, S_G. The primary link is activated by hunger, and its analyser is responsive to cues originating ultimately in a replete stomach; therefore it will transmit excitation until such a condition has been reached. The analyser to the first secondary link is responsive to cues from the last stimulus, $\mathbf{S}_G$. But the animal is still at the start of the maze and is not receiving such stimuli; therefore the excitation is transmitted to the second secondary link corresponding to **S**, etc. The last link in the chain is the one whose analyser is responsive to $\mathbf{S}_1$. Therefore the animal approaches $\mathbf{S}_1$. Before the stimulation from $\mathbf{S}_1$ is maximal, the animal will be receiving cues corresponding to $\mathbf{S}_2$ and to the specific programme of the analyser of the next link to the last. The animal will therefore approach $\mathbf{S}_2$. And so on till it reaches the food. If the animal were to suddenly find itself nearer the goal-box, it would not go back to the start; and if it sees a short-cut it will take it (under (6)).

Let us now consider the additional assumptions which enable Deutsch's model to learn.

(8) Any link will tend to take over behavioural control when it is stimulated by its own analyser even though it is not at the same time receiving excitation from a primary link. But unless it is receiving such excitation, adaptation is rapid, which means that the link will be active only for a short period. While it is active it will function exactly as it would when in an excitatory state, i.e. it will cause behaviour to vary in such a way as to maximize the inpute from its own analyser. This rule taken by itself will account for curiosity or what Pavlov called the what-is-it reflex.

(9) When a secondary link controls behaviour under (8) and immediately thereafter the control of behaviour is assumed by another link which already forms part of a behavioural chain and which is in an excitatory state due to stimulation from a primary link (as well as its analyser), the first link will tend to attach itself to this chain. On a future occasion excitation from the primary link will tend to pass through the established link and be transmitted to the hitherto independent link. The more frequent the couplings the firmer the association. This, of course, is a sort of conditioning principle.

(10) If a secondary link ceases to control behaviour having maximized the input from its analysers (under (7)), but this is not followed by excitation in the link which is proximal to it (in the direction of the primary link), the association is weakened in this part of the chain. This is obviously a sort of principle of inhibition which will account for the fading of connexions that have ceased to be adaptive because they no longer correspond with the environmental conditions (cf. Ashby's definition of ultrastability referred to in the footnote on p. 167).

Taken together, these three rules show how behavioural chains may be formed in the first place and how behaviour in the model will tend to be adaptive, i.e. the model will learn. We cannot within the confines of this chapter give a complete account of Deutsch's theory. But there is one additional feature that needs to be mentioned, since it transforms the model from a machine which will only do one thing (or one thing per 'drive' condition, as defined by the primary links) to one which might show infinitely varied and complex behaviour. This is the principle of 'links in parallel'.

(11) Suppose two or more behavioural chains to have been established having one or several links in common: the result will be either a fork or a detour, or a hierarchy, as in Figure 6.

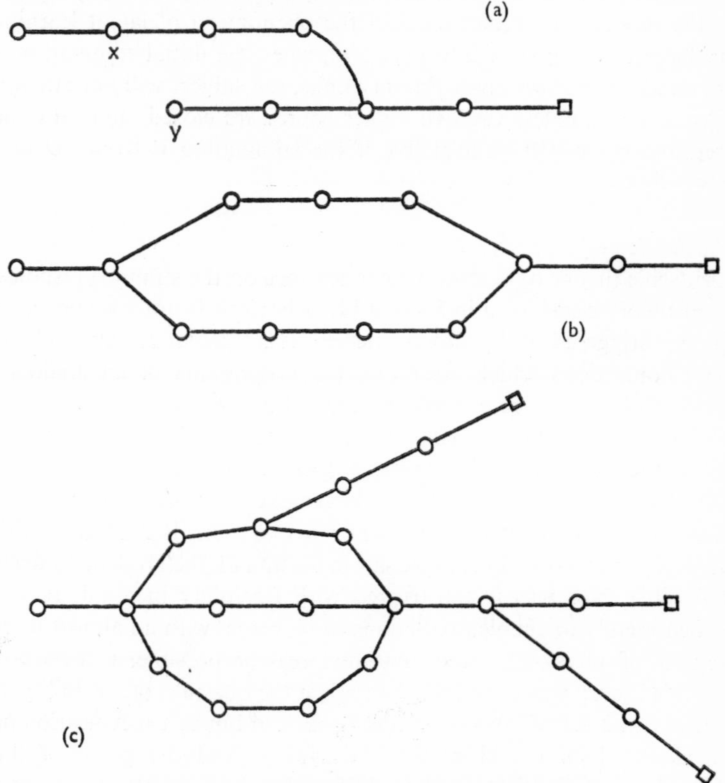

Figure 6 (a) *A fork;* (b) *a detour;* (c) *a hierarchy* (free adaptation from Deutsch, 1960)

These are more complex structures which would inevitably arise in the control mechanism of Deutsch's 'animal', given an even moderately complex environment. It is hypothesized that the excitation from a primary link will be divided among the available alternative chains in inverse proportion to the number of intervening links. For instance, in Figure 6(*a*) the excitation at x will be to excitation at y as 2 : 3. There are two corollaries. (*a*) Where two links are simultaneously and equally stimulated by their analysers, the link which is receiving more excitation from the primary link will control behaviour. (*b*) It will also exert an inhibitory effect on the other (cf. Pavlov's principle of reciprocal induction). Note that there is nothing in the theory which specifies that behavioural junctions will become effective only if both sequences have been built up under the same motivation, or primary link. This means that the model will predict most of the phenomena of latent learning considered in Chapter 1. In Figure 6(*c*), when the initial stimulation is from either of the two lower primary links, the subject will not attempt the lower route unless the two higher routes are closed, and only the uppermost route will be available if the stimulation is from the first primary link.

2. *Evaluation of Deutsch's Theory*

Deutsch's theory represents a clear advance on the stimulus-response type of theory considered in Section II. Behaviour is not a sequence of responses triggered off by stimuli; instead it is the manifestation of the precise connexions which constitute the programme of an analogue computer which is more or less continuously active and responsive both to an internal medium and to its external environment. The pre-programming of the analysers and the precise specification of the variation of control by the link are both features which make the model more credible. It is the sort of model which one has to invoke if one is concerned with problems of feasibility. For, as we saw in Section II, the Hullian model is not feasible. Nor was it constructed with feasibility in mind. It was intended merely to enable predictions to be made, with an almost utter disregard of physiology and anatomy, real or possible. Conversely, Deutsch's theory was constructed with just the question of feasibility in mind, not as a set of laws to *predict* behaviour but as a specification of connexions which would *produce* behaviour. And the proof of the pudding is that following his own specifications, he was able to construct a sort of mechanical rat linked to a restricted environment, which could learn to run a 'maze' in the predicted manner.

Still on the credit side, Deutsch does not assume, as did Hull (and Tolman) that all available response tendencies to every impinging stimulus will be simultaneously effective (if not in response then in the determination of intervening variables). This means that his model admits of the possiblity that two or more links will be realized by different but partially overlapping combinations of the same set of neural elements, and the same for analysers. And this is a necessary condition for feasibility, given the infinite variety of behaviour and the restricted number of cells in the brain. Again, Deutsch's model does away with purely notional (unrealizable) intervening variables such as the drive stimulus and the fractional response with its attendant fractional stimulus. Deutsch's conception of the mechanism underlying the activation and de-activation of behavioural sequences by separate analyser centres which in turn are responsive to specific chemical conditions existing in specific parts of the

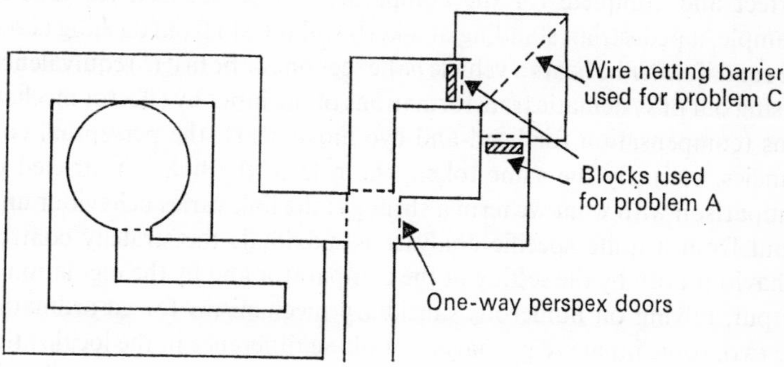

Figure 7. Insight and Ignorance in Rats (from Deutsch, 1960, p. 110)

body is closely modelled on what we know of the regulation of hunger and thirst behaviour by structures in the hypothalamic region of the brain (Rosenzweig, 1963). Finally, Deutsch's model not only accounts for certain apparently insightful behaviour in an economical way, but also predicts correctly some failures of insight, at least in the rat. Thus, in the maze shown in Figure 7, Deutsch and Clarkson predicted correctly that if rats were trained to run all three paths, two short paths leading to the same food-box and a long path leading to a different food-box, then putting a barrier in one of the short paths would have the effect that the rats would tend to try the alternative short path rather than the long path.

On the other hand, they also predicted that if the rats were allowed to run all the way to the food-box only to find their way barred by a wire netting (with the food accessible via the other short path), they would 'foolishly' switch to the long path.

Deutsch's model has the advantage that it is sufficiently precise to allow predictions to be made. It can be confirmed or informed, both by experiment and by reasoning out its implications. This is partly a disadvantage for what is after all a very limited model. Because it is inadequate. I have four main criticisms.

First, the conception of the individual link with its specific analyser is too restricted. It does not allow for perceptual learning. Each analyser is pre-programmed. The difference between the concept of the comparator in Chapter 4 and Deutsch's analyser is that the former is intended to allow for two sorts of equivalences: (*a*) equivalences arising from 'redundancy of input', which means that perception does not need to be perfect and complete for the comparator to be satisfied (to take an example, a pedestrian standing at a kerb will refrain from dashing across the road if *either* he hears a vehicle *or* he sees one *or* both); (*b*) equivalences arising out of systematic transformations of the input by effector mechanisms (compensation for head and eye movements, the perceptual constancies, etc.). By the same token, the role of the link is restricted by comparison with what we term a strategy: the link varies behaviour until input from a quite specific analyser is maximal; the strategy controls behaviour both by the setting of the comparator and by the regulation of output, relying on numerous subsidiary mechanisms for co-ordinating the two, some innate (e.g. analysis of phase difference in the localization of sound), others learned, (e.g. the perceptual constancies). True, like the link, the strategy relinquishes control when certain conditions (which cannot be so generally specified) are satisfied.

Second, the model as it stands cannot account for even the simplest learning of discriminative cues, i.e. learning to do one thing if a given cue is present and another if it is absent, or, even more simply, learning an inhibitory cue once a pattern has been established, e.g. in classical conditioning: light alone = positive; light + sound = negative. In other words, due to the over-specification of the analysers and links, there is no provision for differentiation. Nor for that matter can one see how the model would generalize. If these criticisms are correct they are very damaging indeed, since it is not difficult to see that generalization and differentiation are quite essential to adaptive learning. What is more, like the phenomenon of conditioning itself, they form part of the experimental bedrock upon which further experiment and theory must build. And, sad to relate, there isn't all that much bedrock about in our science.

Third, the specification of a single kind of link connected to only one analyser and with highly circumscribed connexions to other links precludes the existence of strategies, learning sets, or behavioural hierarchies. And this, as we have seen, is one of the principal strengths of ethological theory. There are hierarchies only in the limited sense of Figure 6(*c*), that where several behaviour routes exist, a definite order of preference will emerge. There is no hierarchy in the further sense of a successive determination of behaviour through a series of decision procedures each of which contributes to a narrowing of alternatives by selective facilitation of its successors. Consider a straight-forward concept attainment situation of the type devised by Bruner *et al.* (1956) (see Figure 8). We will

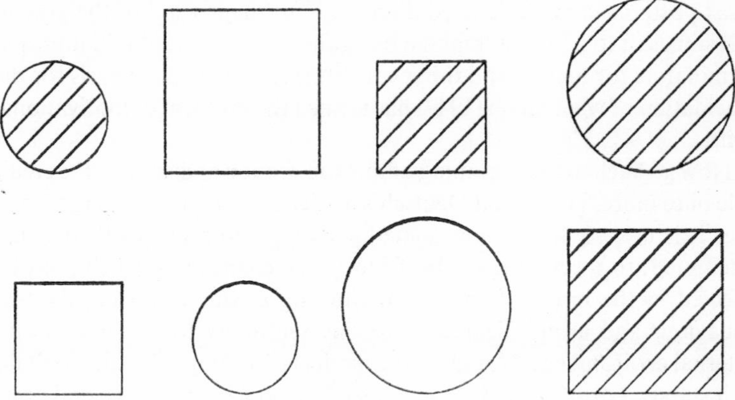

Figure 8. Array of examplars featuring three attributes: colour, shape and size. The subject chooses a figure and is informed whether or not it is an instance of the concept. His task is to 'discover' the concept in the minimum of choices

suppose that the task is to discover the correct basis for classifying negative and positive instances. If there are two attributes, colour and size, each with two values, then the decision to use these attributes rules out, e.g. position (left or right); the decision to use only one rules out the combination of both; the decision to use colour rules out size; red rules out blue. Much the same process must be held to underlie the operation of learning sets in Harlow's discrimination learning experiments using monkeys (see Chapter 5). This is not a high-faluting elaboration of behaviour peculiar to primates possessing language. It is pretty fundamental to the organization of behaviour at a fairly low level. A corollary weakness of the model is that since all links are equal, any link can be connected to any other. In other words, any stimulus can serve as a cue for any behaviour. In an absolute sense this is probably true (it is also Skinner's claim). But it is not at all true in a relative sense. It is quite false to suppose that all cues will be adopted with equal facility. To suppose this would be to ignore all the evidence adduced by ethology concerning innate releaser mechanisms, and all of Broadbent's evidence for the existence of selective filter mechanisms regulating the admissibility of input (cf. also Stott's appraisal strategies in Volume III). Incidentally, the central problem for education is the provision of optimal conditions for selection of the right cues.

Fourth, Deutsch's treatment of motivation is much too limited. We must postpone a more detailed discussion to Chapter 6. For the present it is sufficient to point out that the recognition of the role of initiators and terminators for hunger and thirst constitutes an inadequate basis for the elucidation of what Hebb (1949) has termed the problem of motivational drift.

Now go back to the beginning of this sub-section and go over the credit side once more. To say that Deutsch's model is inadequate does not mean that it is useless. It attempts something which no previous theory had attempted: to specify the kinds of functional connexions which must be effected in the brain of an animal showing a wide range of adaptive behaviour and a high degree of specific sensitivity to its internal and external environment. Not all of the model is for scrap. Since it won't do as it stands, I propose, in Chapter 4, to dismantle it and use several of its parts in a Heath Robinson construction of my own. True, this is not a proper theory or a proper model. It is held together with bits of string and what can only be called faith. But its purpose is not so much to explain as to indicate the general lines which a true explanation must take, and above all to offer some idea of how the parts are likely to fit together. This I regard as a proper pedagogic pursuit, since one can hardly expect a learner to be interested in parts if he cannot be given at least some idea of where they belong and what they do.

VI. SUMMARY

We began by formulating a distinction between the structural and the mechanical approach to behaviour. One of the principal shortcomings of the latter is its failure to take account of the physiological implications of behavioural theory. Psychology cannot make up its own physiology in an armchair, but also physiology cannot interpret its own observations without the intervention of psychology. Structural psychology is concerned with the elaboration and the experimental validation of models of behavioural regulation. Its concepts need to be consistent not only with the behavioural evidence but also with the physiological evidence. Without presuming to trespass on the ground of physiology, the structural approach shares with physiology the concept of the brain as a computer mediating the regulation of behaviour. While the former corresponds to the engineer who seeks to establish the structure of its components and their mode of operation, the latter is more like the applied mathematician who tries to discover the programmes which enable it to do what it does.

It was argued that Hullian theory fails to provide a satisfactory model and should therefore be discarded as an explanatory device. At the same time it was conceded that the descriptive generalizations established in the light of this theory need to be respected – even though their generality may be more limited than is sometimes supposed. Criticisms of Hullian theory were mainly concentrated on the concept of the stimulus, but the conception of behaviour as a sequence of **S-R-S-R** was also shown to be misleading in its analysis of response.

Ethological theory was shown to offer at least two important pointers for psychology: (1) the analysis of behavioural regulation seems to imply a hierarchical structure; (2) the concept of the **IRM** offers a more plausible model for the relations between organism and environment than the Hullian stimulus.

Deutsch's theory of learning, relying as it does on a mechanism similar to the **IRM**, offers a first approximation to the regulation of behaviour through learning. But it was argued that the model is too simple to be more than a starting-point for the understanding of human behaviour.

REFERENCES

ASHBY, W. R. (1960). *Design for a Brain* (second edn.). New York: John Wiley.

BROADBENT, D. E. (1958). *Perception and Communication.* Oxford: Pergamon.

BRUNER, J. S. (1957). On perceptual readiness. *Psychol. Rev.* **64**, 123–152.

BRUNER, J. S., GOODNOW, J., and AUSTIN, G. A. (1956). *A Study of Thinking*. New York: John Wiley.

DEUTSCH, J. A. (1960). *The Structural Basis of Behaviour*. London: Cambridge University Press.

HARLOW, H. F. (1944). Studies in discrimination learning by monkeys: I. The learning of discrimination series and the reversal of discrimination series. *J. Gen. Psychol.* **30**, 3–12.

HARLOW, H. F. (1949). The formation of learning sets. *Psychol. Rev.* **56**, 51–65.

HARLOW, H. F. (1961). The development of affectional patterns in infant monkeys. In Foss, B. (ed.), *Determinants of Infant Behaviour*. 75–97. London: Methuen.

HEBB, D. O. (1949). *The Organisation of Behaviour*. New York: John Wiley.

HESS, E. H. (1962). Ethology. An approach toward the complete analysis of behaviour. In Brown, R., Galanter, E., Hess, E. H. and Mandler, G., *New Directions in Psychology*. New York: Holt, Rinehart and Winston, 157–266.

HILGARD, E. R. (1958). *Theories of Learning* (second edn.). New York: Appleton-Century-Crofts.

LAWRENCE, D. H. (1949). Acquired distinctiveness of cues: I. Transfer between discriminations on the basis of familiarity with the stimulus. *J. Exp. Psychol.* **39**, 770–784.

LAWRENCE, D. H. (1950). Acquired distinctiveness of cues: II. Selective association in a constant stimulus situation. *J. Exp. Psychol.* **40**, 175–188.

LEWIN, K. (1936). *Principles of Topological Psychology*. New York: McGraw Hill.

LORENZ, K. Z. (1952). *King Solomon's Ring*. London: Methuen.

MACKAY, D. M. (1962). Theoretical models of space perception. In Muses, C.A. (Ed.). *Aspects of the Theory of Artificial Intelligence*, 83–103. New York: Plenum Press.

MACKINTOSH, N. J. (1965). Effect of attention on slope generalisation gradients. *Brit. J. Psychol.*, **56**, 87–93.

MILLER, G. A., GALANTER, A., and PRIBRAM, K. H. (1960). *Plans and the Structure of Behaviour*. New York: Henry Holt.

MILLER, N. E. (1959). Extensions of liberalized S-R theory. In Koch, S. (Ed.), *Psychology: A Study of a Science, Vol. II: General Systematic Formulations, Learning and Special Processes*, 196–292. New York: McGraw-Hill.

NEWELL, A., SHAW, J. C., and SIMON, H. A. (1958). Elements of a theory of human problem solving. *Psychol. Rev.* **65**, 151–166.

OSGOOD, C. E. (1953). *Method and Theory in Experimental Psychology.* London: O.U.P.

PIAGET, J. (1950). *The Psychology of Intelligence.* London: Routledge and Kegan Paul.

ROSENZWEIG, M. R. (1963). The mechanisms of hunger and thirst. Chapter 3 in Postman, L. (Ed.), *Psychology in the Making.* New York: Alfred Knopf.

SCHUTZENBERGER, M. P. (1962). Random assembly of logical elements. In Muses, C.E. (Ed.), *Aspects of the Theory of Artificial Intelligence.* New York: Plenum Press.

SKINNER, B. F. (1938). *The Behaviour of Organisms.* New York: Appleton-Century-Crofts.

SPENCE, K. W. (1937). Analysis of the formation of visual discrimination habits in chimpanzees. *J. Comp. Psychol.* **23**, 77–100.

SUTHERLAND, N. S. (1959). Stimulus analysing mechanisms. In *Proceedings of a Symposium on the Mechanisation of Thought Processes,* Vol. II, pp. 575–609. London: HMSO.

SUTHERLAND, N. S., and MACKINTOSH, N. J. (1964). Discrimination learning: non-additivity of cues. *Nature,* **201**, 528–530.

THORPE, W. H. (1956). *Learning and Instinct in Animals.* London: Methuen.

TINBERGEN N. (1950). The hierarchical organisation of nervous mechanisms underlying instinctive behaviour *Symp. Soc. Exp. Biol.* **4**, 305–312.

TINBERGEN, N. (1953). *Social Behaviour in Animals with Special Reference to Vertebrates.* London: Methuen.

YOUNG, J. Z. (1964). *A model of the Brain.* London: O.U.P.

4

The Regulation of Behaviour

I. PERCEPTUAL RECOGNITION AND PERCEPTUO-MOTOR CONTROL

1. *Introduction*

THE QUESTION of the precise limits within which learning can occur in the context of instinctive behaviour is one which continues to divide the ranks of ethologists, and at the same time to provide a focus for much fruitful research. But the chief concern of the present volume is with species in which the part of learning is far from circumscribed, and with one species in particular, one which evinces the greatest variability in directed, purposive behaviour, the greatest sensitivity to modification in its environment, and therefore the greatest capacity for learning.

Two courses seem open. One is to reject the two basic concepts of ethology, the **IRM** and the hierarchical structure of instinctive behaviour. Psychology must then substitute a less structured model for the model proposed by Tinbergen and Weiss. Instead of the intimate union between perception and behaviour implied by the **IRM** mechanism, perception will be seen simply as a function of the reactivity of specialized peripheral neurons to physical stimulation, while behaviour becomes no more than a concatenation of essentially discrete responses. Similarly, instead of the adaptive regulation ensured by the hierarchical structures of instinctive mechanisms, psychology must substitute a pattern of random linkages resulting from external (chance) reinforcement. This is essentially the course taken by **S-R** theory. Over and above the objections already raised to it, we now have the further objection that this would imply a complete discontinuity between the regulatory mechanisms governing the behaviour of lower species and those found in the higher. Moreover the break has the paradoxical character that the latter rely for the evolution of their more varied and structured behaviour on an initial framework which is much more primitive.

The alternative course is to accept that mechanisms similar in function to the **IRM** form the basis of all behavioural regulation. But such mechanisms may differ in their greater susceptibility to modification.

Similarly, structures reminiscent of the hierarchical structure of instincts may be looked for in the programmes of all species. But once again, the programmes evolved by higher species will tend to show greater complexity and greater elasticity. Since this is precisely what has been indicated in our characterization of the second kind of black box, the reader will not be surprised to learn that it is this alternative model which will be explored in the following pages. One aim in this chapter is to bring out some of the more important concepts which I believe to be shared by a majority of contemporary psychologists. A second aim is to produce a working picture indicating a way in which these may be expected to link up with one another in the regulation of behaviour. Such an undertaking is necessarily a very tentative one, and the ideas presented in this chapter should be taken as no more than an approximation. We will begin by introducing a number of key concepts. Chief among these are the comparator and effector systems, the selector link, the strategy, the schema, and the vigilance centre.

2. *The Comparator System*

The essential feature of the **IRM** is that it provides a built-in connexion between a set of environmental cues and the directive to a particular pattern of action. The notion of the comparator system[1] is parallel to this, with the difference that we drop the restriction 'built-in', substituting 'modifiable'. But this does not mean 'infinitely modifiable'. The extent of such modifiability is a function of evolutionary level, while the manner of its occurrence is a problem for scientific inquiry rather than a matter for *a priori* legislation. In human psychology, the concept of the comparator system (and its equivalents) rests on an important distinction between two types of perception: *pictorial perception* and *cue perception.*

Psychologists no less than philosophers are apt to be beguiled by the overpowering impressiveness of visual perception in felt experience. I think both are to some extent the victims of what I would call the painter's illusion. For the painter sets out to reproduce a panoramic view of what his eye can ascertain in his environment and freeze it in a static frame. To the painter's image there corresponds the philosopher's sense datum and the psychologist's 'stimulus' (in its illegitimate usage[2]). (One aspect of the history of modern painting is concerned precisely with the artist's realization of the impossibility of his task. It is a sobering thought that

[1] The term comparator is borrowed from Mackay (1962).

[2] The term needs to be retained for the description of the environment from the point of view of the observer or experimenter, see pp. 134–7.

the artists anticipated the psychologists by something like seventy-five years, while the philosophers have not caught up yet.) Now there seems little reason to doubt that visual perception in the human adult possesses something of the continuity and informational richness contained in pictorial reproduction (although much less than is supposed). But there is every reason to suspect that these qualities of visual perception are very largely the product of learning and that they depend far more on inference than they do on the actual transmission of neural impulses from the retina.

Be that as it may, in so far as visual perception provides an input for the regulation of behaviour, there is evidence that the process involved is bound up with the organism's reactivity to specific cues in the *pattern* of retinal stimulation.

We know rather more of what these cues are in the frog than in the human being: movement, contrast, curvilinearity, size (Maturna *et al.*, 1960). The point about such cues is that they are not direct derivatives of the impact of light rays on the retinal surface but the outcome of analogue computations of relational patterns contained in spatio-temporal sequences of these. So far the findings of modern physiology agree with the theory of Gestalt: perception is relational. But Gestalt psychology went on to ascribe to primary perception the products of the interaction of such relational cues, even to the extent of formulating general 'laws' to determine the perception of the resultant 'wholes'. The observations of ethology compel us to be more cautious: the determinants of behaviour in perception ('wholes') are best thought of as no more than aggregates of such relational cues. The strength with which specific behaviour will be elicited is a function of the relative weighting of each cue in the programme (of the **IRM** or the comparator) and of the extent to which input from the receptor matches the specifications. (For instance, silver colour has less weight than belly shape in the constitution of the **IRM** for the nuptial dance of the stickleback, and the dot over the letter *i* has more weight than its height in the constitution of the comparator setting that enables the reader to recognize it.) The laws of the whole should be seen not as primary facts of perception but as products of learning (Piaget, 1961).

If we cease to confine ourselves to visual perception and consider the characteristics of audial or tactile perception we see at once that in these modalities the cueing role is obvious while pictorial properties are almost entirely absent. There is little to correspond with the visual field in audial perception. The essence of the 'cocktail-bar phenomenon' is that we barely hear the babble of conversation that surrounds us as we bend our ear to our interlocutor so that all else recedes into a background of 'noise'. Functionally, the presence of the noise enables us to switch our attention if something intrudes on our hearing which stimulates our interest. But even this is not a separate mechanism from the comparator settings which enable us to hear our original interlocutor. It is no more than an expression of the general vigilance mechanism which ensures that at any given moment there may be several comparator settings above threshold, and some will be above threshold at all times (danger-signalling cue-combinations).

In tactile and other modalities (taste, smell, proprioception) pictorial perception drops out altogether. For instance we do not feel the pressure of our clothes.

Thus it is postulated that there exist within the brain structures which are differentially sensitive to cues or combinations of cues. Taken together, these constitute a network out of which certain combinations will be sensitized at any given moment. The system is, therefore, sensitized by the organism and at the same time sensitive to the environment. The sensitization is most probably more or less rather than all-or-none (although this does not preclude the possibility that changes in sensitization are quantal). In other words, very strong cues which match well-established recognition patterns in the system can penetrate the 'filter' (the term is taken from Broadbent, 1958) constituted by the existing settings of the system. And so on. This is the basis for the switching of attention. The comparator system is therefore, a detector system which enables a match to be realized between the programme of the organism and the input of the environment.

Since the comparator system (unlike the IRM as conceived by Lorenz) is capable of modification, it is further assumed that existing combinations can give rise to new combinations, following a mechanism which is very close to classical conditioning (see section IV). Finally, a consideration of the gradual co-ordination of sense modalities (Piaget, 1953) leads to the further conclusion that as a result of such co-ordinations the comparator mechanisms come to function increasingly as a unified system, i.e. that there is cue equivalence as between, e.g. visual and audial cues, so that cues arising out of one may eke out or substitute for cues arising out of the other. This of course is what happens if we follow a text in a foreign language while a native speaker is reading aloud, or in following a musical score, or simply in crossing a road, or, significantly, in the combined use of lip-reading and residual hearing by the deaf. However, it is not assumed that this cue-equivalence is there from the start. On the contrary, the observations of Piaget lead inescapably to the conclusion that initially the comparator system is composed of discrete entities existing within the several sense modalities.

3. *The Selector Link*

It has been said that the comparator system is differentially sensitized from moment to moment. The selector link is to be thought of as a switching mechanism governing this sensitization. The link (a term taken from Deutsch, 1960) has two functions: the setting of the comparator system and the control of the effector system. A word about each, beginning with the second.

It seems to me that it is unwise and premature to make any very specific assumptions about the control of the effector system by the selector link. However, a few preliminary statements can be made with a good measure of probability. First, that the link is selective in its control of the effector system just as it is selective in its control of the comparator system. In other words, the simplest link is the reflex, being a specific innate reaction to a specific innate cue (such links exist even at the spinal level). Second, unlike the spinal reflex link, the selector link controls voluntary muscular behaviour. Third, its control of behaviour is perceptuo-motor rather than purely motor; an important function of the selector link is the control of perceptuo-motor scanning movements (of head, eye, and body). Fourth, there is a close co-ordination between the comparator and effector systems, mediated partly by infra-structures at the level of the spinal medulla (muscle spindle and Golgi neuron circuitry, see, e.g. Granit, 1965),[1] but partly by more central (and less well-understood) co-ordinations, such as those which underly the stability of the visual field. Fifth, the effector control may consist in:

(i) a delimited programme of behaviour, e.g. an arm movement, not involving any comparison with the input to the comparator from the external environment;

(ii) the execution of behaviour designed to bring about a modification of input to the comparator (and from the comparator to the link), e.g. to

[1] The muscle spindle is a smaller muscular structure parallelling the main contractile muscle but enclosing a nervous capsule. The spindle moves with the main muscle, causing the nerve to fire when the muscle is stretched. But the tension of the capsule can also be varied independently, so that contraction can be regulated by the spindle setting. Contraction of the muscle is recorded by impulses in the Golgi neurons, which therefore oppose the spindle action, preventing over-contraction. The whole mechanism subserves the adjustment of muscular tension in movement and rest.

further specify the input for the purpose of decision-making (switching control to another link, as in scanning and identification);

(iii) the execution of behaviour which will serve to maintain certain relations in the comparator within limits, while at the same time constituting a modification of the relations between the organism and the environment, e.g. tracing a line (see above, p. 67). We will assume that all of these functions exist, and that they may be mediated by different links, or different combinations of links.

The simplest mechanism would be that envisaged in (i). It is a delegation of control without necessary return to the initial link. The maintenance of continuity and direction in behaviour is assured only by the fact that the comparator system is always active, so that the termination of the given behaviour will invariably result in the inception of some other behaviour (by the activation of some other link), and frequently the behaviour will be functionally related, due to the fact that the overall sensitization of the comparator system is not simply a function of the immediate link, but of the strategy and schema to which this is connected (see below).

(ii) is a control mechanism which pre-supposes feedback. The continuation of behaviour is not left to chance, or to the pre-sensitization of the system as a whole, but is dependent on the reception by the link of precise information from the comparator system. The passage of control to the next link is then mediated by the connexions between links – these being set by the strategy and schema. Often, but probably not always, the link will be acting as a switching device, in the sense that the next link to be activated is a function of the information received. Consider the behaviour involved in studying the signposts at a road-fork – or in glancing at a door to be opened (which may have a handle, in which case the handle may be one of several sorts, or no handle, in which case it may be a push or a pull or either) – or in scanning a telephone directory for a subscriber when we know his surname and his address and his exchange but not his initials: we look down the page for the exchange code; having alighted on a 'possible', we check on the address; if this fits, we note the number, if not we revert to the scanning. (ii) is the type of control mechanism envisaged by Miller, Galanter and Pribram (1960). (See pp. 182ff.)

(iii) is a more complex mechanism involving the simultaneous activity of two or more sub-strategies, and hence of more than one line of links: behaviour is therefore, under a kind of dual control.

Let us now consider the relation between the selector links and the comparator system. With regard to the latter, it was postulated that there exist within the nervous system structures which are differentially sensitive to combinations of cues. It was further postulated that these are sensitized by the organism and at the same time sensitive to the environment. It is now postulated that both processes are mediated in the first instance by the selector link. In the first case, the activation of any given selector link operates so as to lower the threshold for the activation of one or more such recognition structures within the comparator system by the environmental input. In the second, the activation of such a recognition structure when the related link or links are not centrally activated leads to their activation, and therefore, mediates the possibility of change in the direction of behaviour. Both mechanisms have also been envisaged by Deutsch (see Chapter 3, Section V). The second is clearly a more complex relation, subserving Pavlov's what-is-it reflex, and intimately connected with the

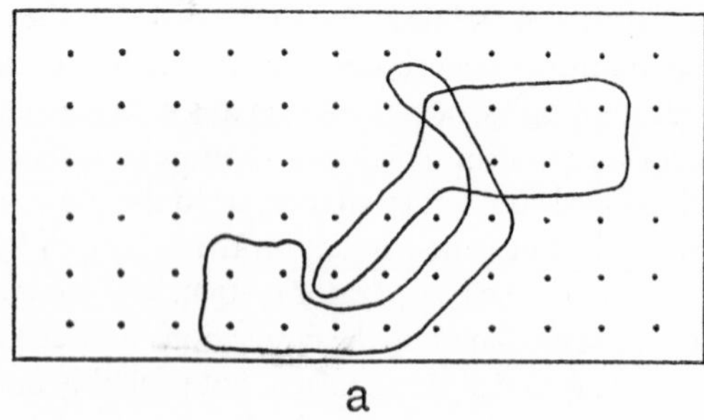

a

(a) Partially overlapping loops

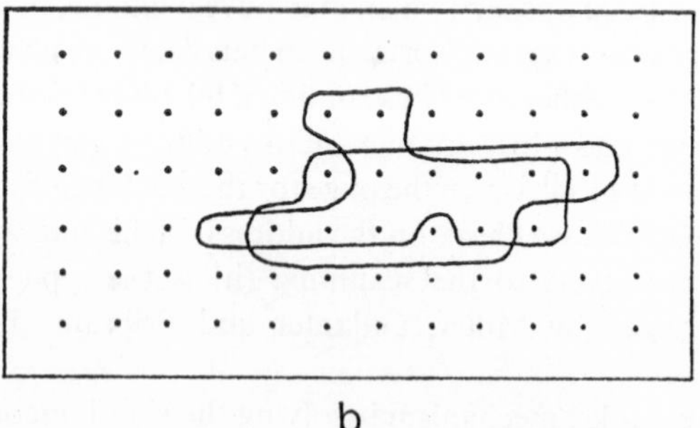

b

(b) Largely overlapping loops

Figure 1. Diagrammatic Representation of Cue-Combinations in the Comparator system.

sources of behavioural motivation. We must reserve its partial elucidation until we have considered the nature of the strategy, the schema, and the vigilance system. Its complete elucidation is of course beyond my competence. But what is meant by the first?

The simplest way of conveying what is intended is to represent the comparator system by an array of dots as in Figure 1. Each dot represents a cue. Any combination of cues may then be represented by a closed loop enclosing some combination of dots. The dots need not be adjacent. The specification of the link could be a single such loop. Perhaps it is in the case of certain simple conditional or unconditional reflexes. But this is only the limit case (just as the limit case for the loop is the loop which encloses only one dot). But any combination of loops can be represented by a Venn-diagram. Two such cases are of especial importance.

The first is the case of two or more non-overlapping or only very partially overlapping loops both of which are sensitized (Figure 1a). Such an arrangement conveniently represents two kinds of situation: equivalent information and alternative information. Equivalent information is provided by the inscriptions '*hommes*' and '*messieurs*', '*exit*' or '*way out*', and so on. But the equivalence of recognition structures is not confined to symbolic material. Are you sitting comfortably? Then stand up; take two paces forward and one to the left; then resume your seat. Now repeat the process, but this time do not turn round to look at the chair. If you have not cheated it is ten to one that in the first case you glanced at the chair before sitting and in the second you felt for it with your leg: the visual cues provided by the edges and corners of the chair and the pressure cues provided by the edge of the seat are equivalent. The alternative information situation is analogous: '*ladies*' and '*gentlemen*'; '*way out*' and '*no exit*'; '*push*' and '*pull*'. Again, the cue combinations are not necessarily symbolic. It just so happens that using symbolic cues enables one to evoke the situation for the reader without going into a long rigmarole. It will not have escaped the reader's attention that '*push*' and '*pull*' are very similar cue combinations. This is not an exception but more often the rule in the case of alternative loops. But it does imply that the sensitization of the two loops is likely to involve an inhibition of the common portion (which contributes nothing in terms of information).[1]

[1] That alternatives have much in common is simply an expression of the unity of opposites. There is nothing very profound about the unity of opposites. It is simply a condition of all structure, of the structure of the world and of the structure of our apprehension of it. Opposites are defined as such in terms of a structure or substructure, and their unity merely reflects their sharing in the structure. The only

The second type of diagram (Figure 1b) represents two largely overlapping loops, only one of which is sensitized by the link. In this case the input will be assimilated to the link which is sensitizing (and to the strategy and schema concerned) and not to the alternative represented by the inhibited loop. And this will occur in spite of the fact that the only cues in fact provided by the environment are those common to the two structures. To take an example, the symbolic combination I3 is recognized as the letter B in a sequence of letters and as 13 in a sequence of numbers (Bruner, 1957). Thus it is clear that the sensitization of some structures involves the inhibition of others. Indeed inhibition is almost certainly more important in the regulation of behaviour than sensitization (the lowering of thresholds in differential sensitization may itself be an inhibition of inhibition). Also, it is apparent that the interaction between regulatory mechanisms and input to the comparator system in no way implies that the information conveyed to the latter must always be maximal, before control is shifted to another link. On the contrary, the reference of behavioural control to the comparator system by the selector link always entails some uncertainty, whether temporal or spatial, with respect to the transmission of control to the next link: temporal meaning when the next step in behaviour is to be entered, spatial meaning which it is to be. Therefore only so much input is required to the comparator system as is necessary to reduce that uncertainty to manageable proportions (allowing decision with respect to 'space' or time).

4. *Regulation via the link*

The selector link is taken to define a set of combinations in the comparator system together with a programme of action for the effector system. At the same time it is supposed that the carrying out of such a programme modifies the comparator system, or else the subject would be unable to distinguish between changes in input resulting from his own movements and those which are attributable to movement or change in the environment. In other words, one must allow an interaction between the comparator and effector systems.

---

interesting feature is that one cannot reflect on the unity without entering a higher structure (meta-structure). Just as the three sisters in *Alice in Wonderland* could not draw treacle from the treacle-well so long as they were in the well. Logical reasoning is not mere behaviour. It is dependent on a monitoring. Actually, on a monitoring of behaviour which is itself contingent on a monitoring of primary, sensori-motor behaviour (see Section IV, and Volume II, Chapter 8).

A corollary to what has been said so far is that besides the feedback implied by the link-effector-comparator triangle, we recognize the operation of proprioceptor feedback mechanisms operating at more peripheral levels, and allowing the effector decisions to control action.

The conception of the comparator system is not consistent with its identification as the set of peripheral receptor organs, viz. the retina, the

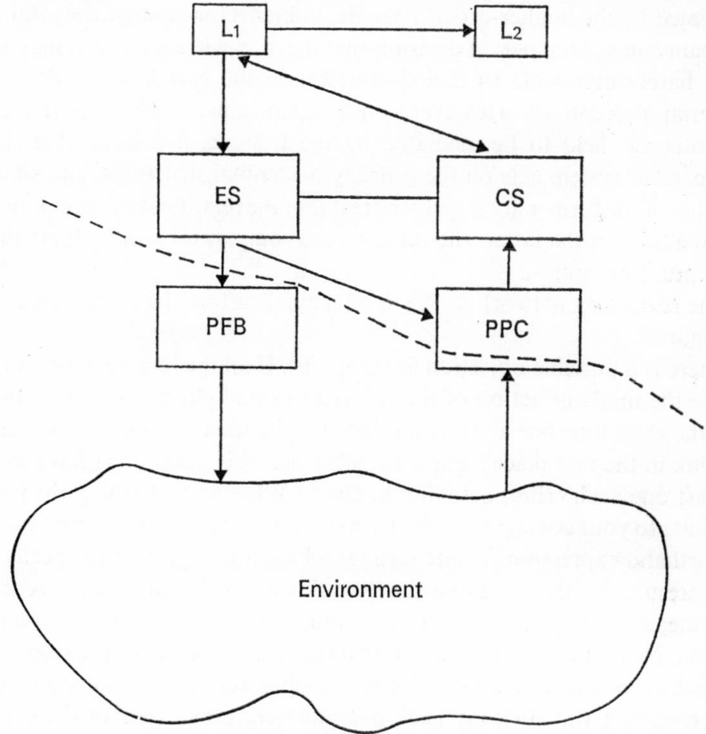

Figure 2. Diagrammatic representation of the Link-Effector-Comparator triangle.

L_1, L_2 = successive links
ES = Effector system
CS = Comparator system
PFB = Physiological feedback mechanisms
PPC = Primary perceptual centres.

The broken line marks an approximate, and probably shifting, boundary between areas of exclusively physiological concern and areas which are the joint concern of physiology and psychology.

basilar membrane, skin receptors, etc. In other words, the comparator system must be thought of as a function of more central structures in the brain, perhaps of what are sometimes called the perceptual association areas (e.g. Hebb, 1949). Peripheral receptor structures, together with their projections in the brain (primary visual, auditory and sensory areas), may be thought of as mediating pictorial perception, in so far as this exists. At any rate, such activity must provide the background for the scanning mediated by the 'higher-order' triangle, link-effector-comparator. But it probably plays little part in decision-making, and what is more, it may be only barely accessible to consciousness (see the earlier discussion of pictorial perception). However, once again, since such activities as focusing are held to be mediated by the triangle, it follows that the comparator system acts on the primary perceptual structures, and since the cues of the former are largely the result of the relations between points of excitation in the latter, the input to the comparator will be from the perceptual structures.

The regulating network at this level may, therefore, be represented as in Figure 2.

There is a possible objection at this point. If all the link achieves is to define the mode of action of the comparator and effector systems, and if at the same time one allows that these two interact, then why postulate the link in the first place? The critic who asks this question (I have met at least one such critic) is saying in effect: What sort of reality do you attribute to your concepts? Is the term 'link' to be taken as no more than a shorthand expression for the settings which it is supposed to specify? And presumably the same questions would be raised later with reference to strategies and schemata. Indeed the link can be thought of as a simple schema. Now of course I have to admit that the evidence for the selector link is less conclusive than that for the comparator and effector systems. Nevertheless I will stick my neck out (not very far in view of the consonance of the ethological evidence, and the fact that the link itself was Deutsch's invention and not mine), and contend that the link does represent a real structure (set of structures) in the brain. And the reason is very simple. What we are trying to do is to arrive at an outline of a cybernetico-psychological analogue of the way the brain works in the regulation of behaviour, and not to write down a list of descriptive 'laws', i.e. empirical generalizations *à la* Thorndike, about the effects of this regulation. An analogy: All of the information contained in the card index of a library is contained in the stacks and the shelves and the books to which it refers. Yet no one in his senses would think of running a library without an indexing system. The same principle would hold for the engineer who wished to construct a hardware analogue for some part of the system being described. The link not only specifies other parts of the system in the verbal description. It must do so 'on the ground' – or something must. And once this is granted it is difficult to resist the implication that it is the selector link (and not its settings of other structures) which is the proximal element of higher-order structures mediating the transition from one segment of behaviour to the next, i.e. of strategies and schemata. Moreover this would be a particularly elegant way of handling things, since it means that the link can be active in certain circumstances (intervene in the setting up of a train of connexions) even though its connexions with subsidiary structures are inhibited. We can sort through or reshuffle the index without interfering with the books. Even more relevantly, a computer programme can set up connexions in the machine with reference to subsidiary programmes or routines which are referred to by name. The machine merely checks to see that the routines exist when setting up the connexions of the main programme; it does not enter the routines.

5. *Direction in Behaviour: the Comparator as a Filter*

It is a commonplace in psychology to recognize the existence of a directional or purposive character in behaviour. It was rightly recognized by McDougall as criterial of the behaviour of organisms when contrasted with the reactivity of inert matter. Tolman's work may be thought of as an attempt to find a place for this directionality while still retaining an orthodox experimentalist **S-R** approach. Hullian psychology is more inclined to set its face against the concept of directionality, treating it as more apparent than real, being no more than the historical by-product of the reactivity of non-directional intervening variables. Cybernetics may be defined as the study of control systems. To it we owe the concept of feedback.[1]

[1] All that is meant by feedback is that some part of the output of a machine is re-directed in such a way as to modify its input. The simplest examples are the thermostat and the governor. In general a system having feedback is one whose output tends to be stable: any large deflexion is self-correcting. Ashby (1960) has introduced the concept of an ultra-stable system. Broadly speaking, an ultra-stable system is one whose feedback system is of sufficient complexity to enable it to adapt to new conditions of input, i.e. to new sets of relations among its several inputs. Given such change in the 'parameters' of the system, the machine reacts, not by maintaining the same output, but by establishing a different one, which is nevertheless stable. A stable system has a single set of outputs, which are stable, but it is restricted as to its input. An ultra-stable system has a family of such sets of output, all of which

Directionality is a property evinced in the behaviour of systems which possess feedback of a sufficient complexity. Cybernetics enables one to pass from the recognition of directionality and its description to its explanation. Psychology becomes very largely a study of decision processes instead of a study of responses. Of course this does not mean that we now know all the answers. We know very few. But we are looking for a different kind of answer.

The triangular system constituted by the selector link, the comparator system and the effector system is really no more than a partial (and very general) representation in cybernetic terms of Piaget's conception that all behaviour involves the assimilation of the environment to a schema. Piaget conceives of the schema itself as a hierarchical system (see next section): i.e. any schema may include sub-schemata which are themselves schemata. Deutsch's concept of the link therefore corresponds to the irreducible schemata at the foot of the 'pyramid'. Now translating Piaget into this kind of language does not result in confusion (like the attempts to render Piaget in terms of S-R theory by Berlyne, 1960b, 1962 and Stevenson, 1962). For the idea that the regulation of behaviour is based on a network of equivalences and non-equivalences among combinations of signals lies right at the heart of Piaget's own thinking.

But the advantage of this kind of representation is that it enables us (at least some of the time) to use a more materialist language in place of Piaget's own which oscillates between the mentalistic and the purely formal or logical. Therefore I think it brings out more clearly the relation between psychology as the study of the structure of functional relations implied by behaviour, and physiology as that of the physical basis which enables them to be realized. Also (though the reader may dispute this) I find one is compelled to be fairly precise about what one is saying, even when this means sticking one's neck out, instead of lapsing into a language so vague that one is apt to delude oneself and one's reader that something worthwhile has been said when in fact what has been offered amounts to no more than a side-stepping of the issues: something which sounds convincing but which depends for its persuasiveness on connotation, where explanation must rely exclusively on denotation.

A second advantage of this mode of representation is that it compels us

---

have a stable form, and is therefore less restricted as to its input. It follows that there are degrees of ultrastability. The implications of these in biological systems, from the virus, through bacteria, coelentera, to the lower and higher vertebrates are discussed by Young (1964, Chapter 18).

to reconsider the relation between perception and behaviour. Which is why the concept of the comparator system as a filter system is fundamental to this account. The present exposition is derived from the ideas of Bruner (1957), Mackay (1962) and Broadbent (1958). Recognition mechanisms in the comparator system are pre-set so that it is sensitive only to a restricted number of patterns at any one time. Such a view is contrary to a number of computational hypotheses (Sutherland, Dodwell, Deutsch) and the analogue devised by Taylor, all of which are described and discussed by Young (1964). For they appear to imply that the receptor centres in the visual cortex are equally sensitive at all times to any of the recognition patterns of which they are capable, each of which, if it were realized (as a result of the computation of relations between point-inputs from the retina) would trigger off its own innate or learned response.

Recent experiments carried out by Neisser on the mechanisms of visual search lend further support to the present sort of view (Neisser, 1964). After a (relatively prolonged) training, a subject can achieve an impressive speed when required to scan an array of random letters and pick out a given one, e.g. the letter K. The speed of performance far exceeds his speed of reading. However, if he is required to pick out either of two letters (say K and L), he eventually achieves an equal rate, even though his task has been doubled. The same result is found when the number of letters to be scanned for is extended to as many as ten, or when the task is o pick out the names of animals from an array of random words.

There are many issues in perception which are less central to our analysis, so that one can afford to leave questions open without affecting the thesis as a whole. One important issue concerns the initial specificity or generality of the cortical pathways involved in perception. This is a question discussed by Sutherland (1959). Whereas Hebb (1949) outlined a theory purporting to show how, starting from a complete indeterminacy in the action modes of cells in the visual cortex, precise connexions with particular classes of retinal input might be developed as a result of learning, resulting in precise 'meanings' (recognition of shapes, etc.), Sutherland advances a number of arguments in favour of a greater initial specificity in cortical centres. Although the pattern-recognition models of Taylor (summarized in Young, *op. cit.*) and of Rosenblatt (1958) are based on the generality hypothesis, the present writer still leans towards Sutherland. Such a view would seem to be supported by the 'innate releaser mechanisms' studied in ethology, as well as by the existence of nerve fibres in the optic nerve of the frog which are responsive to quite specific properties of the retinal input (e.g. contrast at boundary, movement, curvature), being those which have special significance for survival (identification of prey in the form of insects). (Maturna *et al.*, 1960.)

A third problem concerns the precise way in which the feedback system ensures the harmonious interaction of perceptual recognition (in **CS**) and perceptual control (in **ES**), and forms the subject of Mackay's discussion already alluded to. Its treatment far exceeds the scope of this chapter. For we are concerned with the interrelations of the various functions involved in the regulation of behaviour rather than with the detailed analysis of any one. While this is certainly not a very high level scientific pursuit, I believe it to be a justifiable pedagogic one.

6. *Channel Identification*

It is only in the psycho-physical laboratory that subjects are required to maintain a fixed position, to focus their gaze on a prescribed point, and to report on their perception of stimuli that may appear on the periphery of the visual field. Both animals and human beings, as they go about their ordinary business, are constantly shifting the direction of their attention, moving about, altering the direction of their gaze, turning their head in the direction of interesting sounds, and so on. The effect of body, head and eye movements is to minimize the irrelevant stimulation and maximize the relevant. However, in the case of auditory perception, listening, a second effect is to synchronize the phasing of the messages arriving at the two ears. Even if two messages are of equal volume the listener can identify the one he is listening to and exclude the other. This suggests that quite apart from the filtering of irrelevant stimulation which is achieved by maximization of the relevant, one ought to look at the part played by localization of the source in maintaining the direction of attention. Starting from considerations such as these, backed up by a wealth of experimental evidence dealing with the amount of information which the listener is required to handle and its timing, Broadbent was led to develop a 'filter theory' to interpret the use of informational input in the regulation of behaviour (Broadbent, 1958).

Broadbent's thesis is very close to that which is being advanced in these pages, and the several references to it made already underline my indebtedness to him. However, there is a difference in emphasis which is important enough to warrant a word of comment. Our own thesis is that the filtering of input is achieved by the pre-setting of the comparator system as a result of which it is predisposed to the recognition of privileged cue-combinations. Broadbent's theory places far greater emphasis on the identification of the source of stimulation. Starting out from a consideration of communication systems in general, he is led to pay attention to the important part played by the multiplicity of *communication channels.* In engineering contexts, a multiplicity of channels may be achieved either by having several wires, or by using different wavebands for different messages. Biology achieves a similar result principally by providing us with a variety of sensory receptors. In the former context, any specified listener is interested in one channel only, and a filter system is included to unscramble the complex of information arriving at the receiver, and then to decode it, so as to relay to each listener only that which interests him. In the biological context, there is only one 'listener': the subject whether animal or human who must adapt to the relevant input from the environment. Therefore the biological subject must include a sub-system which enables him to 'channel into' the channel which he requires.

The simplest way of distinguishing between channels is that some are visual, some are auditory, etc. But this is not the only way. We have already seen that the source of sound can be identified by the phase relations between the two ears. A message coming from one direction may be thought of as arriving on a different channel from one coming from another. This is the 'cocktail-bar phenomenon' already referred to. Again, where the two messages consist of speech, the fact that the speakers have different voices may enable the system to assign them to different channels.

Does this mean that one can only attend to one channel, or only to one channel at a time? Clearly not. Broadbent adduces a great deal of evidence to show that one can attend to several: for instance a subject can perform a multiple-choice response to a visual signal (press the appropriate key when a light of a given colour is flashed) while carrying on a conversation. But there are limits to this. And these appear to derive mainly from the time-relations between them and from the amount of information handling which they require. In particular, listening to speech does not involve us in enormous amounts of information to be handled because by and large we know what is coming by virtue of the syntactic and semantic constraints of language. Listening to a stream of unrelated words is much more of a job in terms of the information to be handled (see Volume II, Chapter 6). Speaking very roughly, Broadbent's argument in 1958 might be summarized as follows:

(1) Where several kinds of stimulation are impinging on a subject, his normal mode of reaction is to tune into the relevant channel, so that information from that channel passes the filter. Information from other channels may or may not, depending on the state of general vigilance.

(2) How much stimulation the subject can cope with depends largely on the amount of information handling which this entails. Where the transition probability of a given cue-combination (my term) is high following on its predecessor, the amount of information involved is less. Therefore, the subject will be able to cope with more.

(3) Given a high state of general vigilance, and two or more sources of stimulation which, when taken together, do not exceed the information-handling capacity of the subject at any one time, the subject can cope with both. Moreover, in reacting to situations of this kind, the subject normally identifies the channels involved and this identification assists him (*a*) in processing the information that he retains and (*b*) in discarding appropriately if more is offered than he can cope with.

This last point is sufficiently interesting to warrant an illustration. In a classical experiment Broadbent (1954) found that when two sets of three digits were presented simultaneously to separate ears (piped by separate tubes from a twin-track tape-recorder), recall in successive order (i.e. all stimuli in one ear followed by all stimuli in the other) was superior to recall in alternating order (LRLRLR), although the latter order more nearly reflected the original presentation. It looks as if the incoming stream of signals is first identified by its channel of origin and stored accordingly in immediate memory, so that when the subject is required to repeat the list, the ear-by-ear order corresponds to that in which he 'finds' the material, since this re-ordering has already been done unconsciously.

Thus Broadbent's theory, like the view being urged here, draws attention to the importance of selective mechanisms in perception. Moreover, since Broadbent recognizes the part played by 'transition-probabilities' in facilitating or complicating the task, his account involves factors of pre-selection in respect of content (pre-setting of comparator) as well as in terms of channel.

But there is a difference in emphasis. For Broadbent's original thesis only allowed a secondary role to this factor of content, mainly in determining whether some information had to be discarded or not. Also, where Broadbent accepts 'transition-probability' as a statistical fact, external to the model, and influencing its operation, the account given in these pages accords to it a central role, and it is supposed that the machinery itself must include it: the pre-setting by the link.

A number of experiments illustrate that such pre-setting does play an important part in the ordering of information as it arrives. Thus Gray and Wedderburn (1960) used the same technique as Broadbent's (simultaneous messages to two ears), but arranged the stimuli so that a relation of meaningful transitions could be achieved by taking stimuli alternately from the two ears: e.g. **L** EX, **R** 6; **L** 2, **R** TIR; **L** PATE, **R** 9, – where, by crossing from ear to ear, the subject could extract the word EXTIRPATE and the three digit sequence 629. These authors found that subjects who were asked to attend to meanings and group them were just as good at recalling the material as those who were asked to group them according to the channel on which they had been received. Subjects who were given no specific instructions were more liable to group by meaning than by channel.

Treisman (1960) carried out an ingenious experiment to determine whether what I have called the pre-setting factor can overcome the channel factor. The inputs to the two ears consisted of continuous word sequences. These were graded in their degree of transition-probability from second-order approximation to English to narrative text.[1] The subject was required to listen to and shadow (repeat) one track only (left ear or right). But the two texts periodically jumped from one track to the other. In other words, he might be following a text and then suddenly have to follow 'rubbish' while his original text was continuing in the wrong ear – or vice versa. It was predicted, and found, that errors occurred precisely at the nodal points: words from the wrong ear intruded when they completed an anticipated association (jump *from* text) and not when they did not (jump *to* text).

Broadbent and Gregory (1964) accept the implications and offer a revised filter model which comes nearer to the present version. In Treisman's experiment, the tendency to recognize the word from the passage is characterized as a 'response set', i.e. a set to make a particular type of response (when shadowing), as opposed to the 'stimulus set' to tune in to a favoured channel. Both are allowed to play a part. However, the use of these terms is questionable. The subject cannot make the shadowing response unless he has perceived the stimulus. I have urged that the terms 'stimulus' and 'response' are useful only when applied to the operations and observations of the observer. They only confuse when extended to account for the operations of the subject.

The view presented here is not far from Broadbent's revised filter theory, and has the advantage that some account is taken of the mechanism

[1] Starting from a given word, you take the next word following in some sentence, then take that as your starting point and find the successor in a different sentence, etc., see Miller and Selfridge (1953): this yields such sequences as '*singing men and then it was jumping in the tree is idiotic idea of almost there*'.

governing the pre-selection of cue-combinations. On the other hand, Broadbent's work demonstrates quite clearly that the identification of channels does play an important part. I have tried to imply this kind of regulating mechanism by the interaction between comparator and effector systems. Channel identification may be a learned strategy governing the settings of the effector system (which is partly perceptuo-motor), and one which is usually effective in ensuring that the input to the comparator will provide a match to its pre-setting. But it seems to me that this is probably secondary to the pre-setting and not the principal mechanism. In particular, one must not forget that both for human beings and for animals, given a certain level of perceptual learning, the comparator system often acts as a unified system, so that there are cue-equivalences which cross the boundaries between sensory modalities (looking and listening when we cross a road), let alone those between channels within the same modality.

II. SCHEMA AND STRATEGY

1. *Introduction*

One of the possibilities considered in the last section was the activity of a relatively independent link mediating an isolated functional unit of behaviour. But from the point of view of the regulation of complex behaviour a great deal more interest must attach to cases involving the connected and sequential activity of several links, as in the model proposed by Deutsch. Moreover, it was argued that a fuller account of behaviour regulation in higher species is likely to entail the recognition of hierarchical structures parallelling those found by Tinbergen in the organization of instinctive behaviour. And in point of fact those who have tried to deal with the problem more searchingly do suggest such hierarchical structures (Piaget, 1950, Miller, Galanter and Pribram, 1960, and compare Skinner's functional operants, Skinner, 1953).

There is little to be gained from multiplying concepts of speculative validity. Nevertheless, I find it difficult to give an outline of the sort of view which I believe to be shared by a good many psychologists today without having recourse to two concepts which are partially overlapping. The first is the concept of strategy, a term borrowed from Games Theory to denote a line of behaviour (cf. Bruner, Goodnow and Austin, 1956; Piaget likewise makes use of the concept on at least one celebrated paper: Piaget, 1957, see Volume II, Chapter 8). Given the notion of the link-comparator-effector triangle, strategies are taken to define sequences of links. They are essentially decision processes or switching mechanisms. Miller *et al.* use the term Plan in a similar sense. The second concept that we require is the schema. The schema may be thought of as a set of co-ordinate and related strategies. The distinction between strategies and schemata will be considered a little more fully on pp. 186ff.

The schema corresponds to the subject's image of the world, i.e. to his expectations. The purpose of this section is partly to show the lines along which such ideas can be handled without necessary recourse to the method of subjective introspection. Because the concept of the schema is a good deal older than that of strategy, we will begin by discussing this. I believe that by far the most adequate statement we have is that of Piaget. We will therefore, begin by considering this, and then show its close relation with the formulations of British psychologists (Head, Bartlett, Oldfield).

2. *Piaget's Concept of the Schema*

The following account is based largely on that which Piaget himself provides (Apostel *et al.*, 1957; Piaget, 1950, 1959). But I have taken the liberty of translating it into quasi-cybernetic terms similar to those of the last section – a translation which, for reasons already given, involves very little modification and practically no distortion:

(1) All of behaviour is schematic. The initiation of any sequence is a function of input either from the internal medium or from the external environment. But such input is always assimilated to a schema; it is interpreted in terms of its relations with previous inputs, and the behaviour that is initiated is itself structured in accordance with the schema.

(2) The assimilation of a situation to a pre-existing schema cannot fully determine the present behaviour, because behaviour is always an interaction with the environment, and the successive inputs from the environment inevitably differ from occasion to occasion. Therefore, the behaviour is varied to meet the requirements of the changed situation. Such variation is termed *accommodation*.

(3) The accommodation does not leave the original schema unaltered. On the contrary, since the schema is no more than a set of 'if . . . then' equivalences and non-equivalences (e.g. if the object is small and movable pull it towards you and rotate it; if it is large and fixed, go up to it and walk round it; either way, expect to see its rear view), the history of its previous accommodations is what determines its present character.

(4) The range of accommodation is limited by the complexity of the schema (the number of 'if . . . then' alternatives which it incorporates), and by its relations with other schemata. To the extent that the schema

does not admit of the accommodation which a valid (adaptive) reading of the situation would require, the assimilation is distorting. (For instance, the child's inability to differentiate sharply between longer, larger, further, etc. leads to a distorting assimilation in judgements of relative length. There is analogous distortion in the child of nine or ten when the 'deformation' of area is assimilated to the transformation of perimeter, Volume II, Chapter 9.)

(5) Since the schema is a set of equivalences implied in a behavioural sequence, the complexity of a schema is not a fixed quantity. A schema may be made up of sub-schemata, and these sub-schemata are themselves schemata. For instance the schema of related behaviours involved in the identification of an object includes the sub-schema of sucking, rattling, banging, pushing, turning, etc.

(6) In any real situation, if the evocation of a schema does not lead to the realization which is required (either by itself, or by some antecedent schema), so that the 'problem' persists, there is a probability that other alternative schemata will be brought to bear on it (cf. the discussion of continued arousal and of novelty in Section III). Such successive evocation of schemata is what contributes to the construction of more comprehensive schemata, incorporating the new with the old.

(7) But there are two limitations to this tendency and to its import. In the first place, the evocation of a schema tends to inhibit that of others insofar as they do not form part of some larger schema. Therefore, the availability of such alternatives must be a function of a variety of factors, e.g. the degree to which the given schema has become automatized and the plasticity (or flexibility) of the nervous system (of the species, and of the individual).

(8) In the second place, the association between the sub-schemata which a larger schema contains may be loose or precise. It is loose when the evocation of the first sub-schema does no more than facilitate a transition to the second. As examples one may take the passage from one form of action to another in the exploration of objects by the child of six or seven months. Or again, there is the oscillation of strategies in judgements of conservation which is the forerunner of the realization of transformations (Volume II, Chapter 8): it is longer, therefore larger; it is thinner, therefore smaller; it is the same pair of objects, therefore the same (as the subject's attention shifts from one set of cues to another). Conversely, when the association is precise, relations among component sub-schemata are governed by strict implication. The actual transition of behavioural control may then be redundant, since the subject anticipates

its result.[1] Such is the case, for instance, when a child who understands the mathematical relations involved reasons in his head $372 - 48 = 322 + 2 = 324$, and takes it for granted that the written method of equal addition would give him the same result. At the level of sensori-motor behaviour, the initiation of a detour behaviour may be adventitious and exploratory (in circling a barrier), or it may be entered as a function of a fully determined 'if . . . then' equivalence, corresponding to the behavioural realization of the spatial equation: $\leftrightarrows \uparrow = \uparrow$.

3. *The Schema in British Psychology*

The term 'schema' is not peculiar to Piaget, for it is also central in Bartlett's treatment of memory (Bartlett, 1932), and Bartlett himself drew heavily on the work of Head. The concept of the schema in British psychology has been subjected to a searching analysis in a series of articles by Oldfield and Zangwill (1942, 1943) and the following remarks are based largely on their discussion.

The concept of the schema was introduced by Head to account for some of the phenomena observed in connexion with the control of bodily movement and the localization of tactile stimulation. The central problem is to discover a mechanism which will account for the fact that one is able to execute correctly a task such as scratching the left ear irrespective of the hand and arm position from which one starts. The actual movements involved are very different depending on the initial disposition of the body. Therefore, the subject must somehow know where the various parts of his body are in relation to one another before he can initiate such a movement. It does not seem at all likely that the movement itself is preceded by a perceptual act of position plotting. And experiment and observation make it quite clear that the initial knowledge is not dependent on visual perception – at least in the absence of brain damage: for what Head noted was precisely that in some cases of brain damage it is so dependent, and the subject is unable to execute even the simplest of movements if the lay-out of his limbs is disturbed by the imposition of passive movement (which he has not initiated and cannot see). Head therefore hypothesized that the intact subject carries about with him an image of his own body, an image which is constantly and automatically set in such a way as to correspond with the actual disposition of his body. Both perception (in experiments on tactile stimulation) and the initiation of movement are referred to such an image. The actual setting of the

[1] The intervention of 'the subject' in this sentence should not be seen as 'the man in the machine': it is no more than the controlling action of the co-ordinating schema.

image at any one time is simply a function of previous events of which it constitutes a sort of cumulative register. The term 'schema' was used by Head primarily to refer to this body-image.

It is perhaps characteristic of the period in which Head was working that he was concerned mainly with the inadequacies of then current theories of (kinaesthetic) perception. The body schema is itself conceived as analogous to a (visually) perceptible datum, viz. the body itself. Bartlett's extension of the concept derives mainly from his treatment of response. For Bartlett, the sort of response that one observes in skilled behaviour, e.g. in playing a stroke in tennis, is essentially schematic. By this he appears to mean that previous responses made in similar situations have become so integrated as to generate a flexible frame of reference which serves as a guide for the present behaviour. But he goes on to insist that the building of the reference frame is an 'active' process, as also is the reference of incoming data to it, and its further modification in present behaviour to conform with the specificity of the present situation. At least a part of what Bartlett is saying, in contrast to S-R theorists, is that the release of a particular fractional component of response, R_i, is not merely or even mainly a function of the immediately preceding stimulus S_i, or of the preceding response component R_{i-1}, but a function of the 'schema' which determines the whole sequence of responses.

Bartlett's treatment of memory shows a similar dual emphasis: first, on the schematic, or 'whole' character of the memory to be drawn on, and second, on the activity of the subject in reconstructing the events out of the faded cues which are recovered. The notion that what is recovered from memory is predominantly a schematic whole is very close to the conceptions of Gestalt psychology. What is novel in Bartlett's treatment is the recognition of the part played by construction in the process of recall. The rememberer reconstructs the sequence in conformity with a flexible schema of the whole, fabricating such details as he cannot recall to eke out the insufficiencies of what he can recover, and is unable to discriminate accurately between that which is new and that which is truly remembered. The assumption of a constructive element in recall permits a coherent treatment of the difference between recall and recognition. In recognition no construction is necessary, so that the possibilities of error are greatly reduced. At the same time all the details to be identified are perceptually present, which greatly reduces the problem of 'access to store'.

Apart from Bartlett's emphasis on response and the active character of behaviour with reference to the schema, he differs from Head in his suggestion that schematic behaviour occurs at all levels of nervous organization, where Head was inclined to limit it to the highest level. In Bartlett's view the difference between lower and higher schemata is essentially one of flexibility. Thus, in the most primitive forms of recall, the subject is able only to reproduce the responses in the order in which they were learnt, e.g. in reciting tables. A higher level is argued by the capacity to 'turn round upon the schema' and select what is required or relevant, irrespective of that order.

4. *The Schema as an Image of Reality*

Probably the chief limitation of Head's concept of the schema is his failure to take adequate account of the role of the subject in its elaboration. Insofar as the schema is limited to the body image, this may well be unnecessary, since it is altogether possible that the mechanisms for its maintenance are largely pre-programmed in the nervous system so that the part of learning is limited. However, since Head also used the term to refer to the subject's ability to extend his body image in handling tools, etc., the question cannot be avoided altogether. By contrast, Bartlett emphasizes the activity of the subject in the elaboration of the schema, but his stress on the role of repeated sequential response in this process leads to considerable confusion. Thus, as Oldfield and Zangwill remark, is one to assume that the subject constantly rehearses the original sequence in the process of its preservation? Or again, since the eventual reconstruction in recall does not lead to the reproduction of the original order, one is led to ask just what is it that 'turns round on the schema'. Bartlett himself speaks of an 'attitude', but the attitude is suspiciously like the little man inside the machine. Finally, if the essential element in the laying down of the schema is sequential repetition, it is not at all clear just how the overall relations embodied in the schema differ from the elementary order relations of its parts.

It is a little unfortunate that Oldfield and Zangwill's self-imposed limitation to British psychology precluded a consideration of Piaget's use of the concept. For this avoids most of the above limitations. From the functional point of view, Piaget's schema constitutes an internalized image of reality, not just of his own body, but also of objects and of their relations in time and space. But it is not something which is innately given (even though the capacity for its construction must be pre-programmed). It is elaborated in the course of his interactions with reality. Here one rejoins Bartlett's emphasis on response and the activity of the subject. However, the principal difference between Piaget's account and that of

Bartlett is that where the latter looks to the repetition of sequences as the source of the elaboration of the schema, Piaget emphasizes its variability, i.e. that the input-output sequences are non-identical but functionally equivalent. Thus, in the final analysis, the schema becomes the set of equivalences implied by the behaviour of the subject – not, of course, in any single sequence, for no equivalences could be inferred from an isolated observation, but in any adequate set of related observations.

5. *Strategies in the Regulation of Behaviour*

While the need to assume some sort of internalized image of reality is intuitively apparent, it is less easy to envisage the way in which such an image or schema may be realized in the brain. We have assumed that the schema involves a co-ordination of related strategies. Therefore, from the point of view of the structural model, it is the strategy which is the more straightforward notion. The strategy has been defined as an organizational structure which determines the sequence in which links will become active in the actual running off of behaviour. It is useful to keep our feet on the ground by referring the model of behavioural regulation to a reference situation. Since we will be concerned with the role of learning in the regulation of behaviour the example is one in which learning is a relevant factor.

At least at the sensori-motor level, there is general agreement that the learning of discriminative cues underlies much of learning. One of the simplest situations is that in which the subject first extends a routine of behaviour by prefixing the sequence with behaviour appropriate to a set of discriminative cues, and then differentiates the behaviour by prefixing the extended sequence with behaviour appropriate to the identification of a further set of inhibitory cues.

Vince provides a neat example of successive discrimination in finches and in tits. The birds were first trained to remove a white lid from a cup to obtain food and subsequently learned not to remove a black lid (for a brief account, see Vince, 1961). The example is useful in that it will enable us to consider both aspects of learning, positive and negative, corresponding to Pavlov's excitatory and inhibitory conditioning. For the present we may consider the regulation of behaviour in the sequence which is assumed to have been already formed at the outset of the experiment. This includes a measure of taming, probably including the adoption of various procedures designed to secure food from the experimenter, e.g. chirping and approach, and a parallel instrumental sequence enabling the bird to secure food from the cup (without lid).

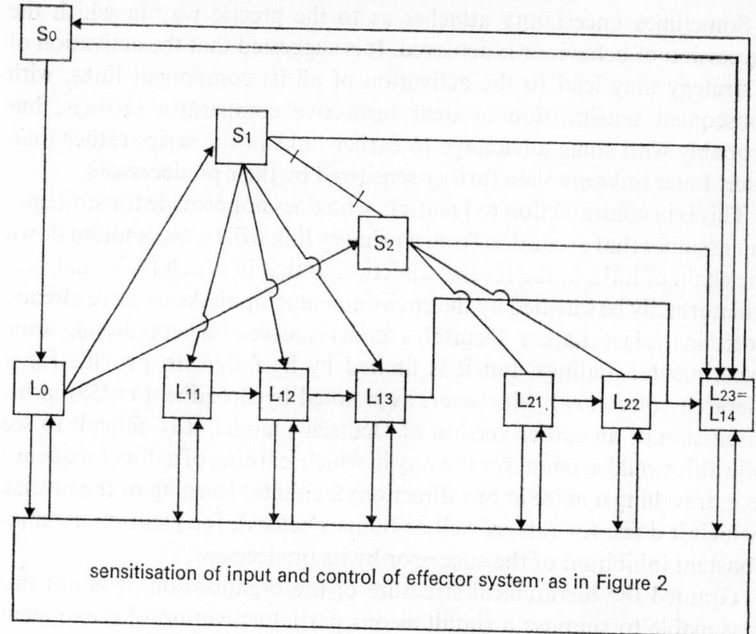

Figure 3. Role of strategies in behavioural control

Taking this situation as our reference point, one way of representing the intervention of strategies in the control of behaviour is suggested in Figure 3.

S_0 is taken to represent the overall strategy designed to secure food. It includes two sub-strategies S_1 and S_2, the former representing securing food from the cup (the favoured sub-strategy, since the experimenter will not normally wish to feed the bird directly when the cup is present), and S_2 represents the more general strategy of securing food from the experimenter. S_0 itself directly controls L_0. This represents a selector link governing the behaviour which determines whether or not the cup is present.

L_0 is therefore a decision link, with alternative outputs. Control passes to S_1 if its comparator settings are satisfied by the environmental input and to S_2 if they are not.

L_{11}-L_{14} represent successive links in the strategy S_1 while L_{21}-L_{23} are links in the strategy S_2: for instance, approach to cup, climbing on it, craning over it and securing food in the first case, and approach to experimenter, leaping at hand, securing food in the second.

Sometimes uncertainty attaches as to the precise way in which the succession of behaviour is achieved. It is suggested that the activation of a strategy may lead to the activation of all its component links, with consequent sensitization of their respective comparator settings, but probably with some advantage to earlier links in the series rather than later. Later links are then further sensitized by their predecessors.

This is in contradiction to Deutsch, who does not provide for strategies but assumes that excitation from a primary link will be transmitted down the chain of links in the reverse direction to that in which their analysers will normally be satisfied by the environmental input. As we have already noted in the last chapter, Deutsch's model is successful in predicting some experimental findings, but it is limited by its failure to provide for a hierarchy of control. Moreover, as is noted by Broadbent (1958) in his discussion of an earlier version of Deutsch's model, it is difficult to see how this would account for the way in which learning of a direct sequence (e.g. travelling a maze in one direction) facilitates learning of the inverse (which it does, for rats as well as human beings), for Deutsch assumes constant inhibition of the successor by its predecessor.

Granted the hierarchical structure of the organization, it is not unreasonable to suppose a simultaneous partial activation of component links by the strategy – in the sense of a lowering of their thresholds, and hence of the thresholds of the comparator settings which they mediate. Most links will be unable to function, i.e. to control behaviour, in the absence of some input from the comparator system, and it is of the essence of this sort of model that the actual control of any link favours assimilation of the input to itself at the expense of any competitors, even within the same strategy. What the present interpretation does allow for is the running off of habitual behaviour with minimal input, as well as the inter-facilitation of links in a common strategy – and hence the organization of schemata. It is important to bear in mind that not all links, and not all strategies, are equally demanding on environmental input. Some, notably general locomotion mediating search behaviour, and, no less important in human behaviour, symbolic representation, are minimally demanding. Few experiments are decisive and the Deutsch and Clarkson result might be 'post-dicted' by the present model just as well, and also, as one of my students observed, by the Hullian r_G mechanism.

6. *Plans*

The present suggestions are not dissimilar to the TOTE concept put forward by Miller, Galanter and Pribram (1960). These writers use the word *Plan* (with a capital *P*) to correspond with what I have called strategies. Like strategies, Plans have sub-plans, which are themselves Plans. Every Plan is of the same form: Test – Operate – Test – Exit (shortened TOTE). This may be interpreted as: test whether certain conditions obtain, i.e. are the cues from the comparator satisfactory; if they are then exit to the Plan next in series or to the higher-ranking Plan; if not operate. Operation may take one of two forms: direct control of behaviour or delegation to a sub-plan. If it takes the first form then the test is repeated and behaviour stays within the cycle until the conditions are satisfied. If it takes the second form then the sub-plan itself (there may be a series of sub-plans) will be of the same form. And so on. The lowest-ranking sub-plans operate exclusively to control behaviour – by definition. But exit from the sub-plan (or from the series of sub-plans) automatically secures re-entry to the higher-ranking Plan.

Figure 4 illustrates the general principle of TOTE hierarchical structure, with a single higher-order Plan and two sub-plans in a series. In practice, it is often necessary to envisage bifurcations in the structure. Applying it to the example under discussion, the sequence might run something like this:

> Is food in bill? – If it is, exit to 'swallow' (same level) – If not, operate: i.e. test: – Is food peckable? – If it is, exit to 'peck' (and back to first unit); if not operate: i.e. test: – Is cup visible? – If not, exit to 'cheep' sub-system; if it is, operate, i.e. test: – Is it near? If it is exit to next unit, i.e. test: – Is it peckable? If not operate, i.e. climb, and exit to higher level (test whether peckable). If, previously, result of 'Is it near?' was negative, then operate (alternative), i.e. approach. Eventually, result will be positive, with exit through the remainder of the structure and eventually back to 'peck-swallow' sequence.

Both the word Plan and its interpretation seem to me to be too rigid, even allowing for the authors' insistence on loose Plans as well as structured ones. My main objection is that the sequence of events in what one might call business-like behaviour is taken as modal and other kinds of behaviour are interpreted by extrapolation from this. The term 'operate', like Deutsch's 'maximize', has an apparent precision which merely serves to cloak over the complex interrelation of perception and effector control. The TOTE sequence brings out the all-important tendency to progressive filtering and coding of the perceptual input by the comparator. But it is not easy to see how the TOTE hypothesis accounts for more or less indeterminate running off of behaviour sequences like the circular reactions studied by Piaget (see Chapter 5, Section II). Is there not some level where behaviour simply occurs, without any precise exit determined by input? And if there is, then do not the same considerations operate to some degree at all levels?

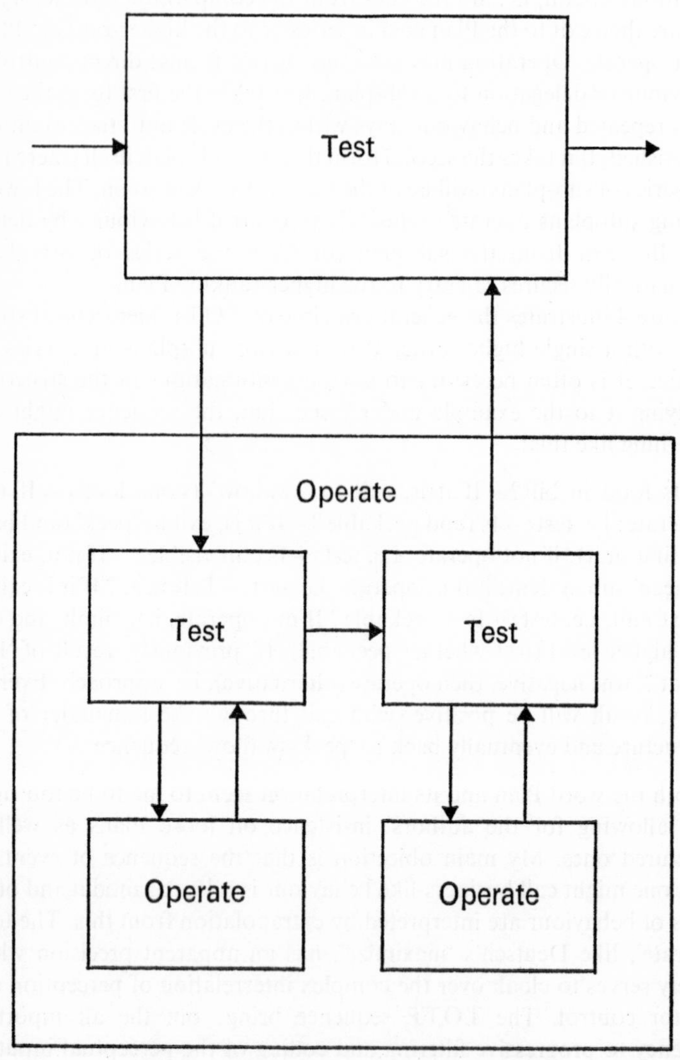

Figure 4. Structure of a hierarchical plan
Based on Miller, Galanter and Pribram (1960)

7. *Simultaneous Strategies*

There is one more point which needs to be brought out in regard to the role of strategies in behavioural regulation. So far we have been concerned solely with unique sequences of actions defined by unique strategies operating alternately or in sequence. However, it will be recalled from the last chapter that the regulation of complex behaviour frequently involves simultaneous controls with respect to its several features. Since this is a ubiquitous feature in the regulation of human behaviour (and probably of a great deal of animal behaviour also) it is worth indicating the general lines along which one would seek to interpret such behaviour in terms of hierarchical strategies.

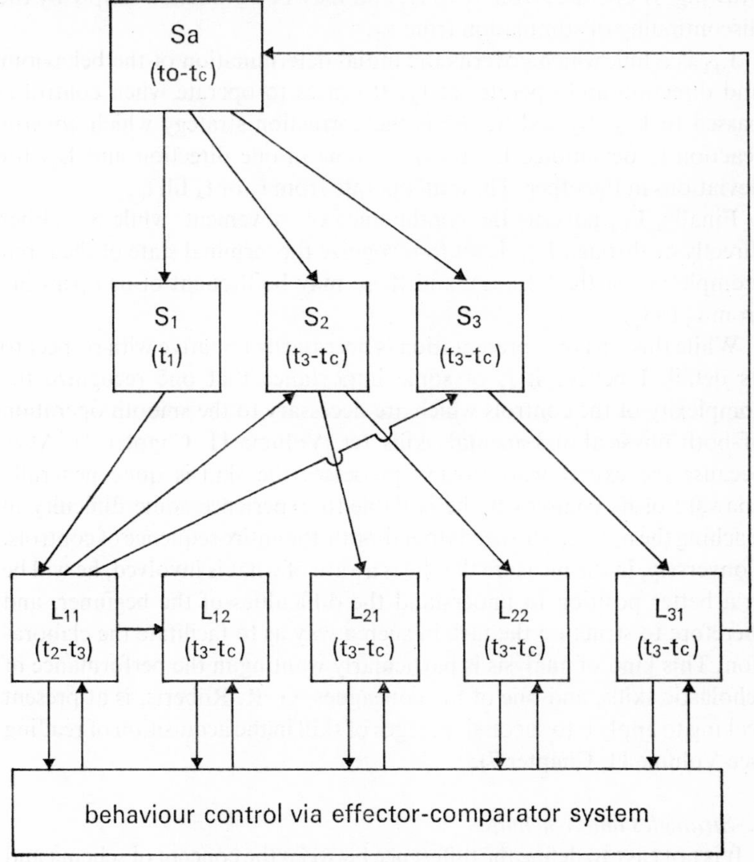

Figure 5. Temporal integration of behaviour

To this end, Figure 5 is introduced as a possible interpretation of the simple example given in the last chapter: tracing a line. In Figure 3, apart from the initiating strategy S_0, the strategies and links were taken to operate either successively or as alternatives. Here we suppose that several will be operating simultaneously. Accordingly, the times over which these strategies may be operative are indicated, with t_0 representing the time at which the behaviour is initiated and t_c that at which it is completed.

S_0 once again represents the overall strategy and operates from t_0 to t_c, being 'switched off' by the input from S_3 or L_{31} (if indeed these are not identical). S_1 is the strategy which initiates and continues the actual drawing. It operates from t_1 to t_c, and may be terminated simply by the discontinuing of stimulation from s_0.

L_{11} is a link which governs the initial determination of the behaviour and direction and operates at t_2. It ceases to operate when control is passed to L_{12}, S_2 and S_3. S_2 is the correction strategy which governs reaction to deviations, L_{21} for deviations in one direction and L_{22} for deviations in the other. These all operate from t_3 or t_4 till t_c.

Finally, L_{12} governs the continuance of movement, while S_3, either directly or through L_{31}, is set to recognize the terminal state of the input (completion of the tracing), and these may be thought of as operating from t_3 to t_c.

While this sort of representation is necessarily tentative with respect to its detail, I believe it is of some importance that one recognize the complexity of the controls which are necessary to the smooth operation of both physical and mental skills (cf. Volume II, Chapter 4). Also, because the expert who already possesses the skill is quite generally unaware of its complexity, he is liable to experience some difficulty in teaching the novice, who needs to elaborate the entire sequence of controls. Conversely, in the measure that he is aware of what is involved, he will be in a better position to understand the difficulties of the beginner, and therefore to structure the task in such a way as to facilitate the elaboration. This kind of analysis is particularly wanting in the performance of scholastic skills, and one of my colleagues, G. R. Roberts, is at present seeking to apply it to successive stages of skill in the acquisition of reading (see Volume II, Chapter 7).

8. *Strategies and Schemata*

It is not easy to define the difference between the concept of schema and that of strategy. Then why have both? The difference is mainly one of emphasis; it is the difference between structure and function. So long as we are describing the actual sequence of events involved in the regulation of behaviour, the language of strategies is quite adequate by itself. However, when we want to describe the connectivity of the various centres which are involved in such strategies, it is more advantageous to use the term schema. The strategy corresponds to the actual operation of the organism at any given time; the schema to its potential for regulated behaviour. The strategy may be likened to the 'flow' of current in any phase of the operation of the machine; the schema is the wiring diagram itself. The strategy corresponds to what Miller *et al.* call the Plan: the schema may be what they call the Image.

Because the schema refers to the potential activation of strategies, its denotation is wider than that of the strategy. The selection of any one strategy within a schema may actually inhibit or exclude that of another; nevertheless their interdependence may be sufficiently complete to correspond to a mutual implication. Since the schema is made up of subschemata and some of these will always be active, it follows that the strategy always corresponds to a schema. To take an example, a rat which has become exceptionally wise with regard to the layout of a maze in the course of prolonged free running in the maze is in a position to take an appropriate route to the goal (or to one of several different goals) irrespective of the point at which it is placed initially. Exactly the same observation was made by Piaget in regard to the spatial organization of an eighteen-month-old child: the child can pick his way freely and appropriately about his home and garden, depending on where he is, where he wants to get to, and what barriers (e.g. closed doors) stand in the way. The schema corresponds to his awareness of the total layout, the strategy to the route which he chooses and the cues which he actually observes in doing so.

There are two corollaries to the above, one of which is epistemological and the other psychological. From the point of view of a description of knowledge and how it is acquired, the elucidation of the equivalences which are implicit in the schemata of a subject at any time constitutes a description of his knowledge of the world, and the study of the way in which such equivalences are acquired constitutes an objective approach to the problem of the acquisition of knowledge as such. In the final analysis, knowledge is not a direct awareness of reality but a set of behavioural implications elaborated in the course of interactions with reality. To ignore the problem of knowledge is to shirk one of the fundamental tasks of psychology. Failure to recognize that the set of behavioural implications amounts to knowledge and exercises a controlling function in the regulation of the course of behaviour amounts to robbing psychology of an essential explanatory tool. Methodologically, of course, one does not study the schema directly – by introspection – but indirectly, by inference from behaviour. This sounds suspiciously like philosophy. But my reply is quite simple: science always implies a philosophy, but the philosophy may be a bad one or a good one. In the case of psychology which is a young science and at the same time deals with the highest organization of matter, the behaviour of man and its regulation, the exclusion of philosophical (or meta-psychological) considerations is likely to lead to bad philosophy.

From the psychological point of view, it is evident that the interconnexions between schemata may be various and overlapping. The set of behaviours which converge on the recognition of particular cues in the context of a variety of strategies defines a given object for a given subject. But these strategies may be very different and the transitions from one sub-strategy to another that they entail may have little in common. If I am looking for a book to verify some elementary point in psychology, then any one of several textbooks may serve, and failing that a set of old notes. But if what I require is something to weight down a collage then only a heavy book will do and it does not matter which, while a brick will serve just as well and a sheaf of notes not at all. Now it is clear that in directed behaviour the transition from one sub-strategy to the next is governed very closely by the settings of a higher-ranking initiating strategy. Conversely, in undirected behaviour the transition from one strategy to the next is only loosely controlled by the higher-ranking strategy ('interest'), and may be largely a function of junctures or intersections of cues at the level of the lowest-ranking strategies, i.e. perceptual similarities and generalized associations regardless of context. Thus the degree of determination of behaviour entailed by variations in strength of the initiating strategy allows a continuum from purposeful behaviour through various forms of play and daydreaming to the apparent incoherence of the imagery of dreams. It does not seem too far-fetched to suppose that individuals differ in the extent to which they can allow free-play to the less directed transitions, by relaxation of control, and yet switch back to more rigorous control, so allowing for the activation of more or less unrelated schemata which can then be integrated into the present overall strategy. For instance, such differences could underlie differences in creativity.

It is tempting, but misleading, to identify the schema with the looser transitions just referred to while reserving the strategy for directed behaviour. All behaviour involves the operation of strategies which vary in their determination, and all behaviour pre-supposes a context of schemata. It is sufficient to recall that the sets of logical implications which Piaget has shown to be characteristic of operational reasoning at the concrete and formal levels do not themselves issue in behaviour (i.e. they are not strategies) but determine the selection of appropriate strategies. Yet there is nothing loose about the mutual implications involved.

It should be added that the schema is taken to represent relations between strategies at every level. It is not a higher-ranking strategy, for corresponding to every node in the regulation of ongoing behaviour (strategy), there are implications representing the intersections of that node with other lines of behaviour (strategies not presently active). In other words, just as there is a hierarchy of strategies, corresponding to various levels in the organization of present behaviour, so there is a hierarchy of schemata, corresponding to functional implications between the possible lines of behaviour at every level. For instance, the schema of an object corresponds to the various lines of behaviour which converge on the input represented by that object. But the object itself may figure only in a minor sub-strategy relative to the main determinant of behaviour: thus, to fetch an object from another room, I have to turn the handle to open the door, to get out of the room I am in. Since I have many behaviours related to door handles, there is a schema corresponding to that object. But it would be nonsense to suggest that this is a 'higher-ranking' strategy relative to the task as a whole.

III. THE ROLE OF THE 'WHAT-IS-IT? REFLEX'

1. *Statement of hypotheses*

The concept of vigilance will be familiar to the reader from Chapter 2. We now have clear evidence that the reticular formation in the brain stem below the thalamus subserves the function of regulating general arousal level (Berlyne, 1960a, Magoun, 1963). In particular, it plays a key role in mediating the transition from waking to sleep as well as the degree of alertness. There is also some evidence that portions of the same structure are concerned with specific arousal, i.e. with the activation of particular schemata. Both the physiological and psychological evidence are well documented in the thought-provoking work of Berlyne.

So far we have been concerned only with maintenance of direction in ongoing behaviour, set off by an initiating strategy S_0. Since such behaviour determines successive settings of the comparator system, it is evident that much of the input from the environment is filtered out by inhibition. By the same token, the activation of a strategy involves the inhibition of irrelevant strategies. But the inhibition cannot be total and continuous from t_0 to t_c or there would be no possibility of learning by accommodation to changes in the environmental input from one occasion to the next. Moreover, while the continuity of behaviour is an obvious fact, it is equally obvious that such concentration is not perfect even when the subject is actively engaged in a task. Sudden changes in input put him on the alert. They give rise to what Pavlov described as the 'what-is-it? reflex'.

Now although we have postulated the necessity for supposing the intervention of a comparator system acting as a filter in the regulation of behaviour, we were not in a position to give any clear account of how it works, beyond the statement that its settings subserve specific recognition patterns. Given the concepts of the schema and the strategy, we can carry the analysis at least one stage further. In terms of the present model, the strategy defines a sequence of favoured outputs for its constituent links, i.e. a passage from one link to its successor (there may be a choice of successor depending on the input to the link). Similarly, the schema defines a family of inputs dependent on the behaviour of the subject, i.e. on the instructions to the effector system. In both cases, the definition must be thought of as partial rather than complete. One may think of the overall schema as the apex of a hierarchy made up of its constituent sub-strategies and sub-schemata while the link itself is no more than the simplest sub-strategy. The activation of this schema rules out all but a favoured sub-set of cue combinations in the comparator, but one which is still fairly large. Successive activation of sub-schemata and sub-strategies has a similar effect on the sub-set. In other words, there is a progressive narrowing of the range of anticipated cue-combinations (favoured by reduced activation threshold) down to the level of the link. But even here the range of possibilities is not completely defined, for the final definition depends on the input. However, because there is partial definition, inputs are recognized, assimilated to the programme, provided that they satisfy at least some of its requirements.

These considerations enable us to hypothesize a little further as to the nature of the 'what-is-it? reflex'. The following seem reasonable hypotheses in the light of the foregoing discussion:

(1) The general vigilance system ensures that the comparator system will not filter out all of the input which is not directly provided for in the

schema that is presently directing behaviour. To take an example, if a person is engaged in reading he is more likely to see the printed characters than irrelevant marks on the page, and he is almost certain to ignore continuous ambient noise (e.g. of traffic), but he will not ignore an alarm bell of even a visual alarm signal.

(2) Peripheral mechanisms within the receptor and comparator systems provide for reactivity to change in input rather than to the absolute properties of input. For instance: sudden movement, sudden noise, etc. At the same time, the organization of schemata and sub-schemata exercises an opposite effect: there is little reactivity to changes in stimulation which are anticipated by the schema. For instance, suppose you are sitting in a railway compartment and engaged in conversation with a friend and happen to glance to the side. Although there may be several passengers seated in the adjoining compartment you barely notice them.[1] But supposing what you see in the adjoining compartment is a horse or a vampire, you are much more likely to indulge in some sort of action.

(3) The passage of information by the comparator to a link which is not a member of the ongoing schema will lead to the activation of that link. (This is essentially what was hypothesized by Deutsch, see last chapter).

(4) Since the link is activated and the link itself forms part of some schema, the activity will not be confined to that link alone but will extend to others with which it is connected through established strategies (behaviour sequences and partial determination of expected input).

(5) Control of behaviour by the interfering schema ceases when the input sequence begins to match the settings of the link sequence. Unless the settings of this intervening schema have disrupted those of the original schema, the previous behaviour will now be resumed.

(6) If the first sequence does not lead to a match, and the input persists, and other strategies and schemata are available (i.e. the disturbing

[1] Glancing from side to side occasionally when engaged in passive, 'cerebral' activity is almost certainly an inbuilt or learnt strategy which facilitates concentration. As in so many aspects of behaviour regulation, the clue to this is contained in the work of Pavlov and Sherrington. Uniformity of stimulation produces local inhibition and if the uniform stimulation is maintained there is a tendency to 'spread of inhibition' to controlling centres, in particular to the central vigilance mechanism. You become drowsy and may relapse into sleep. The tendency to sleep is of course the most universal, although perhaps the least exciting, phenomenon associated with experiments on stimulus deprivation (Solomon *et al.*, 1961). By the same token, the maintenance of general arousal by changes in stimulation probably accounts for the fact that the effect of noise is very often to improve the efficiency of behaviour rather than to reduce it (Broadbent, 1958).

cue-combination partly satisfies these other links, or, alternatively, the link itself forms part of more than one schema), then these will be activated in turn. Taken in conjunction with (5), what this means is that the subject engages in trial-and-error behaviour the effect of which is to reduce the uncertainty arising from the input.

(7) If the input persists and varies without reference to the directing schema, leading to an increase in uncertainty, e.g. by intensification of the stimulus, the subject will engage in behaviour designed to terminate the input: either by flight, or, if this is possible, simply by resumption of the original activity.

2. *Discussion of Implications*

The first four of these hypotheses are entirely consistent with what has been said before. The first is no more than a restatement of the implications of the comparator mechanism, which as we have seen, follows fairly closely the ideas of Broadbent's (revised) filter theory. The third is directly taken over from Deutsch. The fourth brings in the temporal factor which was introduced on page 185. A single link is no more than a more or less arbitrary cross-section of behaviour, so that the assimilation of input to the schema generally implies the sequential activity of one or more strategies. In the measure that a match is to be achieved between the settings of the comparator and the environmental input, it is the congruence of such sequences which becomes decisive. The single link-comparator-effector triangle can be thought of as the limit-case for such sequences (a sequence of one). The second 'hypothesis' is little more than a statement of some of the best-established facts with regard to the operation of the vigilance mechanism.

The sixth hypothesis brings in the concept of trial-and-error. The idea of trial-and-error is of course familiar from the work of Thorndike. But the concept is not limited to S-R theory, and still less to the descriptive and limited version of that theory associated with Thorndike. As Ashby (1960) points out, the very possibility of learning in a system implies that of variation in its behaviour, i.e. of trial-and-error. The term is of course something of a misnomer, since the system must adapt positively to success as well as negatively to failure. Trial and feedback would be more accurate – but 'trial-and-error' has passed into common usage.

Even at the level of formal reasoning (see Volume II, Chapters 9 and 10) a subject cannot resolve a problem without trial-and-error. The point is that at that level successive trials imply an organization of behaviour in terms of a complex schema of interrelated strategies. As a result of these interrelations, the information from any given trial is greater and affects others more. To take an example, in trying to resolve the factors which determine the period of oscillation of a pendulum, the subject who systematically varies the weight suspended from the apparatus while retaining invariant both length and height of release finds that its contribution is negative. However, the negative information ('error') enables him to eliminate the factor in the remainder of his search. The informational possibilities of experimentation have been pre-determined by the directing schema so that they can be stored and retrieved in a compact way (see Volume II, Chapter 9).

Thorndike himself recognized that trial-and-error behaviour is not random but reflects the previous experiences of the subject (see p. 8). The developmental analysis of Piaget which is (broadly) followed in these pages consists essentially in an attempt to elucidate the ways in which learning and development contribute not merely to quantitative changes in trial-and-error, e.g. that more behaviours are tried or that different behaviours are sampled (although both propositions are partly true), but also to changes in its structurization: the lines of behaviour that are engaged on are different in kind, and the resulting input has different effects on succeeding trials, depending on the structure of the schema of which they form a part.

Hypotheses (5) and (7) introduce a new element into the present analysis, at the same time bringing in a view of motivation which will be further elaborated in Chapter 6 of this volume and in Volume III, Chapter 4.

Hypothesis (5) states that the 'what-is-it? reflex' is precisely what it says: an inbuilt determination of behaviour which leads it to function in such a way as to reduce uncertainty. Moreover, it sets forth a terminus to the resultant behaviour: as uncertainty is reduced, so the direction of behaviour alters.

It should be stressed that the 'what-is-it? reflex' cannot be considered something peculiar to higher levels of evolution. On the contrary, it is the mechanism which enables learning to occur and it underlies the search behaviour of organisms at all levels. Moreover, as Pavlov pointed out, it has two poles: it is at once investigatory and defensive. Recent investigations by Harlow and his collaborators into the origins of social behaviour in young monkeys illustrate this bi-polarity most clearly. The infant monkey is placed in an empty room to which it is accustomed and in the presence of its mother. However, the room now contains a variety of new and 'formidable' objects ranging from a crumpled sheet of paper to a large stuffed dog. The characteristic reaction of the infant is to cling to its mother, anxiously regarding the threat stimulus. However, if the situation is repeated, and if the baby is a little older, it will begin to explore and even attack the object – provided it is able to reassure itself periodically by the presence of the mother and by contact behaviour or clinging. A large part of the interest of these experiments lies in the fact that the mother's place may be taken by a clothbound surrogate: a wire cradle bound with towelling to which the infant can cling, but not by a wire surrogate: a similar cradle not bound with cloth, so that clinging is not possible. This holds true even when the latter is fitted with nipples from which the infant has learned to feed (Harlow and Zimmerman, 1958, Harlow, 1961).

Harlow's work demonstrates that there is a primary attachment behaviour in monkeys, and probably in all mammals (there certainly is in humans, see Volume II, Chapter 2) and that such behaviour does not derive by secondary reinforcement from a hunger 'drive'. The following reflex in chicks is analogous.[1] But the second implication is that the new stimulus elicits a progressively more elaborated search behaviour: initially, this takes the form of merely staring at the stimulus; later, i.e. when lines of behaviour have emerged which can be evoked by the input and to which it can be assimilated, the search extends to exploration and attack. Finally, it is apparent that there is a close interdependence between the attachment behaviour and the exploratory behaviour in that the animal deprived of an attachment object shows no exploration (but intense emotional reactions including attempts to bury its head in the floor, so excluding the stimulus), and that such inhibition of exploration extends to later life, i.e. initiative is permanently impaired by deprivation of the 'primary attachment object'. Similar long-term effects have been observed in other species, e.g. dogs (Thompson and Heron, 1954, and see Volume III, Chapters 1 and 5).

Reverting to the general account of behavioural regulation, it seems highly probable that much of the direction of behaviour originates from this primary curiosity reflex, which subserves the goal of uncertainty reduction, but which is at the same time closely bound up with defensive and social mechanisms such as the flight 'reflex' and the attachment 'reflex'.

IV. LEARNING AND BEHAVIOURAL REGULATION

1. *Introduction*

Classical learning theorists like Thorndike or Hull begin their theorizing by postulating some basic mechanism for learning which will be used to

[1] See above, p. 141.

explain the elaboration of complex behavioural organization. Contemporary psychologists like Deutsch, Broadbent and G. A. Miller tend to proceed the other way about. They first take a hard look at the complex system of regulations which seems to be implied by ready-formed behaviour, whether learnt or innate. Only then do they go on to consider the mechanism whereby the interconnexions implied by the system might be acquired. One reason is that the earlier approach tends to lead to a blind alley. Even if the formulation of the learning mechanism is correct, there is a great deal more which is needed to explain the organization of adaptive behaviour. For it is the system as a whole which requires explanation and not merely its ultimate elements.

If one starts from a simple connexionism, one usually ends by a sort of reductionism which is more like explaining away than explaining: it is all a matter of conditioning, or reinforcement, or what-have-you. Of course a concept like Hull's habit-family-hierarchy is a more sophisticated statement, but is still a matter of explaining away. For instance, it tells us little about the integration of concurrent strategies in skilled behaviour, or about the role of novelty in shifting the control of ongoing behaviour, or about the elaboration of a schematic image of the environment, or about the development of representation in human beings to a point where that image can be referred to and reconstructed by the subject by the use of imagery and symbols, so enabling him to anticipate and transform the environmental input at several removes from direct action.

However, to say that the whole is more than the sum of its parts is only a half-truth. For the system as a whole *is* fully accounted for if one can account for the relations between its parts. But what we have seen so far leads us to believe that these parts are not exhausted by the isolation of 'stimuli', modelled on the philosophers' 'sense data' and 'response', the definition of which is even more arbitrary. Nor are the relations between components exhausted by a mere connexionism, even by a connexionism based on reinforcement.

Now it is true that the complex hierarchy of schemata and strategies which one assumes to be operative in the behaviour of even quite young children say twelve months and upwards (see next chapter) cannot be present from birth and must therefore be a resultant of learning. But it is reasonable to suppose that the basic framework which governs the regulation of the more adaptive behaviour is also that which is operative from the start and which subserves its own elaboration and further construction. Four aspects of this are of particular importance.

First, the mechanism of the comparator-effector system: that behaviour is determined right from the start by the selection of effector mechanisms which will bring about at least a partial match between perceptual input and the requirements of the initiating strategy or link, and that input tends to be assimilated to that link.

Second, the existence of embryonic strategies or links, ensuring the possibility of some recognition and some adaptation. These may be identified with the reflex patterns of the newborn infant, patterns which right from the start involve both a perceptor component (connexion with the physical stimulus via the comparator) and an effector component (rudimentary patterning of response via the effector system).

Third, the vigilance mechanism and the what-is-it reflex, with its intimate connexion to the two basic mechanisms which between them subserve the ends of immediate survival (flight with, if possible, social attachment behaviour) and of long-term increased effectiveness (reduction of uncertainty by exploration).

Fourth, the possibility of trial-and-error behaviour in the sense of the successive invocation of the rudimentary strategies or links at the infant's disposal, particularly in the presence of a novel or disturbing input. Because of the lack of intermediate organization between the vigilance system and the available specific links (reflexes), such behaviour will inevitably be more or less formless general activity, which indeed it is – the more so as the effector integrations which are dependent solely on kinaesthetic feedback and not on environmental input (i.e. below the level of the link) have not yet matured.

All this amounts to saying that the apparatus out of which the eventual structure of behaviour is built must include from the start something corresponding to the general organizing framework as well as elements corresponding to the most specific components. What is lacking, and built up in the course of experience, is the vast complex of intermediate structures.

However, the principles governing the operation of the relatively empty system probably operate at all levels. This is possible if (1) they are such as to permit of learning; and (2) the learning which they engender takes the form of the progressive construction of new and intermediate structures mediating between the simple reflex and the central vigilance system. For the present, it is sufficient to consider briefly what these levels are, leaving their more detailed consideration for the next chapter, or for Volume II in the case of the highest levels of integration, which are entirely dependent on the elaboration and availability of an internalized representational input which can substitute for the environmental input.

2. *Successive Achievements of Learning*

The following, then, seem to be the successive levels of integration which are achieved by the human brain, conceived as a partially self-constructing system: at least the first four are shared by other mammals, and the fifth seems to be present in primates, at least in an embryonic form.

(1) *A progressive refinement of the combinations of input and output defined by the link, leading to the construction of new links by differentiation out of the old.* At the level of the simplest animal behaviour, the clearest examples are the differentiations studied by Pavlov: a tone of 500 cycles is conditioned to the salivatory reflex. Initially, the reflex is generalized to other tones, e.g. 750 cycles: i.e. the input combination is not strictly defined. However, if the first tone continues to be followed by food while the second is not, there is inhibition by differentiation. The first input is more strictly defined, and, by the same token, the second input also becomes operative in its own right: as an inhibitory 'stimulus'. In this case, the output is not changed, for salivation is a basic reflex which is available from the start.

It should not be supposed that because this kind of learning is the simplest, therefore it occurs only in lower species, or only during the first period of life. For instance, much the same principle must be held to operate in the acquisition of a second language, involving the elaboration of links, recognition patterns, corresponding to the phonemic and morphemic differentiations which obtain within that language as compared with the mother tongue (e.g. the French *on, in,* and *en* for the English native speaker). Or again, in the acquisition of a new skill, differentiations must be acquired to such combinations of input as determine e.g. the flight of a ball. In both these cases there are also differentiations of output to be made in the form of instructions to the effector system.

It is true that the instances taken from more advanced human learning involve something more than mere differentiations of input and output at the level of the link. They form part of integrated strategies and schemata corresponding to complex skills. But this is quite general. For the construction and modification of performance involving higher levels of integration always involves the operation of lower levels and may involve modifications at such levels. At the same time, since a wide variety of adaptations have already been acquired and integrated into more elaborate schemata, occasions for the formation of new differentiations at the lowest levels are unlikely to arise except within the context of further elaborations involving these higher levels also. To put the matter another way, since existing links may be expected to have become integrated within a number of higher order structures, differentiation of new links out of these links will involve the larger structures.

(2) *The combination of links to form elementary strategies or schemata.* At the level of early development, these are the 'first acquired adaptations' noted by Piaget, frequently taking the form of 'primary circular reactions', e.g. movement of the arm to bring the hand towards the mouth, hand clapping, and so on (see Section II of next chapter).

Again, while such fresh combinations are acquired at all levels of development, they are usually embedded within a higher ranking context, e.g. the acquisition of the perceptual and movement patterns involved in reaching for a spoon and bringing it to the mouth, the movement of a gear lever, the acquisition of the first syntactic patterns of language (see Volume II, Chapter 6).

In so far as we are concerned here with primary schemata, the structures we envisage are built up directly out of links, and not differentiated out of existing strategies, which would involve the next type of learning: instrumental learning. However, as has just been said, the two tend to be closely interwoven once adaptation has proceeded a sufficient way.

(3) *The formation of second and higher order strategies and schemata by the interposition of some other strategy, whether well-established or recently acquired, between the inception of an existing strategy and its completion.* We refer here to the elaboration of means-end behaviour or instrumental learning.

The earliest examples noted in human behaviour frequently take the form of 'secondary circular reactions', or 'procedures to make interesting spectacles last', such as shaking the cot in order to swing a string of rattles suspended from its hood. A large part of the experimental work on animal learning falls into this class also. Notably, discrimination learning, where the strategy of moving in the direction of a food or drink reward is anteceded by a perceptuo-motor strategy involving the selection of the correct direction on the basis of discriminative cues. Or again, maze behaviour, involving the chaining of successive cues. Gagné (1966) classifies such chaining as a higher learning structure arising out of instrumental learning proper. However, where the relevant strategies are homogenous and equally available (in terms of the vigilance mechanism), as in maze learning, chaining may be no more difficult than differentiated or discriminative instrumental learning, and involves similar structures.

Many forms of animal avoidance learning also come under the present heading, e.g. crossing from one compartment of a cage to another to avoid a shock on hearing a buzzer (see Mowrer, 1960). On the other hand, simple conditioned avoidance (raising the paw from an electrified grid on hearing a signal) belongs more properly within the second category, since the paw raising is already an unconditioned reflex to the unconditioned stimulus, so that distinct strategies are not involved.

Once again instrumental learning occurs throughout life in human beings, particularly in the context of the many manipulations required in the context of civilization: tying ribbons and laces, operating door handles, pencils, microscopes, and so on. Or again, embedded within the context of higher-order integrations: arithmetical routines in carrying out operations on numbers involving more than one numeral, and so on. But here a caution is necessary. For such operations as 'borrowing a ten' always involve instrumental learning. But they may involve only this, or they may be acquired within the context of a higher order schema representing the implications of this operation, i.e. the set of equivalences of which it forms a part. The 'meaningfulness' of the learning, and hence its availability in situations requiring transfer depends entirely on whether or not such higher order schemata are activated in the learning process.[1]

(4) *The co-ordination of strategies and schemata which have either links or sub-schemata in common to form more generalized, flexible schemata, with greater possibilities for the transfer of generalized search strategies from one to another.* In the sphere of early human development, the beginnings of this sort of learning seem to occur about the age of seven

[1] There seems little reason to doubt that 'meaningless learning' can occur successfully. Indeed since the mobilization of higher order schemata is not involved, the availability of the strategies to be embedded within their context presents no problems. The pupil is told what to do. Instead of 'learning by discovery' there is limited learning of and for itself. But at a price. For the integration within the larger schema must still be made, as a separate piece of learning. Also at a price of loss in motivation, in the measure that the mechanical skill does little to enhance the pupil's sense of effectance or competence – i.e. in so far as interest is not aroused by the generation of uncertainty affecting many lines of behaviour which the pupil has already made his own and with which he has identified (see Ch. 6, Section V). Or alternatively, the learning does relate to a schema but one which is situational, extrinsic and irrelevant: the pupil learns for the sake of good marks, teacher approval, and so on. Then the very fact of its integration within the irrelevant schema militates against the relevant integrations which will later be required. There is unlearning to be done, and the unlearning is the more difficult of achievement because of the generality of the irrelevant schema. (See also Volume II, Chapter 8, Section V.)

months, when the child successively applies available schemata to any new object in so far as that object permits of such application, e.g. banging, rattling, biting, comparing with another object, and so on (see Chapter 5, Section II). Such co-ordination leads to a far greater availability of alternative strategies in the presence of a given input, and hence to the formation of sensori-motor behaviours attesting the permanence of the object and an adaptation to the general causal texture of the environment: seeking for a hidden object, searching for a means-object when confronted with an end-object (e.g. in an instance not involving a very complex relation between means and end; a stick to beat a drum, a chip to insert in a vending machine (classical chimpanzee study by Cowles, 1937); in a more elaborated context: a stick to retrieve an object out of reach (Köhler, 1925, Birch, 1945)).

There is reason to believe that the co-ordinations involved in the elaboration of object schemata out of strategies which are tied to more or less narrowly delimited situational contexts bring about a sharper differentiation between schemata and strategies. For the schema of the object and its causal relations corresponds to the overlap of many strategies which may be applied to it, depending on the situation, while strategies such as the use of a support or a stick to retrieve an object become available in a wide variety of contexts, i.e. where the input from the comparator system may be very different. This is why one is tempted to attribute the phenomenon of learning set formation to this level of organization (see Sections I and III of next chapter).

In Section II of the next chapter, in which Piaget's outline of sensori-motor development is followed more closely, a further differentiation is made within this level of learning between schemata which are applied to new situations with only so much variation or accommodation as the problem requires (stage IV) and schemata which are deliberately varied to enhance the possibilities of integration, and, using the terminology of this chapter, to increase the area of uncertainty reduction and hence to increase the general effectance of the subject. However, from the point of view of the structurization involved, the difference is probably more one of degree than one of kind, which is why I prefer to lump them together in dealing with successive types of learning as distinct from its successive achievements.

(5) *The elaboration of representational planning: i.e. the running off of strategies which rely on successive input of a representational character (imagery, imitation, language) to precede strategies acting directly on objects, allowing the solution of problems by 'mental combinations': in*

other words, planning. It must be borne in mind that any form of representation has a dual character. In the first place it is itself a form of behaviour, in the second, it acts as signifier for that which it represents. From the first point of view, imitation and language differ from other forms of behaviour only in one respect: the input upon which they rely is less dependent on the environment. Hence it is not surprising to find that the beginnings of speech as well as the beginnings of imitation reach right back to the first few months of life. For instance, there is no difference in kind between the differentiation of cue combinations obtained by hearing a word uttered by the subject himself and the differentiation of cues arising out of his behaviour upon objects. Similar considerations apply to the effector combinations. Therefore at the very same time as the child differentiates combinations to form links in relation to other aspects of his environment, he also learns new differentiations of sounds in the form of a new vowel and consonantal forms. A while later, he experiments with new morphophonemic combinations of these to achieve certain effects, viz. consonance with the language sounds uttered by those around him, exactly as he experiments with other forms of movement to achieve desired effects. Both are instrumental behaviour and belong to our category (3). The recognition of a contextual equivalence between the sounds uttered and the situational input to which they correspond ('Mamma' means a person, 'Teddy' a toy, etc.) corresponds to the behavioural equivalences which determine the identity of the objects themselves: our category (4). The fact that the input for representational behaviour is less limited by the environment probably contributes to an accelerated acquisition of these schemata. For instance, all observers of children's language are agreed that deliberate experimentation with language occurs in young children from the age of six months (see Volume II, Chapter 5), yet deliberate experimentation in relation to behaviour upon objects is taken by Piaget as characteristic of a later 'stage': viz. from eleven months onwards (see next chapter, Section II).

However, the distinctive feature of representational behaviour is its significatory relation to the behavioural schemata as a whole. In the field of direct behaviour, once a sufficient co-ordination of strategies and schemata has been elaborated (level 4), the activation of a given schema, say grasping an object, may be sufficient to evoke that of a number of other related strategies, say rotating, surface exploration, hitting against another object, and so on. But the junctures between such related strategies and schemata are generally limited: sharing a common input at the level of the link (definition of object as the intersection of the strategies which may be applied to it), or sharing an organizational strategy (learning set). Conversely, representational behaviour in general, and language in particular, has junctures with the behavioural system at any and every level: the input combinations (naming of objects and their properties), sequences of input (events), elementary strategies (description of simple actions), higher order strategies and schemata (description of sequences of actions; anticipation of such sequences and planning). It is this multiplicity of junctures which enables it to function as signifier, defining a particular segment and substituting for it (whether in communication or in planning).

Failure to realize the dual character of representation and language inevitably leads to distortion in the analysis of its development. Language in particular is an elaborate skill in its own right and subject to its own internal constraints. These need to be learnt by the child in their own right. The observer must therefore be wary of identifying language elements and language patterns with the objects and relations of the signified system. For instance it is an error to suppose that the meaning of language consists in a succession of 1–1 correspondences between the elements of the language and those of the system (organism + internalized schema of environment), e.g. in the sentence 'John loves Mary', 'John' = the boy, 'loves' = observed sentiment, 'Mary' = the girl. What about more complex and abstract sentences such as any in this text (or any other, if you think my text is meaningless)? And what about transformations such as 'Mary is loved by John', 'Does John love Mary?', and so on. There are semantic relations between *some* words and an object or event. And these do contribute in some measure to the signifying property. But the semantic relation derives in part from the morphemic and syntactic structures in the utterance as a whole, and these structures in their turn have a behavioural aspect as well as a significatory aspect. Indeed the study of the child's earliest acquisitions of syntax suggests that these have little to do with the sequential representation of the order in which he apprehends the elements invoked, and much more with the strategies that he elaborates regarding what words go with what (Braine, 1963, and see Volume II, Chapter 6). Generally speaking, it is the sentence rather than the word which conveys meaning in the sense of reducing uncertainty: i.e. usually one sentence carries one 'thought', or bears on a particular schema, invoking a particular modification of it, at whatever level.

It follows from this that the acquisition of language *qua* behaviour does not constitute a distinct level of learning, even though it clearly does demand the availability of specific language centres to supply the physical mechanism out of which language links, strategies and schemata are to be evolved, and these simply do not exist in lower order species. It is even doubtful whether the significatory aspect of language, taken by itself, implies a different order of schema from that which is entailed in the elaboration of complex sensori-motor schemata such as those which correspond to the causal texture of the environment (our level 4). However, the use of language and representation to substitute for action does entail the elaboration of higher-order strategies as a result of which the strategy which consists in direct action is anteceded and modified by the strategy which consists in the representational sequence. The fact that representation can be used in this way is probably bound up with the fact that (*a*) it is, or tends to be, infinitely flexible, and therefore (*b*) it is not merely evoked by, or associated with some aspect of direct behaviour, but, in a suitably determined form, is evoked only by that aspect – and may therefore substitute for it, while, finally, (*c*) it is behaviour which is, or tends to be, free of the constraints of environmental input, depending only on the input provided by the subject's own behaviour. Each of these three attributes of representative behaviour is relative, and the degree to which they are attained is a function of experience, i.e. learning. Initially, neither imitation nor language are flexible, unambiguous, or free of environmental constraints. But these are the asymptotes which define the tendency of representation and which underlie its functional properties right from the start. Hence, the acquisition of representational anticipation as a form of planning may be thought of as constituting a new level of organization from the moment it appears, resulting from the application of a particular type of instrumental strategy (the representative behaviour itself) to the co-ordinated schemata elaborated previously.

It is not always easy to be certain at the most primitive levels whether or not a particular sequence of overt behaviour implies an antecedent representation. I suspect that the making of a sandcastle does, since the child fills the bucket before overturning it and patting it down to ensure that the castle will be firm. At the stage where he is still filling, the anticipatory realization of the eventual construction enables him to compare the sand in the bucket with the form of the future castle. Two-year-olds make quite successful sandcastles. At slightly later ages, the intervention of planning is more clear cut, and this indeed constitutes the most significant difference between the play of younger and older children in the age-range two to five years (Barker, Dembo and Lewin, 1941; Lunzer, 1955). Here is a typical example:

> 'He (age 4·7) has been playing in the sand-pit. He notices an ammunition box near by. He collects a whole row of these and aligns them to form a causeway to the sand-pit from which he removes all other toys. He tells another boy to jump and the boys now take it in turns to run along the causeway and jump into the sand-pit.'
>
> (Lunzer, 1955, p. 181)

The use of planning in the behaviour of children at this age level deserves more attention than it has had, since the information that we have is for the most part observational rather than experimental. However, the phenomenon does point to a new articulation in the regulation of behaviour: the intervention of representational strategies.

(6) *The combination of representational strategies to derive systematic categorizations.* I refer here to what Piaget terms the formation of concrete operational structures of reasoning. Some of the most significant instances of co-ordination at this level take the form of the elaboration of operational definitions of properties of objects which remain invariant under a wide variety of transformations; the conservation of substance, weight, number, length, area, time, etc. To cite a typical experiment: two rods of equal length are placed side by side and judged equally long by the child: one of the rods is then advanced a couple of centimetres: younger children now judge this rod to be longer because it projects while older children (in this case, from about $7\frac{1}{2}$ years on average) recognize that the change of position leaves the length invariant. Other examples are discussed in detail in Volume II, Chapter 8.

It is well known that in all such situations the younger child expresses his judgement on the basis of a single perceptually predominant cue (the projection at one end, the length of a row of counters, the height of a column of liquid or of cubes, etc.), while the older child takes into account a compensatory relation in some other aspect of the situation (projection at the opposite end, intervals between counters, cross-sectional measurement). To this extent, the judgement of conservation is a reconciliation of two judgements. However, as I have pointed out elsewhere (Lunzer, 1965), this in itself is not sufficient to guarantee equality, for the compensations need not be exact, and perceptually they are not. The conservational judgement depends in equal measure on the recognition of the continuity of the objects and the reversibility of the changes imposed on them. Instead of being content with the not always predictable changes in input following on the implementation of his own strategies upon the object, the child discovers a schema which consists in selecting among those strategies one which is always available to him and which yields an invariant recoverable relation. Generally speaking, in the typical conservation experiment, it is the initial disposition which constitutes the operational definition of the invariant relational property: equality or inequality of length, number, weight, etc. Length is defined by the (recoverable) operation of parallel alignment, number (at this level) by enumeration, weight by putting on scales, etc. It is surely no accident that the consistent conservation of an equality is always found alongside that of the corresponding inequalities (e.g. if one of the rods is longer when measured it is judged longer whatever rearrangement is imposed).

At the previous level the child acquired the capacity to engage in representational strategies which enabled him in some measure to precede overt action with internalized behaviour (involving self-produced cues in the comparator system, whether verbal or imaginal), and, in some cases to revise his actions in the light of such experiment (cf. the example of putting down an object and moving it to open a door cited in the next chapter, Section II). The development of the present level consists essentially in the elaboration of strategies the input to which consists of the final output (relational judgements) of the earlier representational sequences. The systematic co-ordination depends on the juxtaposition and evaluation of such outcomes in relation to the strategies of which they are the product. Such juxtaposition clearly requires the availability of these outcomes in immediate memory. Therefore I am inclined to the view that the input from the comparator system is not necessarily passed back immediately to the strategy from which it results but may be stored for a period in immediate memory. This may not greatly affect the regulation of behaviour at the simplest levels, where the capacity of the immediate memory system is limited to one or two representational elements. It becomes crucial at the point where a co-ordinating strategy determines the successive evocation of several subsidiary strategies each of which results in a distinct input and the final decision depends on a comparison of these. Such considerations lend considerable credibility to the view of McLaughlin (1963) that the development of concrete operational reasoning, and subsequently of formal thinking is intimately bound up with the growth in the immediate memory capacity (see Volume II, Chapter 8).

(7) *Development of formal reasoning*. Little need be said here about this final development in co-ordination since we devote two entire chapters

to it in Volume II. Suffice it for the present to note that with the advent of formal reasoning, the systematic co-ordination achieved at the concrete level become the point of departure for the construction of rigorous hypotheses concerning the necessary relationships that are envisaged to obtain between various aspects of reality, and hence between various aspects of input following on the implementation of precise output strategies (scientific experiment, historical research, etc.). One of the points stressed in Volume II, Chapter 9 is that such hypothesis testing necessarily involves the co-ordination of alternative hypotheses to arrive at comparisons which will be decisive between them. However, for the present it needs to be stressed that however impressive the achievement of reasoning, it is still a form of behaviour of the brain exactly on a par with other activities, but involving a further co-ordination. It depends for its elements on the systematizations achieved at the previous stage, and therefore the demands that it makes on immediate memory are greater. Nevertheless, the strategies which it involves are clearly learnt in exactly the same way as are those of earlier levels. And the facility of its execution is still dependent on the availability of the relevant strategies.

V. BASIC MECHANISMS OF LEARNING

If the account given so far is anything like a reasonable approximation, then the successive achievements entail successive co-ordinations, with the emergence of new centres in the brain corresponding to the higher-order strategies and schemata which are elaborated. The result is that the regulation of behaviour is greatly transformed in the course of development. Included in the regulation of behaviour will be the determination of trial strategies which are essential to learning, and the incorporation of these in the overall schema in so far as they are successful. But what of the mechanism of learning itself?

I would like to make four points. The first is that the fact that the achievement of learning is different at successive stages does not imply that the basic mechanism of learning is different. There is little reason for supposing that it is different, and good ground for supposing that it is the same. Secondly, tentative suggestions will be made as to the way in which learning might be incorporated in the schematic system outlined in Sections I–IV. Third, it will be stressed that most of the fundamental problems regarding the *basic* mechanisms of learning are still unresolved. Fourth, while their solution probably depends on further work in physiology, this does not prevent us from studying and making useful discoveries about the co-ordinations which are achieved as a result of learning. Fifth, one point which emerges with abundant clarity from research is that the most effective way to ensure that behaviour will be integrated into a higher structure through learning is to see that it has first been initiated in the context of that structure.

1. *Conditioning and the 'What-is-it? Reflex'*

Ideally, the unimpeded running-off of an activated schema may be thought of as a determinate sequence: effector activation results in a pre-programmed input to the comparator system, so ensuring transition to the next link. So long as there is agreement between the pre-settings of the comparator system and the environmental input, there is no occasion for learning. The argument holds even of those more complex regulations which involve the simultaneous interaction of several strategies.

However, this sort of perfect marriage between input and programme may be no more than an ideal. Since the organism is subject to constant stimulation from the environment (including its own internal environment), and both undergo continuous change, the problem is first to account for the predictability of behaviour. This is why the comparator system is thought of as having a dual function, serving not only as template for the recognition of matching between programme and environmental input, but also as a filter, so that by and large relevant input will be assimilated to the programme and irrelevant input will be neglected. Even here, it was noted in the discussion of the 'what-is-it? reflex' that the filter is not perfect. Sudden changes in input are noticed. If the assumption is correct that all behaviour is schematic, then it follows that such changes themselves are assimilated to links and strategies, although these may be initially unrelated to the schema which is presently directing behaviour. It was argued that the effect of the novel stimulus is to bring about a temporary switch in the control of behaviour, leading to the reduction of uncertainty.

The 'what-is-it? reflex' was first noted by Pavlov as the unconditional response to a conditioning stimulus in classical conditioning. As a result of conditioning, the cues which initially gave rise to this form of behaviour come to elicit the response which previously was attached only to the unconditional stimulus. Because conditioning represents a change in the regulation of behaviour, it is a form of learning (by definition). It is often held that classical conditioning governs the regulation of involuntary autonomic behaviour, typified by salivation or emotional arousal, while that of directed, 'operant' behaviour is governed exclusively by a different principle: reinforcement in the Thorndikian sense (Skinner, 1938). It is true that conditioning by itself cannot lead to new behaviour but only to changes in the signals which give rise to behaviour. Nevertheless it seems to follow in terms of the schematic model outlined in the previous pages that conditioning constitutes an important element in all learning. Thus one may suppose that the constitution of the recognition patterns which are represented in the link are essentially the result of a conditioning process.

Suppose that a novel cue-element arising within a familiar context is not assimilable to some already differentiated system so that complex investigatory behaviour is minimal. Then, as the stimulus persists and is accompanied or followed by the anticipated input, it will be assimilated to it. The cue-combinations determined by the existing link are thereby enlarged to include the conditioned signal. On the other hand, if there is differentiated investigatory behaviour but this does not lead to a radical change in input, such behaviour will tend to be inhibited by virtue of adaptation. Again the conditions exist for the redefinition of the relation between comparator system and link by conditioning.

This statement is fairly close to Pavlov's characterization of conditioning as the process which gives rise to the formation and differentiation of (temporary) signals. But there is the important difference that the link cannot be thought of as eliciting motor behaviour in a simple reflex way, for it is itself part of a larger organization of strategies and schemata responsive both to the internal states of the organism and to the environment. Such a conclusion is of course consonant with what I said earlier (in Chapter 1): the salivation reflex was used by Pavlov to study the organization of behaviour precisely because the conditioned behaviour is overt, unambiguous, and measurable: the processes revealed, including conditioning itself, extend to forms which are less unequivocal. An agreement which proves nothing except that I can occasionally avoid contradicting myself. But it is also consonant with the fact that conditioned reflexes can be established in a curarized animal (when overt behaviour is impossible), suggesting that the process is central rather than peripheral.

2. *Instrumental Learning*

However, while the progressive definition of the relations between the comparator system and links can be thought of as resulting from a process akin to classical conditioning, such a process cannot account for the formation of strategies and the differentiation of schemata. Such learning is better thought of as resulting from the incorporation of previously independent elements into existing schemata. The elements themselves may be small units: the simple strategies for which I have borrowed the term 'link' from Deutsch, or they may be larger units: sequences of such links, forming more clearly recognizable strategies, or complex strategies like the representation of an intended action.

Once again, the extended forms of behaviour mentioned earlier in the context of the 'what-is-it reflex' may underlie the formation of such new integrative sequences. Suppose, for example, that a blockage occurs in the running-off of a well-established sequence. This means that the comparator system fails to provide the appropriate cues for the continuation of the sequence. It is easy to imagine that the ensuing behaviour will be directed by the schemata evoked by the cues which are in fact passed by the comparator system, and in particular by those which are furnished by that region in the environment upon which the subject is concentrating (the bars blocking the way to food in a Thorndike puzzle-box, etc.). Now we suppose that the running-off of one such strategy results in the removal of the blockage, so that the original behaviour may be resumed. The previously independent strategy tends to be incorporated into the original schema. This is the recognized principle of (Thorndikian) reinforcement learning, slightly paraphrased to conform with the terminology of this chapter. If our analysis is correct, then reinforcement implies not only the strengthening of the successful behaviour, but, more importantly, that it tends to be evoked when the original schema is evoked: the subject learns to search for cues to instrumental behaviour. By the same token, if this is the mechanism which gives rise to the formation of schemata, then, as a result of its operation, the chance activation of a previously independent schema which has been incorporated as a 'means instrument' into a larger schema will result in the activation of that schema. For it has been supposed that a schema tends to be activated when one of its constituent links is activated by input from the comparator system. Once again, there is nothing new in this, for it is no more than a rephrasing of the Hullian principle of secondary reinforcement.

However, if this account is no more than a restatement of well-established facts, and is more descriptive than explanatory, it does entail certain points of departure from conventional (Hullian) learning theory. One is that there is no mention of drive reduction, and a second is that the principle of reinforcement is expressed in terms of cues and not of stimuli.

Extensive work carried out mainly by Olds and his associates at the University of Michigan puts the fact of instrumental learning beyond doubt. Direct electrical stimulation of certain regions of the brain, and especially of the lateral portions of the hypothalamus, may be used to teach an animal an activity, e.g. pressing a lever, and to maintain that activity at a very high level (the rat will continue to depress the lever which results in brain stimulation until it reaches exhaustion). Brain stimulation can also be used to teach a sequence such as maze running. Moreover, if the animal with implanted electrodes is subjected to random electrical stimulation while running a maze for a food reward, the course of learning is severely disrupted. There is still uncertainty as to the way in which such reinforcing centres react on previous behaviour, but a recent suggestion is that the strengthening caused by electrical stimulation results from a double inhibition (i.e. an inhibition of an inhibition). The 'fore-brain bundle' which passes through the lateral hypothalamus is held to be spontaneously active, but inhibited by processes associated with an avoidance centre, the 'mid-brain bundle'. Direct stimulation of the mid-brain centres results in activity which would terminate such stimulation – although this activity is more random and less directed than that which is promoted by stimulation of the fore-brain bundle. Activation of this latter, or enhancement of its activity, results from the activity of a third centre, the effect of which is to inhibit the inhibition from the mid-brain. The evidence for this hypothesis is complex but impressive (Olds and Olds, 1965).

Since electrical stimulation may be substituted for conventional reinforcers, and since random stimulation disrupts their action, one may be certain that the centres studied by Olds play a crucial part in ordinary instrumental learning. But the precise role that they play is far from clear. Hullians would no doubt relate their activity to drive reduction. We ourselves have argued against the hypothesis of independent entities termed 'drives' which would somehow interact with 'habits'. Instead it will be argued that what is termed drive intensity corresponds simply to the strength of activation of a schema (Chapter 5). In line with this, one would argue that the strengthened association between an instrumental strategy and a schema occurs when such a strategy has resulted in the unimpeded running-off of that schema: a position quite close to that of Deutsch.

3. *Activity of the Subject in Instrumental Learning*

Turning to the isolation of cues in the evocation of instrumental strategies, recent evidence indicates that the process involves an active isolation of cues on the part of the subject and is not an automatic response to the physical properties of the stimulus (Sutherland and Mackintosh, 1964, Mackintosh, 1965). In one experiment, eighteen rats were trained in a Lashley jumping apparatus to jump towards a card featuring a white horizontal bar, avoiding one with a black vertical bar. They were then tested for transfer in four situations: A: white horizontal versus black horizontal, B: white vertical versus black vertical, C: white horizontal versus white vertical, D: black horizontal versus black vertical. Thus A and B tested the learning of the cue of brightness and C and D that of orientation. Simple re-testing yielded 96 per cent success, brightness only (A, B) 86 per cent, and orientation only (C, D) 72 per cent. It seems to follow that some animals learned both cues. On the other hand there was a negative correlation of 0·56 between success in brightness transfer and success in orientation transfer, indicating that the cues were learned separately, and at any rate in some cases response to one cue inhibited response to the other (Sutherland and Mackintosh, 1964).

The fact that animals could respond to both cues is consistent with what was said earlier in this section regarding the role of conditioning in the constitution and definition of the link. If the animal has begun to respond to brightness and chances to notice horizontality, the latter cue can be conditioned to the link. But the point is that such learning is not inevitable, and the reverse may also occur: the subject learns to ignore the irrelevant cue.

That instrumental learning is contingent on the active evocation of strategies is highlighted by a number of brilliant studies by Held and Held and Hein to which reference has already been made in Chapter 2. These authors showed that in perceptual learning the proprioceptive stimulation arising from passive movement of the limbs is not equivalent to that of stimulation arising from active movement: whereas the latter leads to effective learning, the former does not. In one study, Held and Hein (1958) investigated the effect of perceived hand movement on the correction of errors in perception produced by distorting prisms. Subjects are seated in front of a pattern of crossed lines which they see not directly but as reflected in an oblique mirror: although the pattern is vertical and in front of the subject, it is seen as a horizontal drawing on the table at which they are seated. The task is to plot the intersections of the lines (or rather the image of these intersections produced by the mirror). But the perception of this image is displaced because the mirror is viewed through a prism which displaces the virtual image to one side. Training consists in moving the hand and watching its movement through the prism. Such training is carried out under two conditions: half of the subjects move their arm backwards and forwards through an arc with the elbow as pivot; the other half of the subjects rest their arm on a lever and allow the pivoting to be imposed by the experimenter. The actual movements and the proprioceptive stimuli are the same for both groups. The effectiveness of this experience may be measured by the extent to which the subjects allow for the distortion produced by the prism when asked to indicate the virtual image of the intersections of the test pattern after training. Subjects who moved their arm themselves show significant corrections, while those who suffered passive movement do not.

Even more revealing is the experiment of Held and Bossom (1961) in which these authors investigated the effectiveness of locomotion for spatial learning. Subjects wore special glasses fitted with aniseikonic lenses the effect of which is to displace the image of seen things through 11° to the right or left. Köhler had previously made extensive studies of the effect of such lenses and the way in which subjects adapt to them (Köhler, 1963). Initially, subjects make gross errors of localization, and naturally tend to bump into things and so on. However, after a period of wearing the special glasses and going about their ordinary business, they adapt to the lenses in the sense that they learn to make automatic corrections for the distortion. It should be added that a similar but shorter period of adaptation is needed to re-adapt to normal vision when the lenses are removed.[1]

Held and Bossom tested the effectiveness of walking along a path wearing the lenses as compared with being wheeled along the same path in a wheel-chair. To test the error of localization the subject was periodically seated in a swivel-chair which he was asked to rotate until he was looking straight ahead at a slit in a circular curtain surrounding the chair. The initial error for all subjects was of course around 11°. After four days of periodic exposure to the training (walking or being wheeled while wearing the lenses) eight out of fifteen subjects who walked about made zero errors (this in spite of the fact that the lenses were not worn continuously during the training period). The subjects who suffered passive movement made no improvement. More recent experimental work by the same authors, cited in Chapter 2, shows that active involvement of perceptuo-motor strategies enters not only into perceptual

[1] The thoughtful reader should take this for granted: the image that we see without distorting lenses is the 'real' one only in the sense that there is co-ordination of movements and of vision with respect to that image; that co-ordination was acquired in the first few months of life. All that is happening in Köhler's experiments is that a similar re-learning is made necessary by the introduction of the lenses.

re-learning (adaptation to aniseikonic lenses, etc.) but also into initial perceptual learning. Although some controversy remains as to whether kinaesthetic feedback is the necessary ingredient in such learning, as argued by Held, the evidence is conclusive that learning depends on perceptuo-motor feedback in general (Wohlwill, 1966).

While the evidence that instrumental cues and strategies are not learned unless the subject makes active use of them rests mainly on simpler forms of learning (simple discrimination and perceptuo-motor co-ordination), there is little reason to doubt that the principle holds true of all learning. Hence its importance. Often in education it is assumed that much of the pupil's learning can take place incidentally. For instance, such an argument has been used in defence of the look-and-say method in teaching reading. Of course, if the pupil learns to read at all, he will have acquired some strategies and cue-combinations. But it does not follow at all that these will be the most effective for continued progress. Nor does it follow that, having gained a certain facility in using wrong or inadequate cues, he will necessarily 'pick up' the correct cues with practice (presumably by conditioning). It is quite possible, and indeed probable (in view of the complexity of the schema) that the partial success of the inadequate strategies will actively inhibit the recognition of those cues which might subserve the more adequate.

Similar arguments (incidental learning) have been used to defend mechanical methods in teaching arithmetic, lack of teaching in grammar, scientific method, composition in the native language, and so on. The point is not that the relevant skills must be taught separately in the form of isolated drills: rules of grammar, spelling of isolated words, Bacon's principles, and so on. On the contrary, if a behaviour is to be incorporated in a certain context, it must be learned in that context. The point is rather that if the conditions for learning are to be improved then the sequence must be programmed, and that such programming can afford to take little for granted, least of all the essentials. While impressive progress has been made in the field of mathematical teaching both at primary and secondary level (see Volume II, Chapter 13), systematic teaching in the idiomatic usage of English has hardly begun.[1]

[1] This book is concerned with pscyhology and education and is not a handbook for curriculum development. Even if it were, it would be impertinent to expand very much on the above criticism without a background of curricular research. But the shortcoming can be made clearer. Exercises in the writing of English tend to concentrate on such limited areas as the combination of simple sentences to make compound ones, the insertion of 'vivid' adjectives in composition, and so on. Hardly any attempt

4. *Discrimination Learning*

Instrumental learning, and especially the role of the isolation of cues in instrumental strategies is relevant at all levels of learning because it enters as an element into higher levels. Discrimination learning is a variant of it which is nearly as ubiquitous and demands a word on its own, since it adds a further dimension of complexity which is not always realized.

The classical conditioning situation is optimal for producing discrimination. Even a simple stimulus such as a pure tone may be thought of as producing an aggregate of cues: pitch, intensity, timbre, etc. The formation of a conditional reflex implies the determination of a link which assimilates some of these cues to the (eating) schema. Discrimination is a secondary process superimposed on this. A differential signal, say a tone of a different pitch, is introduced without being followed by food. At first there is generalization, which may be complete. But with the onset of differential inhibition, the inhibition may extend to the original positive stimulus also. The formation of the stable differentiation seems to entail either the determination of two distinct links, both related to the schema, but one of which is positive while the other is inhibitory, or else the elaboration of a more differentiated link, with two outputs corresponding to the two types of input. However, in classical conditioning, the differentiation is favoured by the fact that the hungry animal is confined in the situation, that distracting stimuli are minimized, and that the single schema of hunger predominates throughout. Just as this situation favours the extension of positive cue-combinations to all of the features of the stimulus, so it favours the differentiation. This is because the transition from assimilation of cues in the comparator system to the final effector component is brief, and particularly because (except in delayed

---

is made to teach and exploit the flexibility of language: the variety of constructions, of substitutions and of transformations which it allows, and above all their effectiveness or ineffectiveness in particular contexts. For instance, at an elementary level: the effective use of pronoun substitution, of synonyms, of the passive transformation, of the interrogative transformation and the various ways of expressing doubt or uncertainty, and so on. At a slightly less elementary level: transformations of compound sentences and groups of sentences, including the decomposition of unwieldy sentences, when nesting (subordinate clauses inside main clauses) is effective, when it is clumsy, and the transformations which can be used to circumvent nesting. None of this is a matter of teaching 'grammar' for its own sake, although in the course of substitution and transformation exercises the meaning of some grammatical terms may become quite clear, and the introduction of these terms at some stage in the learning may facilitate further elaboration as well as transfer. I have to stress that this footnote is not a recipe for programming the curriculum in this field. It merely points a need.

conditioning) the stimulus persists throughout the experiment. (The ideal situation for conditioning is that where the onset of the **CS** anteceded that of the **US** while its termination follows the administration of the **US**.)

Discrimination learning in an instrumental situation parallels classical differentiation in that it involves both a positive component, incorporation of an instrumental strategy within an established schema, and a negative component, the isolation of inhibitory cues or the differentiation of positive and negative links. But the conditions for differentiation are less favourable in that the stimulus does not persist throughout the behaviour but is terminated by the instrumental behaviour itself, which gives rise to changes in input and the activation of different links. The simplest situations are those in which the positive adaptation is acquired first and the negative differentiation is introduced later. This is essentially the design of Vince's studies of learning in birds to which reference was made in an earlier section (Vince, 1961). In the experiment already described it was found that generally speaking older birds were more successful in learning the inhibitory discrimination, i.e. not to remove the black lid. No differences are given regarding the acquisition of the positive strategy, removal of the white lid, but other experiments are cited showing that positive investigation of stimuli is both more intense and more persistent in younger birds and in younger animals generally – after a certain age, corresponding in some species to the age of weaning, but perhaps in all to the establishment of simple strategies involving voluntary movement. Positive exploration appears to decline with age (reaching a peak at about ten weeks in birds), and this may be due to adaptation resulting from the incorporation of cues from new stimuli to established schemata. The evidence for a parallel decline in the acquisition of differentiation is too thin to be reliable. But there is good evidence both from Vince's own work and from related work with other species that animals reared under conditions of relative deprivation are poorer, particularly in learning a negative discrimination (showing greater perseveration of an unadaptive response), while animals reared in an enriched environment (e.g. aviary-reared birds, dogs reared as pets) show a greater flexibility in learning. (See Volume III, Chapter 5, for an evaluation of related work in regard to children.)

Discrimination learning is not an independent form of learning, different from instrumental learning, for the principle of reinforcement applies to both. But it does involve an additional, negative, component: differentiation. It therefore seems reasonable to regard it as a two-step process, and the regulatory mechanism in which it eventuates may be similar to that illustrated in Figure 3, with a discrimination strategy L_0 anteceding an extended instrumental strategy S_1 (removal of lid followed by search for food) as alternative to S_2 (original food-seeking behaviour). Because it is a complex learning, and because the selective, negative component is more difficult than the positive, it cannot be regarded as necessarily simpler than the chaining of approach behaviour in maze learning. Which of the two is easier must depend on the complexity of the maze and the difficulty of the discrimination as well as on species differences. For most species, the acquisition of orientation responses with respect to relatively invariant cues (distant visual, olfactory, kinaesthetic) is easier than that of visual choice discrimination (with respect to near objects, the disposition of which in relation to the environment is deliberately randomized by the experimenter). (Hebb, 1949; Bitterman, 1965.)

The importance of discrimination learning is that, like instrumental learning, it enters into learning processes at every stage, even though (or because) it is relatively elementary. For instance: the differentiation of visual forms in reading, etc., the differentiation of characteristic forms seen under a microscope, the differentiation of phonemes in language and of sounds in music, and so on. Moreover, the techniques (sometimes) used in education for the facilitation of such learning have a sound basis in laboratory experiment: heightening contrast to begin with and then gradually reducing it, isolating contrast or sharpening it, e.g. in the use of colour combined with form in diagrams, and so on. These are the techniques which Skinner calls 'bringing the operant under the control of discriminative stimuli'. They are ways of raising the probability that the cue-combinations which are passed by the comparator system and incorporated into the schema will be those which are relevant for further adaptation. (Once again, a criticism of 'look-and-say' methods in reading is their failure to take advantage of such techniques.)

5. *Summary*

After outlining the successive achievements of learning, we have been concerned in this chapter only with the most elementary, sensori-motor acquisitions. But there is reason to believe that the fundamental mechanisms of conditioning and positive and negative instrumental learning are quite general. I myself share the commonly accepted view (stated most sharply by Skinner, 1938), that these are different and cannot be assimilated to one another. On the other hand, this does not necessarily imply that conditioning is irrelevant to voluntary behaviour.

Probably the most significant conclusion to be drawn is that learning at any level depends on the active participation of the component (cue, link, strategy, schema) which is to be incorporated in the schema (total behavioural co-ordination) as a result of positive and negative reinforcement. This corresponds to Skinner's dictum that learning consists in the increase in the probability of evocation of an operant response in the presence of a discriminating 'stimulus', and that for a response to be learned it must occur. But, once again, there is an important difference. For the strategy or schema is not itself an observable response, and the latter (representing a co-ordination of strategies) in particular is inferred only from observation of the patterning of different, related behaviours. Moreover, the work of Held illustrates that the occurrence of overt behaviour is not by itself sufficient to assure learning. In other words, if a particular higher-level co-ordination (strategy or schema) is to be learnt, then the conditions must be such as to ensure the probability of that co-ordination, and not merely of its constituents. This means, first, that the constituents must be initiated by the subject in the context of the activity of the schema into which they are to be incorporated, and, second that the neural equipment of the subject must be such as to allow the elaboration of the new structures.[1]

[1] The constitution of new links, strategies and schemata must depend on the elaboration of new connexions in the brain, and, in particular, on the determination of centres which are linked with others but which can be activated independently of these (i.e. the activation of a schema does not entail that of all its constituent links). The work of Lashley (1929) proved that, in the rat's brain, and with respect to the co-ordinations involved in maze-learning, there is equipotentiality over a large part of the cortex: loss in acquired learning, and loss in the capacity to learn, depends more on the actual amount of excised tissue than on its location. This led to the field-hypotheses of Köhler and other Gestalt psychologists, denying the specificity of neuronal connexions. But the fact of synaptic transmission and the complex ramifications of axons militates strongly against any theory of vague diffusion. Also, the existence of specific centres (visual, somaesthetic, motor, and especially speech) is just as well attested as that of equipotentiality. More important considerations are the enormous number of synapses which exist between neurons, i.e. every neuron makes connexions with hundreds of others and could receive impulses from hundreds. This makes it probable (*a*) that what happens is that the effect of learning is to select out of the many connexions some which will be privileged, while the remainder are inhibited, or inactivated, (*b*) that there is considerable redundancy in the system (i.e. that the activation of a group of nerves depends on the activation of a proportion of another group, the probability being a matter of more or less, and not all or none), and (*c*) that equipotentiality is relative, i.e. not all neurons or neuronal systems are available for all purposes: if an animal has no speech centre, it will not learn to speak, and so on. See Chapter 2, and compare Zangwill, 1961, for a fuller discussion of equipotentiality.

What this means is that incidental learning is not a different kind of learning but learning of the same kind which is distinguished only by the fact that it is chancy and inefficient, a point which is forcibly argued by Skinner.

Second, although the basic mechanisms of conditioning and positive and negative instrumental learning underlie all learning, this does not mean that their elucidation is sufficient for an understanding of the more complex co-ordinations to which they give rise. For instance, it seems probable that the phenomenon of learning set, described in the next chapter and in Volume II, Chapter 3, depends on the existence, or elaboration, of centres which monitor the strategies of the subject, and the differential reinforcement of these. It is even more probable that the systematic representational strategies which characterize operational reasoning depend on such monitoring. The systematic equivalences which they entail could not have been predicted from a consideration of the basic nature of learning.

Finally, although the evidence that we have strongly suggests the pervasive influence of certain basic mechanisms, this by no means implies that the nature of these is fully understood. In particular, while the fact of instrumental learning is well established, its mechanism is far from clear. It is almost certain that the activity of reinforcing centres controls the differentiation of connexions, but we know all too little about what it is that activates these centres themselves during spontaneous behaviour (as opposed to direct electrical stimulation). Any simple theory of drive reduction related to needs is untenable in the light of recent work on the complex regulations governing eating and drinking. Such work suggests (*a*) that there are separate excitatory and inhibitory centres governing onset and offset of these behaviours; (*b*) that these are overlaid by learnt discriminatory patterns; and (*c*) that the two sets of mechanisms are partly independent (Rosenzweig, 1963). The position taken here is that reinforcement may be contingent on the supply of the feedback which permits unimpeded running-off of a schema at any level, which is a sort of confirmation view. But this is no more than a speculation. It is not a statement of proven fact.

VI. CONCLUDING REMARKS

The concepts and structures described in the present chapter are necessarily tentative. So also is the model of their relations with one another which is put forward. Indeed the two are inseparable, for the structures themselves are thought of primarily as mediating functional relations. Nevertheless, I believe that the kind of regulation envisaged here not only reflects a great deal that is common to many psychologists of the present day, but also that it provides a closer approximation than **S-R** theory to the way in which the several functions executed within the brain relate with one another.

Apart from certain structures whose existence and function may be taken largely for granted (primary perceptual and effector mechanisms) the principal structures envisaged were the comparator system – closely linked with motor regulations through a corresponding effector system, a primary switching device: the link; a hierarchy of strategies governing the connexions between links, and a corresponding network of relations among these, forming a hierarchy of potential strategies or schemata.

Neither the equivalences and non-equivalences of cues elaborated in the comparator system nor the interconnexions of strategies intervening in the regulation of behaviour and mediating the activation of links and hence the settings of the comparator and effector systems, nor yet the equivalences and non-equivalences of strategies that we have termed schemata, are taken as inbuilt. Rather, it was argued that all of the relevant connexions are established largely in the course of learning. It was suggested that a process quite close to Pavlovian conditioning must be assumed to mediate the development of cue-equivalences. The association of links and strategies argued the operation of reinforcing centres, as described in the work of Olds and his associates. But this association was not conceived of as solely, or even mainly, a matter of purely linear sequence. A hierarchical organization was envisaged. For the complete determination of behaviour often involves the simultaneous activation of determinants at several levels. It was suggested therefore that reinforcement acted in such a way as to facilitate all of the connexions which were operative at the time of, or immediately prior to, the activation of the reinforcement centres. In other words, it is not only the immediate sequencing of overt behaviour which is reinforced, but the decision processes which structure and regulate the sequence. Finally, in this connexion, it was suggested that reinforcement was likely to depend not only on the presentation of satisfiers of bodily needs, but mainly on the facilitation of the regulatory process itself: behaviour which is engaged on during the activation of a higher-order strategy and which results in the successful running-off of that strategy is reinforced, and is thereby assimilated to the original structure.

It was argued that representational behaviour could only be understood if one takes into account the fact that it is not merely evoked by the concrete situation but involves the activation of an independent behaviour, conditioned to an input which is largely under the control of the subject, but the elements of which (links and strategies) are able to substitute for those of overt behaviour, and therefore determine the eventual settings in the original behaviour: anticipatory planning. It was suggested that the further development of systematic equivalences at the concrete and formal levels of reasoning is contingent on the formation of strategies co-ordinating several successive inputs, and is therefore closely related to development in the span of immediate memory, as argued by McLaughlin.

Finally, although these considerations were taken somewhat earlier in the chapter, shifts in attention were thought of as basic both to switching in the control of behaviour and to the trial-and-error which is essential to the elaboration of new connexions. Such shifts were possible on the assumption that the determination of sensitivity to environmental cues by selective inhibition was never absolute, and that the reception of cue-combinations associated with a given link (not activated centrally), would lead to the activation of associated strategies, on the lines indicated by Deutsch. It was hypothesized that such activation tended to the reduction of uncertainty, and that assimilation to well-established lines of behaviour (schemata) was sufficient to enable control to pass back to the original strategy. On the other hand, it was suggested that the mechanism was closely linked with the primitive 'what-is-it? reflex', and to the extent that greater uncertainty occurred, there appeared to be a switching of behaviour to very general flight and security-seeking mechanisms, elaborated out of inbuilt attachment behaviours.

All this implies a mode of approach, suggesting the sorts of questions which may reasonably be asked. The central principle behind this mode of approach is that the ultimate concern of psychology is not with segments of overt behaviour, for these are no more than a phenomenal given, but with the elucidation of the functional connexions between them. The systematic functional relations between these decision processes constitute a proper scientific statement of the regulation of behaviour at the level of psychology. Physiology is concerned with the physical mechanisms that render the regulations possible. Since everybody would like to be a behaviourist, I would say that the standpoint is behaviourist in so far as the decision processes are taken to be 'real' changes of state in the organism, and in so far as the functional connexions are no different in principle from those which could be envisaged in a purely physical system. It is not behaviourist if the term is restricted to views which accept the phenomenal datum, the segment of molar behaviour, as the only real psychological event, all others being either purely physiological, or mathematical constructs – 'intervening variables'.

Although I regard the present framework as a very open-ended and inadequate approximation, it seems to be sufficiently comprehensive to accommodate the more detailed interpretation of perceptual behaviour in animals and in human beings as well as the more complex regulations involved in the exercise of human intelligence. In particular, it offers a bridge between the cybernetically oriented studies of skilled human performance which are a distinctive feature of British experimental psychology since Bartlett, and the experimental, but cognitive analyses of intelligence contributed principally by Piaget. In other words, it spans a gulf which might otherwise be suspected between Chapters 4–6 of Volume II and Chapters 8–10 of the same volume. Together with my colleague, G. R. Roberts, I have attempted a more direct application of the model to the analysis of the complex skills involved in reading in Volume II, Chapter 7.

The remaining chapters of the present volume (excluding the very general concluding chapter) are concerned, first, with a review of the principal changes in the regulatory connexions that seem to be manifest in phylogenetic development and in early ontogenesis in human beings (Chapter 5), and, second, with the consideration of the motivational aspects of behaviour, which have received only very perfunctory treatment here (Chapter 6).

REFERENCES

APOSTEL, L., MAYS, W., MORF, A., and PIAGET, J. (1957). Les liaisons analytiques et synthétiques dans les comportements du sujet. *Etudes d'épistémologie génétique* **4**. Paris: Presses Universitaires de France.

ASHBY, W. R. (1960). *Design for a Brain* (second edn.). New York: John Wiley.

BARKER, R., DEMBO, T., and LEWIN, K. (1941) Frustration and regression. *Univ. of Iowa Studies in Child Welfare* **18**, No. 1.

BARTLETT, F. C. (1932). *Remembering*. London: Cambridge University Press.

BERLYNE, D. E. (1960a). *Conflict, Arousal and Curiosity*. New York and London: McGraw-Hill.

BERLYNE, D. E. (1960b). Les équivalences psychologiques et les notions quantitatives. In Berlyne, D. E. et Piaget, J., Théorie du comportement et opérations. *Etudes d'épistémologie génétique* **12**, 1–76.

BERLYNE, D. E. (1962). Comments on relations between Piaget theory and S-R theory. In Kessen, W., and Kuhlman, C. (ed.), Thought in the young child. *Mon. Soc. Res. Child Dev.* **27**, No. 2 (Serial No. 83), 127–130.

BIRCH, H. G. (1945). The relation of previous experience to insightful problem-solving. *J. Comp. Psychol.* **38**, 367–383.

BITTERMAN, M. E. (1965). Phyletic differences in learning. *Amer. Psychologist* **20**, 396–410.

BRAINE, M. D. S. (1963). The ontogeny of English phrase structure: the first phase. *Language* **39**, 1–13.

BROADBENT, D. E. (1954). The role of auditory localization in attention and memory span. *J. Exp. Psychol.* **47**, 191–196.

BROADBENT, D. E. (1958). *Perception and Communication*. Oxford: Pergamon.

BROADBENT, D. E., and GREGORY, R. (1964). Stimulus set and response set: the alternation of attention. *Q. J. exp. Psychol.* **16**, 309–317.

BRUNER, J. S. (1957). On perceptual readiness. *Psychol. Rev.* **64**, 123–152.

BRUNER, J. S., GOODNOW, J., and AUSTIN, G. A. (1956). *A Study of Thinking*. New York: John Wiley.

COWLES, J. T. (1937). Food tokens as incentives for learning by chimpanzees. *Comp. Psychol. Monogr.* **14**, 1–96.

DEUTSCH, J. A. (1960). *The Structural Basis of Behaviour*. London: Cambridge University Press.

GAGNÉ, R. M. (1966). *The Conditions of Learning*. New York: Holt Rinehart and Winston.

GRANIT, R. (1965). Central control of muscular movement. In Monnier, A. M., and Laget, P. (ed.), *The Human Machine: Mechanisms*. Volume 5 of *The Living Universe, An Encyclopaedia of the Biological Sciences*. London: Nelson, 130–132.

GRAY, J. A., and WEDDERBURN, A. A. I. (1960). Grouping strategies with simultaneous stimuli. *Q. J. exp. Psychol.* **12**, 180–184.

HARLOW, H. F., and ZIMMERMAN, R. R. (1958). The development of affectional responses in infant monkeys. *Proc. Amer. Phil. Soc.* **102**, 501–509.

HARLOW, H. F. (1961). The development of affectional patterns in infant monkeys. In Foss, B. (ed.), *Determinants of Infant Behaviour*. 75–97. London: Methuen.

HEBB, D. O. (1949). *The organisation of Behaviour*. New York: John Wiley.

HELD, R., and BOSSOM, J. (1961). Neonatal deprivation and adult rearrangement: complementary techniques for studying plastic sensori-motor co-ordinations. *J. Comp. Physiol. Psychol.* **54**, 33–37.

HELD, R., and HEIN, A. V. (1958). Adaptation of disarranged hand-eye co-ordination contingent upon re-afferent stimulation. *Perceptual and Motor Skills* **8**, 87–90.

KÖHLER, I. (1963). The formation and transformation of the perceptual world. *Psychol. Issues*. **3**, No. 4

KÖHLER, W. (1925). *The Mentality of Apes*. London: Routledge and Kegan Paul.

LASHLEY, K. S. (1929). *Brain Mechanisms and Intelligence*. Chicago: University of Chicago Press.

LUNZER, E. A. (1955). Intellectual development in the play of young children aged 2 to 6. Ph.D. Thesis. University of Birmingham.

LUNZER, E. A. (1965). Problems of formal reasoning in test situations. In Mussen, P. H. (ed.), European research in cognitive development. *Mon. Soc. Res. Child Dev.* **30**, No. 2 (Serial No. 100), 19–46.

MACKAY, D. M. (1962). Theoretical models of space perception. In Muses, C. A. (ed.), *Aspects of the Theory of Artificial Intelligence*, 83–103. New York: Plenum Press.

MACKINTOSH, N. J. (1965). Effect of attention on slope of generalization gradients. *Brit. J. Psychol.* **56**, 87–93.

MCLAUGHLIN, G. H. (1963). Psycho-logic: a possible alternative to Piaget's formulation. *Brit. J. Educ. Psychol.* **33**, 61–67.

MAGOUN, H. W. (1963). *The Waking Brain* (second edn.). Springfield, Ill.: Charles Thomas.

MATURNA, H. R., LETTVIN, J. Y., MCCULLOCH, W. S., and PITTS, W. B. (1960). Anatomy and physiology of vision in the frog *Rana Pipiens*. *J. Gen. Physiol.* **43**, 129–175.

MILLER, G. A., GALANTER, A. and PRIBRAM, K. H. (1960). *Plans and the Structure of Behaviour*. New York: Henry Holt.

MILLER, G. A., and SELFRIDGE, J. A. (1953). Verbal context and the recall of meaningful material. *Amer. J. Psychol.* **63**, 176–185. (Reprinted in Sol Saporta (ed.) *Psycholinguistics*. New York: Holt Rinehart and Winston, 1961, 198–206).

MOWRER, O. H. (1960). *Learning Theory and Behaviour*. New York: John Wiley.

NEISSER, U. (1964). Visual search. *Scientific Amer.* **210** (6), 94–102.

OLDFIELD, R. C., and ZANGWILL, O. L. (1942). Head's concept of the schema and its application in contemporary British psychology. Parts I, II and III. *Brit. J. Psychol.* **32**, 267–286, **33**, 58–64 and 113–129.

OLDFIELD, R. C., and ZANGWILL, O. L. (1943). Head's concept of the schema and its application in contemporary British psychology. Part IV. *Brit. J. Psychol.* **43**, 143–149.

OLDS, J., and OLDS, M. (1965). Drives, rewards and the brain. In Barron, F. *et al. New Directions in Psychology II.* New York: Holt Rinehart and Winston, 327–410.

PIAGET, J. (1950). *The Psychology of Intelligence.* London: Routledge and Kegan Paul.

PIAGET, J. (1953). *The Origin of Intelligence in the Child.* London: Routledge and Kegan Paul.

PIAGET, J. (1957). Logique et équilibre dans les comportements du sujet. In Apostel, L., Mandelbrot, B. et Piaget, J. Logique et équilibre. *Etudes d'épistémologie génétique* **2**, 27–117. Paris: Presses Universitaires de France.

PIAGET, J. (1959). Apprentissage et connaissance: première partie. In Gréco, P. and Piaget, J. Apprentissage et connaissance. *Etudes d'épistémologie génétique* **7**, 21–67. Paris: Presses Universitaires de France.

PIAGET, J. (1961). *Les mécanismes perceptifs.* Paris: Presses Universitaires de France.

ROSENBLATT, F. (1958). The perceptron: a probabilistic model for information storage and organization in the brain. *Psychol. Rev.* **65**, 386–408.

ROSENZWEIG, M. R. (1963). The mechanisms of hunger and thirst. In Postman, L. (ed.) *Psychology in the Making.* New York: Alfred Knopf, pp. 73–143.

SKINNER, B. F. (1938). *The Behaviour of Organisms.* New York: Appleton-Century-Crofts.

SKINNER, B. F. (1953). *Science and Human Behaviour.* New York: Macmillan.

SOLOMON, P., KUBZANSKY, P. E., LEIDERMAN, P. H., MENDELSON, J. H., TRUMBULL, R., and WEXLER, D. (1961). *Sensory Deprivation.* Cambridge, Mass.: Harvard Univ. Press.

STEVENSON, H. W. (1962). Piaget, behaviour theory and intelligence. In Kessen, W. and Kuhlman, C. (ed.), Thought in the young child. *Mon. Soc. Res. Child Dev.* **27**, No. 2 (Serial No. 83), 113–126.

SUTHERLAND, N. S. (1959). Stimulus analysing mechanisms. In *Proceedings of a Symposium on the Mechanisation of Thought Processes*, Vol. II, pp. 575–609. London: Her Majesty's Stationery Office.

SUTHERLAND, N. S., and MACKINTOSH, N. J. (1964). Discrimination learning: non-additivity of cues. *Nature* **201**, 528–530.

THOMPSON, W. R., and HERON, W. (1954). The effects of restricting early experience on the problem-solving capacity of dogs. *Canad. J. Psychol.* **8**, 17–31.

TREISMAN, A. M. (1960). Contextual cues in selective listening. *Q. J. exp. Psychol.* **12**, 242–248.

VINCE, M. A. (1961). Developmental changes in learning capacity. In Thorpe, W. H. and Zangwill, O. L. (ed.). *Current Problems in Animal Behaviour*. London: Cambridge U.P., 225–247.

WOHLWILL, J. (1966). Perceptual learning. *Annual Review of Psychology* **17**, 201–232.

YOUNG, J. Z. (1964). *A Model of the Brain*. London: O.U.P.

ZANGWILL, O. L. (1961). Lashley's concept of cerebral mass-action. In Thorpe, W. H. and Zangwill, O. L. (ed.). *Current Problems in Animal Behaviour*. London: Cambridge U.P., 59–86.

5

Development in Learning: Introduction

THE SCOPE of the present chapter is more limited than its title would suggest. For the most part, changes in the content and character of human learning will be considered in Volume II. The present chapter will simply extend the analysis of learning processes contained in Sections IV and V of Chapter 4 by reviewing three areas of inquiry all of which point to the the existence of phylogenetic and ontogenetic changes in the regulatory mechanisms controlling behaviour. The first section is concerned with recent research bearing on qualitative differences in the character of learning shown by individuals of widely different species. The second is a summary of Piaget's analysis of developmental changes observed in children up to the age of eighteen months. The two sets of data invite comparison, and such a comparison is attempted in Section III. The fourth section deals with imitation. Imitation is important for two reasons. First: it is a form of behaviour which has been first misinterpreted and then neglected in psychology, largely because it is confined to the higher species. As I have indicated earlier (Chapter 1, Section VII), the assumption of biological continuity has been fully justified for it is part of the foundation of psychology as an experimental science. But the further assumption that there are no qualitative differences between species is quite unwarranted, and tends to act as a break on the scientific investigation of human behaviour by limiting inquiry to those aspects which are least distinctive. The second reason for focusing attention on imitation is that the capacity to imitate appears to be intimately bound up with the process of representation itself, which transforms the entire character of human behaviour, both cognitive and motivational. The last section is devoted to a brief overview of the nature of this transformation and its implications.

I. PHYLETIC DIFFERENCES IN LEARNING

1. *Limitations in the Learning of Fishes*

Throughout the first half of the century it was assumed that the laws of learning are the same for all animals. Not all animals are equally suitable for experimentation and none more so than the rat: easy to rear in captivity, to breed, to maintain. The assumption that it made little difference what species one studied led to an ever-increasing concentration of research on this one species as the typical example. Moreover, such studies as were made of learning in other species, e.g. conditioning and discrimination, tended to confirm the belief that its character was identical throughout the animal kingdom. The principal challenge to this view comes from the studies of Bitterman and his associates. Their results show clearly that the laws of learning may be shown to differ quite fundamentally if one compares individuals of widely differing species. Bitterman's strategy (Bitterman, Wodinsky and Candland, 1958) was to begin by choosing a species which differed widely from the rat on the phylogenetic scale, and compare the learning of this species with that of the rat. The first experiments were conducted with fish (the African mouthbreeder). Now it was already clear that the simplest kinds of learning (classical and instrumental conditioning) would be unlikely to reveal differences at least among vertebrates. It was supposed that behaviour requiring a measure of flexibility might be more revealing. Therefore the earliest studies dealt with reversal learning.

Reversal learning is an extension of discrimination learning. Suppose an animal is repeatedly placed at the start of a forked runway with the two forks clearly differentiated by contrasted stimulus cards, e.g. a card bearing horizontal stripes and one bearing vertical stripes. From trial to trial, the position of the two cards (left or right) is varied in random fashion. The pattern of reinforcement is held consistent: either the animal invariably finds a pellet of food if it selects the left (or right) fork, irrespective of the discriminative stimulus, *spatial discrimination*, or the food is invariably placed beyond the horizontal (or vertical) stimulus, irrespective of its position, *visual discrimination*. From trial to trial, the animal learns to match its behaviour with the pattern of reward, so that 'errors' are eliminated, and it obtains 100 per cent reward (apart from very minor aberrations). Suppose now the experimenter reverses the pattern of reinforcement, i.e. left position instead of right, or vertical stimulus instead of horizontal. The animal's first run will now be an error. The reversal requires new learning. Once the reversal has been learnt, a new reversal is made (yielding the original pattern), then a third, and so on. At each reversal, the animal must accommodate. Typically, the rat requires longer to learn the first reversal than the original learning (interference). But successive reversals are made with fewer errors. In time, for spatial reversals, the learning of the rat becomes near-perfect, errors occurring only on the first run after reversal (one-trial learning).

Bitterman *et al.* (1958) reports the findings of visual and spatial reversal experiments with fish and rats as subjects. (Instead of running down an alleyway the fish swim towards one of two plexiglass windows.) The most telling of these involved sixty daily reversals on the spatial problem followed by forty on the visual, or *vice versa*, the whole series extending over one hundred days. The learning series for each day consisted of twenty trials on the same problem. Figure 1 shows clearly the difference between the two species. Each curve represents a block of ten days. The

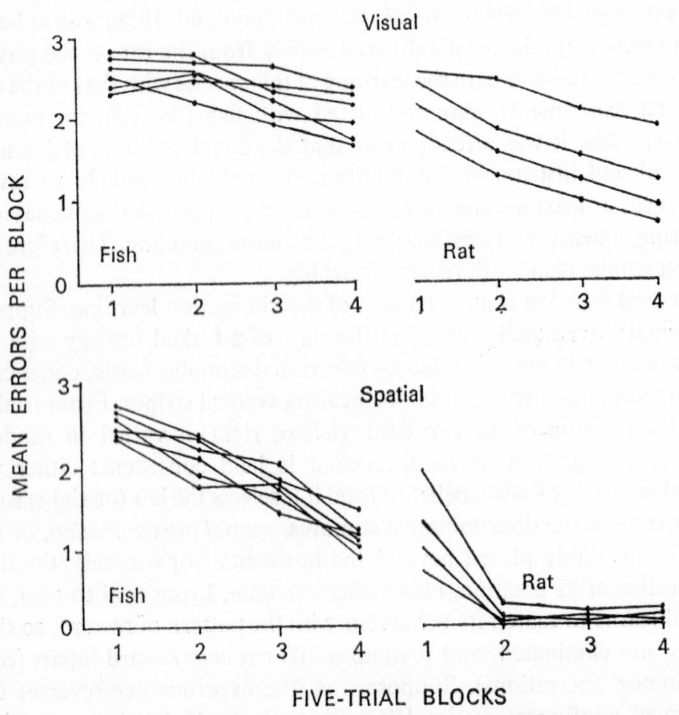

Figure 1. Daily visual and spatial reversal in fish and rat (from Bitterman, Wodinsky and Candland (1958), p. 100)

performance of the rats improved with continued experience of reversal. That of the fish did not. Although it is very clear that, at least for the spatial problem, each problem was mastered quite well within the twenty trials, each learning was separate from that of the previous days. Conversely, the curves for the rat subjects are perfectly ordered. Learning on days 11–20 was superior to that on days 1–10, and so on. Even more striking is the evidence of one-trial reversal learning in the spatial problem.

Figure 2 differs from Figure 1 in that the record of each of the first five trials on successive blocks of days is shown separately. Not only is performance on days 31–40 clearly superior to that on days 1–10 right from the start of each day's problem, but performance from trial 2 on is practically errorless for the spatial problem. The authors do not give the corresponding figure for the fish, since it would be uninstructive. 'Plots for the fish corresponding to those of [Figure 2] present four indistinguishable sets of points hovering about the 50 per cent error level'.

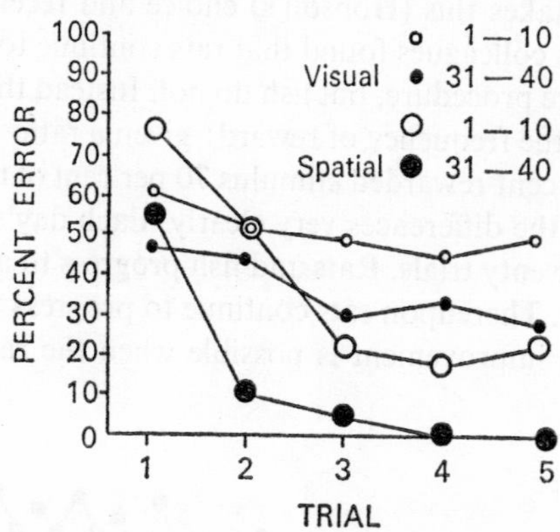

Figure 2. Daily visual and spatial reversal in the rat: per cent errors on each of trials 1–5 (*ibid.*, p. 101)

Other experiments show that when the animal subject is required to learn fourteen reversals on two successive days, each to a criterion of seventeen errorless runs, both rats and fish show improvement from the first day to the second; but whereas the rats show improvement from one reversal to the next, the fish do not. Thus all results point to the conclusion that the rats learn the reversal as such whereas fish learning is limited to separate problems.

A second group of problems which is found to differentiate between the two species is concerned with probability. Given the same type of discrimination learning situation as that used for reversal, the experimenter distributes reinforcement between the two stimuli (spatial or visual) in such a way that one of them is reinforced more frequently than the other, but at a rate which is less than 100 per cent, e.g. 70 : 30, or 60 : 40. The actual sequence is kept random, with the restriction that over a run of trials the ratio remains constant. Under these conditions, given a series of training trials of sufficient length, both fish and rats learn to 'maximize' reward, i.e. to choose consistently (at a level above 90 per cent) the stimulus which receives the more frequent reward. But this result obtains only when the experiment is performed in standard fashion, failure on a given trial being followed by administration of its successor. The two species behave very differently when the experiment is conducted using a 'guidance' procedure: failure on a given trial is followed by a brief black-out, whereupon the animal is presented with the positive stimulus only, it takes this (Hobson's) choice and receives the reward. Bitterman and his colleagues found that rats continue to maximize even under the guidance procedure, but fish do not. Instead their behaviour is such as to match the frequency of reward: given a ratio of 70 : 30, they choose the 70 per cent rewarded stimulus 70 per cent of the time. Figures 3 and 4 illustrate the differences very clearly. Each day's training represents a series of twenty trials. Rats and fish progress to a matching ratio within a few days. Thereupon rats continue to progress to near 100 per cent so that little improvement is possible when the ratio is shifted to

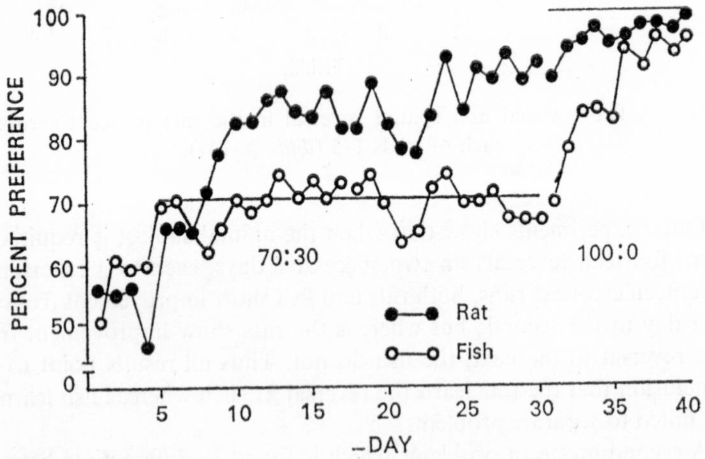

Figure 3. Preference of fish and rat for the more frequently reinforced stimulus (70 : 30 and 100 : 0 visual) (from Bitterman *et al.*, 1958, p. 105)

100 per cent. Fish remain stationary at the matching level, so that the shift is dramatic (Figure 3). Similarly, rats show little fall-off when the ratio is shifted to 60 : 40; fish, maintained at the original ratio, show a dramatic change when guidance is discontinued (Figure 4).

Reverting to the reversal experiment, striking differences were noted between the performance of the rats under spatial as compared with visual reversal, the former showing far more rapid and effective learning. Such differences are systematic. They reappear in quite diverse experiments, with diverse species. For instance, in experiments on delayed-response, Nissen, Riesen and Nowlis (1938) found that chimpanzees learned to select one of two spatially contrasted containers, having seen a reward concealed beneath it to a criterion of 90 per cent success, even after thirty seconds of delay; improvement in a visual delay problem

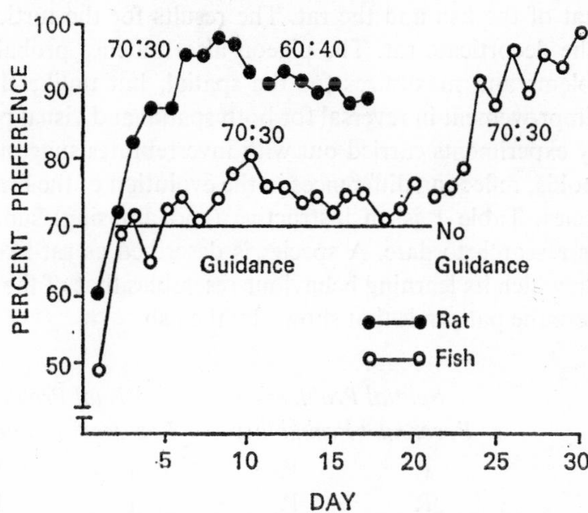

Figure 4. Preference of fish and rat for the more frequently reinforced position (70 : 30 and 60 : 40 spatial) (*ibid.* p. 106)

(contrasted containers on a rotating table) was very slow, reaching only the 70–80 per cent level, and with delays as short as three seconds. Hebb (1949) argues that spatial response represents discrimination with respect to more distant visual cues, these being the more permanent features of input as the animal shifts its gaze.

The difference between spatial and visual problems appears strikingly in control experiments carried out by Bitterman and his colleagues and reviewed by Bitterman (1965). After extensive cortical ablation, rats were given reversal and probability problems under spatial and visual reinforcement. Differences in performance were dramatic. For spatially differentiated rewards, the rats showed no impairment in reversal, and continued to maximize on the probability problem, but for the visual reward, performance regressed to the level of the fish: no improvement for successive reversals and random matching of reinforcement pattern in probability problems.

The same article summarizes results from a number of other experiments (published and unpublished) involving different species. Suitable forms of apparatus and reinforcement were devised to study reversal and probability behaviour in pigeons and in painted turtles, on the plausible assumption that the behaviour of these species might be intermediate between that of the fish and the rat. The results for the turtle parallel those for the decorticate rat. The pigeon also matches probability for visual problems and maximizes for the spatial, but unlike the turtle, it exhibits improvement in reversal for both spatial and visual problems. Preliminary experiments carried out with invertebrates suggest that the hierarchy holds, reflecting differences in the evolution of the brain of the several species. Table 1 is an instructive (and amusing) summary of Bitterman's research to date. A species is described as rat-like (R) for situations in which its learning behaviour resembles that of the rat, fish-like (F) where the pattern is that shown by the fish.

	Spatial Problems		*Visual Problems*	
Species	*Reversal*	*Probability*	*Reversal*	*Probability*
Monkey	R	R	R	R
Rat	R	R	R	R
Pigeon	R	R	R	F
Turtle	R	R	F	F
Decorticated rat	R	R	F	F
Fish	F	F	F	F
Cockroach	F	F	—	—
Earthworm	F	—	—	—

Table 1. Phyletic differences in learning (from Bitterman, 1965, p. 408)

Before considering the next body of evidence on development in learning, attention may be drawn to two of Bitterman's observations. First, whatever their interpetation, Bitterman's data are very clear-cut, being based on an unusually sound methodology. The behaviour of any animal (including our own species) in this sort of discrimination situation is the product of a number of unknown factors. In particular, there is no means of equating drive and incentive or difficulty of stimulus for species as widely different as rat, fish, pigeon and turtle. Differences in learning might therefore be attributed to any one of these causes. Therefore a single comparison of group averages is quite inconclusive. Bitterman's conclusions rest on qualitative differences which he finds to be remarkably consistent regardless of the conditions of experimentation. Having repeated the experiments under varying drive conditions, with and without correction procedure (for reversal), and so on, he finds there are no conditions under which the fish behaves like the rat and none under which the rat behaves like the fish for these four experiments. This rigorous control is very necessary when making comparisons between species, and likewise when interpreting data within species (e.g. with children matched for C A but widely different in M A). It is rarely found, and it is difficult indeed to establish differences which withstand the test. That is the importance of Bitterman's work.

The second observation is a rather obvious one. The four experiments do not differentiate between the rat and the monkey, and there may be invertebrates whose learning is inferior to that of the fish. Others are needed for further and finer differentiation. In point of fact, however, there is one respect in which the behaviour of monkeys does appear to differ from that of rats. One of the major differences between the rat and the fish in probability learning is this. In so far as the fish matches, its choices are random, unrelated to the previous trial, reflecting only the gross ratio of reinforcement. The rat, too, does not maximize until after many trials. But during the period of acquisition its behaviour is non-random. Instead it exhibits a consistency, e.g. a position choice where the reinforcement is visual. Often its behaviour is related to the preceding trial. It repeats the previously reinforced behaviour. This observation recalls the much earlier observation of Krechevsky (1932): rats learning mazes act on 'hypotheses' (= 'strategies' in Chapter 4). Monkeys also reflect the previous trial in their choices, but often their strategy is the reverse: they avoid the previously reinforced response. Although this difference is less well-established than differences between lower species, it is none the less suggestive, particularly as it is relevant to the very different behaviour found in human children and adults in probability experiments, often deceptively fish-like. We reserve its discussion for Section III. For the present let us consider a group of experiments which has been found to differentiate quite sharply between lower mammals and primates.

2. *Learning Set*

Experiments on learning are quite generally conducted on the assumption that the subject entering the laboratory has something to learn, and the mechanism of this learning can be fully revealed by studying the effect of the experimental manipulation of variables (deprivation, incentive, reinforcement, discriminative stimuli) during the course of the experiments themselves. Little account is taken of the effect of previous learning experiences on the present learning. It is not very difficult to find isolated researches even before 1940, when Harlow embarked on the study of learning sets, which would force one to qualify the generalization. But they were isolated, and Harlow was the first to systematically explore the effect of repeated exposure to a learning situation. The subjects were rhesus monkeys, and the experiments were variants of discrimination learning.

Learning set experiments have been carried out with a wide variety of subjects, but mostly with primates (for reasons which will appear). Human beings are included in this order. But the original work used monkey subjects, and their data provide the base-line for comparisons. The experimental procedure devised by Harlow may therefore be taken as typical. The subject reaches for a tray through the bars of his cage. The tray contains two food wells differentiated by the stimulus objects which cover them (e.g. a yellow cross versus a blue triangle). The stimuli may be solid or two-dimensional. (For monkeys, and for immature children, the former are easier to differentiate and the course of learning is more rapid.) The subject removes one of the lids. If his choice is correct, he finds a food reward. Usually (non-correction) he is not allowed to remove the other. This concludes a trial. A screen is lowered and the next trial is prepared. The objects are the same but their position may be reversed in accordance with a predetermined random sequence. The second trial is followed by a third and so on. The learning continues until a specified number of trials has been reached, or until the subject has attained a predetermined criterion of success (e.g. five errorless trials). This concludes a problem. The procedure is identical for the next problem, but the stimulus objects are different (e.g. a red circle versus a white square). Problems may be continued to a specified number or, again, to a predetermined criterion of success, e.g. not more than one or two errors on five consecutive problems.

The data for the most celebrated of Harlow's inquiries (1949) are reproduced in Figure 5. They are based on work with eight monkeys, who began with no previous experience of discrimination situations. They were given a series of 344 problems: fifty trials for each of the first thirty-two problems, six on each of the succeeding two hundred, and an average of nine on each of the remaining 112.

Each point represents a percentage of errors on a given trial totalled

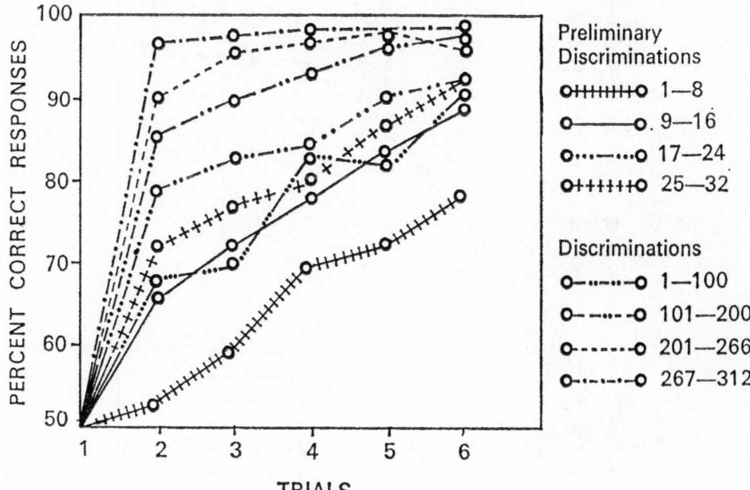

Figure 5. Discrimination learning curves on successive blocks of problems (from Harlow, 1949, p. 53)

over subjects and problems. As may be expected, each curve has its origin at the 50 per cent ordinate, because the subject has no means of predicting which of the objects will be correct on the first trial of a new problem. If we look at each curve separately, we see a representation of the average course of within-problem learning: errors decrease in frequency from trial to trial in accordance with the usual negatively accelerated function (see Estes, 1959). If we look at the relation between curves, we see a representation of inter-problem learning (or 'transfer' between problems of the same class – as Harlow (1959) is careful to specify, but whereas the specification of the data is of the utmost significance, the specificity of the description simply begs the question: for how is one to define 'same class'?). Again, there is a gradual improvement: the acquisition of the learning set follows the same negatively accelerated course as does single problem learning.

One is free to plot one's data how one chooses, and Harlow makes the point clearer by simply reversing the representation of blocks and trials,

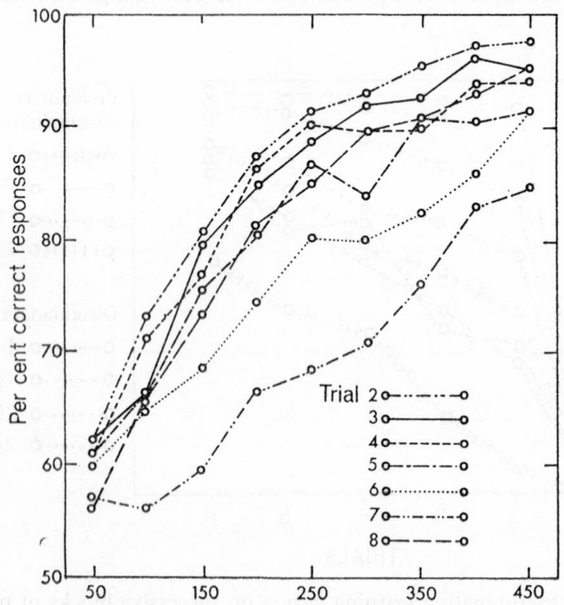

Figure 6. Learning set curves with problem blocks as the parameter (from Harlow, 1959, p. 498)

so that each curve represents improvement for a given trial as the subject proceeds to the next: Figure 6.

In general the curves of Figure 6 resemble those of Figure 5. Learning is a trial-and-error process, but one which takes place at more than one level: here the two levels are discrimination learning and the formation of the discrimination learning set. (Both are 'strategies' in terms of the conceptual system described in the last chapter.) There are two points of difference. The curve for trial 2 in Figure 6 is sigmoidal, exhibiting an initial flat: this is attributed by Harlow and Warren (1952) to a difficulty which the animals have in discriminating between the two forms during the first few trials of the first few problems (the curves of Figure 6 relate to planometric stimuli). In other words, the true learning is negatively accelerated, and the flat portion simply points to a more elementary learning which is not directly shown up in performance.

The second difference appears in the curves of Figure 5 relating to the last blocks of problems. Here learning is sudden, showing an apparent discontinuity: from 50 per cent on trial 1 to 90 per cent or even 100 per cent on trial 2. Consistent 'one-trial learning' can easily be obtained from some monkeys (after many problems), more easily from chimpanzees (Hayes, Thompson and Hayes, 1953), and almost invariably from children, at least after a mental age of approximately six (*ibid.*; Roberts, 1933; Stevenson and Swartz, 1958; etc.). Harlow (1951, 1959) likens this to insight. Learning appears sudden instead of gradual. And he draws the conclusion that insight is invariably a result of previous (trial-and-error) learning. The conclusion is perfectly correct so far as it goes. But the discrimination learning procedure has not so far proved equal to the elucidation of all the characteristics of what Köhler described as insight. The argument from the graph is specious, because the data for trial 1 antecede the learning and do not form part of it. Harlow himself has shown (1944b) that monkeys can learn in zero trials: after being shown the food going into one of the wells, or after seeing the experimenter point to the correct well (always of course after the establishment of the learning set). A further characteristic of insightful learning in Köhler's (1925) observations is that it frequently follows a pause in overt behaviour, being a product of interiorized trial-and-error, as well as of the combination of behaviour segments (see Chapter 1, Section V and Chapter 7).

But the universality of trial-and-error as the condition of all unguided learning stands. (Skinner's technique of shaping behaviour is really a matter of building on previous learning and at the same time adjusting the criteria of 'success' to match the progress of the learner.) At the same time, the significance of the work on learning set (which antedates Bitterman's) is that it provides a clear specification of at least one broad area of learning behaviour which differentiates quite sharply between species.[1] Thus, chimpanzees have been found to form learning sets more rapidly and more efficiently than monkeys (Hayes, Thompson and Hayes, 1953).

[1] One might well go further, for its relevance is general. But the general statement cannot but entail a partly speculative extrapolation from the data.

Children aged two to five are at least as efficient as chimpanzees (*ibid.*) and may be more so (experiments reported by Harlow, 1949). But experiments on learning set formation using children as subjects often give conflicting results (Lunzer and Hulme, 1967). It is practically certain that inter-species comparisons between even higher animals and human children are seriously vitiated by differences in motivation as well as differences due to the fact that children, possessing language and a considerable experience of interacting with an adult in a play situation, are apt to react to the situation as an interpersonal one, involving themselves and the experimenter. Both factors must operate in such a way as to lower the efficiency of learning set formation, at least up to the age at which children begin to form conscious hypotheses and test them. This is a level which is of course never achieved by sub-human species (see Section V, 5). The fact that, at least under optimal conditions, the performance of younger children equals or surpasses that of other primates is consistent with comparative results of animal studies, and this is one instance where one is inclined to attach more weight to successes (arguing a higher potential) than to relative failures (attributable to failure of motivation, etc.).

Harlow (1959, pp. 505 ff.) summarizes the evidence on the developmental significance of learning set. On the side of ontogenetic development, rhesus monkeys do not form learning sets below the age of 150 days. although they are capable of single problem learning by sixty days of age. Full capacity is not attained until well into the second or third year of life. On the side of phylogenetic development, experiments using the more primitive marmoset and squirrel monkeys reveal that efficiency in **LS** formation corresponds to cortical evolution of the species: the squirrel monkey is superior to the marmoset and the rhesus monkey is vastly superior to either. Ontogenetic and, especially, phylogenetic differences appear in two ways: the rate of **LS** formation increases with the level of cortical functioning, and the asymptote to the curves of performance for the first few trials on each problem, and especially the second trial, rises correspondingly (see Figure 6). Experiments with sub-primates (rats and cats) indicate that these species do show problem to problem transfer (**LS**), but the rate of such improvement is very slow and even after many problems (340 in the cat study) the asymptote for trials 2–10 is only about 70 per cent (20 per cent above chance) as compared with over 90 per cent for trial 2 in rhesus monkeys and apes.

The interpretation given to these phenomena by Harlow is based on what he terms 'error factor theory'. Each 'error factor' is taken to represent a reaction tendency in the subject, and the response that is made on any given problem reflects the factor which was operative at the time. Error factors are closely related to Krechevsky's 'hypotheses' to which several references have been made elsewhere in this volume. An error factor is very obviously one sort of strategy in the sense in which I have defined this term in the last chapter. In order not to confuse myself or the reader I will stick to the term 'strategy' because it has (I think) a wider range of application. A number of such strategies can be identified: e.g. repetition of the previous choice (stimulus perseveration), alternation of the previous choice (response shift), positional preference (for right or left stimulus), and preferences based on a discriminative cue. It is supposed that the animal subject approaches the problem with a repertoire of such strategies and that the effect of learning is to lead to the gradual elimination of 'error' strategies, presumably through non-reinforcement.

It is presumed that the differential strengths of such strategies may vary at the start of the series. Which strategy operates at any time cannot be stated in absolute terms, but the frequency with which it is selected reflects its strength (within the situational context). Having operated, it is returned to the 'pool', but with diminished strength if unreinforced. Clearly, the more complex a situation the more strategies it will be capable of evoking (compare a simple object-choice with the case where a choice must be made in terms of one attribute from objects varying in several: colour, shape, size, etc., or with the 'oddity problem', where the choice must be in terms of a relation between three objects, two being identical and the other different). Error-factor theory therefore offers a first approach to the problem of quantifying task difficulty. But it is only a first approach, since it tells us nothing about how a (higher-order) strategy arises in the first place, nor what determines its probability of evocation in the given situation.

Be that as it may, error-factor theory enables one to predict with some accuracy the course of later learning from that of initial error, and not only for the correct response but also for the frequency with which an error strategy (factor) will appear (Harlow, 1959). Restle (1962) has shown that, mathematically, the same predictions will result whether it is assumed that only one strategy is sampled on each trial, and returned to the pool, or that several are sampled simultaneously, and all are strengthened simultaneously. Both probabilistic models yield excellent fits to **LS** empirical data. The interpretation of Restle differs from that of Harlow in that his, like that of Estes (1959) is a reinforcement theory. Harlow's is an inhibition theory, in which non-reinforcement has the effect of further inhibiting error factors. Positive learning is indirect. Current physiological theory certainly favours the increased recognition of the role of selective inhibition in the implementation of positive (because uninhibited) connexions (Young, 1964). But the evidence for positive reinforcement at the behavioural level seems to me to be too strong to discount (see Section IV of last chapter). In other words, it is difficult to maintain that no learning occurs when a response is rewarded.

This glimpse into error-factor theory and related probabilistic models has taken us a little away from the facts about learning set. We have to retain three points of anchorage. First, learning set discriminates both in terms of ontogenesis and in terms of phylogenesis, where 'single-problem learning' shows little discrimination. Second, learning set phenomena cannot be explained without recourse to some sort of strategy interpretation, e.g. error-factor theory. Third, both error-factor theory and the probabilistic models of Restle assume the availability of such strategies as well as the generalizability of modifications to their relative strengths across problems (inter-problem learning). Yet it is precisely these characteristics which most sharply differentiate the higher from the lower species.

I have of course been quite deliberate in describing the phenomena of learning set immediately after Bitterman's findings on reversal and probability learning. Everything points to the conclusion that the processes fit end on to one another. Bitterman's experiments differentiate between lower orders and *mammalia* while those of Harlow differentiate within the latter order, and especially between primates and non-primates. Presumably there are further kinds of organization of experience which differentiate between human beings and other primates, and within the former, between successive ontogenetic levels. Indeed there are, and it is their elucidation which constitutes Piaget's main contribution to the problem of development in learning.

Clearly, we have to consider a little more closely the relation of learning set to reversal learning and of both to single problem discrimination. In other words, we need to consider the nature and origin of strategies which are generalizable across problems of a 'similar class' and the nature of those co-ordinations which result in the constitution of such a class. For it is not enough that the psychologist be able to define it; we need to know how the subject arrives at it. In fact, we will not be able to give any very definitive answers to these problems. But we can begin to pinpoint their salient features. We should be in a better position to do so after considering the successive achievements in ontogenetic development. These have been most closely analysed by Piaget, and, conveniently, in the human species. To which studies we now turn.

II. ONTOGENESIS OF HUMAN LEARNING

In the present chapter we will be concerned only with the development of behavioural organization through learning in the course of the first eighteen months of life, i.e. with what Piaget has termed the sensori-motor stage in ontogenetic evolution. Further development forms the topic of Volume II as a whole. It is hardly necessary to add that it is the earlier phase of development which offers the more striking analogies with what we have just seen in phylogenetic developments. But there is a further reason for devoting some attention to it: for it is not the case that sensori-motor organization gives way to representational behaviour and that the more primitive kinds of representation give way to the more systematic kinds of operational organization. Rather, the co-ordinations which are achieved in the earlier stages remain active throughout life and their importance is twofold: (*a*) they form the basis for the co-ordinations entailed in later, more elaborated structures; and (*b*) they continue to operate independently, albeit in slightly modified form, whenever the situation is such that higher-order co-ordinations are not required. To put the matter plainly, be I never such a clever fellow, the co-ordinations which I invoke when I blow my nose are sensori-motor co-ordinations; and I spend rather more of my time on this order of activity than in constructing and testing sometimes tenuous hypothetico-deductive models.

Piaget (1950, and, more especially, 1953) distinguishes six 'stages' in the evolution of sensori-motor co-ordinations, although the sixth of these really amounts to a first characterization of representation. They are:

Stage I (0–1 month): extension of reflex behaviour.
Stage II (1–3 months): primary circular reactions.
Stage III (4–7 months): secondary circular reactions.
Stage IV (7–11 months): co-ordination of secondary schemata.
Stage V (1 year–17 months): tertiary circular reactions.
Stage VI (18 months–): beginnings of representation.

The ages are only approximative and each of the stages is thought of as shading into its successor. Indeed, the comments just made on the role of the sensori-motor co-ordinations at later stages of development also apply to the successive phases within the former. Every 'stage' is characterized by the highest level of co-ordination that becomes habitual at that level, even though lower levels of co-ordination still operate. Moreover, the term 'habitual' is used deliberately, for Piaget regularly quotes isolated instances of higher-order co-ordinations occurring at earlier stages.

The following account will adhere closely to Piaget's own although I will try, wherever possible, to fit his account to the model used in Chapter 4, and later, to trace the relevance of the analogy between phylogenetic and ontogenetic evolution.

Stage I (extension of reflex behaviour). Typical of the behaviour which Piaget finds as characteristic of this stage is the extension of reflex in the course of a groping which involves only those effector combinations which are already present in the reflex itself. The principal example cited is the movement of head and mouth in the direction of the nipple when this is withdrawn or when it is applied to the cheek, the upper lip or the chin. A second example is the movement of the hand towards the mouth when it happens to touch the face. Piaget interprets such behaviour patterns as a matter of *accommodation* of the reflex to the related contingencies in the environment and *assimilation* of the latter to the reflex, as a result of which this takes on the character of a primitive schema. He notes that assimilation is at once *generalizing*, by which he means that where a particular stimulation has been incorporated into the schema, other similar stimulations will be likewise; *recognitive*, in the sense that once a stimulation has activated a reflex it will more probably reactivate it on future encounters; and *reproductive*, in the sense that the reflex itself tends to function whenever circumstances permit. This tendency for activities, or schemata, to function, and thereby to assimilate to themselves whatever features of the environment lend themselves to such assimilation, is taken by Piaget to be the fundamental, biological, basis of motivation (O I, p. 42. References to O I are to Piaget, 1953).

The analysis of the simplest forms of behaviour is not the easiest task of the psychologist but the most difficult. As I have already noted, the basic notion of assimilation – accommodation is present in any structural interpretation of behaviour (**IRM**, analyser, comparator system) even though the terminology may vary. Moreover within this mode of analysis, as will be apparent when we consider Piaget's description and analysis of subsequent stages, his interpretation has been followed fairly closely in our description of the comparator system, as opposed to, e.g. Deutsch's analysers or Broadbent's filter. Nevertheless I am inclinded to urge two modifications to Piaget's interpretation of these primitive behaviours, whose import may be considerable.

In the first place, Piaget traces the origins of motivation to a functional tendency: 'The reflex must be conceived as an organized totality whose nature it is to preserve itself by functioning and consequently to function sooner or later for its own sake.' (O I, p. 38). Few would object to the first part of this statement which is descriptive. But the last phrase constitutes an attempt at explanation, and it is one which would probably command little support among psychologists or physiologists. What Piaget is saying in effect is that the functional tendency is a primitive biological datum which transcends psychology. He later refers to a similar property of the eye: 'Things seen constitute nourishment essential to the eye since it is they which impose the continuous use to which the organs owe their development. The eye needs light images just as the whole body needs chemical nourishment' (*ibid.* p. 43). Taken at its face value, the statement is false: animals reared in darkness do not lose the power of sight. It is true that such animals, and also human beings after removal of a cataract have to learn to make adequate use of their restored vision (Hebb, 1937; von Senden, 1960). But this means only that perceptual discrimination depends on higher level organizations acquired in the course of learning. It tells us nothing about the causal mechanism underlying the functional tendency.

It seems to me that what Piaget is trying to do is to establish a continuity between certain other processes in biology, notably the assimilation of inert matter by eating and breathing, and psychology, and in so doing somehow to by-pass altogether the question of the material basis for both. Now there may be some idealist biologists who would lean to such a viewpoint; but the biologist who is in the least interested in physiological mechanisms is unlikely to do so. If it were indeed the case that there is a sharp break between the biological and the non-biological, so that one could not conceive of any material basis for the relative independence of an external trigger to which Piaget is referring, we might be driven to this sort of conclusion. But it is perfectly possible to conceive of a mechanism which periodically charges its own batteries as also of one which seeks stimuli to which it reacts in specific ways. Therefore there is no such break. It is true that, by invoking the concept of the functional tendency, Piaget is able to avoid the **S-R** fallacy of assuming all motivation to be 'external' in origin. But it also robs his theory of any explanatory power it might have to account for the subtleties and varieties of motivation. A mere assertion of the tendency for schemata to be active is quite inadequate as a basis for the explanation either of animal or of human motivation.

My second objection concerns the independence of the reflex. Having isolated this as a functional entity, Piaget finds that it 'extends itself' by incorporating the environment to itself, e.g. by assimilation. Now the meaning here is obscure if we consider only the behaviour at stage I. It becomes less so if one contrasts this with behaviour at a subsequent stage, e.g. at stage II when the child learns to compose the directed and voluntary activity of arm movement with that of sucking to construct the integrated schema (or strategy) of moving the hand to the mouth and rotating the hand to suck the thumb. Piaget counterposes this to the earlier behaviour with characteristic insight. For the later behaviour argues the juxtaposition and co-ordination of two more or less organized systems whereas the earlier does not.

The distinction is an important one. Can it be made without attributing a sort of a life of its own to the reflex which will enable it to extend itself without having recall to other mechanisms within the subject? It seems to me that we can do just this. For the reflex is a primitive kind of link, involving of course an input (cues from the still very limited comparator, which is as yet more of a set of disparate cue combinations than a co-ordinated system) and an output, the co-ordinated behaviour which is the reflex itself. But such reflexes are not the only behaviours which the young infant exhibits. For over and above this there are the more or less unco-ordinated motor and vocal activities, etc. which may be presumed to reflect the degree of general arousal. As a result of these it will sometimes happen that tactile cues occur and are followed by movement concerned with the variation of stimulation in the comparator, however diffuse this may be. When these result in the adequate input for the sucking reflex, this is activated. When the input is lost (the child loses the nipple) there is general arousal. And so on. This is the first phase, and it is one which must persist so long as the child has not yet elaborated the effector control mechanisms for oral search. When later a measure of control has been achieved, the arousal results in movements which are repeatable, at least immediately after their occurrence, and which in any case are more delimited and integrated. In other words, new links have been constructed involving some association between comparator and effector and some integration. When this has happened the way is open for conditioning. One must suppose that some mechanism exists whereby if the sucking reflex is active and unable to function for lack of input, and if the activity of some other link precedes the input which enables it to resume its function, the second link tends to be 'assimilated to' the sucking reflex itself, in the sense of a lowered threshold for its activation when the first is active.

This sort of 'conditioning' would indicate a very primitive instrumental conditioning. And Piaget observes it about the age of three weeks. It is interesting to note that this is also the age at which the earliest conditioned reflexes have been obtained by classical conditioning in Soviet research according to Elkonin (1957). The limitations of the first sort are important. The cues for the conditional link belong to the same 'channel' as those for the original reflex. And the chaining is minimal. The embryonic schema comprises only one or two strategies, and these involve only two links. This interpretation diverges from Piaget's own, for Piaget denies that the extension of schemata involves conditioning, evidently on the ground that there are restrictions as to the type of cues which can be conditioned. This is of course a matter of definition. But the mechanism seems in all other respects essentially similar to that of later learning. For Piaget himself notes the tendency to generalization (for which one might read: sensitivity to cue combinations similar to the original), to recognition, which is no more than the fact of conditioning itself, and to reproduction, which simply expresses the fact that the extended reflex now consitutes a schema which can be activated as a whole, either by input from the external environment or by modification of the internal environment (hunger, boredom, uncertainty).

Stage II (primary circular reactions). This stage is marked by the appearance of co-ordinated behaviour. In this sense there is little that sets it off from the primitive strategies and schemata noted in the last paragraph and characterizing the fourth week of life. But the co-ordinations are more numerous and involve larger segments of behaviour. What sets it off from the third stage is the fact that the schemata which are formed are isolated. They imply the existence of strategies in a single context which are not transferable to other contexts. Moreover, and consequent upon this, the schemata are simple in the sense that they are not compounded of sub-schemata which are themselves schemata.

Primary circular reactions constitute only one aspect of this phase of development to which Piaget gives the more general title of 'first acquired adaptations'. The phenomenon of circular reactions was noted by Baldwin, although it was Piaget who is responsible for their categorization as primary, secondary and tertiary. A circular reaction is simply an activity which terminates by producing the very cues which are sufficient for its onset. Hence the tendency to circularity. The simplest primary circular reactions are rhythmic movements such as kicking, waving the arm back and forth, rocking from side to side, and so on. The cues for many of these simpler reactions may be taken to be largely proprioceptive. But not entirely. For this period also sees the beginnings of the co-ordination of sensory modalities, as when the child watches his hand as he moves it, or as he learns to move his hand towards his mouth and rotate it for the purpose of thumb-sucking. In the same way, Piaget notes how the child will first respond to the nursing situation by moving in response to tactile cues, but later in response to visual cues. It is also during this period that the child acquires conditioned reactions to auditory signals: his movements anticipate the reaction to nursing when he hears the adult's approach. It may be noted in this context that it is unlikely that this reaction is entirely learnt. The mechanism for the localization of sound depends on a precise analysis of phase differences between the sound waves reaching the left ear and those to the right, consequent upon the screening of the head itself: the two waves are in synchrony only when the source of sound lies in the sagittal plane of the nose. This fine analysis is not learnt in the ordinary sense, although it may depend on the maturation of relevant nervous structures. Hence turning the head in the direction of a sound (approximately six weeks) is an unconditional reflex. But what is learnt is the assimilation of the sound cues characteristic of approach by an adult with the visual and tactile cues.

From the point of view of the structural analysis which we have taken as our standpoint, this phase of development may be thought of as characterized by the formation of simple strategies and schemata composed of several links (i.e. subject to several successive and distinct checks on environmental cue combinations in the interval from t_0 to t_c[1]), and also by the beginnings of integration in the comparator system (equivalence of cues from distinct sense modalities or channels).[2]

Stage III (secondary circular reactions). This stage, together with the two following, is characterized by Piaget as exemplifying intentional sensori-motor adaptations. Typically, if a child is engaged in a particular activity, e.g. he goes to grasp a hanging object, and a new and interesting result follows on his manoeuvres (e.g. he does not manage to grasp the

[1] See Chapter 4, p. 185.

[2] The reader who is familiar with the work of Piaget and Inhelder (1956), of O'Connor and Hermelin (1963) and of Birch and Lefford (1963), on the integration of sense-modalities will not need to be reminded that the development with which we are concerned here is far more primitive that that which is entailed in the tactile recognition of shapes presented visually, the visual recognition of shapes presented by touch, etc. Such recognition depends on the representational reconstruction of the object, as well as on the progressive analysis of generalizable cues (angularity, curvilinearity, relative size, etc.). The comparatively late acquisition of such representational equivalences testifies to the correctness of Piaget's thesis that all that the child acquires on the sensori-motor 'plane' during the first eighteen months needs to be painfully re-acquired on the plane of representation during the ensuing three–four years.

object but hits against it, causing it to swing to and fro) he repeats the behaviour which led to the interesting spectacle. There is continuity with the behaviour of the preceding stage since this too is a circular reaction as defined. The novelty lies in the intentionality. Failure of accommodation does not invariably result in abandonment of the original schema: if the failure is accompanied by a novel input, there is a modification of the original strategy which appears to be a function of that result itself. Behaviour may be said to have become instrumental.

A second feature of behaviour at this stage is the appearance of a dependency relation between strategies. For instance a child may be seen grasping a doll and shaking it in order to rattle the cradle-top from which it is suspended. The proof: that he looks at the cradle top and not at the doll. Or again, a child will pick up a new object (e.g. a knife) and use it immediately to further some well-established schema (e.g. rubbing it against the side of the cot, or banging it).

The period between four and seven months is of course the age at which the child acquires sufficient motor control to sit with some support and to grasp small objects when he sees them (Gesell, 1940). Hence, a third and related feature of this development is the further elaboration of the comparator system as a system of cue equivalences involving a co-ordination of sensory modalities. From the point of view of the elaboration of the skills themselves, one aspect of this is the substitution of kinaesthetic cues for environmental (visual or tactile) cues. It seems altogether probable that this is a necessary feature of the growth of behavioural co-ordination, and hence, of the elaboration of intelligent behaviour. Thus there is reason to believe that the amount of information that can be assimilated from the comparator system within short intervals of time is limited (see Broadbent, 1958). This limitation does not apply to the feed-back mechanisms which exist within the effector system itself. Hence the elaboration of skilled behaviour depends on the automatization of its components in the precise sense of relative independence of environmental input. More generally, of course, the entire evolution of behaviour may be thought of as a progressive liberation from the restrictions imposed by the contingencies of the immediate environmental input (Wohlwill, 1962). But such an observation is probably too sweeping to be of more than heuristic value, i.e. more than indication of what to look for. Thus representation and language bring a considerable liberation from these restrictions inasmuch as the input upon which they depend is one which the subject can provide at any time (by imaging, speaking, thinking, etc.). Similarly the development of systematizing categories enables the subject to dispense with trial-and-error observations and solve problems by reasoned deductions even where observation would be difficult or impossible. But this does not absolve one from examining the mechanism of these more advanced co-ordinations which are very different from those of the automatization of habitual movements.

To return to secondary circular reactions. In terms of the analysis given in these pages what distinguishes these from primary circular reactions is that they imply the evolution of new strategies and schemata by the juxtaposition of existing ones. More specifically, a strategy engaged on for its own interest (uncertainty reduction as described in Chapter 5, Section III) is found to lead in to a second, and more interesting strategy (one in which the combination of novelty and familiarity is more 're-warding'). From this point on the two combine to form a single schema. At the same time the integrity of the original schemata is to some extent preserved. In the example given, the close observation of movement is a self-sufficient visual schema and the manipulation of seen objects is another. The juxtaposition of the two and the subordination of the second to the first constitutes the new development. Moreover, characteristically, the input to either of the original schemata may activate the new strategy: the child may look for the object to shake when seeing an object swinging, or, alternatively the sight of an object may induce him to shake it in order to cause another suspended object to swing. We have already indicated that the mere juxtaposition of links in the co-ordination of extended reflexes can be regarded as a primitive instrumental conditioning. Yet it is the present behaviour, involving the subordination of schemata and strategies, which corresponds more closely to the situations studied by psychologists since Thorndike under the rubric of instrumental learning.

Stage IV (co-ordination of secondary schemata). If we were correct in ascribing the first conditioned reflexes to the end of the first stage, then the second stage is in fact intermediate, since it only extends the strategies and schemata which were embryonically present from the third week. The third stage clearly marks an advance since it involved the first subordinations of one schema to another. By the same token, the fourth stage might again be thought of as intermediary: it is marked by further co-ordinations and subordinations of the kind already noted. But there appears to be this difference. Whereas earlier the schema which served as means was hit upon by chance, one now finds a more or less active experimentation; presented with a new object, the child explores it by applying successively the schemata that he already possesses. The following observation of one of Piaget's children, Laurent, at an age just short of nine months, is particularly revealing:

> 'He examines a series of new objects which I present to him in sequence: a wooden figure of a man with movable feet, a wooden toucan 7 cm. high ... a beaded purse. I observe four quite constant reactions. (1) In the first place a long visual exploration: Laurent looks at the objects which are at first stationary, then looks at them very rapidly while transferring them from one hand to the other. He seems to study their various surfaces and perspectives. In particular, he folds the purse in two, unfolds it and refolds it in order to study the transformations; as soon as he sees the hinge he turns the object over to see it full face, etc. (2) After the visual exploration, a tactile exploration begins. He feels the object, especially the toucan's beak, the little man's feet, and gently passes his finger over any unevenness. Some places he scratches (the case of the box, the smooth wood of an elephant). (3) He displaces the object slowly. (4) Only at last does he try the various familiar schemata, using them each in turn with a sort of prudence, as though studying the effect produced. He shakes them, swings them, rubs them against the cot, draws himself up, shakes his head, sucks them, etc.'
>
> (OI, p. 254)

The deliberate and cautious approach to a new object seems to be a characteristic of this subject. But what is common at this age is the application of several schemata to new objects. From the point of view of the child's awareness of the world, this development is crucial. Instead of serving merely as an input for a particular schema, *the object becomes the intersection of all the schemata that can be applied to it. It is for this reason that the conservation of the object is consolidated at this stage.* At seven months the child looks for an object when it has dropped out of sight. But at eight or nine months his behaviour takes into account its causal connexions with other objects: an object concealed under a cover is looked for in the place where it was hidden and not just anywhere, e.g. where it was hidden on a previous occasion. An object seen to disappear behind a screen is looked for at the far end of the screen as might be expected if it continues in its line of motion, and not at the end where it was first hidden from view. And so on.

To speak of an object as the intersection of all the schemata that can be applied to it (this is not a direct quotation from Piaget although it undoubtedly expresses his point of view) is to enunciate an epistemology which is true at all levels: we only know the world by interaction with it.

Once again, however, it is important to stress that the knowledge implied at the present level is fully accounted for by the behavioural anticipations observed. There is no symbolic representation of object and relations.

As to the mechanism underlying these developments, we are still uncertain. But it looks as if what happens is that the greater mobility of schemata points to a finer adjustment between activation and inhibition: the activation of one schema no longer implies the total inhibition of all others. Similarly, the readiness to apply one strategy in order to achieve another, often involving different objects, e.g. seizing one object to hit another, or removing an obstacle to reach a coveted object (both of which are characteristic of this stage), seems to argue a persistence of the schema in the absence of immediate input from the comparator (the child may be looking at the means object) and is closely related to the beginnings of immediate memory. Whether this depends on the elaboration of reverberatory neural circuits, as Hebb has suggested (presumably at the level of the link and strategy and not at the level of the comparator system itself) is still a matter for speculation.

Finally, from the point of view of motivation, the increased availability of schemata shown by the application of familiar schemata to new objects may be taken as marking the beginnings of a transfer of the uncertainty associated with the immediate input and its assimilation to particular schemata to more central mechanisms concerned with what Stott calls the 'effectance' possibilities of the subject. In a recent article, Schaffer (1966) has shown how fear of strangers develops progressively from the age of six to seven months onwards. Along with the increased certainty and security which springs from the recognition of the conservation of familiar objects and people, there is the (central) uncertainty and fear which stems from the unfamiliar and, more especially, from stimuli which (*a*) combine a certain mixture of familiar and unfamiliar, and (*b*) are liable to behave in unpredictable and uncontrollable ways, i.e. strangers and animals.

Stage V (tertiary circular reactions). At stage IV the schemata are sufficiently mobile to enable the child to apply a wide variety of schemata in succession to a new object. We have seen how this fact plays a crucial part in the behavioural definition of the object as the intersection of schemata and hence in its conservation. Once again, the development which Piaget notes as characteristic of the beginning of the second year of life is not a sudden change but a gradual refinement of what went before. There is an increasing tendency to variation of behaviour in the presence of the unfamiliar. Experimentation is more active. The child seems to conduct his explorations not merely to assimilate the new to existing schemata but to find out. Here is an illustrative example.

> 'At 0 : 10 (29) Laurent examines a watch chain hanging from his finger . . . He starts it swinging a little and at once continues this . . . But instead of stopping there, he grasps the chain with his right hand and starts it swinging with his left while trying some new combinations (here the 'tertiary reaction' begins): in particular he slides it along the back of his left hand and finds that it falls when it reaches the end. He now holds the end of the chain with finger and thumb of his right hand and lets it slide slowly between the fingers of his left. He studies it carefully at the moment when it falls off the left hand, and repeats the movement ten times over.'
>
> (O I, p. 269)

The interest in novelty and the experimental variation of the situation which it engenders leads to a more rapid transfer of acquired schemata to further objects. For instance a child who has experimented with dropping one object readily transfers this behaviour to other objects. In the process he discovers their similarities and differences: those which make a noise when they drop, those that are liable to roll off a surface by themselves, and so on. Nevertheless the initial impetus to these discoveries is the activity itself and the differentiations which come to be made are likewise established in the course of action.

This is why Piaget characterizes these developments as circular reactions. The definition of circular reaction which I gave earlier is in some ways a little narrow when applied to the present behaviour. A true circular reaction is one whose termination produces the conditions necessary for its replication. The present reactions are circular only in the wider sense that they are dependent on the provision by the environment of the conditions necessary both for their onset and their continuation. Discoveries are made in the course of ongoing behaviour. There is still no problem solution by mental (i.e. representational) experiment.[1]

[1] Developments during this stage and the preceding are clearly bound up with that of short-term and long-term memory. Piaget's observations reveal that new relations are discovered only by overt trial-and-error, i.e. with adequate direct input to the comparator. Both animals and human beings, at levels of behavioural organization comparable to stage IV, are capable of behaviour in which the present input evokes a search for an absent input necessary for the operation of an established schema: a dog will fetch his lead when he hears 'Walk', and so on. This sort of behaviour does not involve the discovery of new relations, only the operation of well-established schemata. Moreover, in this everyday example, the animal does not 'remember' where

The active experimentation characteristic of stage V enables the child to gradually structurize his environment in terms of general causal relations operating between objects and no longer only in terms of those operating between his own actions and the objects (as at stage II). This enables him to solve several of the problems of 'insightful' learning observed by Köhler in the chimpanzee. In particular, the child discovers and generalizes the relation of object to support, that of object to its extension, the rotations of a stick-like object enabling it to pass through certain kinds of obstacles (bars). Thus the child learns gradually, by trial-and-error in the course of active experimentation, that an object can be brought within reach by pulling a cloth or a cushion on which it rests, and even by pivoting a board. Similarly, he discovers the 'behaviour of the string': an object can be pulled in. Similarly again, in the course of experimentation like that of Laurent with the watch chain, he learns how to rotate an object so as to pull it in through the bars of his play-pen. Finally, Piaget quotes at least one of his children who discovered how to draw an object nearer by using a stick as a rake (OI. p. 298).

Before one can pass from the merely descriptive enumeration of these behaviours to an attempt at analysis, two facts must be borne in mind. The first is that the relations between objects are not 'observed' by the child by a simple 'structurization' of the visual input. They are discovered very gradually in the course of active experimentation. In this respect, Piaget's observations exactly duplicate those of Birch (1945) in his investigation of insight in chimpanzees. The second, which operates in the opposite direction, i.e. to speed the learning, is that the application of newly acquired schemata to new situations is now much easier than it was. Also, the child's active experimentation enables him to establish the limits of such generalizability. What this means is that insight is not a *sui generis* kind of learning, different from trial-and-error, but simply an extension of trial-and-error, characterized by finer differentiation of the relations between output strategies and the resulting input, and a far greater capacity for 'transfer'. In this respect, the behaviour studied by Piaget recalls that of 'learning set', and may well be dependent on similar mechanisms, even though there are important differences between the two phenomena (see next section).

---

the lead is: what he remembers is the series of actions which lead him to its discovery. If an object is concealed alternately under one of two objects with an animal watching and the animal is restrained from going to it at once, one finds that unless its orientation is maintained throughout the delay period, its capacity for short-term memory is very limited.

Stage VI (beginnings of representation). In spite of the obvious importance of representation in enabling the subject to go through a sequence of actions with the aid of image, gesture or language, and anticipate the requirements of the situation before embarking on overt action, the differences which Piaget observes between the trial-and-error discoveries of stage V and the representational discoveries of stage VI are by no means sharp. All that one can say is that solution of problems is generally more rapid and is apt to involve an extension to or modification of an existing strategy which enables this to be applied to the problem without prior overt experimentation. The actual accommodation (modification of the strategy) is not different in essence from what was already seen at stage V. The difference lies only in that it precedes action instead of following it. So long as the input necessary for the solution of a problem is present from the first, it is not easy for the observer to decide whether or not there has been such anticipation. The principal criteria for decision consist, first, in the fact that the accommodation has not been made before and is not a member of a set of variations which the subject has already practised by overt trial-and-error experimentation, and, second, in that there tends to be a break between an initial period of unsuccessful experimentation and the eventual solution. These of course are the criteria of novelty and suddenness observed by Köhler and confirmed by Birch. But the novelty is invariably limited.

> 'Jacqueline, at 1; 8(9) arrives at a closed door – with a blade of grass in each hand. She stretches out her right hand toward the knob but sees that she cannot turn it without letting go of the grass. She puts the grass on the floor, opens the door, picks up the grass again and enters. But when she wants to leave the room things become complicated. She puts the grass on the floor and grasps the door knob. But then she perceives that in pulling the door toward her she will simultaneously chase away the grass which she placed between the door and the threshold. She therefore picks it up in order to put it outside the door's zone of movement.'
>
> (O I, p. 119)

It is the second part of this observation which is characteristic of stage VI. The point is that the door has not yet touched the grass when the child sees the need to move it. (My dog has learnt to go to the kitchen to fetch a biscuit, return with it to the living-room door, put it down to scratch his muzzle against the door, then, when the door has been opened, he turns round to pick up the biscuit before entering. I assume that every portion of this behaviour has been learnt gradually in the course of overt trial-and-error, and that the total acquisition therefore corresponds to Piaget's stage IV).

Perhaps the best known of the observations noted by Piaget is Lucienne's use of imitation to further the process of solution.

> 'I put the chain inside an empty matchbox (where the matches belong), then close the box leaving an opening of 10 mm. Lucienne begins by turning the whole thing over, then tries to grasp the chain through the opening. Not succeeding, she simply puts her index finger into the slit and so succeeds in getting out a small fragment of the chain; she then pulls it until she has completely solved the problem.
>
> Here begins the experiment which we want to emphasize. I put the chain back into the box and reduce the opening to 3 mm. It is understood that Lucienne is not aware of the functioning of the opening and closing of the matchbox and has not seen me prepare the experiment. She only possesses the two preceding schemata: turning the box over in order to empty it of its contents, and sliding her finger into the slit to make the chain come out. It is of course this last procedure that she tries first: she puts her finger inside and gropes to reach the chain, but fails completely. A pause follows during which Lucienne manifests a very curious reaction bearing witness not only to the fact that she tries to think out the situation and to represent to herself through mental combination the operations to be performed, but also to the role played by imitation in the genesis of representations. Lucienne mimics the widening of the slit.
>
> She looks at the slit with great attention; then, several times in succession, she opens and shuts her mouth, at first slightly, then wider and wider! Apparently Lucienne understands the existence of a cavity subjacent to the slit and wishes to enlarge that cavity. The attempt at representation which she thus furnishes is expressed plastically, that is to say, due to inability to think out the situation in words or clear visual images she uses a simple motor indication as 'signifier' or symbol....
>
> Soon after this phase of plastic reflection, Lucienne unhesitatingly puts her finger in the slit and, instead of trying as before to reach the chain, she pulls so as to enlarge the opening. She succeeds and grasps the chain.
>
> During the following attempts (the slit always being 3 mm. wide), the same procedure is immediately rediscovered. On the other hand,

Lucienne is incapable of opening the box when it is completely closed. She gropes, throws the box on the floor, etc., but fails.'

(O I, pp. 338–339)

The fact of interiorized, mental, combination in Jacqueline's behaviour (if it is a fact) and the use of imitation in experimentation by Lucienne mark the beginnings of representation: substitution of a sequence of actions relative to an input which is auto-determined for a sequence which is dependent on environmental input, and transfer of relations of implication (anticipation) gained from the first sequence to the determination of effective strategies in relation to the second (action based on thinking ahead). Both the mental combination and the imitiation are embryonic, and both are, to some extent, open to doubt in the given instance. The point is that whether or not Piaget's interpretation of these particular behaviours is sound, representation does become more and more apparent from this age onwards, and, sooner or later, the use of mental combinations and of verbal and imaginal planning comes to play an ever greater role in the regulation of behaviour. Also new strategies emerge which are entirely dependent on such interiorized action, viz. systematic strategies based on the formation of 'operational' schemata (Volume II, Chapters 8, 9, 10).

However, as we will see in Section IV, the use of imitation itself is not an entirely new development. And for the present, rather more interest attaches to the sequence of development which antecedes the emergence of representation, for it is these earlier stages which present the closer analogies to the phylogenetic developments reviewed in Section I.

III. DEVELOPMENT IN GENERALIZATION[1]

1. *Learning Sets as Higher-order Strategies*

Comparing the observations of the last two sections, two conclusions emerge very clearly. First, that development in learning, whether in phylogenesis or in ontogenesis, takes the form of extension in generalization (from initial learning to reversal, from one discrimination problem to another, from co-ordinated strategy applied to one object to its application to another). Second, that both in ontogenesis and in phylogenesis, the development is gradual. There are no sharp breaks between the stages noted by Piaget. On the contrary, behaviour appropriate to a later stage appears in isolated instances at earlier stages as of rule. By the

[1] This section may be omitted on first reading.

same token, there is continuity in phylogenesis. Discrimination reversal, as we shall see, is a kind of learning set. Pigeons and turtles are midway in this respect between fish and rat, since they are capable of reversal learning in spatial but not in visual problems. Doubtless there are species whose developmental level will be found to be midway between pigeon and rat, given problems which will pinpoint the differentiation. Learning set itself is a gradual development, for it is present to some degree in all mammals so far studied, but more pronounced in the primates, with further, quantitative differentiations within this order.

Development in learning is a matter of change in generalization. The evidence for generalization is transfer. What needs to be explained is not only the fact of generalizations (and transfer) of various kinds, but the fact of phylogenetic and ontogenetic changes in generalization. Error-factor theory taken by itself is not enough. For it assumes the existence of the strategies (error-factors) which are eliminated in the course of learning. It predicts the mathematical form of learning set formation within species, but fails to explain why species differ from one another. It seems to me that a similar criticism holds of any purely mathematical theory of learning.

What follows is speculation. But it is the sort of speculation which is essential if we are to know what to look for in theory construction and experiment. We begin with a tentative analysis of learning set.

We have supposed in the last chapter that the action of any link or strategy is one of selective facilitation, probably by inhibition of irrelevant centres. But reinforcement is positive. In other words, the strengthening of strategy **X** may be effected by weakening (inhibition) of strategies **Y** and **Z**, but it takes place directly, as a result of the activity and reinforcement of strategy **X**, and not indirectly, following the unreinforced activity of strategy **Y** or **Z**. We have also supposed that the control of behaviour is mediated by a hierarchy of strategies, and not by a simple **S-R** bond. We apply the model to **LS** behaviour. Suppose that the subject is faced with a discrimination between a cross and a circle, and suppose further (*a*) that on a given trial he selects the cross, and (*b*) that this selection was mediated by a strategy (link) determining the selection of the cross (as opposed to, say, selection of the object on the right, or selection of the previously unreinforced object, etc.). Now that link operates by selective facilitation of certain visual pattern cues, inhibiting other patterned relations of visual input. But the activation of that link in turn was a function of a previous and higher-order strategy, facilitating the visual pattern link by selective inhibition of other links of similar order (position, alternation, perseveration, etc.). What happens on the next trial of the same problem? The cross is again present, which means that there is perceptual input which can be assimilated directly to the reinforced link (for we assume that there was reinforcement). But suppose now that the next problem presents the alternatives of a square and a triangle. The specific visual cues of the cross are no longer present, which means that if transfer is to occur it must do so indirectly *via* the higher order strategy. In other words, the cues deriving from the experimental situation as a whole (or certain aspects of it), including the subject's orientation in the situation, activate links which in turn activate the higher-order strategy determining which cues shall be neglected. For, supposing the square to be positive, the cue-combinations relevant to squareness cannot have been selectively reinforced by reinforcement of the cross (apart from primary perceptual generalization, which is irrelevant, since **LS** formation is general). Thus, if there is problem-to-problem transfer, it must be through the suppression of irrelevant strategies.

Which takes us back to error-factor theory. But it is error-factor theory spelt out, so that the role of the hierarchical structure of behavioural determination is apparent. There remains the question of why learning set is not universal. But although we cannot presume to give a definitive answer, the problem becomes much more tractable. For it reduces to such questions as: (*a*) Under what circumstances does the reinforcement of a (lower-order) decision procedure (link or strategy) communicate with a previous decision procedure, so converting it into a higher-order strategy? In the example, under what circumstances will reinforcement of the selection of square communicate with selection of the decision to neglect position, etc.? (*b*) Under what circumstances will input to a link **Y**, activate a higher-order strategy **J**, even though not previously associated with **J** directly, when the activity of **Y** is analogous to that of other links **W**, **X** and **Z**, in the precise sense that all are compatible with, and liable to be facilitated by the activity of **J**, since the action of **J** is to inhibit the incompatible strategies **P**... **V**, given that at least one of these links (**W**, **X**, **Z**) has been activated by **J**? Once more the translation into concrete terms is obvious. For **Y** substitute *square*, for **J** read *object strategy*, for **W**, **X** and **Z** read *cross* etc., and for **P** ... **V** read any relevant 'error factors'. Now it certainly looks as if the factors that are relevant will be of two sorts.

First, factors concerned with the duration of the trace of the higher-order decision procedure and its relation to lower-order links. In other words, if the action of **J** is terminated by the activation of **X** or **W**, then it is no longer available for reinforcement; in a sense it functions not as a higher-order strategy but as no more than an antecedent element in a series, and a series is not a hierarchy. On the other hand, if **J** remains active throughout the activity of **X** or **W**, we have the conditions for feedback following reinforcement of **X**, activation of **Y**, etc. It is reasonable to suppose that the duration of **J** and its relations with **W** . . . **Z** will be a function of the complexity of cortical structure, whether by virtue of Hebb's reverberatory circuits (of which Harlow is most suspicious) or through some other mode of neural action. Even the existence of a strategy corresponding to **J** is likely to be a matter of cortical development. For we may suppose that strategies of the order **W–Z**, could exist independently, the activation of any being governed only by selective inhibition mediated by the most general mechanisms of specific arousal. However, if centres are available which could take over the functions of **J**, then sooner or later they will chance to be active simultaneously with **W**, **X**, etc., and this alone (by virtue of conditioning) will gradually come to circumscribe their mode of activity, integrating them within the system of interdependencies as a whole. In other words, lower order species simply have not the brains to form learning sets, and those that have can only acquire them gradually.

The second set of factors relates to the similarities of the primary links **W–Z**, to their intensity, to their prior relations to alternative strategies **P–V**, and so on. For instance, a novel and interesting stimulus will be more readily responded to as a stimulus, but may inhibit the higher-order object strategy, or it may by virtue of previous experience evoke a position strategy, and so on. In other words, the formation of learning set will be a matter of chance as to its details, even though its overall form is determined by the experience and above all the capacity of the subject. More specifically, if the transfer situation differs from the original learning situation across several dimensions, then learning set formation will be more difficult. Likewise, if the cues to be learnt are not easily discriminable by the subject, thereby rendering the selection of alternative cues more probable. All of which is plain common sense, and accords well enough with the facts, such as the greater difficulty of object learning set formation (in rhesus monkeys) when planometric stimuli are used, or the fact that reversal learning is easier than learning set formation. But the question of the relation of Bitterman's work to **LS** deserves a special word, and we will consider it along with the rather more problematic questions raised by the ontogenetic stages in the human infant.

2. *Learning Set, Reversal, Probability and Ontogenetic Development*

The phylogenetic order of their attainment suggests that if reversal and probability are to be thought of as forms of learning set, i.e. as instances of the formation and operation of higher-order strategies, then they argue a simpler structure, or a more limited generalization, than the situations studied by Harlow. In the case of reversal, it is not difficult to see that whether or not the former is true, the latter certainly holds. Experiments on learning set require transfer to problems of a 'similar' class; reversal learning requires transfer in a situation which is the same – apart from the contingencies of reinforcement. Nevertheless reversal learning is not universal, for it is absent in fish. Let us look at the situation more closely, from our new vantage point of (modified) error-factor theory. Assume that the subject (fish, rat or whatever) has mastered the initial discrimination. Since his performance is error-free, we infer that he is using a consistent strategy. This may be (*a*) to respond to the perceptual cues of the reinforced object as a whole, or to some part of these cues, i.e. a specific object strategy. Or it may be (*b*) a strategy of choosing the object he chose on the last trial, or (*c*) a strategy of choosing the object reinforced on the last trial. We infer also that several error strategies have been eliminated, viz. position strategies, etc. What happens when the pattern of reinforcement is reversed? Strategies (*b*) or (*c*) would still serve, although specific object strategies would not. We do not know whether the former are more difficult than the latter; for instance, alternation is a primitive mode of behaviour.[1] However we do know that the non-reinforcement of the originally positive stimulus constitutes a change in input, and the only input which could reinforce the effective strategy must have the previously unreinforced stimulus as its proximal antecedent. The evidence is that in the fish, this change in the proximal antecedents of reinforcement is sufficient to render ineffectual the previous learning: lower-order strategies involving reponse to cues from the previously unreinforced stimulus do not communicate with the higher order strategies mediating the inhibition of position responses, etc., and the entire learning must be done anew. At the same time there is interference from the originally positive strategy, so that initial reversals are more difficult than the original learning. From reversal to reversal there is a gradual improvement, but this is entirely attributable to the separate learning of the two habits. Conversely, in the rat, although the first reversal may be learned more slowly than the original problem, due to

[1] Although it may be primitive when it is simply the result of 'reactive inhibition' or a refractory phase and less primitive in other forms.

interference, the higher-order strategies continue to be effective, so much so that, at any rate for spatial problems, the subject approaches the theoretical optimum of one-trial reversal.

On the other hand, the rat shows very limited improvement in problem to problem transfer when the two stimuli are no longer identical from one problem to the next. Clearly, the difference in input renders communication with the higher-order strategies more difficult. To be frank, I do not see how this could have been known *a priori*: interference effects might have been such as to more than offset the similarity of the situation in reversal. But the facts of reversal improvement in the rat have been known for a long time. Theory does not arise *in vacuo*. Explanatory models are devised to account for known facts, and having been constructed, they suggest new areas of inquiry, not only to confirm or infirm the model, but often to make it more precise. In the present case, allied problems which merit investigation include transfer when the stimulus is similar but the situation is different (e.g. from **T** maze to Lashley jumping stand, and so on), and transfer when one of the stimuli remains constant and only the other is changed.

As we have seen, one of the variations the effects of which are known appears in the difference between visual and spatial problems. Orientation in terms of more distant visual cues (being the stable features in the situation, as Hebb, 1949 remarks) leads to spatial response, as would reaction responsive to internal cues from effector feedback. The importance of the latter is shown in the primitive tendency to alternation. The finer accommodation necessary for learning new detailed cues in the near visual stimulus[1] may be a phylogenetically later development, an intrinsically less probable strategy, and one whose suppression is more readily achieved, whence the greater facility of the higher-order positional (*left or right*, not the lower-order *left* or *right*) strategy relative to the higher-order visual. The 'explanation' is *ex post facto* and therefore suspect, but the facts are incontrovertible.

The interpretation of the probability data is even more problematic. But there is one pointer. When learning takes place under conditions of non-guidance, both rat and fish maximize. In other words, the two first-order strategies (the more and the less frequently reinforced response) are learnt independently, and, because one is more frequently rewarded, it simply becomes more probable, with the result that the other is inhibited and the situation becomes one of partial reinforcement, the periodic reinforcement of the alternative being irrelevant. When guidance is used

[1] As opposed to the unlearnt IRM of Chapter 3.

the situation differentiates between species. For the fish, the guidance procedure (forced response to the less probable alternative) has the effect of preventing stabilization of the inhibition of one response, and the behaviour now becomes one of chance matching. The rat's behaviour is unaltered. It is reasonable to conclude that the rat discriminates between the 'choice' situation and the 'guidance' situation: one is marked by the presence of both stimuli, and the precedent higher-order strategy of scanning for its presence or absence enables it to evolve two stable alternatives, economical maximization when both stimuli are present, response to the alternative when the favoured stimulus is absent. Thus, where reversal learning depends on the comparison of two situations yielding similarity, the probability problem depends on the differentiation of two total situations versus the lower-order reaction to cues which happen to be common to both.

That partial reinforcement learning itself may be more dependent on a higher-order strategy in some species than in others is apparent from further work of Gonzalez, Eskin and Bitterman (1963) on fish. Under conditions of partial reinforcement higher order species yield more trials to extinction than under constant reinforcement even when the total number of trials is matched, the fish only when the number of reinforced trials is equalled (see Chapter 1, Section VI for a general introduction to partial reinforcement).

It should be added that probability maximization in animals is an economical strategy mainly in the sense that there is economy of effort. Both rats and monkeys show an initial tendency to systematic as opposed to random matching (systematic matching being an obviously higher-order strategy), and, as Bitterman noted, monkeys are more liable to choose the previously unreinforced stimulus, while rats prefer the previously reinforced stimulus. Maximization corresponds to a still fairly elementary strategy: viz. constant response under partial reinforcement. Children and human adults behave very differently from either fish or rats. Adults match probabilities even when no guidance procedure is used (Grant, Hake and Hornseth, 1951). When required to predict whether a second light will come on following a first warning light under conditions where the actual appearance of this second light is random, but with a probability varying from 0 through 25 per cent, 50 per cent and 75 per cent to 100 per cent, the predictions of adult subjects stabilize rapidly about a proportion of '*Yes*' which accurately reflects the true incidence of yeses. Of course, they are wrong more often than they would be if they replied '*Yes*' every time for 75 per cent and '*No*' for 25 per cent.

Since no guidance is used, they are not like fish. In effect, they are taking all the information into account even though, in a sense, it is uneconomical to do so. Fish take the easy way out when they can and rats are more effective than fish at taking the easy way out. Children, likewise, try to arrive at a higher-order strategy which takes account of both alternatives even without guidance, and even when the alternative is in fact never reinforced. This is the situation used by Stevenson (Stevenson and Zigler, 1958; Stevenson and Weir, 1959). Children are presented with three alternative knobs to press: two are never reinforced, and the reinforcement of the third is random at 33 per cent, 66 per cent or 100 per cent. In spite of the fact that the alternatives are never reinforced the children do not maximize. Neither do they match. The rate of choice of the correct button varies from 0.97 for 100 per cent, through 0.79 for 66 per cent to 0.53 for 33 per cent. Adults evidently behave similarly to five-year olds in this situation. The later article shows some growth with age, but in the direction of matching: older children and adults are more inclined to vary their behaviour when the anticipatory strategy is shown to be at variance with input.

All this is very different from fish or rat. The maximization of the latter should not be taken as the resultant of a calculation of profitability. Piaget's studies of the development of the concept of chance suggests that even in the human being, it is not until about the age of formal reasoning (twelve and later) that the child comes to the realization that if the incidence of reinforcement is random, then the best prediction will be an all-or-none for all ratios other than 50 per cent (see Piaget and Inhelder, 1951).

In general, the whole burden of this chapter is that one needs to be cautious in the analysis of developmental data, whether phylogenetic or ontogenetic. Continuity is a premise. But superficial analogy is dangerous. Analogous behaviours in analogous situations by different species (and by children of different ages) may be due to quite different causes.[1]

Accordingly one must be cautious in drawing analogies between the phylogenetic data of Section I and the ontogenetic data of Section II.

[1] In Section III of Volume II, Chapter 9, there is an instance of a mode of response in six- or seven- year-old children which is in all respects similar to that of ten- and eleven- year-olds, and different from that of eight- and nine- year-olds for quite different reasons. The younger children have an insecure hold on the notion of perimeter; intermediate ages assimilate its transformations to transformations of area; the older groups make a clear differentiation.

But it is very probable that there is a relation. Even simple choice discrimination is a behaviour of some complexity, involving the subordination of the initial scanning and instrumental activity to the terminal consummatory behaviour (e.g. eating in the goal-box). Piaget's observations of the limited co-ordinations achieved in the course of the first three or four months of human life suggest that this kind of subordination corresponds more properly to the achievement of Stage III. By the same token, the next stage, Stage IV, is marked by the application of familiar schemata to new situations (I would prefer to call them 'strategies', reserving the term 'schema' for the pattern of implications taken to underlie the whole set of related behaviours). This is clearly a case of transfer, and of transfer which is based on something more than mere perceptual generalization. One is therefore tempted to draw an analogy between this development and the formation of learning sets. Certainly, the deliberate experimentation of Stage V argues the operation of a higher-order strategy leading to the discarding and modification of lower-order strategies. For instance the variation of the movements of Laurent's hands are subordinated to the higher-order strategy of achieving the sudden drop when the watch is no longer supported by the left hand.

However, although I believe the search for more precise analogies of this sort to be a proper line of inquiry, one must beware of hasty conclusions. The suppression of error-factors is more apparent in learning set than it is in object manipulation. And there is no evidence as yet that the child handles positional transfer more readily than visual. He may not. Perhaps because of difficulties of motivation, it has so far proved impossible to demonstrate true learning set formation in children below the age of two to two-and-a-half. It is possible that the level of co-ordination underlying learning set is available to them before that, but equally it may not be. There is no warrant for crude equations relating the total behavioural organization of the child at successive developmental stages to successive phylogenetic levels: e.g. 1 month = invertebrate; 4 months = fish; 7 months = rat or monkey. Human beings differ from other species in their great capacity for manipulation and tool-using and in the capacity for language. Neither development is simply superposed on a 'rat-like' behaviour. For the former grows out of prehension and the latter out of imitation, and both of these develop very gradually throughout the first year of life, i.e. long before the integrations which enable human beings to discover modes of transfer which are inaccessible to lower orders. It is possible that the child's greater aptitude for differentiated modes of prehension and for the reproduction of perceptual input by the implementation of perceptuo-motor strategies (imitation) actually militates against the early formation of relatively narrow learning sets. Therefore, before taking a very general look at the course of further development in human learning, we need to examine briefly the origins of representation in imitative behaviour.

IV. IMITATION

1. *Imitation and Following*

Imitation was a popular topic in nineteenth-century psychology. The establishment of the experimental tradition in studies of learning, and especially of animal learning, coincided with the growth of a much more sceptical attitude in regard to imitation. Thorndike (1898) was encouraged to develop his connexionist psychology by the observation that cats, dogs and chicks frequently learned to solve problems by repeated overt trial-and-error and were never helped by mere observation of the correct solution in other members of their species. It looks as if such animals have neither an instinct nor what McDougall (1908) called a 'natural propensity' to imitate. Moreover, they do not learn by imitation. Nevertheless rats can learn to run a maze more rapidly through following a 'maze-wise' leader than they do in the course of unguided trial-and-error. Miller and Dollard (1941) attribute the phenomenon to what might be termed pseudo-imitation. The behaviour of the leader (who 'knows' the maze) is conditioned to cues in the environment. That of the follower is initially conditioned to cues originating from the leader, not in the sense that he imitates the leader but that he literally follows the leader. In time the cues to which the latter is responding acquire secondary reinforcing powers for the former, so that he can run the maze more efficiently on his own. Miller and Dollard argue that this sort of pseudo-imitation underlies learning by imitation in all species, and notably in human beings.

However, it is difficult to see how this sort of explanation can be stretched to cover the important part of imitation in human learning. For instance, we saw in Chapter 1 that Skinner's account of the origin of language relies very heavily on the assumption of 'echoic behaviour'. Instructional techniques take it for granted that pupils can repeat a correct performance following a 'prompt' (demonstration), while more recent programming methods extend the process further by the introduction of gradual 'fading'. It is interesting to quote the more cautious remarks of Nissen, a comparative psychologist who has concentrated principally on the study of the chimpanzee:

'Comparative psychologists of the post-Darwinian period were much concerned with the problem of imitation. In more recent literature, however, one finds little mention of it. Like 'instinct' the term is considered by many a bit disreputable, or at least out of fashion. One reason for this may be that psychologists have thought of imitation as a single process or mechanism, whereas actually there may be many degrees or kinds of imitation, not all conforming to the same criteria. Aping of "motor acts" – operating a water-faucet, spitting, using keys, scribbling with pencil and paper ... – is very frequently seen in monkeys and apes. On the other hand, it is extremely difficult or impossible for a chimpanzee to learn, purely by observation of another animal, that response to a triangle is correct, response to a square incorrect. Imitating hand-clapping is easy; imitating certain human vocal sounds (which are within the capacity of the animal) is very difficult. Imitation is obviously of critical importance in human learning; its limitations and potentialities in anthropoid behaviour remain to be explored.'

(Nissen, 1951, pp. 444–445.)

Clearly, the study of imitation is not easy, and its comparative study is rendered more difficult by the fact that there are inter-species differences in the various aspects of imitation. As for learning by imitation, this is a very crude concept which one cannot begin to analyse until one has achieved a clearer perspective with regard to imitation itself.

One might begin by enunciating two criteria of imitation as distinct from the pseudo-imitation shown in following behaviour. The first is matching and the second is spontaneous reproduction of cues. The second can occur without the first, and whether the process should then be called imitation is simply a matter of language. The more extended use is favoured by common usage, and the fact that some very important forms of imitation make little use of matching, notably imitation in the acquisition of the phonetic aspect of language.

Matching, or the 'aping of "motor acts"' is more than mere following. The first difference is that aping implies an assimilation of the cues provided by the form and movements of the model to cues provided by analogous movements by the subject. This is a sort of a transfer, and we have just seen that transfer is the principal yardstick of phylogenetic evolutionary level. The second difference relates to sequencing. In general, the mimicry of apes involves very little sequencing, but the up and down movements of scrubbing windows or scribbling do involve the minimal sequencing of a circular pattern (of two elements), and the use of a key to open a door seems to involve more. Reference will be made later to an experiment on learning by imitation in which sequencing is the crucial feature.

The third difference between matching and following behaviour is that matching pre-supposes the spontaneous reproduction of cues, although the converse is not true. It is difficult to resist the suggestion that where aping is general, as in anthropoids and human beings, the behaviour is not unrelated to the increased part of curiosity (uncertainty reduction) in the motivation of these species. Clearly, in the measure that the sequence and antecedents of a set of cues provided by the behaviour of another can be reproduced by the subject and assimilated to his own behavioural strategies, there will be assimilation of the postcedents of the former to the familiar postcedents of the latter. In plain English, if I know just what you're doing because I can do it myself, I have less cause to worry about what you're going to do next.

Matching of behaviour always involves matching of result, since result is no more than the perceptual input which contributes to the match. But it is a more articulated matching, usually involving some sequencing. The imitation of hand-clapping is a case in point. The final result is the matching of sound, but the imitation also involves the deliberate matching of visual input provided by the movements of the subject's hands to that provided by those of the model. Matching of results, or the spontaneous reproduction of cues can occur by itself. This would seem to be the mechanism involved in the imitation of birds, and also in vocal imitation by the human infant. In both cases, there is trial-and-error. The counterposition of imitation and trial-and-error is one factor which is responsible for much of the confusion in this area.

Thus the distinguishing features of imitation turn out to be (*a*) the assimilation of model-cues to own-behaviour cues, (*b*) articulated matching or sequencing, and (*c*) matching of results. One might add a fourth: generality of imitative behaviour. Pseudo-imitation occurs where there is no articulated matching, but the IRM (see Chapter 3) or the learned releaser for the behaviour of the follower *happens to be* the execution of similar behaviour by the model. It is like the difference between walking along and walking in step. Because the coincidence is chance, there is no generality. Imitation of song by birds is nearer to true imitation because there is deliberate matching of results. But the imitation is partial and not general. In human infants it is general, and in the chimpanzee it can be, as we are about to see. The question whether the generality is due to an inbuilt matching schema or the formation of an imitation learning-set is difficult to answer and may be less important than it appears. For if the latter then the capacity to form the learning set in question is of crucial significance in phylogenesis.

This introduction should be of some help in evaluating the significance of the ontogenesis of imitation in the human infant.

2. *Imitation in the Human Infant*

Piaget (1951, Chapters 1–3) traces the growth of imitation in the human infant from birth to the end of the sensori-motor period, based on careful observation combined with *ad hoc* experimentation designed to test the accuracy of interpretation. He finds that the earliest imitative behaviours are precisely the result of chance coincidences between the behaviour of the 'model' which provides the cues and that of the subject. It is pseudo-imitation in the sense we have just defined. By the end of the period under study, the imitation is general, articulated and deliberate. Also it is deferred, so that imitation provides the starting-point for representation. Yet there is complete continuity in the development of imitative behaviour, just as there was continuity in the elaboration of the more general behavioural schemata reviewed in Section II.

The nearest behaviour to imitation in the very young infant (up to one month) is contagious crying. That one baby's crying should set off crying in another is a clear case of chance coincidence. In fact, of course, crying on the part of another baby is only one of several stimuli which may elicit crying. But this behaviour shades imperceptibility into a pre-imitative behaviour in which the coincidence of results is more apparent. Thus, even at the beginning of Piaget's Stage II of the sensori-motor period (one to four months), the child is observed to stop crying when the other stops and to resume when the other starts. This is the forerunner of those 'primary circular reactions' which are characteristic of this phase. The child vocalizes when he hears himself vocalize, and, by the same token, when he hears another vocalize. There is little or no articulation in the behaviour, and the child's vocalization may be a poor match of the model's. Nevertheless, the circular reaction is maintained more readily when there is a match, e.g. when the adult initiates the sequence by correctly imitating the child. Following a nodding or shaking movement of the head is another instance of circular reaction which is in some measure provoked by the behaviour of the model and is at the same time similar to it. Movement of eye or head or hand which apes the oscillatory movement of a swinging object falls into the same category.

Imitation of hand movement is more dependent on the co-ordination of movement and vision and consequently it is not observed until the age of three months. The need to rely on observational data makes interpretation difficult. Nevertheless it looks as if this sort of imitation has a twofold origin. First, it is a 'procedure to make interesting spectacles last', akin to the 'secondary circular reaction'; second, it derives in part from the similarity of the visual cues provided by the subject's own hands and those of the model. Piaget notes isolated instances of imitation of hand movement as early as three months and four days.

Although he reports this observation along with others of Stage II, it seems to be closer to the behaviour of the next stage (four to eight months). The characteristic gain is that the imitative behaviour is differentiated: the child matches sound for sound and movement for movement (e.g. hand-clapping, opening and closing hand.) Its limitation is that there is no deliberate effort of accommodation: when the behaviour of the model is within the child's repertoire, the input elicits the appropriate strategy rather than any other; but there is no trial-and-error, or rather there is no correxion of error to make the behaviour conform to the model. Thus we are told of one child who had not spontaneously learned to open and close his hand as a distinctive behaviour; this child (T) imitated finger movement and hand opening with the same movement, although he differentiated clearly between waving good-bye, hand-clapping, thumb raising and finger movement. In general, there appears to be accurate imitation when the input from the model is assimilated to a well-defined unitary schema. But there is no differentiation within the schema and a behaviour which has not been practised on its own cannot be imitated as such even though the child can perform it spontaneously when it is in the context of a larger sequence ('strategy'). Imitation of mouth and eye movements is limited by the lack of differentiation and deliberate search for a match. Therefore it occurs only to the extent that the adult deliberately reinforces the child's own spontaneous behaviour by himself imitating the child, and especially when there is an audial cue to facilitate the assimilation. Nevertheless imitation is not confined to empty movement and Piaget quotes several instances of imitation involving the handling of objects (e.g. swinging an object, scraping one against another) at the age of seven to eight months, and an isolated instance at three months.

Deliberate matching of behaviour to the behaviour of the model seems to be a development which begins at Stage IV (eight months) and is perfected in the course of the following stage; i.e. about the turn of the first year of life. The significance of developments about this period has already been highlighted by the discussion at the end of Section III. From seven to eight months on, the child systematically applies familiar strategies to new objects (transfer), and this itself leads directly to the conservation of the object (as the intersection of strategies appropriate to it) and to a differentiation between strategies and schemata in two senses. First, a schema corresponding to the apprehension of an object in its relations with the environment is now compounded of many strategies. Second, the schema corresponding to the subject's alternative behaviours *vis à vis* the object is likewise differentiated into several alternative strategies. The differentiation between strategy and schema corresponds therefore to a differentiation between subject and object: the subject can experiment with his own behaviour or he can experiment with the behavioural potential of the object. In general, it is the latter which is most evident. However, in imitation, considerable interest attaches to the child's growing perception of himself, by analogy with other human beings whose parts and whose behaviour resemble his own.

Thus among the developments characteristic of the last third of the first year are the imitation of eye and mouth movements, and the recognition of parts of the body, as in imitation of pointing to chin, mouth, etc. It is interesting to note that one child tries to imitate opening and closing of eyes by opening and shutting his mouth (*op. cit.*, p. 36). Seeing the adult rub his eye with the back of his hand, the same child is unable to do this but examines the back of his own hand (articulation). The following quotation illustrates the more successful and deliberate discovery of movement involving hidden parts of the child's own body:

> 'At 1 : 1 (19) J. was in front of me when I touched the tip of my tongue with my forefinger. She at once tried to imitate me, doing so in three stages. She first touched her lip with her forefinger (a schema with which she was familiar). She then put out her tongue without moving her finger (another schema she already knew), and finally she again brought her finger towards her mouth, obviously felt for her tongue, and succeeded in touching the tip.
>
> The same day I put my tongue against the left commissure of my mouth. J. at once put out her tongue, moved it about and finally pushed it against the right commissure (which was natural, since I was opposite her).
>
> At 1 : 1 (23) she tried to imitate me when I touched my chin. She

began by feeling in the direction of her ear, which she found, then she took hold of her nose. She then touched her eyes, and with her eyes on me, brought her hand down towards her mouth. She then took hold of her lips, and stopped there. At 1 : 2 (3), however, she started from her mouth and, carefully moving her hand downwards, finally reached her chin.'

(*op. cit.*, p. 57.)

The example brings out clearly the characteristics which have been cited as critical of true imitation. The assimilation of cues in the model to those of the subject, and the articulation of sequencing of behaviour, as well as the deliberate matching of the result. The last, however, is more obvious in the deliberate rehearsal and improvement of language (phonation).

The importance of imitation does not derive primarily from its value in learning. (As a matter of fact, when we 'learn by imitation', all we do is to take advantage of a 'prompt'.) Its importance is rather that imitation enables the subject to reproduce the environment and therefore provides the first instrument of representation. However, representation cannot be said to occur until the imitation is deferred.

'At 1 : 4 (3) J. had a visit from a little boy of 1 : 6, whom she used to see from time to time, and who, in the course of the afternoon got into a terrible temper. He screamed as he tried to get out of a play-pen and pushed it backwards, stamping his feet. J. stood watching him in amazement, never having witnessed such a scene before. The next day, she herself screamed in her play-pen and tried to move it, stamping her foot lightly several times in succession. The imitation of the whole scene was most striking. Had it been immediate, it would naturally not have involved representation, but coming as it did after an interval of more than twelve hours, it must have involved some representative or pre-representative element.

At 1 : 4 (17), after a visit from the same boy, she again gave a clear imitation of him, but in another position. She was standing up, and drew herself up with her head and shoulders thrown back, and laughed loudly (like the model).'

'At 1 : 6 (23) J. was looking at an illustrated paper and her attention was caught by the photograph (much reduced in size) of a little boy with his mouth wide open, gaping with amazement. She thereupon attempted to reproduce the action and at once managed to do so most successfully. The observation is interesting, because the situation was one in which there was no suggestion of imitation: J. was merely looking at pictures. It was as though she felt the need to mime what she saw in order to grasp it.'

(*op. cit.*, p. 63.)

3. *Imitation in the Chimpanzee*

There is evidence that the development just considered is often paralleled in the behaviour of chimpanzees, although it may be that the generalization of imitative behaviour is less spontaneous in anthropoids than it is in the human infant. Hayes and Hayes (1952) recall the conviction of Yerkes and Yerkes (1929) that chimpanzees imitate spontaneously and with ease, but add that in the ensuing decade comparative psychologists become increasingly sceptical. However, Hayes and Hayes add that the discrepancy between Yerkes and Yerkes' observations and those of their critics may be largely attributable to the more limited environment of typical chimpanzees reared in the laboratory. Hayes and Hayes report the results of observations made on a single chimpanzee Viki, brought up by the authors and reared as a human child. Their observations fall into three categories: records of spontaneous imitation, the effects of deliberate formation of an imitation learning set, and the results of a series of controlled experiments on learning by imitation.

It appears that at about sixteen months of age, Viki began to imitate household routines: dusting furniture, washing clothes and dishes. From the age of seventeen months until thirty-four months she was given intermittent training on a series of seventy tasks in an effort to establish an imitation learning set: the experimenter executed some piece of behaviour (e.g. hand-clapping, eye-blinking, head-tapping), and rewarded Viki if imitation followed within a few seconds. To begin with it was necessary to manipulate her hands, i.e. there was no true imitation. After eleven learning tasks, the chimpanzee imitated provided the behaviour was already present in her spontaneous repertoire (saying 'Mama'; a 'Bronx cheer'). This of course recalls identical behaviour in the human infant at Stage III. Beginning with the twentieth task, at least ten items were copied immediately, even though they had never been performed independently (stretching mouth with two forefingers, whirling on one foot, rubbing sandpaper against a piece of wood). Such behaviour is analogous to behaviour of the child at Stage V.

However, the authors also note several instances of delayed imitation. These include going through the motion of sharpening a pencil in a pencil sharpener, spraying a window with a spray can (interval of fifteen minutes), inserting photographs in a book as if to flatten them (delay of six hours), and using a screwdriver to open the lid of a paint can (delay of one hour, but the use of a screwdriver as a lever is familiar to Viki in other contexts). Taken together, these results indicate that imitative behaviour in the chimpanzee reaches levels comparable with that of the human infant in the sensori-motor period, but the development is slower and generalized imitation is less spontaneous.

4. *Learning by Imitation*

Between the ages of twenty-eight and thirty-four months Viki was given six problems involving learning by imitation. These were also given to four children of similar age and to a single cage-reared chimpanzee nine months older. These problems included a stick and tunnel problem (bait inside a tube which can be poked through with a stick which is provided, but which cannot be reached by hand), and a series of sequence problems: a box would fall open if a series of three levers were operated in a particular order, as demonstrated, (e.g. left, middle, right). Viki solved the stick and tunnel problem after two demonstrations, and the majority of the remaining non-sequential problems in one to three. There was little to choose here between her response and those of the children. However, even after thirty-two demonstrations she was unable to imitate any of the sequence problems without hand guidance, but the three oldest children solved the left-to-right and right-to-left order after one to four demonstrations. The cage-reared chimpanzee learned only one of the non-sequential problems and was not given the harder, sequential ones.

The comparative success of Viki in learning by imitation contrasts with the failure of sub-primates and of the chimpanzee Fran which lacked relevant experience. It will be recalled from Chapter I that insight occurs only as a result of prior learning. The chimpanzee which had not previously acquired the behaviour of using a stick as an arm-extension was unable to profit from observation of the model behaviour. It follows that the success of demonstration in the case of Viki and the human children is of the nature of a 'prompt'. After observing the demonstration, the subject assimilates the stick-using behaviour to the food-reaching behaviour, so that the stimulus of the food in the tunnel elicits the instrumental stick-behaviour. Learning by imitation is therefore akin to insight since it involves the putting together of two or more schemata. (One might say strategies, but there is evidence of spontaneous accommodation to the new situation, indicating a more generalized system rather than a unique line of behaviour: see the discussion of Birch's inquiry in Chapter I, Section V.) At the same time, observation of the model behaviour acts as a prompt, enabling the subject to apply the correct strategy from the start, and allowing for accommodation and consolidation through active experimentation. The provision of a model for imitation is a form of guidance: the general character of learning is trial-and-error with reinforcement of effective strategies, but the general character of instruction consists in the guidance of trials to minimize error.

To say that there is no learning by imitation is rather like staring hard at a giraffe and exclaiming 'There ain't no such animal'. The problem is rather to analyse the nature of the process and the conditions under which it occurs. It turns out that learning by imitation can only occur where there is imitation, and this in turn depends on a phylogenetic and ontogenetic evolution which will allow the assimilation of the behaviour of the model to that of the subject, this being a form of transfer akin to learning set, and characteristically absent in sub-primates. It also transpires that, at any rate in the chimpanzee, the process can be facilitated by the fostering of a general 'imitation learning set', which may develop spontaneously in the human infant.

It is highly revealing that the one task which differentiated most clearly between the chimpanzee and the children was that of sequence. The reconstruction of a sequence argues an articulation which is more than the minimal analysis of input demanded by imitation in general. Also it depends on the availability of strategies where the cue to behaviour arises not out of the environmental input (which remains substantially unaltered) but out of the trace of the previous behaviour of the subject, i.e. it depends on some sort of monitoring process. Finally, the reproduction of a sequence depends on the preservation in immediate memory of several elements or 'bits' of information, corresponding to the elements of the sequence. The first of these three developments may be no more than the resultant of the other two. Both the growth of immediate memory and the elaboration of higher order strategies and schemata which depend on the behaviour of the subject rather than the character of the object are critical in the formation of representational intelligence. It would be ridiculous to suggest that our understanding of these later and crucial developments is adequate. But we have tried to show that the way to further advancement of such understanding lies in the realization that the structurization of experience which is most characteristic of human intelligence builds on an organization which is common to other species and carries it further.

V. FROM CHIMPANZEE TO MAN

1. *Functions of Language: The role of Representation*

The most salient difference between chimpanzee and human being is the fact of language. There is little reason to doubt that the evolution of human intelligence is bound up with the possession of language. Language begins as communication. The communication of threat or of comfort. To start with, variations of stress and of pitch are probably more important than phonemic differentiation: a mother can comfort or frighten her child as well by nonsense or random words as by an apt choice of vocabulary. But by the end of the first year of life there is differentiation of some words and phrases. By the same token, although a little later, the child himself can communicate requests, e.g. for specific objects, or, by appropriate naming, for approval. Except for the relatively rapid growth of spontaneous single word vocabulary in the second year of life, these uses of language are not species specific. There are differences, but the differences are quantitative rather than qualitative. Domestic animals are capable of differentiating the affective tone of the human voice, and likewise of recognizing a number of words. Chimpanzees are capable of reproducing several. In general, communication by sound is common to many species. In the human being there is greater differentiation and a greater part of learning (as compared with e.g. vocal communication in birds).

However, language in human beings develops further functions. Beginning about the age of twenty-one months (on average), when the child elaborates the beginnings of syntax by stringing two words together, language is used increasingly for the representation of experience. The child describes what he is doing, what he has done, or a little later what he is about to do. Piaget (1926) has shown that the function of language in such instances is not primarily one of communication. Language may be used when the child is alone, in which case it is true monologue, or it may occur when he is in the company of others. But, if the latter, there is often no intent of communcation. More accurately, there is no intent of differentiated communication, for the child does not vary his remarks by observing the effect that they produce. On the contrary he takes no notice of the reply when there is one. Such language is termed by Piaget 'collective monologue'. The fact of its existence has been confirmed by numerous studies (including observations of the present writer, 1955), the majority of which have been reviewed by McCarthy (1954). Much rather futile controversy has sometimes centred on the question of just how prominent it is in the language of young children. Futile, because language as egocentric representation does not displace the use of language as primary communication, but merely features alongside it as a new development, so that the ratio of the two is as much a function of the situation (child-child or child-adult, co-operative or parallel activity, etc.) as it is of development level (see the more recent remarks of Piaget in the new edition of the 1926 volume).

A second development which is a feature peculiar to human language is the use of language in the auto-regulation of behaviour. Two groups of studies are relevant. The first is the work of Luria (1961) dealing with the use of language in the acquisition of skilled (controlled) behaviour. By way of example, a child is required to press a bulb when a light appears. Children of two can achieve a controlled sharp movement as opposed to a diffuse continued squeezing by uttering the word '*Press*' when the light is shown. The use of the word '*No*' to aid in differentiating a negative signal (do not press if the light is red) is a later development. Initially, the excitatory process in the second, representational, linguistic system simply spills over into the effector, sensori-motor system, and cannot function to inhibit it. By the age of four, the child can use the semantic function of language to regulate his own behaviour: e.g. '*I must press twice*', where previously a similar result could be achieved only by '*Press, press*'.

The second is the group of studies by Kuenne (1946), Kendler (1963), and others to which reference has been made previously (Chapter 1, Section V). The availability of language as a mediating behaviour facilitates transfer of learning in far transposition and in discrimination reversal. Both are in part instances where the categorization of events is facilitated by the assimilation of representational, linguistic categories from adult language. By the same token, although primates can learn a discriminative response to a class of dissimilar objects (e.g. red objects irrespective of shape) and even to scan an array and inhibit the overt choice when a representative of the rewarded class is not present (Weinstein, 1945), there is abundant evidence that children from the age of two or three are superior to all non-human primates in tasks involving 'concept attainment', i.e. discriminations where reinforcement is for some aspect of the stimulus objects (colour, shape or size) rather than for the positive or negative object as such.[1]

A third feature of language in human beings is the communication of

[1] See Volume II, Chapter 3 for a fuller review of the relevant literature.

precise information, allowing for the accumulation of knowledge through vicarious experience. This book or any other similar is an obvious example: it is hoped that the reader can learn vicariously from the work of the writer, and the latter in turn is indebted for 95 per cent of what he communicates to the experience of others. This is clearly a different type of communication from that in which language originated. What has happened is that the representational function of language has been taken over in the process of communication itself, allowing for the communication of generalized relational systems. But the latter in turn are no more than instructions for the potential reconstruction of experience out of actions. Since the communicative function of language is present from the start, it follows that the transition from primary communication in the form of requests relative to a present input ('*Give me the teddy*', etc.) is a gradual evolution. At every stage in this development communicative language is able to take advantage of the degree of structurization of relations that has been elaborated by representation as a whole. Thus there is progress when the speaker can communicate differential relations between objects '(*Put the button under the cup*', '*Find the thimble inside the box*', etc.) or instructions for a sequence of actions ('*Put the book on the chair, then open the door, then hand me the pencil.*'). There is further progress when the speaker can communicate a systematic rule: e.g. '*Two are the same and the other is different; it is always under the one that is different*' in the solution of the oddity problem (see below). It is important to note that such a development does not arise directly out of communicative language, and the proof is that the hint is not immediately effective, even though it may be so in the long run, at least with children of four, who are capable of solving the oddity problem. In other words, the linguistic message functions exactly in the same way as the behaviour of the model in imitation, as a prompt for the selection of appropriate strategies by the combination of available behaviours in more or less accessible ways. Finally, the evolution is complete when the child can himself produce a generalized linguistic formula to prescribe rules for his own behaviour, e.g. when he can describe the rule for the solution of problems such as learning set (Hayes, Thompson and Hayes, 1953; Lunzer and Hulme, 1967), reversal, relational transposition (Kuenne, 1946), or the oddity problem (Inhelder and Piaget, 1964; Lunzer and Astin, unpublished). But as we will see, this development is intimately connected with a gain in representation as a whole, the ability to reconstruct a systematic relation by focusing on the criteria of one's own actions.

Fourthly, there is the use of language in thinking. Thinking has been described by Piaget as a form of internalized action. Vygotsky (1962) has shown that the use of sub-vocal language in thinking evolves out of representational, egocentric language as a result of the internalization of language itself and the differentiation of language as communication from language as planning. This is in contradiction to Piaget's (1926) contention that egocentric speech merges into 'socialized language', i.e. adaptive communication. The proof is twofold: in the first place, the communicative function of language is present from the start; secondly, as the incidence of egocentric speech begins to wane, so its structure tends to approximate that of internalized thinking in adults, at the same time as communicative language becomes increasingly grammatical. Thus, in the overt egocentric language of four- and five-year-olds, Vygotsky notes an increasing tendency to a truncated language in which what he calls the 'psychological subject' is omitted and only the 'psychological predicate' remains, i.e. the subject expresses the end-state envisaged in the representation, omitting the starting-point (e.g. '*Brush*', rather than '*I'll use the brush*'). This is not a regression to 'baby-talk' but a progression to the form of language used in internalized representation. However, thinking in the sense of problem-solving or thinking out is more than mere representation, for it consists in part in the formulation and application of rules, in the formulation of results, the further processing of these, and so on. In other words, as Skinner rightly recognizes, thinking tends to be a form of communicative language in which the subject functions both as speaker and as listener (even though he fails to recognize the developmental complexity of communication itself, see Chapter 1, Section VI).

The significance of this overview of the functions of language and their development is this. It is not enough to argue that the superior intellectual achievement of human beings is due to their possession of language, or that language functions as a mediating process. Both statements are true but not sufficient. For it is apparent that the mediating functions of language (in communication and in thinking) do not grow directly out of language as communication, but out of representational function of language. Moreover, as the power of representation evolves, so the subject is able to receive and to communicate more complex or more abstract messages. The language of communication and of thought always amounts to a set of instructions (or auto-instructions) for the execution of sequences of action, often internalized action involving a representational or symbolic object, but its availability to the subject, either as listener or as speaker, depends on the elaboration of the representational function as a whole.

This is not to argue that language is irrelevant to that development. On the contrary, it is relevant and useful in that it serves continually as a 'prompt', in the sense outlined above. The reader will find a further discussion of the relations of thinking and language in Volume II, Chapter 5, and especially of the evidence for the development of thinking where language is absent or deficient, viz. in the deaf. For the present, we must turn to a consideration of the development of representation itself, of which language is only one 'vehicle', albeit the principal.

2. *From Imitation to Representation: The Evolution of Play*

A landscape painting is a representation of a scene, but it is not the scene itself. A murder-play is a representation of a dastardly deed but not the deed itself. The sentence '*The cloth is on the table*' must not be confused with the fact which it represents. Human beings paint pictures, we write plays and act them, and we speak to one another in sentences. Since illustration, dramatization and linguistic description are the very stuff out of which the communication of knowledge is built, representation deserves very careful attention. Both ontogenetically and phylogenetically, the evolution of representation underlies the distinctive achievements of the human adult. And it is clear that representation is more general than language.

To begin with the painting. The representational character of the picture derives from visual similarity between its parts and the parts of the landscape, and from similarity in their dispositions relative to one another. These correspondences enable the artist and the beholder to pass readily from one to the other: from signifier to signified. As a result there is communication, for the viewer is helped to 'see' the original scene and others 'with the artist's eye'. Of course, there will be failure of communication if the correspondence which exist for the artist between signifier and signified are not shared by the viewer, if they do not possess the same 'language' (in the wider sense of 'vehicle of communication'). But by and large we do, so long as we share similar cultural backgrounds. In any case we are more concerned at present with the nature of representation itself than with individual differences within it.

If we examine the sentence we again find correspondences: between '*cloth*' and cloth, between '*table*' and table, and between the relation of these conveyed by the sentence (as opposed to, say, '*The table is on the cloth*') and the relations obtaining between the things. Since we are not concerned at present with the distinctive features of language, we can afford to simply note the fact that all of these correspondences rest on learnt conventions instead of similarities. Leaving this aside, it is the fact of the correspondences which leads us to characterize the sentence as representational in the same sense as the painting or the play. It is this fact which led us in the last sub-section to draw a sharp distinction between the primitive communicative functions of language and the use of representational language in communication. It is the difference between the young child's request for '*biscuit*' or '*mummy*', or his triumphant response '*all gone*' (which is no more than a differential verbal reaction to a global situation), and the articulated correspondences of such sentences as '*The cloth is on the table*'.

It is instructive to carry the analysis one stage further. If we allow that the child uses words appropriately in one-word sentences towards the end of the first year of life, we have to allow that his behaviour is mediated by correspondences between the situations and the words that they evoke. The difference between this level of language and the level which concerns us now is that the correspondences are multiple. Instead of a single 'bijection' between the set of words and the set of situations we have a 'partial isomorphism' between the system of relations implied by direct action upon objects and direct perceptions at the sensori-motor level and a system of relations embodied in the vocabulary and rules of language. The latter is what is intended by 'representation'. It is obvious that in the field of language the origins of representation must be sought in the beginnings of the child's syntax, i.e. in the first appearances of substitution behaviour when the child starts to experiment with primitive sentence frames (e.g. '*Mummy gone*', '*biscuit gone*', '*Teddy gone*')' Taking the wider context of representational behaviour, the origins are in imitation, for here too we found a direct elaboration of behaviour from pre-imitation where the behaviour of a model simply cues behaviour in the imitator which happens to coincide, to true imitation involving correspondences between the parts of the model and those of the subject and between their respective actions.

Harking back for a moment to the discussion of Chapter 4, the very fact of the regulation of behaviour which enables the subject to adapt to the contingencies of the environment at the sensori-motor level implies just such a correspondence of systematic relations, or partial isomorphism, as that under discussion: an isomorphism between the connexions mediated (in one way or another) within the subject's brain, i.e. the equivalences and non-equivalences implicit in his schemata of action, and the objective state of affairs to which they correspond. The sensori-motor schemata themselves therefore constitute a 'first signalling system', signalling – because of its correspondence with systematic relations within the object (or environment). By the same token, the elaboration of several ways of representing or re-constructing reality (in imitation, play, graphic symbolization, language) constitutes a 'second signalling system', entailing a second-order correspondence with reality, mediated by the first. The terms 'first and second signalling systems' are Pavlov's. The emphasis given here to representation derives from Piaget; but Pavlov anticipated Piaget in the recognition of a qualitative difference between the organization of behaviour in animals and in man, save that Pavlov emphasized language instead of taking into account all of representational behaviour.

We are now in a better position to formulate the problem of the psychological interpretation of representation. If one can assume that we already know the specifications for an organism which will show adaptive behaviour and adaptive learning so that its inbuilt programme 'reflects' the relations of reality, being isomorphic with them, as a result of learning, what must one add to our model of this organism to enable it to reconstruct or represent its environment by significatory behaviour? The assumption of understanding in so far as sensori-motor behaviour is concerned is of course quite unwarranted, since what has been conveyed in previous chapters is still a very inadequate approximation. Also, given the assumption, a formulation in these general terms is very far from a solution. But it is a first step. It helps us to ask more precise questions and to see what sorts of phenomena are likely to be relevant.

Contrasting representation with imitation, one notes that the latter implies a significant development in the range and connectedness of the significatory behaviour itself. In the case of immediate imitation, the behaviour of the model constitutes the input which initiates a specific representational behaviour, being the imitative behaviour of the subject. Even in deferred imitation, so long as a particular object initiates a specific imitatory action, e.g. pretending to iron clothes or read a book, the representation involves only a single line of behaviour. It is a representational strategy, to use the language of this chapter and the last. This is in some contrast to the fluidity of representation in dramatic play. The imitation of individual actions passes over into the representation of experience, implying a greater availability of representational strategies and a greater interconnexion between related representational lines of behaviour. The relation of this form of play to imitation parallels that drawn already between the strategy and the schema.

The incidence of play as the representation of experience has been noted by nearly all observers of children's play (e.g. Buhler, 1947;

Lowenfeld, 1935; Piaget, 1951). Not surprisingly, it is impossible to draw a sharp distinction between deferred imitation and this form of play. However, to the extent that the behaviour features a number of related activities and experiences, to the extent that one incident of play serves as the cue for another (e.g. laying the table followed by a doll's tea party), to the extent that the behaviour shows a sequential order mirroring the order of the child's experience, one is inclined to say that the child is not simply imitating but engaging in dramatic play. This is the dimension characterized as 'constructiveness' by Barker, Dembo and Lewin (1941), and as 'organization' by the present writer (Lunzer, 1955, 1959; Hulme and Lunzer, 1966). Another index of play maturity which is relevant is imaginativeness in the use of materials. If imitation itself is a representational strategy and representation in dramatic play depends on the availability of an increasing number of related strategies, forming representational schemata, then it is understandable that one shades into the other. Thus, speaking generally, the development of representation argues a progressive autonomy in imitative behaviour: delayed imitation shades into representational behaviour in the measure that it becomes increasingly cued by a minimally supportive perceptual input (freer use of materials) and in the measure that the subject's own previous actions provide the cues for a variety of alternative representational lines of behaviour (organization or constructiveness of play).

One may readily conclude that the development of representational behaviour is intimately related both to an increased capacity for behaviour implying a recognition of order and to an increase in the capacity for delayed response. These are among the areas of experimental inquiry which are most relevant to the development under consideration. Hence the following brief digression.

3. *Delayed Response and Double-Alternation*

The comparative (= inter-species), experimental study of both these elaborations in behavioural regulation originated with the work of Hunter (1912, 1928) and most of the earlier literature has been excellently reviewed by Heron (1951).

Delayed response is usually studied by showing the subject a reward which is hidden behind one of two or more stimulus covers. Often, but not always, a screen is then interposed between the subject and the stimuli. The test, following the delay, is whether the subject will choose the correct path to the reward. Hunter first believed that the rat is incapable of delayed response in this type of situation, but subsequent studies have shown this conclusion to be false. Nevertheless, there is abundant evidence that the capacity for delayed response increases with the level of phylogenetic evolution. Also, a considerable difference appears between spatial and nonspatial (visual) delayed discrimination behaviour. So long as the correct reaction depends on the discrimination of a stimulus in a particular place (e.g. left, right or centre alley), preservation of the discrimination over the period of delay is very much easier (and this appears to be the case even when precautions are taken to exclude the maintenance of bodily orientation, which would of course assist the subject). The difficulty is greatly increased when the subject is shown the correct stimulus but not the position to be chosen. It has been contended (Harlow, 1951) that animals below the level of primates are incapable of nonspatial delayed response. Even in the chimpanzee, this type of response is not easy to achieve, and the delays are severely limited (Nissen, Riesen and Nowlis, 1938), although it may be that the procedure used to rule out spatial cues adds an interfering dimension of complexity (Harlow, *op. cit.*). The fact that capacity for delayed response is closely related to the level of ontogenetic development in human beings is well attested by the work of Pascal and Stolurow (1952), who studied the capacity for spatial and non-spatial delay in a sub-normal group of twenty-seven defectives having a CA range of 5:11 to 31:10 and an MA range from 2:1 to 7:1. Delays achieved ranged from zero (failure to maintain even a delay of one second), for subjects having an MA below 3:0 and for nonspatial delay, to several days. Correlation (rank-order) between MA and maximum delay was 0.61 for spatial and 0.88 for non-spatial delay.

Interest in delayed response stemmed out of the realization that here was an experimental situation which could be administered to a variety of species (with appropriate modification) and which seemed to be very relevant to the question of symbolic processes. There is little need to question its relevance to the use of symbols in representation, but it remains a far cry from the fact of delay to the attribution of symbolic behaviour to the subject. Indeed one cannot be sure just what is meant by 'symbolic behaviour' when this is used to refer to, say, the rat. The difficulty of delay problems is in fact closely related to the formation of learning set as discussed in Sections I and III of this chapter. For the correct solution implies a learning set: that the reward will be in the same position or pointed by the same stimulus as that shown before the delay, where position and stimulus vary at random from trial to trial. Hence it is not surprising that delayed response in the rat is poor. Even in the chimpanzee criteria of 90 per cent success are unrealistic. For the fact of delay presents an added complication, which is the necessity to 'bridge the gap'. Where the delay interval is short (say less than a minute) one must assume some form of continuing intervening activity (e.g. imagery) which enables the subject to produce the correct response after the delay. But where the interval is longer (and we have seen that in children it may extend to days), what we need is some mechanism for the storage of the information and for subsequent retrieval from store. It is here that it seems essential to invoke the use of symbols, whether in the form of language or in the form of some other behaviour which functions in such a way as to reconstruct previous experience by reinstating the strategies involved, using an alternative, representational input, one which is more fully under the control of the subject.

The insufficiency of our knowledge compels us to be vague about the precise nature of delayed response, even though we can be more certain of its intimate connexion with imitative and representational behaviour. Equally certain is that development in the capacity for maintenance of delay is closely related to cortical evolution and especially to frontal lobe development. Frontal lobe development differentiates more sharply than any other gross brain characteristic between sub-primate and primate and between chimpanzee and man. The role of the frontal lobes in delayed response was first shown by Jacobsen (1936) and has since been confirmed in many studies. For instance, delayed response problems discriminate more sharply between animals operated on by the removal of frontal lobe tissue and animals with posterior lesions than do other tasks such as double-alternation or the oddity problem (Leary, Harlow, Settlage and Greenwood, 1952; and cf. Pribram, Mishkin, Rosvold and Kaplan, 1952).

Delayed response is of particular relevance to the investigation of the development of processes mediating the storage and recall of information in the absence of direct input. Double-alternation is a form of experiment relevant in particular to the growth of ordering strategies. The situation devised by Hunter is shown in Figure 7.

The problem is essentially one of serial order. What this means is that the strategy which regulates the decision for the direction of the next turn operates on an input which is itself the trace of a previous strategy of the subject. The mere fact of order, as when three buttons are placed in the order, red, blue, yellow, is of course an aspect of the environment. But any response on the part of a subject which implies a recognition of that order is necessarily a second-order strategy acting on his own actions as input. For nothing compels him to follow the sequence in one order rather than another. We have just seen an instance of the difficulty of problems involving order in the contrast between the imitatory behaviour of the chimpanzee Viki and human children. The dependence of order on 'second-order strategies' is even more apparent in the Hunter problem. If the subject is required to learn to run the maze L L R R, even the trace of a left turn is of no use as a cue since everything depends on whether it is L following L or the first L. Hunter had found that the rat was unable

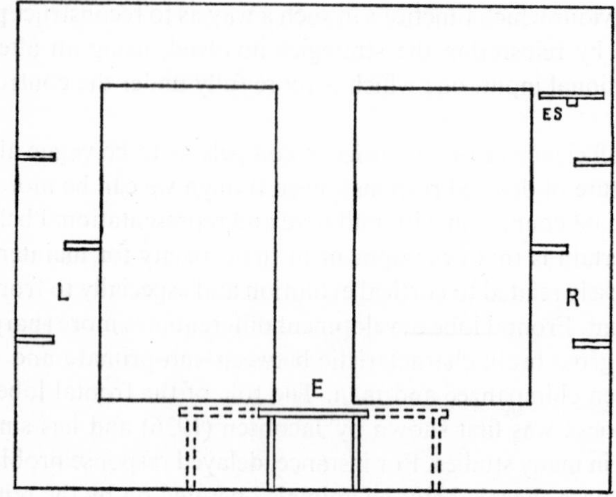

Figure 7. Temporal Maze (after Hunter, from Heron, 1951, p. 160)

to learn the double-alternation maze even to the extent of L L R R, as opposed to a double run (L L R R L L R R). More recent work (e.g. Palmer, 1965) indicates that some rats can achieve a fairly high level of performance, especially if every part-circuit is rewarded during the training. The behaviour of raccoons is clearly superior (Hunter, 1928). Analogous problems show vastly superior performance in chimpanzees (Gellerman, 1931; Leary *et al.*, 1952). However, it should be added that not all double-alternation problems present the same difficulties: in particular, the task of depressing one lever twice then another twice may argue no more than the formation of a 'double-pressing response', and this is one which is soluble by many species.

Both delayed response and ordering problems are of interest because they afford an experimental approach to the progressive auto-regulation of behaviour in phylogenesis and in ontogenesis. More work would seem to be needed in these fields. However, the same tendency to progressive auto-regulation is apparent in the development of representational behaviour, where its significance is more apparent, even though the control of observation is of necessity less rigorous.

4. *Significance of Representation*

The foregoing discussion should not be taken to imply that the development of representation is a secondary phenomenon, dependent on delayed response and the capacity for ordering. The relation is rather that all these behaviours are dependent on a similar extension in the functional capacity of the nervous system: viz. the elaboration of strategies the input for which consists in the trace activity of other strategies, and of strategies for re-activating others. This is what we have termed the auto-regulation of behaviour. It has been suggested that the principal factor in this development is the evolutional maturity of the nervous system itself. However, in so far as such a development depends on experience, i.e. on the provision of opportunities to form the necessary connexions, it is probable that such experiences occur more often in play situations than in situations resembling controlled laboratory experimentation.

Reverting to the consideration of play as the earliest overt form of representation, we have to remember that the child of eighteen months to five years spends a great deal of his time playing, and that a fair proportion of this is representational play. It has been suggested (Chapter 4, Section III) that from the motivational point of view the switching of attention and the maintenance of new directions in behaviour can frequently be explained in terms of a principle of uncertainty reduction. As the child moves about his environment, so the objects that he experiences (sees, hears, etc.) are assimilated to the strategies and schemata which he possesses. Where the lines of behaviour which he might engage on are clearly defined, there is little uncertainty and little challenge. But to the young child, new contexts often imply new situations, whence a constant challenge to experimentation in the form of play. It has long been known that the duration of play episodes reflects the child's maturity, which means that shifts of attention are more frequent in the two-year-old than in the four-year-old and so on (Van Alstyne, 1932). Our own observations confirmed this expectation, although it also transpired that organization of behaviour is a surer measure (Lunzer, 1955).

That a great deal of children's play is representational seems to be due to two causes. The first, and theoretically less important, is that the materials themselves which he encounters suggest human activity and therefore provide a challenge to imitative, representational behaviour. The second derives from his perception of his own activity. We have already noted that imitative behaviour depends on a kind of transfer in which the subject establishes analogies between the body and movements of others and his own, so that the same strategies are applied to both. Among the things which the child can imitate one is himself. It is common in the second year of life for children to pretend to go to sleep, or to pretend to sit on the pot, etc. Sometimes, the child uses his own body as the signifier, sometimes a doll. The effect of such representation which includes the self among the objects of the environment is a growth in self-awareness. The result is that any object or situation in the environment can present a challenge to the subject: is he capable of appropriate actions in respect of it? The difference between this sort of experimentation and that referred to in the last paragraph is not merely one of emphasis. In both cases there is uncertainty with respect to the subject's lines of behaviour. But in the former case (sensori-motor experimentation which reaches its culmination about the end of the first year of life), the uncertainty is purely objective and it is immediate in its action. It is an uncertainty in the 'system' inferred by the observer, and not accessible to the subject. In the second case, the uncertainty is mediated by the subject's self-reference, by the fact of his observation and representation of his own actions.

The fact of self-reference may well be crucial in transforming the character of behaviour, since all of behaviour becomes subject to representation. The child acts on the object, and can be immediately aware of his action, i.e., of his role as cause. At the same time, the object itself, i.e. the fluctuations in the situation which impinge on his receptor system, may be immediately assimilated to schemata which are not only schemata for potential action but schemata for representation. By imitative (play) behaviour, probably combined with imagery, and rapidly supported by the representational use of language, the child extends the retro-active awareness of his own actions to a pro-active anticipation.

The term anticipation can be used very loosely, as if to describe a timeless 'idea' which somehow duplicates the interaction between subject and object, but is not itself an action at all. In fact, anticipation always implies an action, viz. the activation of a line of behaviour with respect to a representational input. However, anticipation differs from imitation in that there is a greater independence in the representational behaviour, and there may be a return from representation to direct action (as when one solves a problem by going over the moves verbally). The greater independence derives from the fact that the representational strategies which originated as a mere duplication of sensori-motor events as they were experienced rapidly extend to representations of experience as it might have been. It is easy to see that once the behaviour acquires its representational character, the subject is in a position to forego the attempt at exact reduplication of the model at any time, and simply accept what he has done as adequate, valid for a possible model – and perhaps a better one.

In point of fact, every observer of children's play (Buhler, 1947; Lowenfeld, 1935; Piaget, 1951) notes the tendency for play as the representation of experience to shade very readily into play as the transformation of experience, or compensatory play. When the child plays at being mother, and doling out sweets or punishment, or when he plays at being a powerful engine or aeroplane, his representation is inaccurate because it implies a transfer of roles. But the role taken enables him to assume a greater control of reality by manipulating its contingencies (in the representation) in ways which are not open to him in reality. To this extent, the play operates to reduce uncertainty. At the same time, the false assumption of reciprocity also acts backwards so as to afford him a greater control of reality itself, in so far as, having reconstructed the sequence of events, he is in a better position to anticipate it stage by stage, and to adapt to it without excessive uncertainty, even when its direction is not strictly under his control.

One very striking, and early, instance of this tendency to reduce representational uncertainty by assuming imaginary control of the situation is the bedtime ritual, common in children from at least the age of two onwards. Uncertainty is aroused by the anticipation of loss of consciousness (with unpredictable dream imagery), darkness and isolation. Compensation takes the form of ritual, which may be more or less elaborate, in which the child produces an artificial certainty by executing a pattern of stable actions and surrounding himself with a stable input (teddy in one corner, bed-clothes tucked in just so, etc.). Needless to say, the child is not aware of 'why' he is doing this, since this type of introspective self-awareness is a much later development, being dependent on the ability to dissociate the critical moments in a line of behaviour, and thereby discover the criteria of one's own actions (see next section), and probably on the further tendency to reflect on the sources and implications of one's own identity (see next chapter and Volume II, Chapter 11). But it is clearly different from pre-programmed instinctive ritual behaviour in animals (dogs execute one or more complete turns before settling to sleep), as is apparent from the fact that it does not appear until the child is capable of representation, and that in spite of its ritual character, it is capable of infinite elaboration – especially if parents don't put their foot down!

Thus the significance of representation is that the child becomes progressively more able to anticipate the contingencies of experience by a process of active reconstruction, first in imitation and play, and later in language. From the motivational point of view, what we see is an increasing tendency to reproduce sequences of events as experienced or as anticipated, in ways which will enhance the subject's sense of control. It seems to me that much of human motivation is rendered less obscure on the simple assumption that, faced with input which threatens the subject's sense of control (as he anticipates the possible sequences), he acts in ways to alter the situation either by transforming it, or by avoiding it, and that faced with input which promises to increase his sense of control, he acts in ways which will promote the situation. Often the enhancement of control is achieved most readily by the provision of inputs of graded uncertainty, such that problems will be met but overcome. This is the main thesis of Berlyne (1960). It is these considerations which lend the utmost relevance to Stott's discussion of effectance mechanisms in Chapter 4 of Volume III.

Outside the work of Piaget, failure to take a developmental standpoint for the analysis of behaviour has led to a comparative neglect of representation. Indeed, it is particularly easy to overlook the reality of representation precisely because, in the human adult and in the child above the age of two, it is omnipresent. Not in the sense that sensori-motor behaviour does not occur (for all overt behaviour is sensori-motor even if it is representational as well), but in the sense that the transitions from sensori-motor to representational behaviour are frequent and rapid, and that, frequently, at least in the adult, sensori-motor behaviour may be accompanied by representational behaviour in the form of sub-vocal language and imagery which may or may not be related – as when we perform tasks mechanically while thinking about something else. Overlooking the distinctive character of representation led to the attribution of symbolic thought to animals in the nineteenth century (as, for instance, in the work of Groos) and to its identification with mere language in the twentieth.

5. *Analytical and Reversible Representation: the Oddity Problem*

Strictly speaking, the further development of cogntion in children falls outside the scope of this chapter. But there is one well-defined experiment which has been investigated both from the point of view of infra-human generalization and as a pointer to the systematization of representational thought in children of school age. This is the oddity problem. A brief look at the data on this problem will serve as a fitting conclusion to the present survey and as a bridge between the developments considered here and the further elaborations examined in the central chapters of Volume II.

In the main, subjects in investigations of the oddity problem have been monkeys. The first inquiry was that of Robinson (1933), but there have since been many elaborations, due principally to the work of Harlow and his associates (Harlow, 1951, 1959; Harlow, Meyer and Settlage, 1951). In the study of learning in monkeys and of children under five, the oddity problem is best thought of as a particular instance of learning set formation (Harlow, 1959). The following description is taken from Harlow, 1951.

> 'Two different pairs of identical stimuli are used, but only three stimuli are presented together. The odd stimulus, the stimulus singly represented, is rewarded, and trial sequences are so arranged that a member from each pair of stimuli is odd on half the trials. On any given trial there is reward of the position, the object, and single representation, but over the series of trials only single representation is rewarded 100 per cent of the time. The other stimulus and situation variables – the position of the reward and the particular object rewarded – must be disregarded by the animal if he is to master the problem.'
>
> (Harlow, *op. cit.*, p. 190.)

Harlow finds that monkeys take from 400 to 1500 trials to reach a criterion of 90 per cent correct responses. For the data presented in Figure 8, thirty problems were used, with twenty-four trials per problem.

It is apparent that the oddity problem is more difficult than the object discrimination learning set considered in Section I. Indeed, from the point of view of learning set theory, perseverative object choices constitute one of the error strategies to be overcome. A number of investigations using sub-primates show failure to make any improvement on this problem. As to monkey learning, we note that progress is gradual and slow, but the eventual criterion achieved is as high or nearly as high as that reached in other learning set problems. One feature which is especially noteworthy is that even with twenty-four trials per problem, problem to problem transfer seems to be very gradual.

Before looking at the data on children, mention should be made of an inquiry on an analogous problem: non-oddity or matching (Roberts, 1933). Roberts' inquiry, designed as a comparison between children

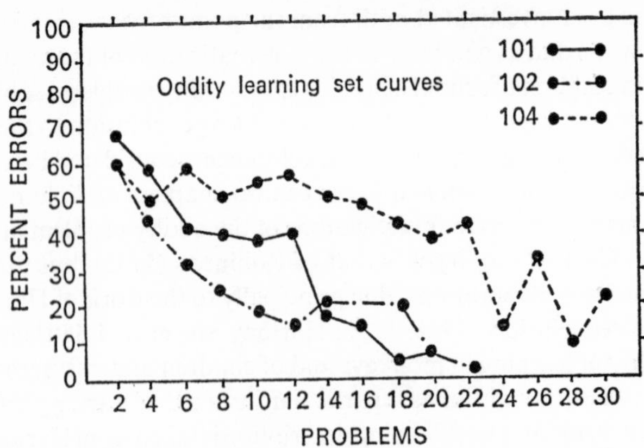

Figure 8. Oddity Learning by Three Representative Monkeys

raised in families and orphanage reared children, used only nine problems. The situation consisted of an array of six double cupboards, one mounted over the other. The lower cupboard held a toy which could be removed and played with if the child chose the right cupboard. This could be identified by the fact that the colour (or the shape) of the stimulus on the upper cupboard differed from that seen in the lower cupboard for all bar the correct, rewarded couplet on any trial. CA of the twenty-one pre-school children ranged from 3:6 to 4:6; the nineteen orphanage children were a year older. However, in terms of MA there was little difference, and no child had an MA less than 4:0 or greater than 6:4. The performance of these children is illustrated in the data of Table 1.

Table 1. Performance of Pre-school and Orphanage Children on a Non-oddity Problem

	Problem								
	1	2	3	4	5	6	7	8	9
Mean trials to criterion	36·8	7·1	2·5	9·0	0·7	0·9	1·2	1·3	0·8
Median trials to criterion	39·0	0·0	0·0	3·0	0·0	0·0	0·0	0·0	0·0
Per cent given hints	53	11	0	0	0	0	0	0	0
Per cent achieving zero-error solution	0	56	68	20	75	77	68	82	92

(Based on data from Roberts, 1933)

Roberts' data are not strictly comparable with the monkey data for several reasons. (*a*) The problem is a non-oddity or matching problem (but the two are probably of a similar order of difficulty); (*b*) each successive problem was given for as many trials as needed to achieve criterion (four successive correct choices) before proceeding to the next; (*c*) a correction procedure was used throughout, i.e. the child was shown the correct solution if he made a wrong choice; (*d*) after thirty-six trials, hints were given after each failure, i.e. the child was told to look for the two matching stimuli in language that he could understand.

Nevertheless, there is clear evidence of the superiority of the children. In particular, although mastery of the first problem was slow, problem to problem transfer was considerable, as is especially apparent from the last row of the table. In general, hints were required only for the first problem, but it is interesting to note that where hints were given, they did not in general lead to immediate solution, the maximum number of hints for any child being twenty-two, and the mean about six – for the pre-school children, for the orphanage children, being older, were superior on problem 1, and 47 per cent required no hints compared with fifteen per cent of the other group.

It is interesting to note that none of Roberts' subjects was able to give her a general verbal rule for the solution of these problems – although her criteria for generality seem to have been rather strict. However, many solved the problems correctly and could give no account of how they did so. For further light on this question we turn back to the oddity problem.

Inhelder and Piaget (1964) report an inquiry which is essentially identical with the oddity procedure. Children were shown an array of three or six cards, all but one of which were identical in colour and asked to find the card which had a cross on the reverse side. This card was always the odd one. Apparently, none of their subjects had any difficulty in mastering the problem after one or two trials. But the five-year-olds could give no account of how they did so, and generally gave quite incorrect explanations, while children of seven to eight were able to formulate the rule of solution. Moreover, when asked to turn the tables on the experimenter and make up their own oddity problems, the older children could do so but not the younger (who would present an array of two reds and a green and put the cross under one of the reds, etc.).

The qualitative difference between the performance of younger and older children is clearly important. But a careful reading of Inhelder and Piaget's account indicates that their methodology was so rough and ready that little reliance could be placed on the accuracy of their conclusions.

It was therefore decided to replicate the inquiry, with more rigorous experimentation.

The inquiry was designed by the present writer and executed by J. C. Astin. The procedure was closely modelled on Harlow's Wisconsin studies. The apparatus consisted of a tray with three removable boxes. The boxes had slide-on lids, and variation of trials and problems was achieved by using lids of different colours. Each problem, featuring two exemplars of two colours was given for exactly six trials, any one trial featuring only three stimuli. A new problem was introduced every six trials irrespective of performance on the previous problems. Two criteria were used: (*a*) not more than three errors in three successive problems (eighteen trials); followed by (*b*) errorless solution of five successive problems presented at the rate of one trial per problem. The reward was a 'Happy Family' card (to build up an interesting collection) and a marble to be inserted in a tube (the height of the column indicating the child's success). Following Roberts, hints were given after every failure beyond trial 30, and a non-committal hint after trial 20 ('There is a trick to get it every time'). A non-correction procedure was used up to trial 40, and a correction procedure thereafter. The subjects were six children at each of the ages four, seven, eight, nine, and ten, selected by their teachers as of 'average intelligence'. Up to 120 trials were given. Only one child (a four-year-old) failed to reach both criteria. In addition each subject was required to explain his method of solution at the end of the series (and helped to verbalize what was 'in his mind' where necessary), and to make up five problems of his own. The results may be seen in Table 2.

All but one of the thirty children reached both criteria within 120 trials. In each case, the second criterion, involving only one trial per problem, proved no harder than the first. Even the four-year-olds reached criterion after a mean of only 49·4 trials. This figure may be contrasted with the 400 and upwards needed by monkeys. As against this, more trials might have been needed had no hints been given. But this is not true of the older children.

However, the principal finding is that Inhelder and Piaget's conclusions are fully borne out. The improvement in terms of trials to criterion is gradual. But the ability to give a verbal explanation and above all to reproduce the structure of the problem by turning the tables on the experimenter shows a dramatic change about the period seven to eight.

The solution of the oddity problem is attributed by Harlow to the formation of learning set. There is no need to assume the intervention of representation – although this is not to say that monkeys are incapable

Table 2. The Oddity Problem in Children

	Age				
	4	7	8	9	10
Mean trials before criterion	49·4	33·2	18·0	10·8	5·0
No. given at least two hints (2)	6(6)	5(6)	3(6)	2(6)	1(6)
No. failing to reach criteria	1	0	0	0	0
Verbal explanation*	0,1,5	2,4,0	6,0,0	6,0,0	6,0,0
No. giving correct reversals†	2	1	5	6	6

(Lunzer and Astin, Unpublished Data)

* In each column, the first figure represents the number (out of six) who gave a spontaneous adequate explanation, the second the number of those whose explanations were taken as adequate but only after appropriate supplementary questioning, and the third figure those who could give no proper explanation of their method of solution.

† Subjects were required to produce five successive 'problems' for the experimenter. The criterion for correct reversal is four out of five. In most cases, the odd error did not appear.

of minimal representation. The actual solutions of the children seem to be analogous. Very clearly, representation is quite advanced even at the age of four. Nevertheless, it does not lead to a different kind of learning. The chief gain is that the children can profit in some measure from the hint (representational communication) but even here it is obvious that the hint is not understood in its full sense since (*a*) it is not effective immediately and (*b*) the children cannot explain their solution (although the hint itself was a sufficient explanation), nor can they reproduce the situation. The hint is therefore no more than a prompt, favouring the correct strategy at the expense of error strategies. Since solution is far better than explanation (as it was in Roberts' data), one may conclude that representation lags behind performance in terms of the intelligent organization of behaviour.

The position is quite otherwise after the age of eight (on average) when the children can give a satisfactory verbal explanation and can also reconstruct the experiment themselves. The two measures agree well with one another, and the second is simply a more objective measure of the same thing. What they involve is more than the mere representation of the actions involved ('*I chose the red one,*' '*... the middle one,*' etc.), or even their anticipation ('*I'll try the blue one*'). They imply the ability to reorganize the moments of behaviour and to represent the strategy or decision process itself. Representation, as we have seen, is more than the mere activation of a trace: it is an active reconstruction of the situation using an alternative, representational input. But to begin with, the reconstruction simply follows the lines of the action itself: the order of elements is largely dictated by the original sensori-motor associations. The new development depends on progress in re-ordering the moments of experience, analytical representation, to the point where the child is capable of deliberately selecting the moments of decision and comparing one with another, or of anticipating them (as at the age of ten when the child solves the problem without any experience at all).

In a word, the child of eight (in this problem) is able to represent the criteria of his own actions. This is clearly a new kind of second-order strategy which is dependent on progress in ordering. We have already noted that the growth of representation itself is bound up with that of minimal ordering. But because representation creates its own input, the actual order of experience is less binding as the child becomes more fluent in the exercise of representational strategies (language and imagery). The new development substitutes a logical order for an experienced order. It results in new kinds of transfer, as in the reversal or 'table-turning' of the present experiment, in imaginative extensions to different points of view of an object seen in one perspective, in conservation of criterial properties, and so on.

The reader will need to consult Volume II, Chapter 8 for a fuller account of concrete logical thinking. This experiment has been reported in some detail because it brings out the representational character of logical solution. Psychological inquiry is often narrowly compartmentalized. This is one reason that experiments on learning have so often appeared irrelevant to human beings. One result is that comparative psychologists are apt to leave the study of human learning to educational psychologists (often conceived of as an inferior breed, all too liable to eke out observation with empathy). For their own part, human learning is then thought of as a simple extension to animal learning (cf. Mandler, 1962, who argues that cognition of structure is an elaboration of learning set). It is nice to recognize the continuity of behavioural organization. Indeed it is essential. But it is equally essential to recognize the existence of qualitative growth. To reiterate: the progress in actual solution of the oddity problem to the age of seven is indeed fully paralleled by the animal data, and does not involve representation; the understanding and transfer shown by the eight-year-olds is entirely due to progress in representation, and has no parallel in the behaviour of the monkey (just as the latter has no parallel in that of the fish).

VI. SUMMARY

The work of Bitterman and his associates reveals clear differences in the learning of different species. Whereas fish, like rats, are capable of discrimination learning, fish show no improvement in reversal learning while rats do. Similarly, fish fail to maximize in probability problems when one stimulus is reinforced more frequently than another, unless the conditions of experimentation are such as to enable them to eliminate experience of the less rewarded stimulus; rats maximize regardless of the conditions of experimentation. Differences are shown between spatial and non-spatial problems, and the behaviour of turtles and pigeons is intermediate between that of fish and rat. Harlow's studies of learning set formation bring out further phylogenetic differences in learning. While studies of simple discrimination (single problem learning) show no differences between members of different species, transfer due to the formation of learning set, as in object discrimination, shows clear differences even within the primate order. Although sub-primates such as the cat do show some problem to problem improvement, progress is very slow and the asymptote of such learning falls far short of that shown by primates. Studies of learning set formation in children show that improvement even in four-year-olds is superior to that shown by monkeys and chimpanzees.

A review of the ontogenesis of sensori-motor development in the human infant based on Piaget's observations suggests certain analogies between ontogenesis and phylogenesis. Thus the primary adaptations and circular reactions of the child at Stage II (1–4 months) permit a co-ordination of sensory modalities which is essential for the instrumental behaviour shown at Stage III (4–7 months), in some ways analogous to a stage of single problem instrumental learning. Application of familiar schemata to new objects at Stage IV (7–11 months) leads to the conservation of the object and to a behavioural awareness of a stable causal, spatial and temporal framework. From the strictly materialist point of view taken in Chapter 4, the behavioural object which is conserved is defined as the intersection of the strategies which it permits. There is therefore a clear differentiation from now on between the line of behaviour or strategy and the pattern of related lines of behaviour or schema. At the same time, the ease of transfer of strategies which appears in the application of familiar strategies or schemata to new objects suggests an analogy with learning set. Stage V, from eleven months to seventeen months, sees an elaboration of behaviour already present at Stage IV, but with a more active experimentation which permits the appearance of some 'insightful behaviour' reminiscent of the problem solutions made by Köhler's apes. Stage VI is in reality the beginning of a new phase of behavioural organization, when behaviour is supplemented by the intervention of imagery and imitative gesture, both of which feature alongside language as vehicles of representation.

A careful but admittedly tentative theoretical analysis of all these developments suggests that the principal feature of development in learning is a development in generalization. It is suggested that such development is due to the activity of higher-order strategies or links. While the mode of activity of such elements is likely to be by the suppression of others at the same level, as suggested by Harlow's error factor theory, it is argued that their facilitation is due to positive reinforcement. It is further supposed that the appearance of generalization of this sort is contingent on the availability of suitable connexions in the nervous system, although on the ontogenetic side these cannot become effective until lower order strategies (upon which they act) have been perfected. Both reversal learning and probability learning are seen as simpler cases of learning set, simpler because of the greater similarity of the situations to which they apply. It is stressed that the further equations between human ontogenesis at Stage III and instrumental learning, and especially between Stages IV and V and learning set involve a speculative leap which is not fully supported by the evidence that we have.

Returning to the analysis of behaviours which differentiate between species, considerable attention was devoted to the nature of imitation. The importance of imitation lies in the fact that it is the forerunner of representational behaviour. It is possible to account for apparent imitation in sub-primates on the assumption that the behaviour of the follower coincides with that of the leader only as a result of conditioning: the follower is conditioned to attend to the same cues. Imitation in primates cannot be accounted for on this basis. The principal differences between true imitation and pseudo-imitation are that the former involves the assimilation of cues arising from the behaviour of the model to cues arising from the subject's own behaviour (a sort of transfer), a deliberately articulated matching of the moments of input, a deliberate selection of behaviour so as to favour a matching of the results with those yielded by the behaviour of the model, and a generality of imitative behaviours.

A survey of the development of imitative behaviour in the human infant based on Piaget's observations reveals that the growth of imitation is gradual. To begin with, the imitative behaviour is simply cued by that of the model and imitation is coincidental. Subsequent development passes through a stage where behaviour is favoured by the similarity of its results with the input from a model, to the deliberate and systematic variation of behaviour in the effort to produce such similarity.

Learning by imitation is shown both by the chimpanzee and by the human child. It is suggested that in the former species generality of imitation may be less spontaneous, so that learning by imitation is more contingent on the deliberate formation of an imitation learning set. However, it is stressed that learning by imitation is not a separate kind of learning distinct from learning by reinforcement. The imitative behaviour simply acts as a prompt, facilitating the activation of 'correct' trial-and-error behaviour. The provision of a model for imitation is therefore a form of guidance akin to Skinner's shaping of operants, and indeed is used by Skinnerians in this fashion for the more efficient instruction of human beings.

It is frequently argued that the distinctive achievements of human intelligence are due to the role of language as a mediating response. A closer analysis of the functions of language reveals that its use in the planning of behaviour, in the communication of structured knowledge and in thinking does not derive solely from its primitive communicative functions but rather from the development of representation as a whole, of which language comes to serve as the principal vehicle. Representation begins as an extension of deferred imitation, when new connexions develop among representational strategies themselves (as opposed to the old connexions mediated by sensori-motor schemata). The growth of representation in play is shown by a freer use of materials (greater independence with respect to the perceptual input) and, above all, by a greater autonomy: representation acting as cue to further elaboration of representation, as measured by 'constructiveness' or 'organization' of play behaviour.

Perhaps owing to the relative neglect of developmental changes in learning, and within this of the significance of representation, relevant experimental studies are few. It is suggested that the emergence of representation may be bound up with developmental changes shown in the phylogenesis of two forms of behaviour well-known to laboratory investigation. They are delayed response and double alternation. Capacity for delayed response is bound up with frontal lobe development and is therefore a good candidate for the study of the most differential human characteristics. Both delayed response and double alternation seem to depend on the availability of strategies which will act on an input resulting from the trace of previous strategies, or of strategies for storing such traces and reactivating them when required.

Nevertheless it is stressed that the development of representation is a spontaneous tendency and does not depend on the provision by an experimenter of temporal mazes and delayed-response problems. Rather it appears to be bound up with the new turn taken by motivation due to the formation of a primitive representation of the self. Even from the age of two, the child spends a portion of his time not only in representing experience as lived, but in modifying and distorting it in ways which will reduce tension or threat resulting from uncertainty of input. It is argued that from now on, much of the motivation of human behaviour may be attributed to the selective facilitation of strategies and schemata conducive to self-enhancement – and to the avoidance or circumvention of situations which are assimilated as threatening. A typical and revealing instance is the bedtime ritual in young children.

The final sub-section in the chapter illustrates both the continuity of human intelligence with that of other species and a relative discontinuity due to the emergence of a new use of representation: the systematic ordering of experience. Both the similarities and the differences are highlighted by experimental studies of the oddity problem and its complement the non-oddity or matching problem in monkeys and in human children. The behaviour of monkeys is fully accounted for in terms of learning set theory, and the same holds of children up to the age of seven or eight on average, in spite of their possession of language and in spite of the ubiquity of representation in their behaviour. It appears that for a long time, representational intelligence actually lags behind the highest achievements of sensori-motor intelligence. However, the behaviour of older children reveals a new found capacity to systematically reorder their experience. In the oddity problem, this is evidenced by their ability to explain their rule of action and to reverse the situation. It is argued that the growth of logic (which this implies) results directly out of representation: for representation is increasingly free to reconstruct the moments of experience in any order, so that in the end there is a tendency to substitute a logical sequence in representation for one which is random or contingent on experience. The essence of the latter is that attention is focused on those moments of behaviour which are the criteria of the subject's own actions. To the question 'why?' I would again answer: reinforcement, for this second-order strategy and no other leads to a consistent prediction and control over experience, and hence to a maximal reduction of uncertainty. The discerning reader may discover a certain similarity between this formulation and Piaget's 'doctrine of equilibration' as described in Volume II, Chapter 8.

This concludes our discussion of learning and its development in this volume, apart from the summary final chapter. The chapter which follows takes up anew the questions of motivation, and especially of human motivation, for it is clear that they demand a separate discussion in their own right.

REFERENCES

BARKER, R., DEMBO, T., and LEWIN, K. (1941). Frustration and regression. *Univ. of Iowa Studies in Child Welfare* **18**, No. 1.

BERLYNE, D. E. (1960). *Conflict, Arousal and Curiosity.* New York and London: McGraw-Hill.

BIRCH, H. G. (1945). The relation of previous experience to insightful problem-solving. *J. Comp. Psychol.* **38**, 367–383.

BIRCH, H. G., and LEFFORD, A. (1963). Intersensory development in children. *Monogr. Soc. Res. Child Dev.* **28**, No. 2 (Serial No. 92).

BITTERMAN, M. E. (1965). Phyletic differences in learning. *Amer. Psychologist* **20**, 396–410.

BITTERMAN, M. E., WODINSKY, J., and CANDLAND, D. K. (1958). Some comparative psychology. *Amer. J. Psychol.* **71**, 94–110.

BROADBENT, D. E. (1958). *Perception and Communication.* Oxford: Pergamon.

BUHLER, C. (1947). *From Birth to Maturity.* London: Kegan Paul.

ELKONIN, D. B. (1957). The physiology of higher nervous activity and child psychology. In Simon, B. (ed.), *Psychology in the Soviet Union.* London: Routledge and Kegan Paul, 47–68.

ESTES, W. K. (1959). The statistical approach to learning theory. In Koch, S. (ed.), *Psychology: A Study of a Science*, Volume II. *General Systematic Formulations, Learning, and Special Processes.* New York: McGraw-Hill, 380–491.

GELLERMAN, L. W. (1931). The double alternation problem: III. The behaviour of monkeys in a double-alternation box apparatus. *J. Genet. Psychol.* **39**, 359–392.

GESELL, A. (1940). *The First Five Years of Life: A Guide to the Study of the Preschool Child.* New York: Harper.

GONZALEZ, R. C., ESKIN, R. M., and BITTERMAN, M. E. (1963). Further experiments on partial reinforcement in the fish. *Amer. J. Psychol.* **76**, 366–375.

GRANT, D. A., HAKE, H. W., and HORNSETH, J. P. (1951). Acquisition and extinction of a verbal conditioned response with differing percentages of reinforcement. *J. Exp. Psychol.* **42**, 1–5.

HARLOW, H. F. (1944a). Studies in discrimination learning by monkeys: I. The learning of discrimination series and the reversal of discrimination series. *J. Gen. Psychol.* **30**, 3–12.

HARLOW, H. F. (1944b). Studies in discrimination learning by monkeys. II. Discrimination learning without primary reinforcement. *J. Gen. Psychol.* **30**, 13–21.

HARLOW, H. F. (1949). The formation of learning sets. *Psychol. Rev.* **56**, 51–65.

HARLOW, H. F. (1951). Primate learning. In Stone, C.P. (ed.).*Comparative Psychology*. (Third edn.). New York: Prentice-Hall, 183–238.

HARLOW, H. F. (1959). Learning set and error factor theory. In Koch, S. (ed.) *Psychology: A Study of a Science. Vol. II General Systematic Formulations, Learning and Special Processes.* New York and London: McGraw-Hill, pp. 492–537.

HARLOW, H. F., MEYER, D., and SETTLAGE, P. H. (1951). The effects of large cortical lesions on the solution of oddity problems by monkeys. *J. Comp. Physiol. Psychol.* **44**, 320–326.

HARLOW, H. F., and WARREN, J. M. (1952). Formation and transfer of discrimination learning sets. *J. Comp. Physiol. Psychol.* **45**, 482–489.

HAYES, K. J., and HAYES, C. (1952). Imitation in a home-raised chimpanzee. *J. Comp. Physiol. Psychol.* **45**, 450–459.

HAYES, K. J., THOMPSON, R., and HAYES, C. (1953). Discrimination learning set in chimpanzees. *J. Comp. Physiol. Psychol.* **46**, 99–104.

HEBB, D. O. (1937). The innate organisation of visual activity: I. Perception of Progress by rats reared in total darkness. *J. Genet. Psychol.* **51**, 101–126.

HEBB, D. O. (1949) *The Organisation of Behaviour*. New York: John Wiley.

HERON, W. T. (1951). Learning: general introduction. In Stone, C.P. (ed.), *Comparative Psychology*. (Third edn.). New York: Prentice-Hall, 137–182.

HULME, I., and LUNZER, E. A. (1966). Play, language and reasoning in subnormal children. *J. Child Psychol. Psychiat.* **7**, 107–123.

HUNTER, W. S. (1912). The delayed reaction in animals and children. *Psychol. Monogr.* **2**, 1–85.

HUNTER, W. S. (1928). The behaviour of raccoons in a double alternation temporal maze. *J. Genet. Psychol.* **35**, 374–388.

INHELDER, B. and PIAGET, J. (1964). *The Early Growth of Logic in the Child. Classification and Seriation.* London: Routledge and Kegan Paul.

JACOBSEN, C. F. (1936). Studies of cerebral function in primates. *Comp. Psychol. Monogr.* **13**, 3–60.

KENDLER, T. S. (1963). Development of mediating responses in children. *Mon. Soc. Res. Child Dev.* **28**, No. 2, 33–48.

KÖHLER, W. (1925). *The Mentality of Apes.* London: Routledge.

KRECHEVSKY, I. (1932). 'Hypothesis' versus 'chance' in the pre-solution period in sensory-discrimination learning. *U. of California Publications in Psychology* **6**, No. 3, 27–44.

KUENNE, M. R. (1946). Experimental investigation of the relation of language to transposition behaviour in young children. *J. Exp. Psychol.* **36**, 471–490.

LEARY, R. W., HARLOW, H. F., SETTLAGE, P. H., and GREENWOOD, D. D. (1952). Performance on double-alternation problems by normal and brain-injured monkeys. *J. Comp. Physiol. Psychol.* **45**, 576–584.

LOWENFELD, M. (1935). *Play in Childhood.* London: Gollancz.

LUNZER, E. A. (1955). Intellectual development in the play of young children aged 2 to 6. *Ph.D. Thesis.* U. of Birmingham.

LUNZER, E. A. (1959). Intellectual development in the play of young children. *Educ. Rev.* **11**, 205–217.

LUNZER, E. A., and HULME I. (1967). Discrimination learning and discrimination learning sets in subnormal children. *Brit. J. Educ. Psychol.* **37**, 175–187.

LURIA, A. R. (1961). *The Role of Speech in the Regulation of Normal and Abnormal Behaviour.* Oxford: Pergamon Press.

MCCARTHY, D. A. (1954). Language development in children. In Carmichael, L. (ed.), *Manual of Child Psychology.* New York: Wiley, 492–630.

MCDOUGALL, W. (1908). *An Outline of Psychology.* London: Methuen.

MANDLER, G. (1962). From association to structure. *Psychol. Rev.* **69**, 415–427.

MILLER, N. E. and DOLLARD, J. (1941). *Social Learning and Imitation.* New Haven, Conn.: Yale Univ. Press.

NISSEN, H. W. (1951). Social behaviour in primates. In C. P. Stone, (ed.), *Comparative Psychology*. (Third edn.). New York: Prentice-Hall, 423–457.

NISSEN, H. W., RIESEN, A. H., and NOWLIS, V. (1938). Delayed response and discrimination learning by chimpanzees. *J. Comp. Psychol.* **26**, 361–386.

O'CONNOR, N., and HERMELIN, B. (1963). *Speech and Thought in Severe Subnormality*. Oxford: Pergamon.

PALMER, F. H. (1965). On the behavioural foundations of mathematical concepts: Discussion. In Morrisett, L. N. and Vinsonhaler, J. (ed.), Mathematical learning. *Monogr. Soc. Res. Child Dev.* **30**, No. 1. (Serial No. 99) 96–102.

PASCAL, G. R., and STOLUROW, L. M. (1952). Delayed reaction for form and place contrasted. *J. Comp. Physiol. Psychol.* **45**, 294–299.

PIAGET, J. (1926). *The Language and Thought of the Child.* (Third edn.: 1959). London: Routledge and Kegan Paul.

PIAGET, J. (1950). *The Psychology of Intelligence.* London: Routledge and Kegan Paul.

PIAGET, J. (1951). *Play, Dreams and Imitation in Childhood.* London: Heinemann.

PIAGET, J. (1953), *The Origin of Intelligence in the Child.* London: Routledge and Kegan Paul.

PIAGET, J., and INHELDER, B. (1951). *La genèse de l'idée de hasard chez l'enfant*. Paris: Presses Universitaires de France.

PIAGET, J., and INHELDER, B. (1956). *The Child's Conception of Space.* London: Routledge and Kegan Paul.

PRIBRAM, K. H., MISHKIN, M., ROSVOLD, H. E., and KAPLAN, S. J. (1952). Effects on delayed-response performance of lesions of dorsolateral and ventromedial frontal cortex of baboons. *J. Comp. Physiol. Psychol.* **45**, 565–575.

RESTLE, F. (1962). The selection of strategies in cue learning. *Psychol. Rev.* **69**, 329–343.

ROBERTS, K. E. (1933). Learning in preschool and orphanage children: An experimental study of ability to solve different situations according to the same plan. *Univ. Iowa Stud. Child Welf.* **7**, No. 3, 1–94.

ROBINSON, E. W. (1933). A preliminary experiment on abstraction in a monkey. *J. Comp. Psychol.* **16**, 231–236.

SCHAFFER, R. (1966). The onset of fear of strangers and the incongruity hypothesis. *J. Child. Psychol. Psychiat.* **7**, 95–106.

SENDEN, M. von (1960): *Space and Sight*. London: Methuen.

STEVENSON, H. W., and SWARTZ, J. D. (1958) Learning set in children as a function of intellectual level. *J. Comp. Physiol. Psychol.* **51,** 755–757.

STEVENSON, H. W., and WEIR, M. W. (1959). Variables affecting children's performance in a probability learning task. *J. Exp. Psychol.* **57**, 403–412.

STEVENSON, H. W., and ZIGLER, E. F. (1958). Probability learning in children. *J. Exp. Psychol.* **56**, 185–192.

THORNDIKE, E. L. (1898). Animal intelligence: an experimental study of the associative processes in animals. *Psychol. Rev. Monogr. Suppl.*, **2**, No. 4 (whole No. 8).

VAN ALSTYNE, D. (1932). *Play Behaviour and Choice of Materials of Pre-School Children.* Chicago: Univ. of Chicago Press.

VYGOTSKY, L. S. (1962). *Thought and Language.* New York and London: John Wiley.

WEINSTEIN, B. (1945). The evolution of intelligent behaviour in rhesus monkeys. *Genet. Psychol. Monogr.* **31**, 3–48.

WOHLWILL, J. F. (1962). From perception to inference: A dimension of cognitive development. In Kessen, W. and Kuhlman, C. (ed.), Thought in the young child. *Monogr. Soc. Res. Child Dev.* **27**, No. 2 (Serial No. 83), 87–112.

YERKES, R. M. and YERKES, A. W. (1929). *The Great Apes.* New Haven, Conn.: Yale Univ. Press.

YOUNG, J. Z. (1964). *A Model of the Brain.* London: O.U.P.

6

Problems of Motivation

E. A. LUNZER AND J. F. MORRIS

I. THE COMMON-SENSE VIEW OF MOTIVATION

1. *Statement*

FROM THE common-sense point of view, the problem of motivation hardly exists, at any rate as psychologists understand it. People can usually give a very good account of the reasons for their behaviour. We are familiar with such experiences as following our desires, making up our minds or struggling with our consciences. In the end the course of action that we embark on can usually be traced back to some kind of mental decision, whether it be easy or more difficult, appearing to involve a definite act of will. The more philosophically minded might well be taken up with such problems as the origins of conscience and the sanctions for its dictates or the existence of free-will. If mental events, like physical events, are the result of a causal process, the association of ideas under the influence of habit, in what sense can a man be held morally responsible for his actions? But the origin of habitual, more or less pleasurable or necessary behaviour can be taken for granted. We eat when we feel hungry, we go to work to earn a living, we collect stamps because we are interested, we pass the time of day with a neighbour either for amusement or out of regard for convention, and so on. In each case, we can give a rational account of the causes of our behaviour. The feeling of hunger, the desire to make ends meet, the interest in stamps, and so on are all mental events. It seems to stand to reason that such mental events are the causes of action.

Without prejudicing this mentalistic framework, we may go on to ask the reason for, say, our interest in stamps or our adherence to social convention. If we do, then we will very likely find our way to a more general 'theory' of motivation, probably hedonistic. We may wish to test the idea that quite generally people engage in activity from which they expect to derive pleasure, or through which they expect to satisfy their bodily needs, so avoiding pain.

If we go on to consider the course of events in the sphere of social interactions in which we may feel a deeper sense of involvement, we note that our actions are very often accompanied by more or less strong feelings: of affection and sympathy, or of love, or of anger or jealousy or fear. We note that these emotions, like the pleasure that we seek and the pain which we seek to avoid, are often accompanied by physiological changes, and we take it for granted that these, like the behaviour, are the result of the feelings, being more immediate than the actions to which they give rise.

Probing just a little more deeply, we find that while we do quite often act on impulse, under the sway of immediate emotion, we usually think it wiser to curb our emotions, to weigh up the consequences, for ourselves and for others, and to follow the dictates of reason. We have advanced from a simple hedonism to a hedonistic utilitarianism.

Now it is a little embarrassing to find that behaviour has both *aims* (pleasure and the absence of pain), and *causes* (the emotions of anger, love, etc.). But one can reassure oneself by noting that both aims and causes are clearly emotional. One may argue that the various special emotions are somehow subordinated to the ultimate aims of pleasure and pain-avoidance. Reason is invoked only to ensure that this more general satisfaction is achieved. Thus all motives are clearly bound up with emotion, and we end up with the conclusion that in the final analysis, the impulse for all behaviour is emotional in origin.

At no time have we abandoned the position that the processes with which we are concerned are mental ones, and that they are accessible to a special kind of observation: introspection. Wishes and fears, as well as the special emotions which move us to behaviour and the pleasure which is its end are all open to introspection. They are the subject of a special science: the science of psychology, being the study of the mind.

Such is the position of common sense, and such also was the position of most psychologists in the nineteenth century. For it was accepted that psychology was the study of mental events. Even the use of experimentation was consistent with this. Thus nineteenth-century psychophysics was concerned mainly with finding the correlates between an introspectible mental datum: sensation or perception, and the physical variable. Motivation and emotion were not studied experimentally by psychologists, but the implications of careful introspection were considered by such writers as James and Stout.

2. *Objections to the Common-sense View*

Now there are three reasons why this common-sense line of approach cannot provide a satisfactory starting point for the scientific study of motivation. The first is that the experimental study of motivation in animals becomes impossible. Even if one accepts that animals experience emotions, in the sense of felt emotions, and are capable of wishes and fears, they cannot report on them. And this means that the psychological technique of introspection cannot be used. But if psychology is the science of the mind, then introspection must be its principal technique, for it is only by introspection that we can gain knowledge of private mental events – if indeed such knowledge is possible. (In point of fact, many psychologists find that anything that can usefully be said about private events can be expressed more unequivocally in terms of events which are not private at all: verbal statements, physiological changes, the contingencies of overt behaviour, and so on.) Now the scientific study of human behaviour cannot afford to overlook the fact of biological continuity. Indeed it is reasonable to begin with animal behaviour, since here we have organisms which are simpler, so that the elucidation of the mechanisms which govern their behaviour should be easier. Experimentation with animals is usually easier, and nearly always less equivocal than experiments involving human subjects. (An argument which should not be used, as it was used by Tolman, to infer that experiments with human subjects are unnecessary, for there are differences between species as well as a fundamental continuity.)

The second reason is that even in the case of human subjects, introspective data are unreliable, especially in the area of motivation. It is true that some of the time we can report on the reasons for our actions or on the state of our feelings with some hope of accuracy. But this is plainly untrue of several large and important classes of behaviour. For instance, not even the most hard-headed critic of psychoanalysis would deny that some behaviours are unconscious in origin: the child who is a compulsive eater cannot report that eating is a substitute behaviour engaged in whenever he is subjected to experiences relating to rejection, for he is unaware of the relation. Freud's essay on *The Psychopathology of Everyday Life* (Freud, 1914) shows very clearly that many aspects of quite normal behaviour, e.g. lapses in verbal memory, and especially in memory for names, are often bound up with unconscious associations. As to the argument that such associations are recoverable by free association and especially by psychoanalysis, we have to recognize that one of the reasons for the unsatisfactory scientific status of psychoanalysis is precisely that the process cannot be restricted to the recovery of 'material' but extends inevitably to its transformation, so that securing controlled and repeatable data becomes difficult if not impossible. One might add that neither direct verbal report nor free verbal association under analysis can be made available with young children, and interpretations of motivation based on play depend on a great deal of inference, which may be quite misleading. (For example, elaborate discussions of the child's relation with the 'love object' sometimes ignore that the child does not achieve conservation of objects in general before the age of about seven months.)

A third reason is that a scientific approach to psychology, including motivation, requires a recognition of the continuity of biological regulating mechanisms. Psychology cannot afford to be entirely divorced from the physiological study of the nervous system in general, and of the brain in particular. Many important motivational regulations depend quite certainly on changes in body chemistry and on neural processes which are open to investigation by physiological techniques both in animals and in human beings.

II. STATEMENT OF PROBLEMS

It is probably no exaggeration to say that psychologists are more divided on the subject of motivation than on any other topic. It is the purpose of this chapter to present a number of views which are presently held or have been held in the past, to review some of the evidence, and develop a number of ideas presented in preceding chapters. As we have seen, questions of motivation are closely bound up with questions of emotion. Just as there is controversy over the former, there is controversy over the latter, and especially over the relations between the two. Here, too, an impressive body of experimental evidence has been built up, evidence which one can ill afford to neglect. The evidence is not decisive for any one view. But we would like to state at the outset that taking a broad stand on these issues is more a matter of deciding which questions may be fruitfully asked than of furnishing a set of clear-cut answers.

Traditionally, motivation has been concerned with three problems: the motive power or force which produces behaviour, the directionality of behaviour or its purposive character, and its intensity, as evidenced by the vigour with which it is pursued and its persistence in the face of obstacles. We say traditionally because in the view of many present-day psychologists, ourselves included, the first of these is an unreal problem, and attempts to resolve it alongside the others lead to confused formulations. The second and third are quite central to the study of behaviour. Also, although they are closely bound up with questions of cognition and learning, (one cannot easily separate evidence for purposiveness in behaviour from evidence relating to the subject's knowledge of his environment), they demand consideration in their own right.

The principal views on motivation are four in number. First: that the 'springs of action' are rooted in the mind; conscious purpose or intention is taken to be a sufficient explanation in itself. Second: that motivation derives from instincts which parallel biological needs for the survival of individual and of species; they are independent biological mechanisms with a functional origin. Third: that motivation derives in part from primary drives similar to the instincts in the second view, but in part from secondary, acquired drives; like instincts, primary and secondary drives serve the treble function of initiating behaviour and of governing its intensity and direction. Fourth: that motivation may be identified with the strength of arousal of established action tendencies or strategies, whether learnt or innate; the initiation of behaviour does not imply any separate 'force'; its directionality derives from the character of the strategy itself, which is partly cognitive; its intensity is determined both by specific factors, degree of arousal of the strategy, and by general factors, level of general arousal. As already indicated, it is the fourth view which will be developed in this chapter, after reviewing the other three.

The view that one takes of emotion is largely concerned with the question of the relation between emotionally loaded experience and the physiological symptoms of emotion: increased heart rate, perspiration, vasodilation and constriction, muscular tremor, etc. Again, there are four ways of approaching the problem. First: that the physiological accompaniments of emotion are caused by psychological experience or felt emotion. Second: that felt emotion is epiphenomenal, being merely the reflexion in consciousness of the physiological symptoms; psychological experience is therefore caused by the latter, it reflects the nuances of physiological change, but is not itself a cause of anything (the James–Lange hypothesis). Third: that since psychological experience is a private phenomenon available only to the person concerned, and since his reporting is notoriously unreliable, felt emotion is not itself a proper subject for scientific inquiry; the study of emotion is therefore concerned exclusively with the conditions that lead to changes in its physiological correlates. Fourth: that psychological experience is an important aspect of behaviour, inferable both from verbal reports and from its observed physiological correlates; that the former are liable to error is a characteristic which they share with all forms of observation and should not be taken as an argument for not studying the correlates of felt emotion (indeed one is interested both in the causes of disagreement in verbal report, implying error, and in the causes of agreement). It is assumed that all psychological phenomena have a basis in physiological events which are observable in principle even though they may not yet be amenable to adequately differentiated observation; in particular felt emotion is taken to correspond to physiological events in the brain. The relation between gross physiological change in emotion and these is one of interaction: change in either may be the cause of change in the other. On the other hand, it is stressed that the relation between central processes (felt emotion and events in the brain) and peripheral processes is not a 1–1 correspondence but 1–many: there are far more nuances in felt emotion than can be shown in gross physiological change.[1]

Finally, the question of the relation between motivation and emotion centres largely on the role of peripheral processes associated with emotion. Again there are four views. First that emotion is an activator and organizer of behaviour, being the physiological expression of instinctual force. Second: that the physiological expression of emotion is disruptive; emotion is therefore more a terminator of organized behaviour than its initiator. Third: that intense emotion is disruptive, but mild emotion serves as initiator and organizer. Fourth: that physiological behaviour in emotion is a reaction to conflict; the question of function is partly misleading, but often (although not always) intense emotion, especially negative emotion (fear, anger, etc.) is a stimulus for aversive behaviour; i.e. it is activating but not organizing. To put the matter another way, adrenergic changes are a functional response to the activation of a schema, being necessary to prepare the organism for action. But this does not make them a cause of action. Intense physiological reaction corresponds merely to the continuance of these processes and the failure of check mechanisms due to the fact that, because of conflict, behaviour of the voluntary musculature is not engaged.

The critical reader may well object that in this initial presentation we have not been strictly neutral, for we have made the fourth view sound more convincing in every case. Agreed; one cannot circumvent one's own biases.

A second objection may be that it all sounds too good to be true. It is suspicious to hear that for each of three problems there are just four possible views. Again, we are bound to agree, but this introduction has

[1] One ought perhaps to add the possibility of a many–many correspondence: i.e. there may be circumstances where on separate occasions one and the same central state may be linked with distinct states in respect of such dimensions as vasoconstriction, perspiration, etc. But this is more speculative.

been somewhat over-simplified. It would be even simpler if we were to argue that psychologists who hold the second view on the first problem also hold the second on the second and third, and so on. But as a matter of fact this is false. In each case the first view is the view of common sense as described in Section I, and in each case the fourth view is the one which we believe to be most fruitful. For the rest, one finds a variety of combinations. For instance, McDougall is strongly identified with the view that motivation is instinctual in origin (the second view), his attitude to the relation between felt emotion and emotional expression is close to our first alternative while on the question of the functional relation between motivation and emotion he may be midway between the first and third of our alternatives, without of course accepting the second, which is antithetical to these. Or again, while the orthodox Hullian position may be nearest to our third alternative in each case, neo-Hullians like N. E. Miller may well retain this view of the nature of drive while being nearer to our fourth position on the questions of emotion.

Be that as it may, it is well to recognize that the naïve point of view described in Section I, being a direct outgrowth of reflexion on the most salient features of motivation in human beings, is able to come to grips with many key issues in a direct way. For instance, the difference between impulsive and deliberate behaviour, or the nature of moral conflict, or the feeling of being a free agent in an 'act of will'. Yet we have seen that it can only do so because it is descriptive, and prescientific, overlooking the continuity of the physiological and the psychological. Starting out from the objective analysis of the mechanisms of behavioural regulation in animals as well as in human beings, one would like to arrive at an explanatory framework backed by experiment which will be sufficiently elaborated to tackle the same issues. It will probably be painfully apparent from the following pages that there is a good way to go yet.

III. MCDOUGALL AND THE DOCTRINE OF INSTINCTS

Beach (1955) traces the notion of instinct back to the Greeks – in an article concerned chiefly to expose its weakness as a scientific concept. However, in the context of modern psychological history, these ideas find their clearest expression in the work of McDougall (1908), and, to a less extent, of Freud (see, e.g. Freud, 1922). McDougall's ideas (based partly on those of James) were influential in shaping some of the notions of Thorndike, and, via Thorndike, of American and British psychology generally. There is a much more direct filiation in the personality theories of Burt and Cattell (see Cattell, 1965). Burt's article on the subject remains one of the most persuasive in the case for the defence (Burt, 1941).

To McDougall, an instinct is an inherited disposition which directs behaviour in a way that is different from a reflex. Where a reflex determines a specific reaction to a specific stimulus, the operation of an instinct is more pervasive and more flexible. An instinct has three aspects: cognitive, emotive and conative (Cattell prefers the term 'dynamic'). It is a disposition to be aware of and pay attention to objects of a certain class, to experience an emotion of a distinctive quality when perceiving such an object, and to act upon it in a particular manner. Both the cognitive and the conative aspects of the instinct are subject to considerable modification by learning; the cognitive, in the sense that the subject learns to recognize objects and their characteristics which are relevant to the instinct; the conative, in that instincts determine the ends of behaviour only and not the means to their achievement. Modification of instinct through learning increases as one rises in the evolutionary scale, being greater in mammals than in insects, and greatest by far in human beings. What is more, in human beings the innate instinctive processes are further modified in that we are capable of reacting not only to objects but also to ideas. Evocation of the idea of an object which has become linked with an instinct tends to arouse the affect and the conative disposition just as the perception might have done.

The picture is further complicated by the suggestion that instinctual tendencies tend to cluster about certain objects which have significance in the life of the subject: mother, wife, child, home, church, ideas of justice, cruelty, etc. Such objects may be invested with emotional attitudes derived from several instincts whose satisfaction they serve. These more complex emotions are termed 'sentiments'. Taken as a whole, these objects form complex structures governed both by the emotional sentiments attaching to them and by the beliefs which the subject has concerning them and their relations with one another. Finally, just as the objects in his surroundings and the ideas to which they give rise become the foci of beliefs and emotions derived from instinctual sources, so the subject evolves a concept of himself, and a self-regarding sentiment, charged with the emotions deriving from the instincts of self-assertion and submission, and linked in varying degrees with other objects with which he has identified himself. Because the self-regarding sentiment is extended to many objects and ideas, it can take on a dominating role in the determination of conduct, mediating idealistic behaviour and self-sacrifice as well as selfish ends.

To condense McDougall's ideas into two short paragraphs is to rob them of much of their conviction. Spelt out *in extenso*, they are most persuasive. Not surprisingly so, for they answer closely to intuitive introspective experience. Complex sentiments are compounded of several emotions derived from the play of primary instincts: shame is a mixture of negative self-feeling (instinct of submission) and thwarted positive self-feeling (instinct of self-assertion); reproach is a fusion of tender emotion (parental instinct) and anger (instinct of pugnacity), and so on. This sort of idea can be made to sound very convincing. Yet it is not self-evident. McDougall often finds himself arguing against opposing interpretations. For instance, vengeful emotion is held by him to be compounded of anger and frustrated self-assertion, but other authors evidently ascribed it to a primary feeling of resentment coupled with an impulse to more deliberate action as opposed to the sudden manifestation of anger. One description is as good as another, and one is naturally led to ask how this kind of descriptive generalization can ever form the basis of a science.

McDougall held that it could, on the grounds that the basic instincts can be identified by a number of criteria. They are present in all members of a species, and often in more than one species, being common to animals and men; they are capable of morbid hypertrophy independently of other dispositions; they are recognizable by primary activities to which they give rise, especially in animals; they are distinguishable from one another by the distinctive flavour of the emotion with which they are associated.

Unfortunately, every one of these criteria breaks down upon analysis unless it is bolstered by the last, and the last is entirely subjective and equivocal. It is true that one could take any human being at random and, for every one of McDougall's instincts, one might with only a little ingenuity discover some portions of his behaviour which could be attributed to it. But one could equally do this with a great many 'propensities' which are not called instincts: play, imitation and exercise, which McDougall rejects on the grounds that they are too general (true of his instincts also) and are not attended by any specific emotion (the last criterion); rest seeking (an unaccountable omission); communication; jealousy; etc. The second criterion is entirely gratuitous (it reflects none of the many and conflicting nosological categorizations that exist), although it is recovered in attenuated form both by Burt and by Cattell as a product of the factorial analysis of individual differences in interest within the normal range. However, of this it must be said that the measures upon which such analyses are based are at present unreliable, and the techniques employed leave rather too much room for subjective interpretation. The third criterion, if it could be applied strictly, would defeat the object of the exercise, which is to categorize a class of activity which is infinitely modifiable. The last criterion, which is the one most heavily used by McDougall, is invalidated by the ambiguity which attends all attempts at the finer analysis of subjective data.

We have to distinguish three questions. The first concerns the existence of an inherited component in behaviour functionally related to the survival needs of individual and of species. The second concerns the distinctness of instincts if they exist. The third concerns their role.

As to the first question, no one denies the importance of genetic determinants in behaviour. But, as Beach (1955) points out, the problem for physiology and psychology is to unravel the interrelations of all the mechanisms which govern the regulation of behaviour, including the part played by hormonal influences, neurophysiological processes, genetic pre-programming, modifications to this determined by the history of the organism, limitations to modifiability whether of genetic or of learnt origin, and so on. This task is not greatly advanced by an *a priori* dichotomy into learnt and innate, and especially one which assigns the ends of behaviour to the innate and the means to the learnt. For on the one hand, the distinction between ends and means is always relative, and on the other, nothing is more certain than the existence of genetic influences in the determination of differences in learning, both between species and within species. Suppose Olav and Sven to be two Swedish lumbermen each of whom operated one side of a two-handled saw to fell the tree which produced the timber to manufacture the paper which went into the very exemplar of this book that the reader is handling. It is not particularly fruitful to ask what part of the book should be attributed to Olav, what part to Sven, and whether their combined parts amount to more or less than the part of the tree.

As to the second question, we have already seen why McDougall's categorization is unacceptable, and the same considerations would apply to any alternative constructed on the basis of armchair speculations as to the fundamental basis of human and animal behaviour. Does this mean that the concept of instinct is useless? Certainly, Beach along with many other students of animal behaviour prefers to do without it. On the other hand, as we saw in Chapter 3, there is a powerful school of animal behaviourists who continue to use it, including Lorenz, Tinbergen and Hess.

However, the 'instinct' of Lorenz is very different from that of McDougall. While McDougall's instincts, like Freud's, are characterized chiefly by their flexibility and their affect, Lorenz's are identified entirely on the basis of their rigidity. Indeed his case for the continued use of the concept rests largely on the observation that the behaviours to which instincts give rise are genetically determined both as to the cues to which they are responsive, the 'innate releaser mechanisms' or **IRM**, and as to the precise form of the 'instinctive behaviour': they are species-specific and species-predictable, and can be used taxonomically to supplement morphological and physiological characters (Hess, 1962). Granted the existence of such instinctive behaviours, larger structures are identifiable by the fact that their thresholds tend to vary in close relation to one another, forming hierarchies, by far the most structured being the reproductive instinct. This sort of analysis is not a great deal of use for the identification of separate human instincts, since very little of human behaviour has the species predictability of 'instinctive behaviours'. Nevertheless it does lead one to hypothesize that the regulation of human behaviour is also governed by a structure which is partly hierarchical in nature, being the schemata and strategies introduced in Chapter 4. And it may well be that this structure will be found to reflect innate regulatory sub-systems relevant to procreation and survival.

But all this leaves the third question largely unanswered. For if one agrees not to rely on the concept of instinct in the study of human behaviour, one is left with the problem of establishing a set of constructs which will enable one to handle the motivational aspects of behaviour. Also, if emotions are not taken to be the central 'affective' core and driving force of instinctual tendencies, one is left with the task of finding an alternative interpretation of the role of emotion in the regulation of behaviour. Various answers have been given to the second problem. The first is most generally considered in terms of 'drives', or of 'needs', or of both.

IV. DRIVES AND NEEDS

The concept of instinct as typified by McDougall reaches back to philosophical origins in antiquity. That of drive has its origin in the experimental laboratory; and is usually attributed to Woodworth. In the form in which it is most generally found in the psychological literature, it is by Clark Hull out of *Mus Norvegicus Albinus*, the laboratory rat – or else it is a recognizable mutant of the Hullian drive. This is an acknowledgement of authorship, not a disparagement in advance.

For the facts of animal learning in the laboratory require an explanation in motivational terms as well as in cognitive terms, and the Hullian concept of drive is designed to provide a framework for such explanation. The speed of maze-running varies directly with the hours of food and water deprivation. The latency of a discrete response such as bar-pressing at a signal varies inversely with the same measure, its amplitude (pressure exerted) directly, and so on. In the extreme case, the satiated animal may not respond at all, yet the existence of learning is sufficiently attested by the fact that it will continue to do so subsequently if deprived. This is the basis for the distinction between learning and performance: performance is a joint function of (*inter alia*) learning and drive. In many experiments, where learning is under investigation rather than drive itself, drive may be operationally defined in terms of hours of deprivation.

One might make an imaginative leap and intuit that in all human and animal behaviour there is some process at work analogous to the drive which arises from food deprivation. But this sort of leap is too large to be scientifically useful. We have to consider how the concept is refined both in Hull's own work and in that of his followers before we can say anything about its general usefulness.

1. *Hull's version of 'drive' and related concepts*

Hull's approach to the study of behaviour as a system was marked by a determination to be as rigorous as possible: to look for variables either on the level of observed behaviour or immediately inferable from it. Hullian theory is not only one of the most influential but also one of the most complex systems in the history of psychology (which is replete with complex systems) – a strange combination of meticulous and even inappropriate precision and ill-defined, overlapping basic concepts. Even though Hull chose to stay, in most of his work, on the level of simpler sub-systems of behaviour, great problems were encountered. He found that although one may work hard to circumscribe the sub-system that one is studying – in his case, the food-seeking behaviour of the laboratory rat under varied and rigorously controlled conditions – the unity of the larger system of behaviour makes classification and interpretation of one's data extremely difficult. But it will be useful to examine this point in some detail. We shall begin, then, at Hull's starting point, not with the concept of drive but with that of a bodily need.

A bodily need can be defined reasonably clearly as an organic requirement of the animal. It needs food (of particular kinds and at frequently recurring intervals), water, air, and a viable range of temperature. It also needs to excrete waste products, to avoid physical damage, and to engage in activities associated with mating. In the case of the laboratory rat, these latter needs are associated in turn with copulatory behaviour and with nest-building.

This set of bodily requirements and readily observable activities is linked by Hull with the conditions of effective survival, both for the individual animal and the species to which it belongs. It is important to remember in this connexion that despite the great specificity of some of his later formulations (for example, some of the postulates in *A Behaviour System*, 1952), Hull's theory is intended to have very general implications. He is primarily concerned, through an accumulation of rigorous specific studies, with the adaptation of living organisms (including man) to a complex and changing environment.

Taking bodily needs as the point of departure, Hull then went on to the states of activation, either specific or general, that are linked with needs. These are termed 'drives'. The relationship between needs and these action-tendencies is clearly very close, but Hull made the distinction because drives seem both more dynamic and closer to the level of observable behaviour than bodily needs. Also, if one takes precise measures of the intensity of a need, such as the number of hours of food-deprivation, one finds that the relationship between needs and these measures is exceedingly complicated. It therefore seemed useful to have a hypothetical construct other than the need itself.

Hull also made a further distinction, between general drive, which he saw as accumulating from the activity of a number of different needs, and specific drives, linked with single needs. The more specific state is called 'drive stimulus'. This gives us three closely related concepts, all of which are hypothetical constructs (in McCorquodale and Meehl's sense, 1948), that is, causal agencies inferred from behaviour. Keeping these concepts apart proved extremely difficult, and in his later work Hull often used them interchangeably. Confusion is increased by a fourth concept, 'drive condition', which is defined as any condition producing a drive. While Hull presumably used this term as an anchor, attempting to specify in as much detail as possible the factors instigating drives, one is puzzled by the relationship between 'drive condition' and 'need', which as we have seen was Hull's original basis of drive. Madsen (1959) commenting on these overlapping concepts, writes, '"Need" is, as can be seen from the above quotations (from the Glossary of *A Behaviour System*) explicitly defined as being synonymous with both "drive" and "drive stimulus", but it is *not* explicitly mentioned in the definition of "drive condition". In my opinion, however, the only unambiguous way to use "need" in Hull's theory is to define "need" as a synonym for "drive condition".' (p. 166).

We thus have four motivational terms, all of which refer to states of activation or the conditions readily eliciting them. The usefulness of distinguishing them seems to be in some doubt. One feels that the whole string of concepts has arisen from Hull's attempt to build on the supposedly solid foundation of instinctual tendencies common to a whole species. The gap between the actual behaviour of the individual organism and the concept of a 'need' turns out to be too great, and as a result Hull's whole motivational sub-system becomes precarious.

This view is strengthened by the fact that states of activation are not always related to the bodily needs from which Hull's theory begins, and to which all action directly or indirectly is supposed to relate. Hull made room in his system for 'secondary drives', differentiated by associative learning from the primary, need-based drives. But this concept does not fit easily into Miller's work on fear as a drive (1948), which cannot be translated into a need-reduction formula. Again, the work of Amsel and his associates (e.g. Amsel and Roussel, 1952) shows that under certain conditions, frustration becomes a drive. Miller and Dollard (1941) have suggested that 'a drive is a strong stimulus which impels action. Any stimulus can become a drive if it is made strong enough. The stronger the stimulus the more drive function it possesses.' (p. 18).

The generality of this view, which later work has amply confirmed, seems to undermine very seriously Hull's attempt to base a precisely articulated structure on the foundation of bodily needs. Needs, themselves, on closer investigation, prove to be far from simple structures, and our earlier comment that a bodily need can be defined 'reasonably clearly' as an organic requirement only holds true if we do not wish to proceed to rigorous behavioural measures as an unequivocal indicator of need. Cattell (1957) has criticized – effectively in our view – the tendency to gain precision at the expense of understanding by using a small number of readily quantifiable measures of a need rather than a more carefully considered pattern of measures. 'In some studies,' he claims, 'this single measure – hours of deprivation of food – contains more error-variance and specific variance than hunger-factor variance. The best measure of intensity of a need is as an estimated factor, from *several* well-loaded manifestations.' (p. 536).

The major difficulty with Hull's theory, then, from the motivational point of view, is that it proves over-restrictive. As McClelland (1964) comments, 'Hull's weakness ultimately lay in the fact that he whittled away at the inductive process until observation became merely a means of checking his previous theoretical assumptions.' (p. 13).

2. *Skinner's treatment of drive*

If we look for an approach that gives us greater freedom to follow the experimental studies, we seem to find it embodied in its most extreme form in the work – one can hardly say the theory – of Skinner (1938, 1953). Skinner has attempted to stay almost wholly on the level of directly observable behaviour, but to manipulate it in such a way that generalizations can be directly observed, as it were. One of the very few concepts derived from inference is drive, and this is brought in mainly for convenience as a classificatory device. As Skinner says, 'In measuring the strength of a drive, we are in reality only measuring strength of behaviour. The "drive" is a hypothetical state interpolated between operation and behaviour and is not actually required in a descriptive system. The concept is useful, however, as a device for expressing the complex relationship that obtains between various similarly effective operations and a group of co-varying forms of behaviour. The properties assigned to the state are derived from the observation of these relations.' (Skinner, 1938, p. 368).

Skinner is particularly reluctant to group diverse forms of behaviour together as indicators of the 'same' drive. If an animal eats different kinds of food, and its behaviour in relation to these foods shows that they are not substitutes for one another, Skinner would want to speak of separate 'hungers' rather than a single 'hunger drive'. For him, the question of 'how many drives' can only be answered empirically by studying the selective behaviour of the organism in specified conditions.

Nevertheless Skinner (1953) finds it convenient to describe a number of broad drive 'groupings' which look very much like those of Hull – hunger, thirst, sex activity, pain avoidance, sleep and exercise. Skinner does not use experimental methods to elicit more differentiated groupings, and his strategy of investigation leaves him relatively indifferent to the whole question.

It will be recalled from Chapter 1, that for Skinner 'drive' is simply a convenient term to refer to the fact that several alternative operants may be affected by the same operations, especially deprivation. Similarly, the strengths of a number of operants may be temporarily affected by frustration or by strong stimulation, and here the term 'emotion' seems appropriate. Although the effects of emotion are in general more transient than those of drive, the difference is not regarded by Skinner as of any fundamental theoretical importance.

Suppose, however, we take the argument further and extend it to the definition of the operant itself. The operant unit is whatever behavioural sequence is made to vary by the presentation of a reinforcer. Operants may be of different lengths and longer operants include shorter ones. Skinner speaks of the texture of behaviour which he is interested in shaping, and this may be fine-grain or coarse-grain. In some cases at least, e.g. the imitation of speech or drawing from copy, it is apparent that reinforcement of coarse-grain operants may strengthen a number of alternative fine-grain operants. For instance the act of sitting is conditioned to the command 'Sit-down' by withdrawal of the aversive stimulus of threat, but the conditioning extends to several ways of sitting. Thus, even reinforcement history may determine concomitant variation in a number of related operants. The point is that Skinner's operant is not a response to a stimulus but a functional unit of behaviour.

Of course, so long as we confine ourselves to the use of 'natural', unconditional reinforcers, e.g. food or particular kinds of food, it is easy enough at least in principle to distinguish between concomitant variations or behavioural equivalences due to drive, and those which are due to reinforcement history. But if we turn our attention to secondary and especially generalized reinforcers, then the difficulty is at once apparent. The search for approval or for monetary gain is attributed to the action of generalized reinforcers. Neither human nor animal subjects exhibit the same degree of love hunger or of greed at all times. Variations in these will lead to concomitant variation in several related instrumental behaviours. Is the relation due to history of reinforcement or to drive? Which term is the more appropriate? Or are we to reserve the term 'drive' for primary or unlearnt manifestations of behavioural equivalences?

These are not questions that Skinner chooses to ask himself – the reason may be partly that their relevance to the experimental shaping of behaviour is at several removes. But it is also due largely to the fact that the range of behavioural variation covered by Skinner's experimental strategy is too narrow. Drive itself plays only a very minor role. Moreover, the implications of his functional definition of operants for the structure of behaviour are not fully realized by Skinner himself. This is the chief limitation of his descriptive attitude. For the structure of behaviour should refer to the structure of the functional connexions mediated by the nervous system within the subject. Too often, for Skinner, the functional unity ceases to be of interest except in so far as it relates to the behaviour of the observer. Skinner (1959) flippantly describes other psychologists as being supremely interested in their own theories often to the neglect of the richness of nature. We accept the characterization as a compliment and the criticism as a rider and a caution. He goes on to criticize himself by saying that he is supremely interested in achieving control. And again we would add, often to the neglect of the richness of nature.

3. *Drive as the activation of behavioural structures*

It would be nice to emerge with a clear-cut definition of drive – or even with a clear-cut rejection of the concept, based on an interpretation of motivation which renders it unnecessary or misleading. But no such clear-cut definition is possible precisely because of the considerations linking drive with emotion and with the structure of behavioural equivalences, whether learned or unlearned. At the same time, the concept of drive would appear to be not only convenient but even essential to characterize variation in reactivity of behavioural strategies. Let us see why.

From the standpoint of the dualism of common sense, cognition is a matter of awareness or knowing (see Section I of the present chapter and Section I of Chapter 7). From that of an objective science of behaviour, cognition reflects the equivalences and non-equivalences among lines of behaviour. Thus it was argued in Chapter 4 that perception itself implied the activation of elementary strategies or links which are specifically sensitive to certain cues or cue-combinations. The mode of action of such links was to activate behaviour through their connexions with effector control mechanisms, and to sensitize further links, leading to the formation of strategies or lines of behaviour. The pattern of connectedness revealed by strategies shows a partially hierarchical structure. At the same time, a recognition of the relations among different strategies having intersections with one another by virtue of the possession of common links led us to posit the complementary concept of the schema. In particular, this mode of analysis led us to a purely behavioural definition of the object as the intersection of all strategies applicable to it. Thus, to the structure of subjective cognition there corresponds a structure of regulations (interfacilitation or interinhibition) mediated by elements in the nervous system.

If we turn to motivation, we find that from the standpoint of common sense, motivation is a matter of subjective interest, desire and so on. From that of scientific analysis, motivation is the study of factors which determine the reactivity of these same elements: the strategies and schemata which govern the regulation of behaviour.

Now to begin with, from the functional point of view, which is that of psychology (since the material constitution of the inferred elements and relations is the concern of physiology and biochemistry), the cognitive structure itself is expressed only by the fact of sensitization or activation, i.e. that activity in one element affects the threshold of others.[1] And this is precisely what we have said is the province of motivation. What does this mean in ordinary language? Simply that when we are engaged in an activity, we have a desire to engage in it, to complete it. This may appear trivial. But it expresses the fact that the system which is the referrent of the analysis of cognition is co-extensive with that which is the referrent of motivational analysis. In other words, drive is an aspect of the structure already outlined. In studying cognition, we study the structure of relations among the elements we infer: what connects with what and in what way, facilitatory or inhibitory. In studying drive, we study the factors which cause excitation to flow along the paths we have outlined. And the principal factor is simply that the system is differentially activated and that the paths are as laid down.

All we have done is to follow the logic of the previous discussion of Skinner's definitions. But already we are in a position to see the fundamental error in Hullian theory. This was to suppose that the stimulus communicates with a separate drive stimulus and that the reaction or response is the product of an interaction between two distinct variables: drive-strength and habit-strength. Contrary to this, we find that the reaction – differentiation of activity within the system – is activated at *a particular strength* and this is what we refer to as drive.

What this means is that whether we speak of a structure of drives or of a structure of cognition depends mainly on the focus of our interest. For the referrent of the two terms is identical: the way in which the elements of the system act upon one another by interfacilitation or interinhibition. At the same time, such tendencies as the increase of activation due to frustration, the arousal of emotion, and so on, presuppose the existence of separate arousal centres within the brain. The action of these is to communicate with the cognitive structure by increasing or decreasing the strength of the process regardless of which sub-system is presently activated.[2]

[1] When one element activates another directly, this is simply a matter of altering its threshold as a step-function, from 0 to 1; it is not different in principle from a quantal increment in threshold within a larger range.

[2] Thus the concept of generalized drive would correspond to a genuine aspect of behaviour while that of the drive stimulus is a figment of the Hullian system.

In terms of motivation: if we are sufficiently hungry, we eat anything edible, if only a little hungry we are more finicky. In terms of cognition: we recognize differences between sweet foods, salt foods and so on, but we recognize all these as foods. Which came first, the chicken or the egg? Of course, in the case of this hierarchy of food appetites, the structure reflects the organization of body chemistry. In other words, the cognitive structure is not entirely learnt (it is partly, for we can 'acquire a taste'). All learning builds on a previously existing structure. In the case of the exercise of certain human skills which reinforce one's self-esteem (e.g. doing a crossword, having a friendly discussion, and critically reading an article may be variants subordinated to the same drive), the part of learning is obviously far greater. But the difference is one of degree.

However, to arrive at a correct analysis of the nature of a problem is not to solve the problem. It would be quite wrong to suppose that if the preceding arguments are correct, then problems of motivation disappear, or that they are fully taken care of by the study of cognition. The two shade into one another but they remain distinct areas of study. If one is interested in cognition, one's concern is primarily with the origin of the structure of behavioural organization and the nature of learning and transfer. If one's interest is in motivation, then one is far more concerned with other aspects of the system. In particular, granted the tendency of behaviour to maintain its direction, what are the factors which cause variation in that tendency, greater or lesser resistance to distracting or irrelevant input, and so on. Above all, what factors govern change in the direction of behaviour, the abandonment of one schema in favour of another, or the resumption of the first, etc.

The model of organization of behaviour outlined in Chapter 4 provides for a two-way activation of strategies. A strategy, at any given level could be activated either by downwards or lateral stimulation from another, due to the operation of a higher-order strategy. But it was also liable to activation by upward stimulation, through the reception of input to the comparator system to which it was sensitive. Since the organism is constantly subject to stimulation, the problem concerns mainly the conditions under which a link which is not activated by a higher-order strategy will nevertheless respond to input, inhibiting the activation of links which are.

It was pointed out that many psychologists treat this as a problem of differential arousal. Shifts of behaviour are less likely to occur if the input is familiar, i.e. if it is readily assimilated to existing schemata.

Very generally, the system acts in such a way as to reduce uncertainty, and this can be done in at least three ways:

(i) exploration of the unfamiliar situation or object, which is then assimilated to known lines of behaviour;

(ii) aggression towards the novel object or situation, which removes the uncertainty either by destroying or transforming the novelty;

(iii) flight, or 'leaving the situation.'

From the point of view of learning, the first is the most interesting.

Exploratory behaviour has been studied increasingly during the last decade, partly as a reaction against the earlier behaviourist view of the organism as responding solely to bodily needs. It is seen by most of the investigators who have worked with it (e.g. White, 1959; Berlyne, 1960) as a reaching out to the environment, a more positive activity than the reduction of stressful drive stimuli by need-satisfying behaviour. The 'need' most often cited in the study of exploratory behaviour is curiosity (see the discussion of the 'what-is-it? reflex' in Ch. 4, Section III). It is interesting to distinguish between exploration as a way of reducing a situation to one that fits in to a class of familiar situations, and exploration as the selection of novelty when there is a choice of novelty and familiarity. The distinction is one between preferences for novelty or familiarity.

Berlyne (1960) in studies of 'orienting responses' shows that both animal and human subjects tend to select (when given a choice) novel as compared with familiar stimuli. They also fixate longer on novel stimuli. Experiments with rats (e.g. Montgomery, 1953) seem to suggest that exploratory activities are not merely the result of deprivation of activity. Nor are they restricted to complex ways of satisfying biological needs, such as hunger and thirst. Although the evidence is difficult to interpret, and does not unequivocally support the view that there is a single 'exploratory drive', it seems highly probable that such forms of behaviour are readily elicited, and form the basis of a great deal of the operant learning studied by Skinner.

The general siting of motivation as an area of study given here is not a clear-cut answer to specific issues.[1] But it is consistent with a number of findings which are inconsistent with Hullian drive theory, but for which there exists solid experimental support. Thus, it is consistent with the numerous studies of Amsel illustrating the role of frustration in the enhancement of drive. For frustration implies failure of the environment

[1] See Cofer and Appley (1964) for an excellent and detailed discussion.

to supply the input for the continuation of a line of behaviour. A mechanism similar to that which operates in curiosity is added to the original activation. It is also consistent with the well-known phenomenon established by Zeigarnik that human subjects show a strong tendency to remember unfinished tasks after interruption as compared with completed tasks (1938).

As to the original activation, it would be ridiculous to argue that because some behaviour is a response to uncertainty therefore all behaviour is a manifestation of curiosity. It is abundantly clear that the activation of many lines of behaviour is a response to input from the internal medium and will therefore continue to be active, and will show a tendency to resumption so long as such activation continues. And this in spite of the fact that the behaviour is terminated by a separate centre, which can be activated independently (see the discussion of hunger by Deutsch, 1960, and Rosenzweig, 1963, already referred to in Chapter 3).

Finally, there is no inconsistency with the findings of Burt (1941) and of Cattell (1965), based on the factor analysis of replies to objective interest tests and questionnaires, that individual differences in these basic drives cluster along lines which reflect their distinct biological function. Thus it seems clear that the bodily needs from which the theorists of animal learning begin are basic elements in human motivation. Cattell (1957) reporting on his investigations of drives in human behaviour, writes: 'It has taken many years of development of factor-analytic methods, adaptively applied to personality, to produce the evidence that drive patterns exist in man, and that they correspond with unmistakable parallelism to those intuited by clinicians like Freud and Murray, on the one hand, and naturalists like McDougall and Darwin on the other.' (p. 535). Cattell prefers to call these dynamic tendencies *ergs*, and defines them (1965) as innate sources of reactivity, such as are often described as drives, directed to a certain goal and accompanied by a certain quality, but established by factor analysis of many motivational manifestations.

These come close to McDougall's instincts or predispositions, and it is perhaps not surprising that the list of *ergs* uncovered by factor analysis of large numbers of attitude items has a distinctly McDougallian flavour. Cattell has distinguished eleven *ergs*, which he names curiosity, sex, gregariousness, protection, self-assertion, security, hunger, anger, disgust, appeal and self-submission. However, the degree to which these 'sources of reactivity' (a term with which we have no quarrel) are innate is open to considerable doubt.

One advantage of Cattell's list is that it includes several *ergs* which have relevance to social relationships. For one cannot but recognize that motivation in human beings is very closely bound up with social interaction, with self-awareness and with the formation of social attitudes. The origin of such drives, and of the cognitions which they imply, must be sought in the human capacity for representation. But before we examine the specific characteristics of human motivation, we need to say a word about the role of emotion.

4. *Mental and Physiological Correlates of Drive*

It has been argued that drives do not represent a distinct set of structures which somehow interact with cognitive response tendencies. Instead it is proposed that the term is a convenient way of referring to the activation of such tendencies. The study of drive is concerned primarily with factors affecting the intensity of such activation and switching in the direction of behaviour. Emotions are evidently included in these factors. What is rather less clear is whether all such factors are to be regarded as emotional or whether the usage of the term 'emotion' should be more restricted. Among proponents of the more extended usage, one would cite Leeper (1948), who maintains that the primary function of emotion is to act as an integrator of behaviour, suggesting that it is only in its extreme manifestations (panic, rage, etc.) that emotional behaviour is found to be disruptive, impeding the implementation of finer behavioural adjustments. The balance of psychological tradition favours the more restricted usage. Leeper's position is in line with that of common sense, which, as we saw earlier, tends to regard all of motivation as 'basically' emotional in character. The more restricted usage reflects more closely the experimental and observational study of emotion. The former has centred on the study of observable physiological reactions associated with intense emotion, being concerned in particular with the effects of physiological measures (lesions or stimulation of the hypothalamus and other regions, administration of drugs, etc.) on such behaviour. Emotional behaviour so defined is clearly not co-extensive with behaviour as a whole.

Alongside the study of physiological manifestations of emotion and their correlates, one finds studies of mood, especially in the form of the perception that people have of their own emotional states. Certainly one of the central difficulties in the study of emotion is that, unlike drive, the concept suggests little by way of general behavioural investigation, so that one is left with a theoretical void between the study of physiological manifestations at a peripheral level (autonomic arousal) on the one hand,

and that of conscious representation of mood on the other. Often the two have gone on independently of each other, the former being primarily an area of physiological inquiry, while the latter lends itself fairly readily to highly speculative elaboration, as in the work of psychoanalytically oriented psychologists. As to the relation between emotion and behavioural organization, there has been remarkably little advance since the enunciation of the James–Lange hypothesis and its rejection in the light of the studies of Cannon. Inevitably, this now ancient controversy continues to occupy an important place in any discussion of emotion.

The James–Lange theory of emotion can be stated quite simply. The pure mentalistic position is that felt emotion causes emotional expression. Contrary to this, James and Lange argued that felt emotion is merely the reflexion in consciousness of visceral changes: we do not tremble because we feel afraid; we feel afraid because we tremble; we feel shame because we blush; and so on (James, 1884).

On the face of it, this looks like a surprisingly modern point of view: mental processes are taken as the outcome of physiological processes which are overt and open to experimental analysis. The theory should more properly be regarded as an attempt to complement the psychophysical approach of the nineteenth century.

Psychology is seen as the study of consciousness, but consciousness must have links with physical reality if knowing and feeling are to be valid. Just as psycho-physics sought to establish a firm connexion between one sort of mental entity or idea, the percept, and the physical characteristics of the environmental stimulus, so James and Lange envisaged the possibility of establishing a parallel link between another sort of idea, emotion, and something outside: visceral states of the body. Given such an anchorage, psychology remains the introspective study of the mind and its traditional faculties (reason, memory, emotion, will) as opposed to the study of the system of regulations implicit in the organization of behaviour, whether mental or physical.

As Zangwill (1950) points out, there are at least three reasons why this theory of emotion cannot be considered as adequate. In the first place the varieties of emotional feeling far exceed the varieties of visceral expression, for the latter tend to be similar for quite distinct emotions, fear and rage, being mediated by the activation of the same excitatory process: the adreno-sympathetic system (Cannon, 1929). Nor do similar emotions always issue in similar physiological reactions. Secondly, there are cases of neurological disease where the patient exhibits an abnormal tendency to laugh or cry which is out of keeping with his feelings. Third, injections of adrenalin lead to physiological reactions characteristic of intense emotion without such emotion being experienced by the subject. Recent experiments by Schachter in which two groups of subjects were given adrenalin with different explanations of its effects showed that their emotional reactions were very different depending on what they had been led to expect. At the same time, control subjects given a placebo reacted differently from either group. One may legitimately infer that visceral changes do affect emotional feeling (it would be remarkable if they did not), but that the latter is by no means merely the reflection of the former. The whole problem has been reviewed fairly recently by Mandler (1962), whose conclusions, as given in the last sentence, do not differ appreciably from those of Cannon in 1929 or Zangwill in 1950.

In spite of the fact that James would probably have allowed that the peripheral manifestations of emotional disturbance are initiated in the brain, the theory still reflects a rather crude opposition between consciousness and the states of the body. Now although consciousness may appear to introspection as some sort of indefinable inner light, the scientific study of consciousness is fully taken care of by statements about the reactivity of the organism – or the things that are lit. A simple organism which has a negative tropism to light is to all intents and purposes conscious of light. A more complex organism that reacts differentially to its own internal states can be said to be conscious of these. Since human beings are able to report the fact that their heart is beating harder, that they are trembling, and so on, it makes sense to say that they are conscious of their own emotions. Since, moreover, reports of emotional states are not confined to these 'visceral' manifestations of emotion, one may conclude that our consciousness of our internal states is not exhausted by the statements about these. But the question which must be asked is whether this further awareness is indeed an emotional awareness and not simply a cognitive awareness. In particular such reports usually include statements describing the causes of our emotions, e.g. what it is we are afaid of, or simply a statement that we cannot explain the cause of our fear. Both statements are representations of things or of our characteristic behaviour in regard to things. They do not imply any privileged access to and reactivity to some more subtle states within ourselves. However, this still leaves open the possibility that emotional awareness includes reactivity to some properties of more central processes within the brain itself, those to which we give the name of 'mood'.

The difficulty is partly that, although there is good reason to believe that moods do correspond to states of chemical balance within the brain, in as much as they are differentially affected by drugs, we still do not know what these states are or even how many different chemical regulatory systems are involved. Conversely, from the behavioural point of view, a mood is no more than a tendency to initiate certain kinds of actions rather than others (including, of course, verbal representation and internalized representation). Once again, as we found with drive, the structure of emotion seems to shade into the structure of the system as a whole. Nevertheless, it seems probable that the number of mood 'factors' will prove to be more limited. For instance, it is not impossible that the finer differentiation of emotion that we term mood will be found to correspond to distinctive physiological processes associated with the most basic differentiations of the system: viz. the differentiation between appetitive and aversive behaviour, the intensity of its activation, and the degree of conflict which is engendered. Given the more extended usage of emotion, to include mood, it becomes difficult to distinguish between emotion and drive, save that (*a*) drives are more differentiated, and (*b*) the study of drive, like that of cognition, is primarily the province of psychology, while that of emotion falls more within that of physiology.

It should be noted that even if one accepts an extended view of emotion to include not only those peripheral manifestations which can be induced by stimulation of the hypothalamus but also some components of mood (not all, since the 'content' of mood is not itself emotional, though it may be provocative of emotion), this still does not entail an acceptance of Leeper's view that the primary function of emotion is to act as an integrator, and that it is only extremes of emotion that are disruptive. As Hebb (1949) remarks, even mild manifestations of emotion may be disruptive of highly skilled performance. The quest for a positive 'function' of emotion may be misleading. From the point of view of introspection there is little to suggest that the untrammelled execution of behaviour is accompanied by any emotion. The association between emotion and conflict has been familiar since long before the work of Freud. Pavlov's demonstration of the experimental neurosis tends to confirm the suggestion that emotion does not depend on any deep significance of the stimuli that induce it, but is primarily an expression of the existence of conflict within the system (e.g. between the positive response to a circle and the inhibitory response to an ellipse – see Chapter 1). If there are distinct variations in chemical processes within the brain corresponding with experiences of mood, then it is reasonable to believe that these represent failures of temporal integration between the various parts of the system, leading, for instance, to excesses of free acetylcholine and a corresponding deficiency of cholinosterase (although biochemists are understandably reluctant to indulge in general speculation of this sort, see Tower, 1958).

Likewise, even the distinctively emotional components of the adreno-sympathetic reaction may be associated with failure of temporal integration. Violent aggression or flight demands the mobilization of physiological resources. It does not demand trembling or excessive palmar perspiration. On the other hand, it is not the case that these are conspicuously associated with violent action, but, on the contrary, with the inhibition of such action due to conflict. Excesses of fear do not occur when we run away, but, precisely, when we stay put. Similarly, the positive emotions of relief and their physiological manifestations are clearly the result of failure of temporal integration, due to the failure of the environment to supply the anticipated input. The fact that aversive or negative emotions seem to preponderate over the positive may be associated with the ambivalence of aversive behaviour which is present from the start – since input which is assimilated to aversive strategies invokes both withdrawal or flight behaviour and aggressive, approach behaviour.

We conclude, albeit rather tentatively, that whether in the form of mood or in the form of violent physiological reaction, the distinctive physiological and experimental characteristics of emotion are closely bound up with failure of temporal integration. This is in opposition to the common-sense view that emotions somehow constitute the 'springs' of behaviour, and that motivational phenomena are basically emotional. There is no evidence that animals actively seek emotion, whether positive or negative. Human beings, who are capable of representing and reflecting on their previous experiences undoubtedly do, at least part of the time. But this is more likely to be a secondary phenomenon, bound up with the fact that emotional arousal inhibits reflexion on painful experience and that willingness to withstand fear may be enhancing to the self-concept, at least in the context of many cultures. Even in human beings, there is little warrant for the suggestion that all or even most of one's behaviours are emotional in origin.

V. HUMAN MOTIVATION

1. *Representation and the Self-Concept*

Psychologists who are concerned with problems of human motivation are compelled to introduce a great many considerations which have little parallel in animal psychology: achievement, social conformity, personal integrity, the reduction of cognitive dissonance and so on. Nevertheless it would clearly be a mistake to suppose that motivation in human beings differs qualitatively from animal motivation right from the start. It is true that much of human motivation is social in origin. But social motivation exists in animals also. There is good evidence for the existence of innate social patterns of behaviour in the human infant. For instance one may cite the clinging behaviour adopted by the child in the nursing situation or the appearance of the smiling reaction about the age of six weeks. The cues for the latter appear to be certain pattern characteristics of the human face, and of the human voice (see Volume II, Chapter 2). It is therefore a social behaviour from the start. The former is actuated by cues deriving from handling by the mother. But animal psychology too offers numerous examples of behaviours which are specifically actuated by cues deriving from members of the same species and which are innate rather than learnt. Among the best known examples one could cite not only suckling behaviour in mammals, but the following reaction in many species and the attachment (clinging) behaviour in monkeys to which reference was made in Chapter 4.

Likewise we saw that exploration, which foreshadows the motivation for the exercise of intelligence in discovery and problem solution is a form of behaviour which is present in rats and monkeys as well as in the human infant. Such behaviour underlies the effectance motivation which plays a major part in the excellent discussion presented by Stott in Volume III, Chapter 4.

However, what distinguishes human behaviour from that of animals is the part of representation. It has been suggested that representational behaviour originates as an elaboration out of deferred imitation. It begins when the child modifies his imitative behaviour, first by chance, and later more deliberately under the influence of the reinforcement given by knowledge of results. It is perfected as he explores the possibilities of such modification by means of the behaviour that we recognize as dramatic or representational play.

The supreme gain which results from representation derives from the fact that it enables the subject to reconstruct the elements of experience (sensori-motor inputs and their relations) using an input which is relatively free from environmental constraints. The objects of the child's imitation include his own actions. By the same token, the objects of his representational activity include himself. Thus it was argued in Chapter 5 that one of the principal achievements of representation is the elaboration of a self-concept.

The very possibility of imitation depends on the greater possibilities of transfer, related to the greater capacity for the formation of learning set (Chapter 5, Section IV). This being so, one may expect the same capacity for transfer to appear in the representational behaviour also. Such considerations lead to a simple definition of analogy: it is transfer in the context of representational behaviour.

If we apply this rather obvious extension to the analysis of the formation of the self-concept, we find that it leads directly to a well-known conclusion: that the child arrives at a better understanding of himself by analogy with others, i.e. by a process of identification. The term is familiar from Freudian psychology. But its use here is intended to be neutral in the first instance. We do not imply a necessary introjection of standards and values, although identification undoubtedly creates the conditions for this. Rather it is a question of the progressive delineation of the self in the child's representation. It is interesting to speculate on the likely course of this elaboration, leaving the details of its consideration to Volume II (Chapters 2 and 11).

1. (*a*) Doubtless the first identification which must be made is the recognition of analogies between the self and other individuals as human begins. This includes the parallelisms between parts of the body and actions which these permit that were noted in the review of imitation (Chapter 5, Section IV). But one must bear in mind that such parallelisms cannot give rise to a self-concept until they are available to representation. The starting point for this development is the use and extension of deferred imitation, for it is this which allows the inception of representational behaviour, relatively independent of input. Among the criteria of this first adumbration of a self-concept one could cite the use of verbal substitution in references to human achievements: e.g. '*Mummy shopping – Baby shopping*', '*Daddy din-din – Baby din-din*', '*Baby ah-ah – Mummy ah-ah*' (reference to bowel movement), and so on. Similarly one would look for a more general and deliberate tendency to imitate the achievements of others, as opposed to their actions, or to extend the imitation of action by using the action itself as a prompt for the elaboration of further behaviour, as in vying. Recent experiments by Bandura *et al.* (1963) reveal that young children are more prone to imitate a person seen as active, a dispenser of rewards and punishment, than as a passive receiver. Moreover the imitation is general, reflecting the attitude of the model, rather than specific, replicating his actions. The condition for such identification is the availability of representational schemata linking a variety of alternative lines of behaviour by their effects on a recipient. Its result is the formation of a representation of the self as an agent (Erikson, 1963), i.e. as determiner of its own input – (although, of course, the child cannot formulate it in these terms).

(*b*) A second phase in the elaboration of the self-concept comes with role-identification. It is a differentiation out of the primary representation of self as agent. There is no need to postulate a different mechanism to account for this further development, for the mechanism of identification is sufficient. However, we cannot account for the elaboration of role identity without experience, i.e. without relevant input which will allow differentiated analogies. The child learns that he is a child, boy or girl, little (but big when compared with a baby)[1] and so on. The necessary experience to role identifications consists in the perception of other children, interaction with other children, and observation of the interactions between other children and adults. The process is one of exploration or experimentation at the level of representation (i.e. using representational input), through language and play. As such, it involves trial-and-error, and transfer by analogy, while its modifier is reinforcement or non-reinforcement resulting from confirmation (success, free-running) of the strategies which are engaged on. In other words the formation of the self-concept makes use of the mechanisms of cognition outlined in Chapters 4 and 5, exactly as was the case for any other concept.

On the other hand, the motivational importance of the self-concept lends special significance to studies of role identification (Sears, 1957; Maccoby, 1959, 1961). This is because the representational counterpart to uncertainty-reduction in the switching of attention is self-reference. There is minimal uncertainty in so far as the situation is assimilated to one in which the subject is effective or one which is irrelevant, presenting neither threat nor promise to self-valuation.

(*c*) Referring once more to the footnote on this page, the fact that the subject engages in representational strategies involving comparison between self and others by no means implies the logical congruence of such strategies. Thus from moment to moment, the subject may represent himself as strong or weak, big or little, loved or hated, and so on. It is only as a result of the progressive systematization of representation that the child can be expected to show an increasing tendency to the resolution of 'cognitive dissonance'. This is a term used by Festinger and others in

[1] Which identification is made depends on the situation. Until the child begins to systematize his representations, the two comparisons are not made simultaneously, and from the point of view of the observer, the child's successive remarks will appear contradictory (see Volume II, Chapter 8).

reference to strategies the effect of which is to modify attitudes and beliefs in such a way as to minimize contradiction (Festinger, 1957; Brown, 1965). Likewise, the child's representation of himself undergoes progressive systematization, first by insertion of the self within specified categories: age (no longer confused with size, Piaget, 1946); nationality (distinguished from town or residence etc., see Piaget, 1928; Jahoda, 1963); religion (Elkind, 1964), and so on.

2. A second stage is reached about the age of adolescence, when the child finds himself cast in a multitude of conflicting roles, a position which is inevitably conducive to a degree of insecurity, whence the term 'crisis of identity' (Erikson, 1963). The word 'crisis', however, is misleading unless taken in a strictly relative sense. For although new identifications are forced upon the subject both by the fact of physiological change and by changes in the expectations of society, and although the latter in particular are often contradictory, their impact upon the subject is episodic and protracted. In other words, the activation of this or that representational identification and the simultaneous activation of conflicting identifications are all contingent upon fluctuation in input. The input includes representational input (the product of the subject's own thinking), and the course of the latter is largely determined by the structure of analogies inherent in the subject's own schematization of his environment (including the self-concept as defined). This is why the observer finds considerable difficulty in interpreting and predicting swings in adolescent 'mood'.

In so far as the social world of the adult is more stable (which itself is in some doubt, see the discussion in Volume II, Chapter 11), the resolution of the crisis of identity is of course greatly aided by the mere fact of growing older and its impact upon the environment: as the adolescent enters adulthood, so he finds himself increasingly accepted in some roles and no longer cast in others which conflict. But the resolution of residual internal contradictions depends on the consolidation of a new frame of reference: i.e. on the extent to which the more stable expectations of the environment are reflected in a more stable schematization of the subject's internal identifications. Which is why some persons remain 'adolescent'. One would predict that 'extraverts', or those who are more inclined to seek environmental input to sustain more frequent changes in the direction of attention, will tend to achieve a stabilization of personality more rapidly than 'introverts', more inclined to explore the possibilities of representational input. But the proper definition of these two terms is still open to some doubt (compare Stott's scepticism in Volume III, Chapter 4 with the excellent summary of the empirical evidence given by Warburton in Volume III, Chapter 3).

Questions relating to the importance of adolescence in personality development are considered more fully in Volume II, Chapter 11. More generally, the motivational significance of the self-concept arises out of the fact that input which communicates with strategies involving comparisons between self and others (the union of which *is* the schema known as the self-concept) is more likely to be attended to, leading to the inception of new behaviours. What these behaviours are will be dealt with briefly in the following sub-section.

Before going on to this, we need to dot an *i*. Why should the self-concept be relevant in human motivation and not in animals? The answer is this. While it is meaningful to speak of a self-concept, it would be meaningless to speak of a self at the sensori-motor level. This is because the schema of any object has been defined as the intersection of all strategies relevant to that object. Since all behaviour is the behaviour of the subject, the sensori-motor counterpart of the self-concept is the system itself. This might suggest that the representation of the self should be equally all-embracing and therefore equally meaningless. A consideration of the history of its evolution shows that the concept is more restricted. It is the schema which comprises all representational behaviours involving a comparison between the subject and other subjects. Representation of actions involving no comparison with others is not included in the self-concept. In other words the self-concept is co-extensive with representational identifications.

2. *Identification and the Moulding of Attitudes and Values*

What has been said so far concerns only what the self-concept is, and not how it functions. In order that our language should not diverge too far from current psychological usage, we need to introduce a somewhat ambiguous concept: attitude.

The term 'attitude' is often used to refer to the tendency of a subject to act in a specified way in relation to an object. More especially, it refers to the function of his preferred mode of action along the axis approach-withdrawal: for attitudes can be positive or negative. From the standpoint of research methodology, perhaps the most important aspect of attitudes is their quantifiability, for attitudes are assumed to vary in intensity from intense positive, through zero (ambivalent or neutral) to intense negative.

There is no need to quarrel with this usage, but to avoid confusion we have to remark that so far the connotation of 'attitude' coincides exactly with that of 'drive'. The difference is primarily that the first term has been preferred by students of animal behaviour and the second by students of human behaviour. One of the principal aims of the present volume is to provide a bridge between these two fields of study, largely by means of our analysis of the nature and significance of representation. In so far as the bridging is successful, one might easily dispense with the duplication of terms.

But the fact is that the appearance of representational behaviour so alters the structure of motivation in a social environment that the kinds of problem which are studied by social psychologists are usually very different from those studied by comparative psychologists. So long as we are concerned with the former, to insist on the term 'drive' would place an intolerable strain on everyone concerned. In particular, many or most of the significant attitudes in child and adult are acquired, or at least modified, by a process of identification. And identification, as we have seen, is contingent upon representation. Secondly, the attitudes of human beings are modifiable even in the adult in response to pressures exerted by others. Again, characteristically, these take the form of representational (usually verbal) information: statements of (contradictory) attitude, of relevant evidence which conflicts with the established attitude, and so on. Even if the stimulus is non-verbal (for one person's attitude to another can be modified by physical attack just as easily as it can by verbal insult), the restructurization of attitudes which results takes place very largely at the level of representation (making allowances, extending the attitude to members of some group with which the assailant is identified, and so on). Third, many studies are concerned primarily with the measurement of attitudes, either as a methodological device to be used in other studies, or as a first attempt at mapping the structure of personality, or as an instrument in applied psychology, e.g. for use in vocational guidance. Again, the tests are most often verbal in form.

Finally, for the most part, the study of attitudes, both in children and in adults has not been concerned with the primary drives aroused by the environment as perceived or as represented. The principal focus of inquiry has been on the activation of secondary processes of an evaluative or moral character. To this extent, the study of attitudes is inseparably linked with that of morality. For instance, attitudes to patriotism, to freedom, to democracy or to family loyalty have a fairly obvious moral quality. The attitude to this or that political party, or to the value of a sense of humour or of modern art may be less obviously moral. But the boundary between them is not easy to draw, nor do we believe that it is of any significance. We will try to show that all such attitudes have a common origin, in identification, and a similar outcome, a tendency towards differentiated identification, coupled with consistency.

(*a*) *Origins of social and moral attitudes.* In view of our earlier recognition of the importance of identification, it is useful to begin with a consideration of the suggestions of Freud. Freudian theory holds that the child's libido gradually becomes centred on the mother, that this gives rise to hatred and jealousy of the father, and that the latter is coupled with (*a*) intense fear of retribution in the form of castration, and (*b*) a partial identification with, and therefore love of, the father. The result is an intense traumatic conflict, the Oedipus Conflict. The original identification with the parent figures leads not only to love, and the desire of union, especially with the mother, but also to the adoption ('introjection') of parental standards of right and wrong behaviour. Moreover, the child's judgement of his own behaviour is harsh and uncritical. In particular, since he is unable to distinguish clearly between wish and reality, he is apt to feel intense guilt over forbidden wishes just as if they had been executed. It is this complex of self-criticism which constitutes the childish super-ego.

The resolution of the Oedipus Conflict takes the form of a massive repression of the primary manifestations of the libido by the super-ego. At the same time the instinctual energy [*sic*] of the repressed drives (the id) continues to press for an outlet. This is achieved by a variety of compromises based on defence mechanisms elaborated by the ego to shield itself from painful clashes between super-ego and id. Among these one finds sublimation, or the substitution of socially approved lines of action (e.g. painting, religion) for the primary behaviours of which they are transformations (e.g. smearing, union with the mother). The adult conscience is a mixture of rationalizations by the ego to justify and support such behaviours and the continuing action of the childish super-ego which sometimes penetrates the disguises.

The term 'rationalization' requires a word of comment. It is used most frequently by Freud to indicate a quite specious line of argument engaged on by a subject to justify irrational behaviour. For instance, if a subject is placed under hypnosis and given a post-hypnotic suggestion to the effect that upon waking he will forget everything that passed but that he must open the windows wide on a given sign (e.g if the hypnotist scratches his head), he is quite liable to invent a reason for his later compliance, e.g. that it was getting very stuffy. Usually the rationalization refers to behaviour already completed.

Now there are two ways in which the Freudian account of rationalization is sometimes extended to cover the phenomena of adult morality. One is to extend the usage of 'rationalization' to include the elaboration of consistent frames of reference not only to justify actions after they have been executed, but to influence their execution in the first instance. The other is to deduce the course of the development of morality from the primitive super-ego in such a way as to (*a*) predict that it will not only be self-consistent but that its consistency will take a particular form, e.g. 'Do as you would be done by', and (*b*) to ascribe to it an independent power (independent of instinctual energy) and an independent (transcendental) sanction. As to the first, it should be noted that Freud himself was little concerned with the form of consistency of rational moral behaviour, and his theory, which is distinctly one-sided, is of little help in accounting for it. To do so, we will need to consider the views of Piaget. As to the second, it is an argument which is entirely contrary to the basic tenets of Freud.

The fundamental point from which to start is the Freudian conception of instinct as initially almost undifferentiated. The accepted translation of Freud's central term '*trieb*' and 'instinct' is a little misleading, suggesting as it does a rigid innately determined structure rather than a flow of energy towards a wide range of goals. In his earlier work, Freud made a distinction between tendencies towards personal maintenance and development and those towards the survival and strengthening of the species (these were termed 'ego needs' and 'sexual needs' respectively). In his later work, Freud was led to postulate two rather different impulses, one directed to the maintenance and enhancement of organic functioning and the other an impulse to the attainment of an inorganic state. The second principle has been variously interpreted as the principle of entropy (Newton's second law of thermodynamics at work in the organism), as aggression, or as a 'death wish'. There has been no real agreement among Freud's interpreters on the precise significance of the latter concept, and it seems likely that it represented little more than a quite diffuse tendency towards escape from tension by cutting off all sources of energy.

Freud inferred the presence of such a drive from observations of apparently gratuitous destructiveness in his own society (Germany during and after the first world war), from his observations of the pervasiveness of destructive activity in human history, and, above all, from his clinical work with self-defeating and often openly self-destructive patients.

Thus an essential element in Freudian theory is the notion that behaviour relies on a special kind of 'force', instinctual energy, of which there is a limited supply, being vested initially in the undifferentiated instincts of the 'id', but which is capable of transformations (as in sublimation). This conception offers no basis for a transcendental morality. However, it is also a conception which is at variance not only with most psychological thinking but also with scientific thinking as a whole. For the distinction made by Freud between physical and mental energy is difficult to sustain. Various forms of physical energy can be measured, or reasonably reliably inferred, but mental energy seems an extremely tenuous, and also unnecessary, concept. Second, the related view that energy forms a reservoir, which is strictly limited and creates painful tension if not released, neglects the extraordinary complexity of the arousal system. Hinde (1960) has a detailed critique of the 'energy theories' of motivation, focusing particularly on their suggestion that the release of energy in behaviour is satisfying, as distinct from the modification of the situation in which behaviour takes place. Such theories tend, however, to be biassed towards non-rationality of behaviour. To this one should add that the universality of the Oedipus Complex and of the massive repression which it engenders has been severely questioned ever since the cross-cultural studies of Malinowsky (1927) and others (see Whiting and Child, 1953) have brought to light the existence of considerable variety in sexual behaviour and *mores*.

This is not to say that the Freudian school has nothing of relevance to contribute to the psychology of motivation. In particular, the mechanisms of defence analysed in detail by Anna Freud (1946) have not only been described as clinical entities but have also stood up fairly well to experimental verification (see e.g. Blum, 1953; Pumpian-Mindlin, 1952). Unconscious tendencies to repression (avoidance of representational input which has painful associations), to projection (attributing attitudes to others which arise initially in the subject himself but are inconsistent with his self-esteem), to reaction formation (assumption of conscious attitudes contrary to those aroused at the sensori-motor level in a powerful effort to inhibit these, e.g. extreme prudery as a defence against sexual arousal) – all these would appear to be manifestations of strategies more or less universally acquired by human beings in order to maintain their self-esteem.

Freud is almost certainly correct in attributing the origin of moral judgement to the uncritical adoption of parental standards as seen by the child. Also he was almost certainly correct in stressing the part played by parental prohibition in relation to early sexual and eliminatory behaviour in his society, and probably in ours. And again it is more than probable that the strength of moral attitudes in later life is very much bound up with the extent and severity of inhibitory, self-punishing attitudes formed in an earlier period. There is good evidence to support such a correlation, e.g. the association between restrictive 'parental attitudes and the prevalence of over-inhibited, neurotic behaviour in later childhood (Hewitt and Jenkins, 1946; Lewis, 1954). Nor is there any necessary conflict between the recognition of environmental factors and that of differences in constitutional personality. In particular, Eysenck (1957, 1960) has repeatedly shown an association between delinquency and measures of extraversion. If the latter is primarily a matter of the extent to which the subject tends to seek new, direct input, as compared with the introvert who is more apt to explore the possibilities of representational input, then one would expect inhibitory attitudes to arise in the introvert more easily. But it is unlikely that the variance in this aspect of personality can be attributed exclusively either to hereditary or to environmental factors.

As to the role of 'the Unconscious' in the arousal of moral attitudes, the anthropomorphic style of Freud's thinking should not blind us to the fact that it is only in logical thinking that the subject represents the criteria of his own decision processes, so that the arousal of indignation or approval is usually unconscious in one sense. Nor is it unreasonable to go further and recognize that logical reflexion itself is likely to arouse inhibition when this entails the admission in oneself of interests that are entirely at variance with those which are accepted by one's fellows and with which one has identified.

Taken by itself, however, Freudian theory does not provide an adequate basis for the understanding of the elaboration of rational, as opposed to irrational, moral attitudes. For even granted the validity of Freud's opposition to a super-scientific, transcendentalist justification of morality, one is still bound to inquire more closely both into the origins of the logical form of acceptable moral codes and into their content. In point of fact we will say rather more about the former than the latter.

In the second place, there is a strong tendency to overestimate and overgeneralize the role of sexual prohibitions encountered at an early age. This is clearly bound up with the Freudian view of instinct as a source of mental energy which must somehow reconcile itself with an independent 'mental' function, that of reality-testing by the ego. The result is a subjectivism, a pseudo-scientific attempt to account for behavioural objective relations in terms of unexplained, *a priori* mental entities, instead of vice versa, coupled with an overweaning faith in the rightness of the analyst's subjective interpretations and a disregard for the necessity for controlled experiment – attitudes which, not surprisingly, have alienated psychoanalytic schools of psychology from the main body of scientific thought.

We turn to a brief discussion of Piaget's account (Piaget, 1932). In a sense, Piaget's account begins where Freud's leaves off. Accepting the notion that the origin of morality is the adoption of moral standards attributed to the parents, presumably through identification, Piaget's studies are concerned primarily with the limitations of childish morality and with the stages by which it becomes transformed to yield an acceptable ethical code. Beginning with a study of children's attitudes to the rules of games, Piaget finds a consistent line of development. The youngest children, aged three or four, have no conception of rules: their play is at best an extension of imitation. Children of five or six are well aware of the existence of rules, yet their behaviour is contradictory. When required to state the rules, they are apt to give them a greater sanction than they in fact possess, as if they were laws of nature rather than conventions. They have no idea as to their origin, and regard them as immutable. By contrast, their behaviour often reveals a sublime indifference to rules, for they break them without realizing it. By seven or eight the contradiction has disappeared; they are capable of sticking to the rules. At the same time, they no longer confuse rules with natural laws, being aware that rules can be broken, but 'must' be kept. On the other hand, the origin of the rules is attributed uncritically to 'them'; grown-ups, etc. They are little concerned with the sanction for their morality, being quite content to follow. Finally, beginning about the age of ten, Piaget found an increasing tendency for children to accept that they are perfectly entitled to make their own rules, so long as the rules once made are respected. The justification for rules is reciprocity.

Passing from the morality of games to that of life, Piaget finds a similar trend from a morality of constraint to a morality of reciprocity. Injunctions against stealing, lying and damage to property are accepted uncritically by the child of five or six. Such actions are wrong, and to be punished. The measure of their wrongness is the 'objective' extent of the offence. In a typical experiment, children are told two stories describing the behaviour of two imaginary child offenders: one tries to help his mother in the home but inadvertenly slips while carrying a tray and manages to break fifteen cups; the other decides to help himself to a pot of jam in the larder and accidentally knocks over one cup. Younger children are almost unanimous in asserting that the first child is 'worse' than the second and deserves the greater punishment. By contrast, older children from the age of seven or eight are much more inclined to extenuate the first child by referring to his noble intentions. Moral laws, unlike natural laws, deal with the behaviour of subjects, and here intentions count: the child who is the victim of an accident continues to accept the law and is therefore less punishable; the other rejects it out of self-interest. The development consists principally in the recognition that a moral law can be accepted or rejected. Hence the tie-up with the games observations. By the same token, the confusion between moral and natural laws is reflected in young children's attitude to punishment. Punishment tends to be regarded as an inevitable consequence of wrongdoing, operating as by natural law, the mechanics of which are not questioned. Hence a ready acceptance of 'magical' retribution. Hence also an acceptance of punishments the severity of which is quite disproportionate to the offence. (The observations refer to children's responses to stories. In other words they refer to their attitudes in a representational situation.) This acceptance of punishment as natural and expiatory gives way first to an attitude of reciprocity, wherein the punishment is made 'to fit the crime', as in Hammurabi's code, and eventually to an ethical morality, in which punishment may be regarded as a measure which must be tempered to fit the criminal as well as the crime, for the maintenance of order, for the reform of the evildoer, and so on. Both developments imply the rejection of magical beliefs in 'immanent justice'.

Although Piaget's findings are based on inquiries in which the presentation of the situation is verbal and the response is also verbal, and although the conduct of his inquiries was unstructured and 'clinical', these observations can be repeated with more standardized procedures, and have been repeated many times since, yielding substantially similar results. (The first replications were the studies of Lerner, 1937; more recent studies include those of MacRae, 1954 and Turner, 1966, and are reviewed in Volume II, Chapter 11.) But the comparative objectivity of this work, as against that of Freud, may easily blind one to the fact that the experiments themselves do no more than describe a series of developmental stages as observed in quite circumscribed types of situations. One must seriously question whether they are sufficient to account for the transformation that takes place from one stage to the next, and especially from pre-logical to logical modes of justification. Equally questionable is the inevitability of the particular form of the development: towards a morality of reciprocity, rules of procedure between equals, sanctioned by the equality of all rational beings.

Piaget's own interpretation consists in the hypothesis that the earlier forms of morality derive from the one-sided experience of rules imposed by parents, the morality of constraint, while the later forms of morality derive from the experience of mutal adaptation to and of rules in social intercourse among one's peers, viz. other children. Which is why the games he studied took the form of 'pediarchic' games (Watson, 1952), games which are transmitted from generation to generation in children's cultures, and only rarely participated in or interfered with by adults, notably marbles and hopscotch (see also Opie and Opie, 1959).

However, one can easily question why early experience should give rise to a morality of constraint. After all, by no means all parents are arbitrary in their handling of children and they are by no means always oblivious of the child's intentions in meting out punishment. Nor is it at all clear why the child should elaborate a morality by reflecting on what he does in pediarchic games. There is an alternative line of approach which consists in analysing the behaviour of children in Piaget's experimental situations in terms of Piaget's own later studies dealing with the elaboration of concrete reasoning (see Volume II, Chapter 8 and the final sub-section in Chapter 5 of the present volume). This is a task recently undertaken by G. N. H. Turner (1966). Referring to experiments like those of the cups cited earlier, Turner suggests that these can be regarded as essentially problems in the development of children's logic. The difficulty is one of arriving at a judgement which is consistent in that it is based on the simultaneous consideration of all the criteria involved. Taking the clumsiness experiment as paradigm, there are four criteria which need to be respected in the solution: the first child has good intentions (1) followed by quite shocking results (2), while the second has evil intentions (3) followed by evil results (4). Turner argued that in order that the child can arrive at the conclusion that the behaviour of the second is more reprehensible than that of the first, he must first be in a postion to compare results with intentions, especially (1) and (2) to arrive at an overall judgement (5) that (2) is compensated by (1). This will be compared with a similar overall judgement (6), wherein (4) is exacerbated by (3). But this means that the final stage implies two levels at which the child must abandon the overt and readily intuitable criteria of extent of damage in favour of his own compensatory judgements: first, in accepting the extenuating circumstances (5), a judgement made only in reference to the behaviour of the first child, and second, when comparing (5) and (6). He therefore predicted that if children were asked for separate evaluations of the conduct of the two children as well as for a comparison, an intermediate stage would appear: thus the youngest children would be unable to take (1) and (2) into account at the same time and would therefore say the first child was wicked altogether (because of (2)); at an intermediate stage, they would compensate for (2) by referring to (1), and would reply that the first child was really good (5), while the second was evil (6) – but they would be unable to retain this purely verbal result (5) when arriving at the final decision; therefore their replies would be self-contradictory, the first child being judged as 'good', the second as 'bad', and the first as 'worse' than the second; the contradiction would disappear when the judgements reached at (5) and (6) were themselves the criteria of comparison between the two children. Turner's inquiries fully confirmed his prediction: the primitive 'results' reply (both children 'bad', but the first 'worse') shows a steady decline with age; the intermediate replies (the first child 'good' but 'worse' than the 'bad') increases from five to eight and then decreases; the consistent 'motive' solution shows a steady increase.

A second feature of Turner's study was his observation that younger children in their replies not infrequently refer to motivation in the limited sense of intention: '*He meant/didn't mean to do it*', while older children more usually referred to the true purpose of the action: '*He meant to help when he broke the cups*'. It should be added that Turner's conclusions are based on rigorous procedures and criteria applied to over four hundred children.

Taken by itself, the second observation might be dismissed as little better than anecdotal evidence, since the experiment was not constructed in such a way as to bring out clearly two ways of representing purposiveness in actions. Its significance, however, is that the older child is capable of dissociating the purpose with which an action was conceived from the action itself, while the judgement of the younger child remains global. Such a conclusion is entirely in accord with the observations of Inhelder and Piaget (1958) in regard to the attempts of very young children to find out about the causes of natural phenomena. Characteristically they are unable to do so because they are unable to separate their actions from their effects, giving themselves time to read the data and co-ordinate them: for instance if a child believes that pushing a pendulum makes it swing faster he pushes it until it does; in the same way another child predicts that a large block of wood will sink in a tub of water and pushes it down when it fails to comply. And so on (see Volume II, Chapter 9). To put the matter another way, in order to give due weight to motivation in moral judgement the child must be in a position to represent his own behaviour and that imputed to others sufficiently clearly to pick out the moments of decision. As noted in Chapter 5, in the measure that he is able to represent the elements of sensori-motor action in any order, he will inevitably be led in time to focus on the moments of decision which are criterial to comparisons between different but comparable situations. This suggests that both the initial judgements implying a rigid morality of constraint and the final judgements which represent a logically consistent morality are attempts on the part of the child to assimilate and identify himself with the moral attitudes which he finds around him. The difference between primitive morality and more mature forms should be attributed primarily to a difference in cognitive capacity.

Let us retrace the development from this new vantage point, beginning with the first adumbrations of moral judgement, e.g. in the fear shown by young children when they have done something 'wrong'. The starting-point for moral judgement is the development of the self-concept, as outlined in an earlier discussion. Granted that the child arrives at a self-concept, even in the primitive form of self as agent, and granted that his capacity for deferred imitation is enlarged to comprise the representation of attitudes, it is inevitable that the inception of primary behaviours will eventually give rise to secondary, monitoring representations of approval or disapproval. Furthermore, we recall that the self-concept is modelled on the concept of others, and that the general tendency of behaviour is to (*a*) reduction of uncertainty, and (*b*) the elaboration of strategies which will tend to reduce the probability of certain kinds of input (those which present a primary threat or conditioned-fear objects (Miller, 1959; Mowrer, 1960) and those which present a secondary threat, that of maximal uncertainty, pp. 323, 349 ff.). It follows that the child will bolster his sense of social effectance and of social security by anticipating the moral attitudes of parents and making them his own . . . in so far as he assimilates them. The restrictive clause is common to the Freudian analysis and to that of Piaget. For the young child is incapable of going back over his own representations and isolating the moments of decision (Chapter 5, Section V.5). Which means that he cannot refer to the motives of his actions as the basis for his moral attitudes. As a result, certain actions, expressive of love or especially compliance, arouse a secondary attitude of approval, while others, especially expressions of aggression, destruction, tampering with forbidden objects, visiting forbidden places, arouse secondary disapproval, coupled with fear. The latter are much the more important. But there is as yet no scale of values, only a scale of conditioned fear based on the action as such, judged in terms of its concrete results. This is the morality which Freud calls the punishing super-ego and which Piaget terms the morality of adult constraint.

How does this sort of morality give rise to the morality of the adolescent and the adult?

(1) The differentiation between things done accidentally and things done on purpose is one that is likely to arise quite early. It corresponds to a difference in the state of the system. For in the one case the input (e.g. corresponding to 'punishable breakage of cups') is assimilated to a link which is already activated by a strategy (corresponding to the intention), while in the other the input communicates with the same link only by virtue of its novelty and uncertainty which enable it to penetrate the 'filter' (see Chapter 4, Section III). Representation of this differentiation is itself a 'global' representation, for it does not deliberately select the critical moments in the sensori-motor sequence but simply registers the end-state. A corollary which could probably be tested by sufficiently ingenious experiment is that accidental 'crimes' arouse more anxiety even in, say, the two-year-old than deliberates ones. (The difficulty is of course to ensure that the latter will still register as 'crimes'.)

(2) The attribution of intention and accident to others follows naturally from the principles which govern the formation of the self-concept (previous sub-section).

(3) A tendency to adopt a morality which takes motive into account is a probable development on two counts. First, by virtue of identification, since such a morality matches the attitudes of others better than one which does not. Second, because it is reinforcing, since it reduces anxiety (uncertainty in the system). It should be stressed that this development would amount to no more than a primitive recognition of 'fair-unfair', and is by no means sufficient for 'motive' replies to Piaget's problems.

(4) The previous development already implies an element of reciprocity. However, Piaget's studies are concerned with a progressive systematization of the elements involved. Such a systematization depends on a cognitive development which enables the child, first, to classify 'good' and 'bad' actions and to seriate them along a continuum, and, second, on the progressive freeing of representation from the order of sensori-motor action, enabling it to select the critical moments of decision, relevant to the evaluation of actions. Only then can the child pass from a practical morality to the acceptance of a coherent moral code.

(5) The further development of morality, in adolescence and in the adult, again reflects the course of cognitive development in other spheres (cf. the final chapter in Inhelder and Piaget, 1958). It is essentially a matter of reconstructing a coherent system, based on the abstraction of general principles, being ways of relating actions rather than the actions themselves

and their relations. This allows the possiblity to transcend the morality of society and to construct new moralities. But, for the most part, this is only a possiblity. There are three reasons for this. First, formal reasoning is difficult and usually unrewarding. It is essential to the species but not to the individual. Second, identification with the morality of society or of accepted groups is anxiety reducing. Hence the presssure to conformity and the tendency, even when attempts at reappraisal are initiated, to 'rationalize', so as to end up with the accepted morality. Third, new moralities can only arise on the basis of changes in social relations. This is obvious. None of us is so clever that he is likely to arrive at a 'new' systematization based on the same old input.

But what is much more common is the tendency to seek evidential support for the morality with which one has identified, and to establish a greater coherence within it. For if this account is even approximately correct, then it is reasonable to look for development in reactions to cognitive dissonance, with younger children showing a greater tolerance of dissonance and a greater incongruity in their valuations of things, or rather the coexistence of several contradictory but internally congruent systems of evaluation (see below).

There are a number of corollaries to this interpretation.

In the first place, since morality is an elaboration out of the arousal of secondary fear, primitive morality, one would expect that where secondary fear is strong, the pressure towards rapid evolution of morality will also be strong. Other things being equal, there should be a positive correlation between moral behaviour, which is more closely linked with primitive morality, and moral judgement.

In the second place, although a positive correlation is to be expected, it is not expected that the correlation should be perfect (cf. MacRae, 1954). For there are other pressures towards the representation and systematization of the attitudes of others besides the reduction of primitive moral anxiety – notably, and quite simply, the reduction of uncertainty concerning their behaviour. Hence one can expect to find the intelligent psychopath, who plays on the morality of others without adopting it for himself. And various shades in between.

In the third place, as already indicated, restrictive régimes will be correlated with strong primitive morality and with strong moral principles in later life. Nor need these be the same in content. Nothing is more common than the consistent and principled atheist with a strong religious unbringing.

In the fourth place, since the development of moral codes and moral principles is a product of identification, it will be fostered by intercourse between equals with whom a more differentiated identification is possible. Which is the principal thesis in Piaget's (1932) exposition. But although peer identification makes the systematization easier, there are other pressures towards it. Notably the maintenance of consistent standards by parents and the prevalence of attempts on their part to give reasons for their discipline. Hence the correlation often found between 'middle-class' (see Bernstein's descriptions of the use of explanatory language in different sub-cultures, 1958, 1960) and moral judgement (Lerner, 1937; Boehm and Nass, 1962).

In the fifth place, since the activation of primitive morality is only the prime factor in the development of morality and is not identical with it, there may be greater or lesser separation between the two. In particular, the realization that punishments are ways of enforcing social norms is not sufficient to counteract the effect of anxiety reduction which it exercised in the young child and continues to exercise in the adult. Hence, the sense of relief following on 'expiation' persists, even though the subject is well aware that it has no foundation in things. (Its foundation is in the system as a whole, which includes his own reactions to things.)

In the sixth place, and for the same reason (the distinction between the sensori-motor manifestation of morality, being the arousal of anxiety, and the systematic formulation of moral codes), one will expect that from a certain age onwards (later than the first systematizations as such, say ten or twelve), the child will tend to make clear representational distinctions between the moral behaviour to be expected in certain circumstances (represented in a story) and that which he accepts as 'correct': between what a subject *would* do and what he *should* do (Morris, 1955).

In the seventh place, since the development of systematic moralities is a function of differential identifications (with sub-groups and with their standards), it follows that there is no warrant for restricting the discussion of morality to the elaboration of some simple universal rule – such as the Kantian rule of mutual respect between rational beings. Moral behaviour and moral judgement cover much more than just one principle. Also, there have been many systematizations evolved in the past, and speaking generally, they have been based on selective identifications, reflecting the conditions of the moralizer and his society. This is no less true today. (When is a being 'rational'? The answer that we give depends on our identification.) There is no transcendental morality acceptable to science. Like Carroll's three sisters, we can draw treacle very well, but only within limits, because we are *in* the well. Of course this does not mean that psychologists must be amoral. Any more than the physiologist who understands the causes of pain is thereby rendered insensitive to pain.

Finally, although moral reactions, whether behavioural or systematic – and the two may be well integrated with one another anyhow – are acquired attitudes (and therefore schematizations, see Section IV), they are none the less drives in their own right. They do not depend on the sublimation of a power source to be found only in primitive 'instincts'. There can be conflict between one drive and another, or, if one likes, between drives to 'err' and drives to moral 'rectitude'. But the mere fact that a person has a powerfully integrated moral code (whatever its content) does not imply necessarily that he is the prey to an equally powerful set of ghastly id instincts just waiting to be released. Some may be. But we should not be blind to the possibility that many individuals who show a singleness of purpose are in fact surprisingly well integrated, more likely to show schizophrenic denial patterns if the input completely failed to match their expectations than to 'reveal their true colours'. It is we ordinary mortals who are the more complicated.

(*b*) *Attitude Measurement.* The measurement of attitudes is a topic which concerns us little in the present chapter. Typically, the subject is required to state his attitude to some person (e.g. Harold Wilson, Picasso), to a group of persons (e.g. Jews or the Ku Klux Klan), or to an institution (e.g. corporal punishment). There are various ways of doing this. One is to require direct open-ended answers to naïve questioning (e.g. 'What do you think of . . . ?' 'Do you agree with . . . ?') – a method seldom used in psychological research. Another is to construct an attitude test which requires either that the subject indicate the extent of his agreement or disagreement with a variety of loaded statements (e.g. 'Spare the rod and spoil the child', 'The operation of a *numerus clausus* for Jews or coloured people is incompatible with democracy', etc.), generally on a 5-point scale from '*strongly agree*' to '*strongly disagree*'. Since the statements all bear on a single topic, the subject's answers yield a single overall score on his attitude to, say, discrimination or formal methods in education (Likert, 1932). Or again, the test may incorporate a wide variety of statements expressive of various shades of opinion on the topic and the subject is asked simply to tick off those which accord with his own views. The statements having been previously weighted by a panel of judges, usually on an 11-point scale from very *pro* to very *anti*, the subject's attitude score is simply the average weighting of the statements that he selects (Thurstone and Chave, 1929). Yet another method is to require the subject to rate a variety of selected concepts (e.g. democracy, family, mother, Negroes, wife, freedom) on a number of scales represented by polarized adjectival pairs (e.g. warm – cold, hard – soft, strong – weak, precious – worthless). Intercorrelations are then calculated between concepts. Factorization of the resultant matrix is taken to yield a map of the 'meaning' which the concepts have for the subject, and especially of his attitude to them. In spite of, or perhaps because of, its sophistication the method works very well (Osgood, Succi and Tannenbaum, 1957; Kelly, 1955). (A fuller discussion of methods of attitude testing will be found in Oppenheim, 1966.)

It is interesting to note that the representational nature of the test can sometimes lead to lack of validity, i.e. the subject's stated or measured atttitude does not represent his behavioural attitude. Such was the case in an inquiry by La Piere and Farnsworth (1949), who found that some subjects who expressed a strong hostility to 'Asiatics', were quite well-disposed to them when they actually met them. However, the fact that even reliable measures of attitude are not always perfectly valid should not be taken to imply that true attitude (= drive as evinced in the validation situation) is unrelated to representation and unaffected by changes in representation. For one must expect imperfect validity since the validation situation itself constitutes a change in input, and therefore an occasion for attitudinal learning.

(*c*) *Attitude Change*. The question of how attitudes change is more central to our purpose. Attitudes may be changed in one of two ways, either as a result of direct (sensori-motor) experience or as a result of representational modification, usually taking the form of suggestion: the suggestion that others hold contrary attitudes or that there are facts which do not support the attitude. Direct manipulation of attitude is simply a matter of learning. For we have seen that upon close analysis, the structure of drive (or attitude) is the same thing as the structure of cognition, the difference being one of emphasis, so that the same principles of learning must hold. The effectiveness of suggestion and that of 'evidence' are specific to representational behaviour and therefore require some comment. We begin with the second.

The schema of an object is the product of the various lines of behaviour (strategies) which it evokes, or permits. Now it is clear that these lines of behaviour may be well-established or not, and they therefore represent varying degrees of uncertainty. So much is true even at the sensori-motor level, i.e. in animal and infant behaviour. Now it is easy to see that representation is a reconstruction of lines of behaviour using a symbolic input, the varying degrees of uncertainty contributing to varying degrees of belief, ranging from minimal uncertainty, or knowledge, to maximal uncertainty. To return to the sensori-motor level, it is clear that from the point of view of the system as a whole, if the input communicates with few lines of behaviour, the relative uncertainty which it generates will be small, and the greatest uncertainty will arise when it communicates with several lines of behaviour but fails to be validated, e.g. by further inspection – because it does not fit. This in fact is what is found. The stimuli which evoke the greatest measure of arousal are those which combine novelty with familiarity (Berlyne, 1960). Reverting to the representational level, we are not surprised to find that individuals tend to seek evidence to support beliefs (reduce uncertainty), especially when these are related to systems of knowledge and belief, i.e. when they are sensed as relevant and important to the subject. Again there is evidence to support *this* belief (!), e.g. Smith, Bruner and White (1956).

However, the range of representation is such that it extends far beyond what can be validated by direct testing. Also, for better or for worse, it is not the case that the representational schemata which are most central and pervasive in the structure of personality are also those which are most readily tested in direct fashion. For these include the self-concept and our conception of the way in which we are regarded by others.

They also include most of our moral attitudes, using the term moral in the extended sense given earlier in this section. For instance many of us hold strong convictions about the political and economic policies pursued by our own governments, about the relative merits of the belligerents in any war, about capital punishment and so on. Indeed we are bound to do so in so far as we are aware that even distant events, if important enough, are liable to affect us, and that we in turn can influence their course in some degree. But our attitude concerning any one of these, such as the merits of the various parties to events in the Congo some years ago, is always bound up with a wide set of beliefs, most of which fall very far short of what we might call knowledge. Both the attitude and the beliefs correspond to lines of behaviour. But the attitude represents, as it were, a proximal line of behaviour, one that we might engage on here and now – for instance: arguing a point of view, writing to the press, and so on. The beliefs are not only statements that we might make, but also anticipations of input which would verify these statements if we entered the appropriate discovery strategies. But since the beliefs may well be complex, such that a single verificatory behaviour is inconclusive, and since they tend to form networks, one belief resting on a number of others, and so on, we do not in fact verify more than a portion of them, and then only indirectly. Which is why they remain beliefs.

However, the verification of beliefs by evidence belongs properly to the psychology of cognition and is discussed more fully elsewhere (Volume II, Chapters 8, 9). The point to retain is that attitudes are taken, and must be taken on insufficient evidence. This is because they represent proximal lines of behaviour – challenges to action in response to input which is present. (Very often, the argument that one should stay action implying a positive attitude until one has all the evidence is used quite speciously by those who hold a contrary attitude; and quite often, inaction is itself a form of action.) Now it is not at all the case that the attitudes which we hold most strongly are those which rest on the firmest foundation of knowledge. For those that do tend to be so trivial that they hardly qualify for the name of attitude: for instance, our attitude to the bus stop round the corner. Strictly speaking, there is an attitude, since a line of behaviour in relation to it can be quite strongly activated – when we have to catch a bus (and an attitude is a drive, which has been defined as the intensity of activation of a strategy). The attitudes studied by psychologists and sociologists are more general, and therefore less verifiable, they are also more closely linked with the self-concept, being lines of behaviour in terms of which people define their own identity by identification with others.

This brings us to the second way in which attitudes may be modified: by suggestion. Reference was made earlier to the work of Osgood *et al.* indicating that attitudes to even quite disparate things can be measured simultaneously, and that such measurement reveals a polarization of the representations of these along a general evaluative axis: good versus bad. The strongest attitudes are entertained in regard to people and things (events or institutions) which are evidently judged as very good or very bad, with others intermediate. However, an interesting finding which emerges from nearly all studies in this field, beginning with the work of Heider (see Heider, 1958), is that positive bonds are established between all the goods, and likewise between all the bads: good people, with whom we identify, approve of good things, and bad people, from whom we dissociate ourselves, approve of bad. Conversely, of course, good people disapprove of bad things and vice versa.

Clearly, so long as this happy state of affairs prevails, there is minimal uncertainty in the system, at least as regards proximal lines of behaviour, the stands we take on various questions will not contradict one another. This equilibrium is disturbed by any evidence which would link a good with a bad, or dissociate two goods or two bads from one another. For instance, evidence that a respected colleague approves of apartheid. The disturbance of equilibrium is what Festinger (1957) has termed 'cognitive dissonance'. The behaviour which follows may be confined to a representational restructurization, especially with respect to the evaluative dimension of the concepts involved, or it may take the form of overt behaviour, calculated to reduce the dissonance, and hence the uncertainty. Osgood has concentrated his attention on the former course: in particular he predicts that the re-evaluation will affect both elements involved in the contradiction (e.g. the respected colleague and the policy of the South African Government). The evaluation of both will tend to change in such a way as to restore equilibrium – both our negative evaluation of the concept and our positive evaluation of the colleague tend to diminish. But unequally. For whichever of the two is more strongly polarized will show less shift. There are a number of other features in the theoretical model, termed 'congruence theory', which render it a very good predictor of attitude change. The chief limitation of this approach is that it takes into account only the evaluative status of the terms directly involved in the contradiction. By contrast, others, notably Festinger, extend the area of study in ways which imply a recognition that any proximal attitude to a single term (e.g. person or institution) implies a wide system of supporting beliefs and attitudes involving other terms. The effect of dissonant evidence pertaining to one term may therefore be to initiate behaviour which will counteract the evidence – for instance, in the fictional example, one way of reconciling oneself is to bolster one's respect for the colleague by a compensatory belief, say, a tendency to overvalue his work (which will enable him to maintain his position in our esteem in spite of his reactionary leanings). One of the features of Festinger's approach is that it not infrequently generates paradoxical predictions of this sort which are confirmed, so accounting for much that is irrational in human behaviour. Yet another way of resolving dissonance is to seek further evidence. This in fact appeared fairly strongly in the studies of Smith, Bruner and White (1956) on the attitudes of ten individual Americans towards the U.S.S.R. over a period.

These remarks constitute no more than the barest outline of what is a growing and fruitful area of investigation in social psychology. The reader will find a brilliant and entertaining general overview in the work of Brown (1965). Developmental factors pertaining to attitude change are considered further in Volume II, Chapter 11, and factors affecting attitude change in pupils in the context of education are treated in Volume

III, Chapters 6–8. It is clear that the central problems for investigation relate to the need for a clearer formulation of the conditions which determine one strategy of dissonace reduction rather than another.

However, enough has been said here to indicate the consonance of these studies with the conceptions of attitude and drive developed earlier in this chapter. The role of identification in the formation and modification of attitudes is not confined to early childhood but persists throughout life.

VI. SUMMARY

From the common-sense point of view, problems of motivation arise only when the behaviour to be accounted for is unusual and unexpected. In general motivation is attributed to mental decisions based on intuitions of pleasure and pain. Strength of motivation is found to be bound up with the presence of emotion. This pre-scientific account fails to provide any theoretical continuity between motivation in animals and human motivation, since the concepts involved cannot easily be applied to animal behaviour. More significantly, it is of little value in promoting advance in understanding through objective research, because of its excessive reliance on introspective impressions.

Historically, the most comprehensive and influential conceptual attack on problems of motivation in animals and in man has been the theory of instincts, especially in the form in which it was propounded by McDougall. Instincts were thought of as very general and flexible action tendencies, more or less closely related to survival needs. Although subject to considerable modification by learning, the distinctness of instincts could be established on a number of criteria: their universality, their comparative independence, their relation to certain primary activities, and the characteristic emotions that accompanied them.

However the usefulness of the concept of instinct in human motivation has been criticized, especially in view of its heavy reliance on the identifiability of characteristic emotions. Even in the sphere of animal behaviour, it is doubtful how much is gained by a simple dichotomy between innate aspects of behaviour and those which are learnt.

More recent thinking, at least in the sphere of animal psychology, reveals that the concept of instinct has been largely abandoned in favour of the more neutral concept of drive. Drives, like instincts were originally thought of as contributing energy and direction to behaviour. But the notion is more flexible, since it is argued, largely on the basis of experimental evidence, that primary drives, which are innate and related to needs, can give rise to secondary drives as a result of learning. The action of the two is similar. More important, the emphasis on enumeration of distinct and basic instincts has little parallel in drive theory, for the concern is chiefly with the evaluation of the effects of variation in drive (regardless of which particular drive is involved) on the determination of behaviour, and especially learning behaviour. Such quantitative evaluation can be achieved, at least in principle, on the assumption that increase in drive can be achieved by deprivation of bodily needs, especially food and drink. One effect of the newer, more experimental approach has been a merging between the general fields of motivation and of learning.

Nevertheless, the question remained whether the identification and measurement of drive could be held entirely distinct from the course of behaviour itself, by simply anchoring its definition to deprivation history. Likewise the notion of a separate structure to form the basis of drive, a structure of needs, is one that cannot easily be made to fit the experimental data. This is the principal reason that psychologists have tended to abandon the Hullian theory of learning by drive reduction or need reduction. Attention was drawn to the extensive work of Miller illustrating the role of the input (or 'stimulus') in the activation of drive, especially aversive fear behaviour, and to the studies of Amsel showing the part played by frustration in increasing drive regardless of deprivation.

While Skinner has been little concerned with direct experimentation on drive, at any rate in his more recent work, his attitude to its definition proves to be of considerable help in clarifying the isssue. The concept of drive is useful in the first instance because it enables one to specify certain distinct ways in which one can alter the intensity of behaviour or its direction. This does not mean at all that drives are separate entities, distinct from habits, or what we have termed strategies or lines of behaviour. Taking this as our point of departure, we have argued in the present chapter that the structure of drives must reflect that of cognition, and that the study of drive should be considered as no more than a definition of an area of psychological inquiry, viz. the study of factors concerned with changes in the intensity of behaviour and with changes in its direction, i.e. shifts from one line of behaviour to another. Cognitive studies are more concerned with the formation of such lines of behaviour and with their interconnexion. This, of course, does not preclude the recognition of specific structures in the brain concerned with the general intensity of behavioural activation, the arousal centres, or with specific activation and de-activation of strategies related to basic needs. But it enables one to discard the notion of a necessary absolute correlation between drive and need, allowing for a more systematic recognition of the part played by such factors as frustration and uncertainty of input in the determination of drive.

In a brief discussion of the nature and role of emotion, it was suggested that while there is good reason for a more extended use of the term to include affective tone or 'mood', as well as its peripheral manifestations in adreno-sympathetic emotional discharge, there is little warrant for assuming that here we have the prime integrator of behaviour, as is suggested by Leeper. It seems not unlikely that mild emotion or mood, like intense emotional arousal, is primarily a physiological reaction symptomatic of failure of temporal integration. At the same time, much of the content of human affect belongs more properly to the study of cognitive representation than to that of emotion as such. It must be admitted that such assumptions are little more than hunches. The experimental study of emotion has barely begun, and most of the work in this field has been concentrated on one area alone: the part played by hypothalamic and other structures in the production of adreno-sympathetic discharge.

In the remainder of the chapter, our attention was turned to the study of human motivation. Partly as a result of differences in emphasis, the central concept of drive is often avoided in favour of 'attitude'. Without quarrelling with this usage, it was argued that the previous definition of drive could be equally applied to attitude in human motivation: factors affecting the intensity of behaviour and the switching in its direction. At the same time, the difference in terminology also reflects a shift in the nature of these factors, due primarily to the development of representation and the elaboration of the concept of self.

The concept of self, like that of any other object or idea, was defined as the intersection of all representational schemata having the self as referrent. Such a concept arises as a result of imitation and identification. It does not refer to all the sensori-motor actions and experiences of the subject, but only to those in which his own part is recognized by comparison with the behaviour of others. A consideration of the development of the self concept suggests a gradual elaboration in which one may distinguish four stages: the undifferentiated recognition of the self as human agent; the intuitive differentiation of the self in terms of child roles: the systematization and categorization of roles; and the resolution of role conflicts in adolescence associated with physiological changes and changes in social expectations. The importance of the self concept derives mainly from the fact that much of human behaviour argues the formation of attitudes whose general direction is to enhance one's sense of security and competence as a person.

Since the most important of these attitudes are evaluative, in the sense that they are concerned with what the subject considers it important for him to do, to believe and to know, the formation of these attitudes comes under the general heading of the development of morality. Nearly all would agree with Freud and Piaget in their claim that the earliest morality derives from identification with adult codes, and that this morality is exaggerated and distorted due to the insufficiency of the child's understanding. Evidence of the adoption of attitudes may be found in Bandura's recent studies of imitation. However, the Freudian account is inextricably bound up with his conception of the instinctual character of behaviour and provides little explanation of the rationality of attitudes in older children and adults. Piaget's studies of the development of moral judgement constitute an excellent characterization of the stages in the development of more systematic moral codes. However, although his results have frequently been replicated, there is comparatively little support for his contention that the growth of morality is based on the experience of reciprocity in the peer society. A re-analysis of some of his data suggests that the development is due largely to the progress in systematization which he himself has illuminated in his later work, i.e. to the growth of logical thinking as a whole. Such an analysis does not preclude recognition either of the continued operation of inhibitions dating back to childish morality – often at variance with reason (Freud), or of the need for relevant moral experience and relevant identifications (Piaget), but these cannot be regarded as sufficient.

The same pressures which act in the formation of attitudes in children, especially the tendency to identification with groups and their values, continue to operate in the modification of attitudes throughout life. They are exemplified in studies of attitude change using a variety of techniques for the measurement of attitudes. Of particular importance is the pressure to form attitudes for which there is insufficient proof, and to bolster these with supporting attitudes and beliefs. The chapter therefore concludes with a brief account of the work of Osgood, Festinger and others, which represent experimental attacks on the precise ways in which human subjects are driven to establish congruence – and to reduce cognitive dissonance.

Both the formation of moral attitudes and the mechanisms of attitude change are taken up again elsewhere in these volumes. Our purpose here has been chiefly to show how these areas of psychological inquiry can be pursued without abandonment of our basic conception of the subject, animal or human, as an objective, self-regulating system. Questions of individual differences in human attitudes and adjustment, barely touched on in this chapter, are taken up by Stott (in Volume III) from the same standpoint of continuity in the regulation of behaviour from animal to man.

REFERENCES

AMSEL, A., and ROUSSEL, J. (1952). Motivational properties of frustration: I. Effect on a running response of the addition of frustration to the motivational complex. *J. exp. Psychol.* **43**, 363–368.

BANDURA, A., ROSS, D., and ROSS, S. A. (1963). A comparative test of the status envy, social power, and secondary reinforcement theories of identificatory learning. *J. Abn. & Soc. Psychol.* **67**, 527–534.

BEACH, F. A. (1955). The descent of instinct. *Psychol. Rev.* **62**, 401–410.

BERLYNE, D. E. (1960). *Conflict, Arousal and Curiosity*. New York: McGraw-Hill.

BERNSTEIN, B. (1958). Some social determinants of perception. *Brit. J. Sociol.* **9**, 159–174.

BERNSTEIN, B. (1960). Language and social class. *Brit. J. Sociol.* **11**, 271–276.

BLUM, G. S. (1953). *Psychoanalytic Theories of Personality*. New York: McGraw-Hill.

BOEHM, L., and NASS, M. L. (1962). The development of conscience: social class differences in conscience development. *Child Developm.* **33**, 565–574.

BROWN, R. (1965). *Social Psychology*. New York: The Free Press.

BURT, C. (1941). Is the doctrine of instincts dead? A symposium. I: The case for human instincts. *Brit. J. Educ. Psychol.* **11**, 155–172.

BURT, C. (1945). Personality, a symposium. I: The assessment of personality. *Brit. J. Educ. Psychol.* **15**, 107–121.

CANNON, W. B. (1929). *Bodily Changes in Pain, Hunger, Fear and Rage*. New York: Appleton-Century-Crofts.

CATTELL, R. B. (1957). *Personality and Motivation: Structure and Measurement*. New York: World Book Co.

CATTELL, R. B. (1965). *The Scientific Analysis of Personality*. Harmondsworth: Penguin Books.

COFER, C. N., and APPLEY, M. H. (1964). *Motivation: Theory and Research.* New York: John Wiley and Sons.

DEUTSCH, J. A. (1960). *The Structural Basis of Behaviour.* London: Cambridge University Press.

ELKIND, D. (1964). The child's perception of his religious identity. *Lumen Vitae.* **19**, 635–646.

ERIKSON, E. H. (1963). *Childhood and Society.* (2nd edition) New York: W. W. Norton.

EYSENCK, H. J. (1957). *The Dynamics of Anxiety and Hysteria.* London: Routledge.

EYSENCK, H. J. (1960). Symposium: The development of moral values in children. VII: The contribution of learning theory. *Brit. J. Educ. Psychol.* **30**, 11–21.

FESTINGER, L. (1957). *A Theory of Cognitive Dissonance.* Stanford: Stanford University Press.

FREUD, ANNA (1946). *The Ego and the Mechanisms of Defence.* London: Hogarth Press.

FREUD, S. (1914). *The Psychopathology of Everyday Life.* London: Ernest Benn.

FREUD, S. (1922). *Introductory Lectures on Psycho-Analysis.* London: George Allen and Unwin.

GOLDMAN, R. (1965). *Religious Thinking from Childhood to Adolescence.* London: Routledge and Kegan Paul.

HARLOW, H. F. (1959). Learning set and error-factor theory. In Koch, S. (ed.), *Psychology: A Study of a Science.* Volume II. *General Theoretical Formulations, Learning and Special Processes.* New York: McGraw-Hill, 492–537.

HEIDER, F. (1958). *The Psychology of Interpersonal Relations.* New York: John Wiley.

HEBB, D. O. (1949), *The Organisation of Behaviour. A Neuropsychological Theory.* New York: Wiley.

HESS, E. H. (1962). Ethology: an approach toward the complete analysis of behaviour. In Brown, R., Galanter, E., Hess, E. H. and Mandler, G. *New Directions in Psychology.* New York: Holt, Rinehart and Winston, 157–266.

HEWITT, L. E., and JENKINS, R. L. (1946). *Fundamental Patterns of Maladjustment. The Dynamics of their Origin.* State of Illinois.

HINDE, R. A. (1960). Energy models of motivation. *Symposia of the Society for Experimental Biology* **14**, 199–213.

HULL, C. L. (1952). *A Behaviour System.* New Haven: Yale University Press.

INHELDER, B., and PIAGET, J. (1958). *The Growth of Logical Thinking from Childhood to Adolescence.* London: Routledge and Kegan Paul.

INHELDER, B. and PIAGET, J. (1964). *The Early Growth of Logic in the Child: Classification and Seriation.* London: Routledge and Kegan Paul.

JAHODA, G. (1963). The development of children's ideas about country and nationality. *Brit. J. Educ. Psychol.* **33**, 47–60 and 143–153.

JAMES, W. (1884). What is an emotion? *Mind* **9**, 188–205.

KELLY, G. A. (1955). *The Psychology of Personal Constructs.* New York: Norton.

La PIERE, T. and FARNSWORTH, R. (1949). *Social Psychology* (Third edn.). New York: McGraw-Hill.

LEEPER, R. W. (1948). A motivational theory of emotion to replace 'emotion as a disorganised response'. *Psychol. Rev.* **55**, 5–21.

LERNER, E. (1937). *Constraint Areas and the Moral Judgement of the Child.* Menasha, Wisconsin: Banta.

LEWIS, H. (1954). *Deprived Children: The Mersham Experiment, A Social and Clinical Study.* London: O.U.P.

LIKERT, R. (1932). A technique for the measurement of attitudes. *Arch. Psychol.* No. 140.

MCCLELLAND, D. C. (1964). *Roots of Consciousness.* Princeton, New Jersey: Van Nostrand.

MCCLELLAND, D. C., ATKINSON, J. W., CLARK, R. A., and LOWELL, E. G. (1953). *The Achievement Motive.* New York: Appleton-Century-Crofts.

MACCOBY, E. (1959). Role taking in childhood and its consequences for social learning. *Child Developm.* **30**, 239–252.

MACCOBY, E. (1961). The taking of adult roles in middle childhood. *J. Abnorm. Soc. Psychol.* **61**, 493–503.

MacCORQUODALE, K., and MEEHL, P. E. (1948). On a distinction between hypothetical constructs and intervening variables. *Psychol. Rev.* **55**, 95–107.

MCDOUGALL, W. (1908). *Introduction to Social Psychology.* London: Methuen.

MACRAE, D. (1954). A test of Piaget's theories of moral development. *J. Abnorm. Soc. Psychol.* **49**, 14–16.

MADSEN, K. B. (1959). *Theories of Motivation.* Copenhagen: Munksgaard.

MALINOWSKI, B. (1927). *Sex and Repression in Savage Society.* New York: Harcourt, Brace.

MANDLER, G. (1962). Emotion. In Brown, R., Galanter, E., Hess, E. H., and Mandler, G. *New Directions in Psychology*. New York: Holt, Rinehart and Winston, 267–343.

MILLER, N. E. (1948). Studies of fear as an acquirable drive. I: Fear as motivation and fear-reduction as reinforcement in the learning of new learning of new responses. *J. exp. Psychol.* **38**, 89–101.

MILLER, N. E., and DOLLARD, J. (1941). *Social Learning and Imitation*. New Haven: Yale University Press.

MILLER, N. E. (1959). Liberalisation of basic S-R concepts: Extensions to conflict behaviour, motivation and social learning. In Koch, S. (ed.) *Psychology: A Study of a Science*. Volume II. *General Systematic Formulations, Learning and Special Processes*. New York: McGraw-Hill, 196–292.

MONTGOMERY, K. W. (1953). The effect of activity deprivation upon exploratory behaviour. *J. Comp. Physiol. Psychol.* **46**, 438–441.

MORRIS, J. F. (1955). A study of value-judgments in adolescents. Unpublished Ph.D. Thesis, University of London.

MOWRER, O. H. (1960). *Learning Theory and Behaviour*. New York: John Wiley.

OPIE, I., and OPIE, P. (1959). *The Language and Lore of Schoolchildren*. London: Oxford University Press.

OPPENHEIM, B. (1966). *Questionnaire Design and Attitude Scale Measurement*. London: Heinemann.

OSGOOD, C. E., SUCCI, G. J., and TANNENBAUM, P. M. (1957). *The Measurement of Meaning*. Urbana: U. of Illinois Press.

PIAGET, J. (1928). *Judgement and Reasoning in the Child*. London: Routledge and Kegan Paul.

PIAGET, J. (1932). *The Moral Judgement of the Child*. London: Kegan Paul, Trench, Trubner & Co.

PIAGET, J. (1946). *Le développement de la notion de temps chez l'enfant*. Paris: Presses Universitaires de France.

PUMPIAN-MINDLIN, E. (ed.) (1952). *Psychoanalysis as Science*. Stanford: Stanford University Press.

ROSENZWEIG, M. R. (1963). The mechanisms of hunger and thirst. In Postman, L. (ed.), *Psychology in the Making*. New York: Alfred Knopf, 73–143.

SEARS, R. R. (1957). *Patterns of Child Rearing*. New York: Harper and Row.

SKINNER, B. F. (1938). *The Behaviour of Organisms*. New York: Appleton-Century-Crofts.

SKINNER, B. F. (1953). *Science and Human Behaviour*. New York: Macmillan.

SKINNER, B. F. (1959). *Cumulative Record*. London: Methuen.

SMITH, M. B., BRUNER, J. S., and WHITE, R. K. (1956). *Opinions and Personality*. New York: John Wiley.

THURSTONE, L. L. and CHAVE, E. J. (1929). *The Measurement of Attitude*. Chicago: University of Chicago Press.

TOWER, D. B. (1958). The neurochemical substrates of cerebral function and activity. In Harlow, H. F. and Woolsey, C. N. (ed.), *Biological and Biochemical Bases of Behaviour*. Madison: University of Wisconsin Press.

TURNER, G. N. H. (1966). A re-examination of certain of Piaget's inquiries on children's moral judgements in the light of his later theory. Unpublished M.Ed. thesis, Manchester University.

WATSON, W. (1952). Society and children's play. *Scottish Educ. J.* **35**, 113–4 and 130.

WHITE, R. W. (1959). Motivation reconsidered: the concept of competence. *Psychol. Rev.* **66**, 297–333.

WHITING, J. W. M., and CHILD, I. (1953). *Child Training and Personality*. New Haven: Yale University Press.

ZANGWILL, O. L. (1950). *A Modern Introduction to Psychology*. London: Methuen.

ZEIGARNIK, B. (1938). On finished and unfinished tasks. In Ellis W. D. *A Source Book in Gestalt Psychology*. New York: Harcourt, Brace and World. (From an original paper in German, published 1927.)

7

Learning and Learning Theory

I

'*Homo sum: humani nihil a me alienum puto*'. Being human myself, I regard everything to do with human beings as my concern. So wrote the Latin poet Terence. Of course he was right, and the universality of such adages as 'There's nowt so queer as fouks' testifies to the generality of his sentiment. And it follows that anyone undertaking a textbook on psychology begins with a great advantage, for he can expect to draw on a fund of interest and goodwill from his reader. If he is dealing with development he is even better off, for while people excite our interest, children excite our love – at least when we are away from them. What a pity it is to throw all this advantage away.

For many a reader who has worked his way through to this point in the book will conclude that we have thrown away our advantage. And so will others who have been put off by some difficult passage encountered on the way and decided to flip through to the last chapter to see how it would all end. Strictly speaking, it is I rather than 'we' who must shoulder the blame, for the writer of Chapter 2 is a somewhat better cook than I am, and better able to serve up scientific fare in tasty fashion.

But enough of this flippancy. For there is a problem and it is this. There are two ways of approaching questions of human behaviour. One is to draw on the fund of our own experience: on our introspective awareness of our own feelings and sensations and on our capacity for empathy – that is to say our ability to observe the expressions and the behaviour of others and to project upon them the same feelings as we have known in ourselves in similar circumstances. The other is to devise a mental construction, using bits which are not themselves psychological but are taken from our experience and knowledge of objects in general, i.e. a model of what is involved in regulating the behaviour of this very complex piece of matter: a human being. We are free to construct the model in any way we choose, so long as we do not surreptitiously slip in a little psychology of the first sort, a bit of our own self-knowledge, a little man inside the machine. And having constructed the model we test it. That is to say, we try to deduce whether a thing ('system') which functioned exactly in the way that we specified would in fact be able to replicate some of the behaviours that we observe in ourselves. More than this, we try to establish whether it would be expected to behave in ways which we have not yet observed in ourselves, and we then want to know whether, given the appropriate conditions, we ourselves behave just as the model predicts. Of course there is more to it than this. For instance, we do not build models *in vacuo*, just any sort of model. There are two points of anchorage: the first is the one mentioned already, the elements used in the construction must relate to ordinary things, they must not be 'psychological elements'; the second derives from the aim of the model. Naturally, since it is intended to be a model of the regulation of human behaviour, we try to use the bits in ways which will replicate this. Or again, one can try to build a real model out of hardware to replicate part of human behaviour. And always the model, real or mental, falls short of what is needed, so we have to adjust it, or start again. And we must beware of cutting corners with mental models. At least we should be aware of the fact that we are cutting them, so that we know what ground we must go back over (I have had to cut many corners in Chapters 4 and 5).

But let us get back to the first approach to human behaviour, which is that of introspection and empathy. It is valid enough: valid in the sense that it leads to accurate prediction a great deal of the time. Valid also in the sense that one is perfectly justified in the assumption that others enjoy similar feelings to our own in comparable situations. But it is not scientific. For three reasons.

The first is methodological. It is completely lacking in rigour. Although it is reasonable to suppose that others enjoy similar feelings to our own, there is no way of proving that they do in any given instance, and there are many cases in which they quite certainly do not: for human beings differ in their personality. One can of course go a step further, and take several incidents into account before proceeding to interpretation. But unless one is systematic about what one observes, taking steps to ensure that one's data are reliable and represent a reliable cross-section of the person's behaviour, the part of unchecked inference is still far too great. Certainly one cannot take people's reports of their feelings at their face value, and as to their sensations when involved in an objective learning situation, too often they have none, or none that they can report. If, on the other hand, we do take steps to ensure that our data are objective and representative, then our inquiries will begin to be scientific – but introspection will be increasingly omitted from them in an attempt to secure reliable data. Which is the point made by Stott in his introduction to Chapter 4 in Volume III.

The second, which is also methodological, derives from the first. If we are to reach valid inferences we must begin from reliable data. This means that we need to be able to specify exactly what it is that we observe and the conditions under which we observe it. The method of introspection hardly lends itself to such specification. Even the observation of behaviour is not enough. In general, in order to ensure that our observations are sufficiently clear-cut to be repeatable by another observer, we find we have to measure and quantify the most relevant aspects of the behaviour and of the situation in which it is observed. In other words, in order to become scientific, psychology is compelled to turn to experimental methods.

But it is the third characteristic of the introspective approach which differentiates it most sharply from the standpoint which is taken explicitly in the present volume but is also more or less implicit in any psychological text. It is not methodological unless we use the term in a very wide sense. It is, strictly speaking, philosophical or meta-scientific: not a part of what one does as a scientist, but part of the assumptions that underlie one's activity. To accept introspective data at their face value and to interpret them in purely mental terms is to accept a fundamental dualism. The language of knowing, of striving and of feeling does not enter into the interpretation of physical events at any level. Nor is it used in chemistry or in biochemistry. The work of Oparin and Miller points the way to the elucidation of the historical continuity between living matter and inert matter. Long before this, Darwin's *Origin of the Species* undoubtedly exercised an enormous influence in compelling scientists to recognize a continuity between the lower and higher forms of life, up to and including man himself. More recently the work of Crick and his associates applies the same monistic approach to the genetics of cellular behaviour. The monism of science is opposed to the dualism of introspection and to attempt to build a science on a dualistic basis is to fly in the face of the history of the acquisition of knowledge.

I have four riders.

In the first place, the materialism of science (which has nothing to do with 'materialism' in the sense of acquisitiveness, in which respect scientists are no better and no worse than anyone else) is not an immediate, intuitive property of experience but a hard-won gain. A mentalistic approach to the behaviour of inert matter is characteristic of the thinking of primitive peoples, just as it is prevalent in that of young children (Piaget, 1929; Laurendeau and Pinard, 1962).

In the second place, I am well aware that many of the greatest scientists of the past and even of the present have failed to extend their materialism to their conception of human behaviour and have been quite content to adhere to some form of dualism. This is irrelevant, so long as they extend it to their work as scientists, which they must. Because the psychologist is directly concerned with human behaviour he has less room to wriggle.

In the third place, the extension of the objective approach to human behaviour is very recent, dating from the turn of the century. As we have noted in Chapter 1, Section II, the major break-through was due to Pavlov and Thorndike. The origin of psychology as a science is usually placed in the nineteenth century, with the opening of the first laboratory by Wundt. In terms of the three criteria of a scientific psychology enunciated earlier, nineteenth-century psychology satisfied the first two but not the third. It was experimental, and therefore productive, but subjective or mentalistic, and therefore limited. (The term 'objective' is often preferred to the term 'materialist', but the two are synonymous, so long as the range of the latter is extended to those properties of matter which are inferred and not limited to those which are immediately sensed. 'Subjective' and 'mentalistic' are widely accepted as the complementary partial synonyms.)

In the fourth place, nothing is achieved by denying the data of human experience: knowing, striving, feeling (some would prefer the more high falutin' 'cognitive, conative and affective aspects'). The point is simply that one must question their sufficiency as irreducible explanatory concepts. The task which science (physiology and psychology) sets itself is to discover what sort of an organization is available to the brain as a result of which it can give rise to behaviour which has these characteristics. The human brain so far as we know, is the most complex system discovered in nature, and the investigation of its functions is a relatively new science. It is ridiculous to claim that it has successfully bridged the gap between the material organization of the brain and the mental qualities of experience. But it has at least discovered a way of advance.

This is to substitute an analysis of the interconnectedness of behaviour for the examination of the qualities of experience. Cognition becomes a matter of reactivity to cues, and ways of processing these cues which result in the elaboration of equivalent or identical behaviours in respect of analogous inputs. Of course one has to arrive at some precision as to the meaning of 'analogous'. But here too the attempt must retain its behaviourist integrity. One looks first at physical similarities in the input or the stimulus which gives rise to it (primary generalization), then to equivalences based on the objective connectedness of things by virtue of which different initial inputs may function as signs for identical consequent inputs (conditioning), then to equivalences which arise out of the fact that different inputs or sequences of inputs can give rise to similar behaviours (logic). (Strictly speaking, true logic exists only when the behaviour is reflexive, i.e. it is a second-order activity the 'input' for which is not the primary cues arising out of perception, but the decision processes or strategies which the subject has elaborated in order to handle them.) (See Chapter 5, Section V.)

Conation becomes a matter of analysing the mechanisms which govern the maintenance, or change in the direction, of behaviour, i.e. the transitions from equivalent to non-equivalent lines of behaviour.

Finally, consideration of emotion or feeling leads to the study of its behavioural and physiological correlates on the one hand, and on the other to a study of attitudes in human beings. That is, to a study of the way in which sensory input is referred to representation (Chapter 5, Section V), and more especially to its implications for the self, giving rise to moods and sentiments which colour the course of further representational activity and which help to determine the strategies that are brought to bear on the assimilation of further, related, sensory inputs (*ibid.* and Chapter 6, Section V).

II

If asked what are the fundamental properties of living matter, one would probably reply: assimilation, reactivity, reproduction, growth. In fact every one of these properties taken singly may be exhibited by non-living matter: assimilation exists in the flame of a burning candle; reactivity is a property of matter at every level, albeit a differentiating property; reproduction could be attributed to any chain reaction; and growth is a characteristic of crystals and many colloids. Probably the term 'fundamental' is entirely misleading, for the study of life begins not with the analysis of its attributes, fundamental or otherwise, but with that of the chemical constitution of living matter. Be that as it may, it is apparent that many characteristics of living creatures present no philosophical problems. Even in the nineteenth century, not only tropisms but instinctual behaviour also could be conceived by analogy with the design of mechanical machinery.

The notion of a purely materialist or objective account of learning, however, continued to present difficulty. For if human beings and animals show an adaptive recognition of the implications of what they perceive and behave accordingly, as in the adage 'The burnt child fears the fire', then this can only be as a result of learning. In one sense, a mechanical view of learning can be traced right back to Aristotle and perhaps beyond, in the form of the theory of the association of ideas. But it was Pavlov and Thorndike who substituted the reflex or the response for the idea. In so doing, they extended the realm of controlled, scientific investigation, by including within its purview the study of systems (human and animal organisms) which were not merely reactive to stimuli, but which were adaptive, showing changes in their mode of response. The way was now open for theoretical and experimental inquiry into the manner in which changes in the connexions mediating behavioural regulation eventuate in the subtle co-ordinations of behaviour, including language, which we call the exercise of intelligence.

Pavlov and Thorndike were the trail blazers in that they showed that learning can be regarded as change in the regulation of behaviour instead of being thought of as a process which can be handled only in the language of ideas. They opened a new era in psychological experimentation which is still with us. But there remained a wide gap between the primary 'laws of learning' and the achievements for which they are taken to provide a basis. Most of this volume has been concerned with the attempt to bridge this gap.

Clearly, a first step must be to integrate the views of Pavlov and those of Thorndike, which appear to provide alternative frameworks, both of which are founded on experiment. It will be recalled from Chapter 1 that Thorndike's principal contribution was his demonstration of the role of reinforcement in instrumental learning: the law of effect. Pavlov, using the involuntary conditional reflex as the experimental model, demonstrated the lawful character inherent in the process whereby environmental cues acquire new signalling properties, leading to the antedating of behaviour appropriate to the signalled experience or event. Hullian theory constitutes a brilliant attempt at such integration.

But it was more than this. For it was also an attempt to elucidate the laws governing the formation of more complex behavioural connexions, such as must be assumed to underlie intelligence. From the thirties on, it became apparent that intelligent co-ordination could not be described objectively by referring only to observed behaviour or 'response' and its observed external antecedents – or 'stimulus'. Both Hull and Tolman were compelled to introduce the notion of inferred events, 'intervening variables' – intervening, that is, between the stimulus and the response. Hull's habit-family-hierarchy is intended as a model of relations among intervening variables which will account for intelligent behaviour even though the basic mechanisms are simply connexions between stimuli and simple behaviours of the organism: responses. Tolman's cognitive map is similar in aim, for this too is based on the intervening variable. The difference is principally that Tolman is less concerned about the conceptual simplicity of his intervening variables (their identifiability with behaviours or events which are not themselves mentalistic). It is sufficient for Tolman that the laws arrived at involving these terms should be objective, verifiable experimentally, anchored in objective features of the environment (stimuli) and observable behaviour (responses).

Since this account must be exceedingly summary, we will recall only four of the major advances in understanding that were achieved as a result of the theoretical and experimental work inspired by these two schools of the thirties. First, the distinction between performance and learning: the fact that a subject, animal or human, has acquired a particular connexion does not imply that the change in the system will be reflected in change of behaviour in all circumstances. Whether it is depends on motivation. This is the positive significance of the latent learning experiments. Second, and related to this, that motivation itself can be modified by learning, as in secondary reinforcement. Third, the connexions that we can usefully talk about, from the point of view of theory and experiment, are not limited to connexions between observed stimuli and observed responses. They include events that intervene within the organism and mediate the final response. In spite of the fact that we have seen fit to question the particular form of the Hullian intervening variables, the fractional response and the fractional stimulus, and the lack of clarity in Tolman's sign-significate relations, their formulations pointed to the existence of an enormous gap – in Thorndike's theory – and showed how the gap can in principle be bridged without abandonment of the objective experimental approach. Fourth, insight was shown to represent, at least in part, a putting-together of previous learnings, suggesting that the phenomena revealed by Gestalt psychology do not necessarily entail the need for a frankly mentalistic explanation.

Nevertheless the principal argument of this book has been that the Hull–Tolman intervening variable model is still quite inadequate to account for the development of human or even animal behaviour and learning. There is no need here to recall in detail the argument of

Chapter 3 demonstrating the physiological impossibility of the system which it implies. One way of summing up the criticisms urged both in respect of the stimulus and in respect of the response is to say that the Hullian model in particular (especially as filled out by Spence) is a sort of switchboard in which all identifiable cues and all distinct responses as well as all the intervening variables must be simultaneously available. Another is to say that the error of S-R theory was to take two perfectly valid criteria of the experimenter's procedure – the need to specify the laboratory set-up (in terms of stimuli) and the behaviour which he records (by means of response measures) – and simply project these end-products into the subject (say the rat). One then imagines that all one has to do is to fill in the links between them.

I must be equally summary in recording the principal features of the alternative model proposed in Chapter 4.

The regulation of behaviour does not begin with the stimulus. The brain is constantly active and constantly reactive. Yet in so far as behaviour shows direction and pattern its activity is non-random. (The restriction is important, since it is highly probable that the direction and channelling is continually altered by the incorporation of random activity within itself, and operates against a background of random activity.) Maintenance of direction depends on the inter-facilitation, and especially the inter-inhibition of elements within the system. Elements which control the activity of other elements sequentially are termed strategies. Strategies represent lines of behaviour. Since, typically, the inception of any line of behaviour allows for the possibility of branching behaviours, depending on the input to the system, the structure of strategies is partly hierarchical. But since any given behaviour, say opening a door, may occur in any number of quite different contexts, it is not a simple hierarchy but a network in which hierarchical connexions play an important part. The set of possible strategies diverging from any node is clearly of the utmost relevance to the operation of the system – especially as the determining influence of higher ranking strategies is never complete. In line with the usage of British psychologists and of Piaget, such sets have been called schemata. Since the nodes occur at various levels in the system, the structure of schemata is also partly hierarchical. The question whether a strategy or a schema is to be identified with the controlling node or with the sub-system upon which it operates is really quite trivial. In a functional interpretation, these are just two ways of saying the same thing.

How does such a system interact with the environment? Clearly there must be elements that are directly sensitive to input and which directly implement output. To all intents and purposes these elements are elementary strategies. Following the usage suggested by Deutsch, I have called them links. But the link is not the eye and the ear or the retina and the basilar membrane. It is to be thought of as a central mechanism which is differentially sensitive to cue-combinations, cues which may be relayed from any receptor modality. The set of possible combinations is termed the comparator system. This too corresponds to central processes. It exists at one remove from the direct responsiveness to perceptual input, e.g. the occipital region of the cortex, where there is evidence of something approaching a 1–1 mapping of the pattern of retinal stimulation. Now the reason for postulating such an intermediate relay station is perfectly straightforward: it lies in the fact that cue-equivalences cannot be rendered by a mere 1–1 mapping. To a dog, a characteristic smell and a characteristic outline or gait are equivalent cues; to a reader an **A** and an **a** (in a variety of types) are equivalent; and there are pattern equivalences which ignore differences in size, in orientation and in locus of projection of the retinal output. The function of the link is simply to act as a decision process. It recognizes whether certain cues are present, or which of several alternatives are present, and directs output accordingly. Often output will be such as to bring into action another link, already pre-sensitized by the preceding link and by the higher-ranking strategy, and so on. Until the line of behaviour is terminated, either by a terminating input relayed to the higher-order strategy, or by the action of a specific terminator (as in eating and drinking), or by the switching of control to some other, overriding strategy. Because the link is differentially sensitized – by downward and lateral stimulation, and because it is differentially sensitizing in turn, and also differentially sensitive, in relation to the possible cue-combinations in the comparator system, the system acts as a variable filter. This is a necessary aspect of the system which has been particularly emphasized in the work of Broadbent. Unlike the stimulus of S-R theory, the universe of links and of cue-combinations which they determine is not to be thought of as simultaneously available. On the contrary, the chief attribute of the system is that its elements tend to be mutually inhibitory.

It should be stressed that the above is not a physiological account. Such an account would specify the anatomical locus and the physiological mode of action of all the elements envisaged. It is a structural and functional account, being an account of the structure of relations among functional elements inferred from the operation of the system. In other words, it is psychological – by my definition, which follows that of Piaget. Of course it does not blindly and stupidly ignore physiological evidence. But it could if sufficiently improved, be translated into quite different concrete terms, e.g. a computer programme.

A contemporary aphorism which commands wide assent is that the brain of the human infant is more like a kit of parts than a machine. It is not a *tabula rasa* waiting to be written on, because nobody does the writing: it constructs itself. To be more precise, it is like a computer in which every element has a very large number of connexions with other elements (but certainly not with all, for the universe of possibilities is more restricted), which is switched on, so that all the elements are liable to fire, but for the most part their order of firing is random – noise. But not entirely, for there are built-in reflexes and built-in co-ordinations. Also, the possible co-ordinations to be acquired are limited by the actual connexions. Learning is a matter of selective inhibition. Of all the possible connexions among elements, some come to be favoured – with the result that the proportion of random activity in the system decreases, and its behaviour tends to show increasing patterning. The cue-combinations constituting the comparator system, the selective connexions between links and comparator and effector mechanisms, the hierarchical relations among strategies of various orders, and the implicatory connexions of schemata are all learnt in this fashion – starting from a minimal basis of innate patterning. This is not gospel truth. Just something which is very probable.

III

One of the most celebrated controversies in the history of psychology concerns the role of reinforcement in learning. Pavlov, it will be recalled, was relatively neutral on this question. Conditioning procedure was used under circumstances where the presentation of the unconditional stimulus *was* reinforcing, and the term 'reinforcement' was used simply to refer to such presentation. In the hands of Hull, the reinforcing power of the **US** was itself called into question, being made contingent on need reduction. At the same time, following Thorndike, Hull was especially interested in the acquisition of instrumental behaviour under the influence of reinforcement. Skinner dropped the formal definition of reinforcement which made it dependent on a dubious intervening variable (drive strength) in favour of an operational definition (any stimulus the presentation of which increases the strength of an operant) which I suggested was circular but not vicious. But reinforcement so defined is the principal factor in learning. On the other hand, Guthrie explicitly denied the significance of reinforcement (in the Thorndikian sense), advancing a theory according to which learning is entirely determined by contiguity: the subject will vary his behaviour so long as the stimulus remains, but whatever chanced to be the final response on the first occasion will be repeated on the next occasion, regardless of reinforcement. Reinforcement appears to be relevant only because its presentation is effective in making the preceding response the final one. We have had very little to say about Guthrie. The theory settled too many questions at a level of very broad generalization and was unproductive in raising questions for research the elucidation of which might have advanced our understanding. And the definitions of 'stimulus' and 'response' were even more improbable than those of Hull. But the importance of reinforcement was also questioned by Tolman, who maintained that the organism learns by building up a cognitive map of what leads to what, i.e. that learning is a function of contiguity. Tolman was not one for committing himself too strongly in a restrictive sense, and he reserved the possibility that reinforcement can be effective by increasing the salience of the stimuli to be connected by the subject. The latent learning experiments were designed to demonstrate learning without reinforcement. As such, their results remained inconclusive.

The startling success of Skinner in teaching instrumental behaviour by means of reinforcement would by itself tend to favour a model in which reinforcement occupies a central place. The contingencies of stimuli and behaviours in the experience of a subject, even in the experimental situation, are very numerous. It certainly looks as if selection among these is determined by the presentation of reinforcement. But the argument is not conclusive. Skinner's work is most telling as a rationale for teaching. What are the reinforcement contingencies when the scientific teacher is not there? And what determines the reinforcing action of the reinforcer?

The issue of reinforcement is one case where a more direct physiological attack has led to a drastic curtailment in the possibilities of interpretation. As a result of the work of Olds and his associates over the last ten years and more, one can no longer maintain that the basis for all learning resides in mere contiguity of input. Direct stimulation of appropriate regions of the brain leads to the repetition of whatever act preceded such stimulation – e.g. in strengthening a bar-pressing response. It can be used to bring about learning of a serial behaviour such as the acquisition of a maze habit. Finally, the random application of **DSB** during the acquisition of such a behaviour under conditions of natural drive, e.g. hunger, has the effect of disrupting the course of learning. One can no longer doubt that the effect of an action is fed back into the system. Such feedback obviously plays a major part, if not the major part in determining changes in the connexions which mediate the regulation of behaviour.

But **DSB** reinforcement by itself will not answer the problem of what it is that brings about reinforcement under natural conditions. In other words we now know that certain kinds of input feed back into the system and strengthen the connexions which were active just before – and the traces of which are presumably still active; we also know that the feedback is mediated by activation of the reinforcing centres (see the brief description and references in Chapter 4); **DSB** by-passes feedback by artificially activating the mechanism which is essential to its operation. What governs the activity of the reinforcing centres when they are not activated directly?

Neither Thorndike nor Skinner has anything to offer, for their formulations are circular. We are left with Hull's attempt to identify the source of reinforcement as the reduction of physiological states of need in the organism. No one would deny that our behaviour is influenced, sometimes quite dramatically, by states of physiological need – e.g. failure of oxygen supply. But the Hullian interpretation goes further than this. It is a formal explanation which provides for the direct action of physiological need in the determination of reinforcement. As such, there are good grounds for rejecting it. In the first place, so far as the basic needs of food and drink are concerned, we have evidence that their action is not immediate but mediate: in particular, detectors for activating behaviour are separate from those which produce its termination. In the second place the direct identification of need and drive makes it impossible to account for systematic variation in drive which is clearly unrelated to need, e.g. enhancement of activation due to frustration (Amsel). Third, there is the evidence of exploratory behaviour which is unrelated to need-reduction. And finally, there is the evidence that social behaviour in animals and in human beings is a primary drive mechanism: it is not a secondary drive mechanism based on the search for secondary reinforcers associated with the satisfaction of primary needs, and this sort of association is incapable of inducing the specific behaviours characteristic of the attachment drive (Harlow). It goes without saying that the concept of need has no explanatory power unless the term is used to refer directly to states of physiological deficit: to invoke the need for love or the need for knowledge, etc., in defence of the Hullian position is no more than a verbal trick.

It has been suggested in the present volume that the proximal condition for the non-artificial activation of the reinforcement centres is likely to be the facilitation of a previously activated strategy, often a higher-order strategy, by the provision of adequate input for the activity of its constituent links. Such a position is of course quite close to that of Amsel, although it is not assumed that there is a necessary and perfect correlation between the amount of antecedent frustration (blockage of an ongoing strategy) and the degree of reinforcement. It is even closer to the position taken by Deutsch. Briefly, our conclusions are these:

The occasion for learning is the failure of the environment to supply the necessary input for the running off of a strategy already initiated. The necessary condition for learning is the inception of 'trial-and-error' behaviour, i.e. the engagement of strategies not already subordinated to the original strategy: the activation of these is taken to be a function of input, related to the assumption that the filtering action of the original control is always imperfect. The use of the term 'trial-and-error' does not preclude the possibility of error-free learning: when the experimenter/teacher structures the input in such a way as to ensure that the input which passes the filter will be assimilated to strategies whose implementation will lead to immediate success – resumption of control by the original strategy. This can be achieved in two ways: by manipulating the subsequent input, i.e. by presenting the reinforcer immediately after the trial behaviour; and by manipulating the contingent input, i.e. by the provision of cues which will render it more probable that the trial behaviour will be the desired behaviour, e.g. by the use of cues, prompts or models for imitation. Skinner makes use of all these techniques. The Skinnerian theory of learning is subsumed under the present as a special case: it is a theory of teaching.

The reference to the relevance of learning theory to teaching suggests two corollaries. The first, which is widely accepted, is that while the present model allows the possibility of incidental learning, as in the latent learning experiments, it suggests very strongly that educational methods which rely heavily on the intervention of such learning are necessarily inefficient. It will be recalled from Chapter 1 that the results of latent learning experiments do not by any means suggest that learning follows inevitably from the fact that the subject happens to encounter the relevant stimulus configurations in the course of his behaviour. In particular, if the association to be formed is irrelevant to the strategies which are currently active in the determination of his actions, then the chances are that learning will not occur. For instance, rats do not learn the position of water in a maze when the maze is run under a strong, irrelevant, hunger drive. But there is a further implication which follows from our conception of the hierarchical character of behavioural organization. It is that higher order strategies, capable of unifying and directing large classes of related behaviours, will not be formed and strengthened when the operation of simpler strategies is sufficient to ensure success. For instance, one would not expect a subject to acquire the higher order reversal learning set under conditions where the operation of the simpler object choice strategy is equally efficient. In the same way, it is unreasonable to expect children to acquire an understanding of mathematical relations by providing them with a series of straightforward routines which enable them to solve the problems they are set without reflexion on their mutual implications.

The second corollary concerns the use of praise and punishment as reinforcers. Both Hull and Skinner have stressed the greater effectiveness of immediate reinforcement, and this is rightly taken as one of the principal grounds for the use of learning programmes which provide immediate knowledge of results. If the drive which is operative in learning is a strategy designed to reduce uncertainty – the 'what-is-it? reflex', then it is reasonable to suppose that knowledge of results is sufficient reinforcement. The effect of delay in weakening reinforcement is one of the many fundamental principles established in Pavlov's laboratory. But the argument can be taken further. Skinner speaks of the capacity of human beings to work for long-range reinforcers, citing the imaginary example of a man who instals a storm shelter in the autumn to guard against a severe winter. There is no denying that we do plan our behaviour ahead. Nevertheless, from the standpoint of a more rigorous scientific theory, it is very much to the point to inquire what can be the mechanism governing the action of 'long-range reinforcers'. Although we are not clear as to the precise nature of the trace upon which reinforcement operates, it is difficult to avoid the conclusion that if reinforcement does occur, then such a trace must be active at the time of reinforcement. Experiment has shown the difficulty of establishing reinforcement of delay involving intervals of the order of one to three minutes. It is inconceivable that the trace continues active over a period of months (reinforcement provided by results of examinations, etc.), or even days (reinforcement provided by teacher correction). Yet such delayed measures do act as incentives in education and similar contexts. Failure to obtain the anticipated 'bonus' leads to a lowering of effort. I do not believe that very long-range reinforcement of this sort should be looked on as a simple extension of a principle of delay. The effectiveness of these incentives must depend on the reactivation of the original behaviours. Since the original input is no longer available at the time of reinforcement, such reactivation is necessarily representational, i.e. it relies on an input which is largely generated by the subject and largely internal. Unless the feedback is accompanied by an immediate renewed opportunity to resume the original strategy under guidance, it is difficult to see how the long range knowledge of results can modify the details of the original behaviour. What is more probable is that the long-range reinforcer acts only as a morale booster or depresser – by reactivating some very general strategies, such as the desire to conform or a general attitude of interest in the work. The force of this argument seems to be missed in many textbooks of educational psychology. On the other hand it is probably recognized intuitively in educational practice, as evidenced by the insistence of teachers on the correction of errors. But if this takes the form of copying the corrected answer, it is not the same set of strategies as that which occasioned the original error, and one must expect the resultant learning to be minimal.

IV

The present volume has been concerned almost entirely with very general questions concerning the regulation of behaviour in animals and in human beings. Questions concerning the formation of specifically human skills have been dealt with only in very general terms, and we have given no more than the barest outline of what appears to be involved in the elaboration of thinking. To confine a discussion of fundamental principles of psychology to a mere statement of the basic mechanisms of reinforcement and of drive amounts to by-passing most of the central problems. The Hullian concept of the habit-family-hierarchy is a formal statement of static relations assumed to exist between all the elements in the system ('intervening variables'). The values taken by each of these at any given moment simply determine the form of the eventual 'response'. This means that behaviour is thought of as a linear succession of atomic behavioural elements. Contrary to this, we have supposed that far from involving all the elements in the system, co-ordination is possible only by the inhibition of all but a few. At the same time, the execution of even the simplest of skilled patterns involves the simultaneous operations of several related strategies. The proper object of psychology is taken to be the elucidation of the interrelations of these inferred processes and not simply the prediction of arbitrarily selected observable 'responses'.

A consideration of the phenomena of phylogenetic and ontogenetic development compelled us to the conclusion that the elaboration of intelligent co-ordinations argues the emergence of higher-order strategies the action of which is to inhibit other strategies concerned more exclusively with reaction to environmental input. The emergence of such higher-order strategies permits a very considerable extension in the power of generalization, as shown in the formation of learning set. Detailed study of development in species and in the individual in a variety of problems shows that development in learning is largely a matter of development in generalization. Generalization cannot be regarded as simply a function of the physical characteristics of the stimulus. The generalizations involved in the operation of higher-order strategies and schemata depend more on the interrelations of the strategies upon which they operate, i.e. on the interrelations among the lines of behaviour which the input allows. The assumption of the regulatory activity of these higher-order elements does not invalidate the basic mechanisms of learning: the former are assumed to be among the terms upon which reinforcement operates. The close analysis of learning suggests that changes in the observed form of behaviour are only an indirect result of the learning: the direct effect of learning is to bring about changes in the connexions among the interrelations of the strategies which direct the overt forms of behaviour.

A further conclusion to which we were led is that even the assumption of the intervention of higher-order strategies in the determination of e.g. reversal and the formation of learning set is not sufficient to account for the special characteristics of human behaviour. These are often attributed to the mediating function of language. But this is an oversimplification. For in so far as language exercises a mediating role in intelligent behaviour, language is only one form of a more general function which plays a predominating role in the regulation of human behaviour, viz. the capacity for the representational reconstruction of experience by means of strategies which depend on a succession of inputs that is largely within the control of the subject, and free of environmental constraints. Non-linguistic representational strategies include deferred imitation, imagery and play. To this one might add systems of signs and operations which are to all intents and purposes languages, although they do not fall into the category of natural languages: for instance, mathematics. From the standpoint of phylogenesis, it seems reasonable to conclude that the evolution of representational behaviour depends on the availability of structures capable of interacting with and affecting the operation of direct sensori-motor strategies, although differing from these in regard to the input necessary for their functioning. From the standpoint of ontogenesis, we have attempted to trace the development of representation out of its origins in imitation, basing ourselves fairly closely on the account given by Piaget (1951). True imitation itself, as opposed to pseudo-imitation which consists in merely following a leader or model, depends on the deliberate matching of input deriving from the body and movements of the subject with that which he obtains from observation of the model. In view of the very large differences which exist between the conditions governing the two kinds of input, it is reasonable to suppose that the capacity for imitation may be related to the capacity for the formation of learning set. To begin with, imitation occurs only in the presence of the model; but deferred imitation is seen in the chimpanzee as well as in children about the beginning of the second year. Representation appears to be a natural development out of this, since the only difference is that the imitative behaviour becomes the occasion for further elaboration instead of being terminated by the achievement of a satisfactory match.

Because representation is relatively free from environmental constraints, the sequence of input which it generates is not bound to reproduce the sequence encountered in direct sensori-motor behaviour. Both in dreams and in play, there is ample room for error, for repetition and for distortion. But one possible consequence of this de-restriction is that sooner or later the child begins to discover more effective ways of contrasting comparable but conflicting events; instead of simply reconstructing first one and then the other (with the aid of representational input) he will tend increasingly to reconcile the conflict by concentrating on the critical elements in the comparison. By means of representation, the child comes to recognize the criteria of his own actions. It is not difficult to see how such a development bears on the progressive systematization of thought which begins about the age of six. For instance, conservation of number, length, weight, etc., is very much dependent on the ability of the child to focus on and retain a clear criterion or operational definition of just what is intended by these terms.

Of course this argument should not be taken to imply that language is irrelevant to the development of logical reasoning. The advantage of language over other means of representation is twofold: because words do not have to resemble what they stand for, they can be made to stand for any of the elements of reality, including the critical relations of logic themselves; and because language is a vehicle of communication long before it becomes an instrument of thinking, the language to which the child is exposed tends to focus his attention on relations which have been found to be critical in the experience of his predecessors. But the mere use of language is no guarantee of logic. Certainly up to the age of six or seven on average there is abundant evidence that representation – and language – actually lags behind consistent or logical action, as we saw in the case of transposition, of the simple object learning set, and of the oddity problem.

V

It is no exaggeration to say that psychology has been dominated by the limited and constricting assumptions of Thorndike and Hull for a very long period, covering nearly all the first half of this century. I have tried to do three things: to lay bare the roots and implications of this traditional approach and at the same time to bring out some of its achievements in the field of learning; to sketch in the outline of a very much more powerful type of analysis, showing how such an approach, termed structural, lends itself to a more unified framework of interpretation of psychological questions and is also far more in tune with the basic assumptions of science as a whole, and especially of the related science of physiology; and, finally, to provide a general and theoretical background for the more detailed survey of the problems of human learning and of education which appears in Volumes II and III.

It is obvious that on every one of these counts there is much more to be said than has been said.

In regard to traditional theories of learning this matters little, for even though many of the 'laws' of learning have a certain limited validity, the interest of these theories is more historic than scientific.

As to the newer approach up to now it is only in the limited but rapidly growing field of psycho-linguistics that one finds a realization of the need for a fresh start, very much on the lines of what has been suggested here – largely due to the influence of the pene-trating theoretical studies of language provided by Chomsky (1957, 1965) – a point well brought out in a recent review by Wales and Marshall (1966).

The work of Piaget tends to be neglected by many psychologists. It looks as if this is precisely because the implications of his analysis of the development of logic and its relation to experience in general is more far-reaching, which means that one cannot simply accept it as a special structural enclave within an otherwise descriptive 'science'. Hence the need for a general and introductory statement of a unified approach.

The third aim has been to provide a basis for the study of practical problems in human learning. This volume is essentially introductory. For there is an important difference between the structural approach and the positivism of **S-R**. The latter sets out with the rather grandiose aim of enunciating the essential relations involved in any learning process so generally in terms of 'stimuli' and 'responses' that one can predict the details of behaviour knowing only the empty theory, provided one can specify the stimulus complex – this in turn being no part of psychology except in the rather trivial sense of psycho-physics. The aim of structural psychology is less ambitious. An analysis of the way in which strategies are formed and interact with one another and with input is in principle quite insufficient to predict the form of learning in any real context, e.g. learning a language, learning mathematics or learning history. Such specification is impossible unless one can also give a proper account of the logical relations implied by the content area to be learned, and of the way in which they can be made accessible to the subject at successive stages in the learning. And this cannot be done *a priori*. Which is why the second volume includes discussions of learning in specific areas such as language, mathematics, reading and social learning.

REFERENCES

CHOMSKY, N. (1957). *Syntactic Structures*. The Hague: Mouton.

CHOMSKY, N. (1965). *Aspects of the Theory of Syntax*. Cambridge, Mass.: M.I.T. Press.

LAURENDEAU, M., and PINARD, A. (1962). *Causal Thinking in the Child*. New York: International Universities Press.

PIAGET, J. (1929). *The Child's Conception of the World*. London: Routledge and Kegan Paul.

PIAGET, J. (1951). *Play, Dreams and Limitation in Childhood*. London: Heinemann.

WALES, R. J., and MARSHALL, J. C. (1966). The organisation of linguistic performance. In Lyons, J. and Wales, R. J. (ed.), *Psycholinguistic Papers. Proceedings of the Edinburgh Conference*, 1966. Edinburgh: Edinburgh Univ. Press.

INDEX